The Common Wor

The Common Worship Lectionary

A Scripture Commentary Year C

Edited by

Leslie Houlden

and

John Rogerson

First published in Great Britain in 2003 by
Society for Promoting Christian Knowledge
Holy Trinity Church
Marylebone Road
London NW1 4DU

British Library Cataloguing-in-Publication Data

A catalogue record for this book is available from the British Library

ISBN 0-281-05327-8

1 3 5 7 9 10 8 6 4 2

Typeset by Wilmaset Ltd, Birkenhead, Wirral
Printed in Great Britain by
The Cromwell Press, Trowbridge, Wiltshire

Contents

Introduction

The purpose of this book is to offer a particular kind of help and stimulus to those who must address congregations and other groups where the Revised Common Lectionary is followed. We provide entries for all the Sunday readings for Year C and for the readings put down for a selection of major Holy Days.

The tone aims to be decently academic, not in the sense that readers are to feel led back to their earlier education, with examinations in the offing, but in the hope of helping them to read a passage in terms of its context and intentions. Of course it would be confusing, and is not possible in the space available, to give a full range of current ways of understanding a text, but the interpretation offered is meant to be neither eccentric nor shallow.

Given this kind of treatment, the entries are emphatically not designed to give instant sermon-fodder; rather, they offer one element in preparation. To it, the speaker will add pastoral experience and a sense of local need – and of course creative imagination. The underlying 'philosophy' of preaching is that, far from being an exegetical plod, it should be seen as, in effect, an art form, with its own special characteristics. The content is the gospel, and the resources and approaches are manifold – but always so that, by way of rhetorical art, hearts and minds are moved. Of course, sometimes a point from the kind of material given here may make a direct appearance in the spoken address, but that will be because it is a telling way of conveying a particular message.

This philosophy seems to downgrade expository preaching as once commonly practised and sometimes still found in (it is to be hoped) appropriate circumstances. But, despite the unparalleled number of opportunities now available for various kinds of formal biblical study, most congregations do not include many people able to slot in, at a moment's notice, to the world of a passage of Scripture that has just been read – at least, as that passage is currently discussed in the academy. Anyway, it is scarcely desirable that this should be the sermon's primary focus. It is an existential act of speech, offered to particular people, here and now.

A further factor is the character of modern biblical scholarship itself – with which the Christian community has always had a guarded relationship. One might say that it exists, for good or ill, and it takes forms that are sometimes informative, sometimes edifying, but often technical and seemingly remote from life and from modern issues. More seriously, it is widely believed to be inimical to faith, especially in the tendency of some of its historical judgements. It is no part of this book's task to enter into a defence or assessment of modern scholarship, and it is unlikely that those who suspect or reject such scholarship, more or less on principle, will be among those who use the book. In part, we simply take it as an inescapable feature of the current scene. But we do also see it as offering great opportunites for the under-standing of the ancient writings that make up the Bible, as well as steering us away from modernizing subjectivism. Our attitude is positive. We also believe that the attempt to grasp the sense of Scripture more clearly is necessary if serious mistakes are not to be made in its use and if mere intuition is not to prevail. The preacher has a responsibility to the text in its own right and decisions to make about its style of relevance, perhaps only of an oblique kind.

Of course modern scholarship is vast in range and multiple in method. The writers of this book have sought to avoid one possible way of reacting to this situation, the method of bland generality. Rather, there has been an attempt to present some of the more stimulating approaches currently in use and to show them working out in practice. The attempt is not rigorously organized. Contributors have written as they thought appropriate to the particular case.

Perhaps the most striking development of recent decades has been to move away from constant attention to questions of mere historicity to an understanding of the minds, intentions and social setting of the numerous writers of Scripture, as well as to seek a grasp of the sheer literary 'flow' of what they wrote. Such approaches are more easily and fruitfully adopted in some writings than in others. Often, in the Old Testament especially, there is too little agreement about the dating or make-up of many of the books that finally emerged. In other cases, notably the Gospels, there is enough discernible homogeneity of mind to offer real illumination if we work along these lines. With the newly adopted sequential reading of one synoptic Gospel in course per year, there is every encouragement to help both preachers and congregations to enter into the thought-forms, ideas and spiritualities of each evangelist in turn – though of course weekly 'doses' of a few verses do not make sermons necessarily the best medium for the conveying of such understanding. (In this respect, liturgists and biblical scholars are not exactly working in tandem.) Our contributors, all experienced scholars and preachers, are identified by initials. They do not conform to one particular method or school of biblical interpretation, and there has been no narrow editorial policy in this respect.

Contributors to the Old Testament readings are Richard Coggins and Rex Mason, in addition to contributions from the overall editor, John Rogerson. The New Testament contributions are from Ian Boxall, Charles Cousar, Ruth Edwards, John Fenton, Beverly Gaventa, Paula Gooder, Andrew Gregory, Anthony E. Harvey, Sophie Laws, Robert Morgan and the overall editor, Leslie Houlden. The contributions from Charles Cousar and Beverly Gaventa have been included by kind permission of Westminster John Knox Press, and are taken from *Texts for Preaching, Year C*. The author's initials are at the end of each entry.

The First Sunday of Advent

Jeremiah 33.14–16; I Thessalonians 3.9–13; Luke 21.25–36

Jeremiah 33.14–16

These three verses raise fascinating critical questions for two reasons. First, they do not appear in the Greek version of Jeremiah, and second, they are almost certainly an adaptation of Jer. 23.5–6, which should be consulted. In Jer. 23 the emphasis is upon a messianic king who will reign and deal wisely. The words about reigning and dealing wisely are missing from 33.15. Another alteration affects the bearer of the new name 'The LORD is our righteousness'. At 23.6 it refers to the coming king, but in 33.16 it is applied to Jerusalem; and note that whereas 23.6 says that Judah and Israel will be saved, in 33.16 the reference is to Judah and Jerusalem. These facts have led scholars to conclude that 33.14–16 is a creative reinterpretation of 23.5–6, probably from the period 500 to 350 BC. The fact that 33.18 refers to Levitical priests and that the stress of the verses is upon Jerusalem has suggested to some scholars that the passage originated in priestly circles.

From a preaching point of view the interesting thing is that it is the city of Jerusalem that is given a new name. This introduces a corporate element into the advent hope, and emphasizes God's graciousness. The passage does not simply look forward to a coming ideal ruler; it looks forward also to a restored and renewed community (Jerusalem) whose citizens will understand, by the new name, that their renewal is entirely the work of God. 'Righteousness' in Hebrew is not so much a passive quality as an activity in which God puts things right and upholds those who are loyal to him. Thus the 'righteous Branch' can be understood as a messianic figure who will contend for what is right and just, and the new name of the city can be seen as an expression of joy of those who live in a community and world in which what is right and true is pre-eminent. JR

I Thessalonians 3.9–13

While Epistles are not narratives in the strict sense of the word (like Gospels), they nevertheless have stories to tell. They often relate what has happened in the past involving the writer and the audience as actors, what is going on in the present, and what might be anticipated in the future. Occasionally the story gets so enmeshed in the 'message' of the letter that it is hard to piece it out. Invariably, however, a plot emerges, and the letter itself becomes a critical event in the very story being told. Sometimes we are left wondering how it all turns out in the end.

The lection for this first Sunday of the year from 1 Thess. 3.9–13 makes sense as we read it in light of the letter's story. The plot begins with Paul's ministry in

Thessalonica, coming on the heels of the rough treatment he had received from opponents in the neighbouring city of Philippi (2.2). The first chapter of the letter relates the diligence, gentleness and steadfastness of Paul's work and the model response of the readers. We learn that Paul, after leaving Thessalonica, becomes anxious for the struggling Christian community because of persecutions they are having to endure and grieves that he cannot come to see them. But he sends his trusted co-worker Timothy to encourage them and to bring a report of their situation (2.17—3.5).

The letter, then, is written in light of Timothy's report, a report that is basically positive and encouraging (though we learn that some readers are despondent over the delay of Jesus' return and the deaths of friends, while others have quit supporting themselves in their enthusiastic pursuit of spiritual matters [4.13—5.14]). The text for this Sunday is a particular expression of delight and gratitude for the progress of the believers at Thessalonica and a petition to God on their behalf for their continued growth.

What gives the passage an appropriate 'Advent' setting is the sensitivity that everything the actors in the story do is done in anticipation of 'the coming of our Lord Jesus with all his saints' (3.13). The plot has a projected closure, and the closure gives meaning to all the events that occur along the way. The return of Jesus is not posed as a threat to keep the troops in line, but as a conclusion to the human story, when the faithful life of the believers will come to light.

Two words occur in the petition made on behalf of the readers that appear (with their cognates) frequently throughout the letter and that immediately get our attention; love and holiness. Love has characterized the life of the Christian community at Thessalonica from its very beginnings. Paul remembers their 'work of faith and labour of love and steadfastness of hope' (1.3). Timothy's report reinforces that perception and prompts Paul to ask God that their love may 'increase and abound' (3.12).

What is striking about the reference is the double community to which the love relates. On the one hand, there is to be 'love for one another'. Within the Christian congregation there are relationships to be nurtured, the despondent to be encouraged, the idle to be prodded. The mutual needs and tensions of church members are not to be ignored in a greater cause of evangelism or social action. The internal life of the community, whether profound or superficial, whether peaceful or strife-ridden, will in fact make a witness, and the critical question is what kind of witness.

On the other hand, the petition asks for love 'for all'. The line between the Church and the world is not one that tells us whom to love and whom to ignore or disdain. The circles God draws are inclusive, not exclusive, and they direct the compassion of the Christian community beyond itself and its own needs.

The second word of prominence in the text is holiness, a word that with its cognates occurs six times in this brief letter. Holiness names the quality of life that distinguishes the Christian community from the world. 'The saints' (or 'the holy ones') are the people chosen and set apart by God, who at the coming of Jesus will prove to be blameless.

The notion of holiness often connotes a rigid style of life that follows a clearly definable code of ethics. One is holy if one does this or that, or refrains from doing this or that. Such a connotation is reinforced by 1 Thessalonians, which some commentators have labelled 'a letter of moral exhortation'. What is particularly noteworthy in this letter is that twice holiness is mentioned in a petitionary prayer (3.13; and 5.23, where 'sanctify' could be rendered 'make holy'). We discover that God alone makes people holy and qualifies them as blameless at the coming of Jesus. All one's valiant efforts to follow the moral exhortations do not produce holiness. It is the gift of a gracious God, whose Son comes at Christmas and yet once again. CC

Luke 21.25–36

Luke's account of Jesus' eschatological discourse speaks of the need to prepare for the coming of the Son of Man at a time after the imminent fate of Jerusalem (cf. 21.2–24). The references to heavenly signs (v. 25; cf. 21.27; also Acts 2.19 where Luke puts signs on the earth below) mark the transition from teaching concerning Jerusalem to teaching concerning last days yet to come. This period of crisis and drama will involve more than the fate of Jerusalem. Jesus speaks now of what is coming on all the world (vv. 26, 35).

Jesus' prediction of the coming of the Son of Man (vv. 25–28) is followed by the parable of the fig tree (vv. 29–31) which underlines the necessity of his coming. As sure and as visibly as the plant comes into season, so the kingdom of God will come. Each passage prepares the way for warnings to be ready to stand before the Son of Man (vv. 35–36). Luke's audience will know that Jesus' predictions concerning Jerusalem have already been fulfilled. This will engender confidence in his predictions for the future, and it underlines the enduring permanence and validity of Jesus' words, to which he refers explicitly (v. 33).

Luke hints at the connection between the Son of Man (v. 27) and the kingdom of God (v. 31). His reference to the coming of the Son of Man picks up Dan. 7.13. It is not unexpected, for Luke has prepared carefully for this climactic announcement as his narrative has unfolded (cf. 9.26; 11.30; 12.8, 40; 17.22, 24, 26, 30; 18.8). The one cloud (not clouds, an 'apocalyptic stage-prop' representing a form of heavenly transport) on which he comes (v. 27) may suggest the divine glory, which indicates God's presence but hides God from human view (cf. Luke 9.34).

The Son of Man comes as judge, but Christians may look up in hope rather than down in fear because he comes to bring them deliverance (v. 28). It is in this context of assurance that the disciples are actively to stand fast and pray that they will have strength to stand before the Son of Man. Luke seems to see both redemption for the believer, and the coming of the Son of Man and the kingship of God that he establishes, as each partially present. There is a tension between the already and the not-yet, and it is within this tension that disciples are to live.

Luke shows no interest in providing a timetable to allow others to chart the outworking of God's purpose. The reference to 'this generation' (v. 32) may have little temporal application. This is Luke's expression for those who resist or turn their backs on God and his prophets (cf. 7.31; 9.41; 11.29–32, 50, 51; 16.8; 17.25). Signs will be self-evident, and Luke's focus is on the need for disciples to live now in a state of constant readiness for what they can be assured is to come.

The place of prayer in the Christian life (v. 36) is a recurring Lucan theme (10.2; 11.5–13; 18.6; Acts 1.14; 2.42; 6.4 etc.). AG

The Second Sunday of Advent

Baruch 5.1–9 or Malachi 3.1–4; Philippians 1.3–11; Luke 3.1–6

Baruch 5.1–9

Whether the lectionary is right to introduce Baruch as a prophet is questionable. Nowhere in the book does the word 'prophet' occur, and in any case the work is pseudepigraphal, that is, composed probably in the second century BC, under the name of Jeremiah's secretary, Baruch (see Jer. 36.4, and compare Jer. 36 with Baruch 1). The book's setting is the Babylonian exile, and it looks forward to the restoration of Jerusalem and the return of the exiles; but in the context of its time of writing, probably soon after the defeat of the attempt by Antiochus IV to suppress Judaism (168/7–164 BC), the book looks forward in hope to a new beginning for a battered land and people.

If, in the Old Testament, Baruch is the secretary of Jeremiah, it is the later chapters of Isaiah that have been the inspiration for Baruch 5. Even without a profound knowledge of the Bible, it is difficult to miss the allusion in v. 7 to Isa. 40.4, in the language about mountains and hills being made low and valleys being filled up to make level ground. There are many less obvious references to Isaiah. The opening words about putting on new robes and a diadem echo Isa. 52.1 and 62.3, and at 62.4 Jerusalem is given a new name. Other Isaiah passages that come to mind include 32.17 and 49.22. The translation of the new names 'Righteous Peace' and 'Godly Glory' in v. 4 is not easy, and it is a pity that the presumed original Hebrew of Baruch no longer exists. The first name probably refers to peace or security which comes from justice. 'Godly' in the second name refers to worship, piety and devotion to God, and thus to the glory that comes from these things.

The fact that the writer has used one occasion of hope after disaster (i.e. the return from the exile in Babylon) to give encouragement for another situation following disaster (i.e. the aftermath of the banning of Judaism by Antiochus IV) is a reminder that life on earth has its ups and downs, and that even the sincerest human hopes are disappointed. Times of hope and expectancy, however, give us glimpses of eternity, and embolden us to face the trials of the present world in the confidence that they are not the ultimate reality. JR

Malachi 3.1–4

The book of Malachi, evidently dating from the late fourth century BC, was written or compiled within a society that contained sorcerers, adulterers, perjurers, and corrupt employers and landowners (cf. v. 5). This state of affairs, together with other unsatisfactory conditions, produces a series of charges and counter charges in the book, as God and the people engage in a dialogue of questions and answers. The passage in 3.1–4 is best seen as God's reply to what immediately precedes (2.17), where God takes objection to the view that he approves of, or is powerless to deal with, evil-doers.

The Hebrew of 'I am sending' implies that something is about to happen. A messenger or angel (the same word in Hebrew) will precede the coming of God to his temple. The function of the messenger is unclear. If it is to prepare the people for the divine coming, then why will it be necessary for God to refine and judge (vv. 2–5)? Perhaps the messenger's function will be to warn the people of the imminence of the divine judgement. At any rate, the divine coming will be painful for those who experience it. People may desire God, but will they be able to endure his judgement?

This judgement will begin with the temple and its worship (v. 3), with the place that ought to know better because it supposedly exists to mediate between the people and God; the place where the experts in prayer, sacrifice and holiness are supposed to be found. The judgement will then pass to the social sphere. A religion in which the cult is acceptable but which tolerates social injustice is an abomination to the Old Testament prophets. True religion is neither an acceptable cult without social justice nor social justice without a worthy cult. The two must go together because they belong together. People who fear God but are indifferent to their fellow human beings, especially those most socially disadvantaged, do not really fear God. People who are only humanitarian workers fail to recognize that the deepest instincts of human sympathy and compassion are God-given. JR

Philippians 1.3–11

It may seem strange to find this prayer of thanksgiving that opens Paul's letter to the Philippians designated as a reading for the Advent season. Normally such prayers represent Paul's adaptation of the traditional letter form of the Greco-Roman period and are often expressed in stereotypical phrases intended as a rhetorical device to build a base with the readers. The prayers anticipate the more meaty matters to come in the body of a letter.

The prayer that begins Philippians clearly telegraphs at least two critical themes of the letter – the reliable God who will see to the completion of what has been begun, and the importance of discernment in the moral life. And yet these two motifs gain their significance because of their setting between the advents, between 'the first day' (1.5) and 'the day of Jesus Christ' (1.6, 10). The eschatological language provides a dynamic framework in which to reflect on God's activity and the demands laid on the Christian community.

The use of 'day' as an eschatological symbol goes back at least as far as the time of Amos, who warns a presumptuous Israel that 'the day of the LORD' can turn out to be darkness and not light (Amos 5.18–20). In the prayer of thanksgiving, 'day' occurs in two ways. The initial reception of the gospel is designated as 'the first day' (Phil. 1.5). Hearing the word of God's grace and sharing with others in its power is like Eden all over again. It is the beginning of life, the creation of something entirely new. But the final day, the day toward which life is aimed, is 'the day of Jesus Christ' (1.6, 10). It is the point of Jesus' return, when the veil will be removed and the good beginnings will be completed.

The Church lives between the two days. The first day is not to be confused with the last day. The personal and moral ambiguities that continually confront us result from the fact that 'the day of Jesus Christ' remains in the future. We live in an expectant, but unfulfilled, world. And yet our confidence in God's promise and our growth in discernment are more than pipe dreams because of 'the first day' and the light it casts on those in-between days in which we find ourselves.

Look at two of the themes developed in this context. First, the great affirmation of 1.6 reminds the readers that the present is a time for God's activity in a venture that God, not the readers, has begun. God ultimately leaves no buildings unfinished, no battles in doubt, no chaos unresolved. The fact that the morning headlines and the nightly news do not always provide obvious reassurance of such a conviction would come as no surprise to Paul or his readers. He is in prison (1.12–14), and they are anticipating suffering (1.29–30). Yet the certainty about God's intentions makes possible a positive interpretation of their situations, even seeing them as gifts of divine grace.

Verse 6 has been understood at various times in the Church's history as implying that the circumstances of people in the world are going to get better and better until they reach an omega-point, the day of Christ, and that it is the task of Christians and other like-minded folk to work for that moment. We are under commission to build the kingdom of God, and its growth can be plotted like an upward-moving line on a graph. The problem with such a reading is that it overlooks the fact that the subject of the sentence is God (and the fact that life does not confirm it). God will bring to completion the good work already begun. God may use believers as agents in the divine mission, but the burden of finishing and the timetable for completion are God's, not the Church's. In this letter at least, the responsibility of believers is much more modest – growth in perception, living in unity, coping with anxiety, demonstrating a servant vocation.

The 'good work' already begun is not to be reduced to what is happening in the life of the individual. The second-person pronouns used throughout the passage are all plural, suggesting that what God has begun is a communal project expressed in the corporate body of believers. To the modern Church faced with a bleak future because of the erosion of membership, the affirmation of 1.6 becomes a word of hope.

The second critical theme emerges in the petition for a love that will 'overflow more and more with knowledge and full insight' to enable the readers 'to determine what is best' (1.9–10). The delay of 'the day of Christ' means that believers are confronted with all manner of moral ambiguities and decisions that demand clear discernment. What is prayed for is not so much a matter of determining right from wrong as a setting of priorities, of distinguishing ultimate from penultimate matters, of sorting out what is important from what is trivial.

Some things in life make a great difference; much is at stake (v. 10). Other matters are relatively inconsequential. Paul later in this letter cites wealth as a matter of little significance (4.11–12). He prays for his readers that they may develop the gift of discernment and do the things that really matter. A Pauline scholar has written, 'Love fills up one's life and informs all moral knowing and doing in such a way that one sorts out and does the things that really matter . . . Living thus, believers confidently arrive at the day of Christ with no fear of judgment' (J. Paul Sampley, *Walking Between the Times*, Minneapolis: Fortress, 1991, p. 83). CC

Luke 3.1–6

This lesson begins somewhat abruptly. No word of transition helps the reader connect chapter 3 with the infancy narrative that precedes it. Once again Luke sets the stage by indicating the names of those who are in charge of the world. It appears that Luke begins his story all over again with the opening of this lesson (3.1).

On the other hand, certain features of this passage do connect it with what has come before, although subtly. John comes on the scene as 'John son of Zechariah' (3.2), ensuring that the reader knows that this is the grown-up child of the astonished Zechariah and Elizabeth. More important, Luke depicts John in a way that unmistakably identifies him as a prophet, indicating that he is now fulfilling the words that were spoken concerning him even prior to his birth (Luke 1.13–17; see also 1.67–80). The one who was intended 'to make ready a people prepared for the Lord' (1.17) stands poised to do just that.

Given these important connections between the infant John and the prophet John, why the elaborate introduction of the rulers' names in 3.1–2 – an introduction that appears to threaten the sense of continuity and begin the story all over again? First, Luke here follows a pattern established in a number of Old Testament prophetic writings, in which the book itself begins by reference to the ruler's name (see e.g. Jer. 1.2; Micah 1.1; Zeph. 1.1). Second, this introduction follows a pattern Luke has already employed twice in the infancy narrative itself. He introduces Zechariah with 'in the days of King Herod of Judea' (1.5), and he begins the story of Jesus' birth with reference to the Emperor Augustus and the governor Quirinius. Third, this most elaborate of the three introductions allows Luke a presentation of figures who will be important later in the Gospel – Pilate and Herod.

This introduction does more than simply fulfil formal expectations or anticipate characters whose real work comes later in Luke's story. By elaborating this list of rulers, Luke provides some indication of who is – or who appears to be – in charge of things. He begins with the most formidable figure of Tiberius, Emperor of Rome. Then he lists the governors of various territories in the vicinity of the ministry of Jesus – Pilate, Herod, Philip, and Lysanias. Then he moves on to religious authorities, Annas and Caiaphas (although how both can be said to be high priest remains a problem, as the commentaries will indicate). The rulers of the earth are in their places.

But wait! In the midst of the status quo, Luke writes that 'the word of God came to John son of Zechariah in the wilderness'. John is neither emperor nor governor nor priest, but it is to John that the 'word of God' comes. And it comes not in Rome nor in any other seat of power, but 'in the wilderness', an unexpected place indeed.

Within the announcement of this prophetic call and its interpretation by means of the quotation from Isa. 40.3–5, three themes emerge that will be important throughout Luke-Acts: the word of God, repentance and the salvation of God. The 'word of God' *(rēma tou theou)* that comes to John consists, in the first instance, of his prophetic call and the proclamation that follows (see also Acts 2.14; 5.20). In the book of Acts, however, a closely related phrase *(logos tou theou)* becomes a way of referring to the gospel and its embodiment in the Church. The apostles proclaim the 'word of God' (Acts 6.2); it grows and multiplies despite persecution (12.24).

John's proclamation concerns 'a baptism of repentance for the forgiveness of sins'. This proclamation not only prepares the way for the coming of Jesus, but anticipates the work of the Church. John's action serves as a prototype of the Church's preaching of baptism and its declaration that in Jesus, God forgives human sins.

What is at stake in the prophetic activity of John is nothing less than 'the salvation of God'. Already the infancy narratives of chs. 1 and 2 have sounded this central Lucan theme of salvation. Zechariah declares that John's role will be 'to give knowledge of salvation' (Luke 1.77), and Simeon addresses God concerning Jesus as 'your salvation' (2.30). As late as Paul's final words in Acts, the 'salvation of God' dominates Luke's concerns (Acts 28.28).

Within Luke's two volumes, then, John 'son of Zechariah' serves as an able 'forerunner' for Luke's theology of the word of God, the preaching of forgiveness and the salvation of all people. In the context of Advent, John serves as the one who reminds Christians of the need to be prepared for the Christ who is to come. The task of making the highways workable again, repairing them so that 'all flesh' can indeed see God's salvation, is a task that the Church dare not neglect.

At the same time, the selection of John as the vehicle of God's word reminds the Church that the word of God does emerge in unlikely places. The rulers of the world and the rulers of the Church continue in their ways, content with things as they are, perhaps lulled into believing that they are in fact the 'rulers'. The advent of the infant Jesus will demonstrate that real power lies elsewhere. BG

The Third Sunday of Advent

Zephaniah 3.14–20; Philippians 4.4–7; Luke 3.7–18

Zephaniah 3.14–20

The prophet Zephaniah is generally assumed to have been active in the early part of the reign of Josiah (640–609; cf. Zeph. 1.1). His prophecies in chs. 1 and 2 and the beginning of ch. 3 speak of the coming day of the Lord and the judgement that will bring, not only upon Judah and Jerusalem, but also upon surrounding peoples such as those in Gaza, Ashkelon, Moab and Ammon. At 3.8 the mood changes to one of future promise; and although it is possible that Zephaniah is responsible for some of the material in 3.8–20, the concluding verses, especially from v. 16, seem to presuppose the situation of the Babylonian exile, with its language about dealing with Jerusalem's oppressors, gathering its people and bringing them home.

Verses 14–15 have been likened to language that could have been used at a coronation. The hopes and expectations that such an occasion would arouse are related, however, not to an earthly king but to the presence of God among his people, among them not for judgement (as in the opening chapters of Zephaniah) but for salvation. The theme of God being with, or in the midst of his people is a powerful one in the Old Testament (cf. Ps. 46. 5, 7, 11). The name Emmanuel – God with us – (cf. Isa. 7.14) is an important instance.

In vv. 16–17, 'holy war' themes appear, in the command to Jerusalem not to fear (cf. the notes on the Second Sunday of Easter), and in the description of God as a warrior who gives victory. Another important theme that is present is the idea that the exile brought shame and reproach upon the people in the eyes of the other nations and, by implication, upon the God of Israel. This situation will be reversed. Israel will receive renown and praise from the other nations when God ends its captivity and restores its fortunes.

However, it would be wrong to read the passage purely in military terms. No doubt the fortunes of war, and matters such as victory and defeat, were important to the Old Testament writers; but the prophetic tradition is not interested in Israel for its own sake, but as the people that will enable the nations to desire and embrace God's rule of justice and peace. The eirenic promises of restoration imply the prior punishment, judgement and purification, so strongly stated in the preceding chapters. JR

Philippians 4.4–7

As one approaches this passage in its own right, it needs a resolute mind to detach oneself from the music of Henry Purcell and the dismissal in the Holy Communion liturgy of the Anglican Prayer Book. It is the classic New Testament passage about both joy and peace.

The proper names, however, counter the feeling of timelessness and give a sense of immediacy to the passage. More than that, Euodia and Syntyche are significant as examples of the prominent place occupied by women in the early days of Christianity, notably in Paul's mission, but also in, for example, the world of the Gospel of John. We have no feeling that they are in any way 'inferior' to male co-workers. With the exception of one or two particular cults, this is remarkable in the culture of the period, especially in view of the Jewish matrix of the Church: though even here, there are exceptions, notably in the synagogues of some cities in Asia Minor where women were particularly active in civic life.

'Peace' is the keynote of the passage, and it has the strong force of the Hebrew *shalom*. It stands for a total well-being of which God is the only true source, and it amounts to the same protective shield as the gift of salvation.

For 'the book of life' (v. 3), see Old Testament precedents in Exod. 32.32 and Ps. 139.16, and then, in a closer apocalyptic connection, Dan. 12.1 and Rev. 20.12–15. This is probably less a memorial book, beloved of town halls in present-day routine, than a record that will be used at the judgement and which will ensure the eternal safety of those destined for 'life'.

It is not easy to know how to take the final verse. Perhaps the two 'if' clauses are best seen as summing up the contents of the 'whatever' clauses. They characterize the desired contents of Christian behaviour. And the expected return of Christ (v. 5) dominates the context in which all – mission, church life, state of mind, moral endeavour – is to be taken. LH

Luke 3.7–18

Luke provides the fullest account of John the Baptist in the New Testament, and he gives the impression that his ministry continued for some time (v. 18). He takes care both to subordinate John to Jesus and to emphasize the continuity between them (v. 16). He seems to emphasize common concerns when he describes John's proclamation, like that of Jesus, as good news (v. 18; cf. 4.18). Such good news consists of John's announcement of God's coming wrath (vv. 7, 9) and the consequent need for repentance that leads to practical action. John is a prophetic figure who emphasizes the moral consequences appropriate to conversion (v. 8a). Repentance is a recurring Lucan motif, as also is the motif that the use of one's possessions symbolizes one's response to the call of God (vv. 10–11).

John's baptism appears to be the outward sign of repentance. Those baptized respond to God by realigning themselves with God's purpose. A new Abrahamic people is being formed, but it is based on the response of lives lived in a manner appropriate to God's call, not on the basis of inherited descent. Such repentance looks to the future and the imminent reality of God's judgement, but it manifests itself in the mundane details of everyday life in the present.

John's vision takes in both personal responsibilities and relationships (v. 11) and the need for the responsible and unself-interested exercise of political, economic and military might (vv. 12–14). God will include even tax-collectors (v. 12) and soldiers among the children of Abraham: they must behave justly, but they are not called to renounce their occupations. Luke blends social conservatism with a radical ethic; the status quo John questions is on the level of individual conduct rather than larger structures. Luke's concern for the possibility of salvation outside Israel emerges once again (cf. 2.32), but the suggestion that not all who claim Abrahamic descent will escape the wrath to come makes salvation universally available but not universally enacted. Abraham's children are those who live appropriately.

Perhaps John's questioning of and challenge to a merely genealogical understanding of God's covenant with Abraham, the Isaianic new exodus context of his baptism (3.3–6: NIV and NRSV omit the 'therefore' that links vv. 6–7) and the eschatological wrath of which he speaks cause those who come to John to ask if he is Messiah. Again Luke subordinates John to Jesus, and now John points to the greater figure to come. He will baptize with Holy Spirit, and with fire. Luke later picks up the promise of baptism with Holy Spirit and appears to see it fulfilled at Pentecost and subsequently (Acts 1.5; 11.16). The reference to fire is more puzzling and is much debated. It is unclear whether Jesus will offer one baptism consisting of both Holy Spirit and fire, or two baptisms for different groups, one of blessing and another of judgement. Certainly John has judgement in mind in his image of the wheat and the chaff. John has separated them in his ministry: another will assign them to their respective places. This good news is not a blank cheque. AG

The Fourth Sunday of Advent

Micah 5.2–5a; Hebrews 10.5–10; Luke 1.39–45 (46–55)

Micah 5.2–5a

The opening words printed in the lectionary, 'The LORD says to his people', do not occur in the text of Micah at this point, and may tend to obscure the fact that in its context, the passage makes a sharp contrast between the fate of Jerusalem in 4.9–10, 5.1, and the promised future for Bethlehem. If 5.2 originally followed on from 3.12, which speaks of the irreversible destruction of Jerusalem, the contrast is even more striking. However, the sense is clear. The city where Davidic kings reign stands under condemnation; the village of which David was a native will provide a future ruler. The Hebrew text of v. 2 (5.1 in the Hebrew Bible) is not without problems, and a more likely reading and translation is 'You who are the smallest of the clans of Judah'. The reference is to Ephrathah, which is held to be the name of the 'clan' to which David belonged (see 1 Sam. 17.12 where David is described as the son of an Ephrathite). The unit so named was probably a group of fighting men, and the fact that it is called the smallest in Judah echoes the story of David's anointing in 1 Sam. 16.11 where David is the youngest, and probably smallest, of Jesse's sons. The point is that God does not work in the same way as humans, and that he uses apparently small and weak things to fulfil his purposes (cf. 1 Cor. 1.26–29). Verse 3 is reminiscent of Isa. 7.14–16, and the image of the pregnant woman symbolizes a time of waiting and, perhaps, suffering before the joy of the expected hope can be experienced. The concluding verses draw upon traditions associated with David, whether written or oral, and play on the fact that 'shepherd' in the ancient Near East is a common symbol for kingship. It is not a random symbol. The ideal shepherd devotes himself exclusively to the needs of the flock. An ideal king should do the same for the people. JR

Hebrews 10.5–10

The author of Hebrews continues to explore the similarities and contrasts between the Levitical system prescribed in the Old Testament and the work of Christ. The models and the expectations of the old system were valid, but ineffective. In particular, he focuses on the ritual of the Day of Atonement, the annual sacrifice for the sins of the whole people presented before God by the high priest in the Holy of Holies. The aim of the ritual was correct, but unsuccessful. One reason, explored in 9.6–10, lay in the character of the high priest, himself a sinner; another, explored in the present passage, lay in the nature of his sacrifice. As a sinner, a blemished thing, he cannot offer himself as a sacrifice, but must use animals instead; and animals cannot take away human sin (10.4). Only a 'human sacrifice' can meet the human need. The author takes for granted the necessity of sacrifice in dealing with sin, and that sacrifice involves death, the shedding of blood (9.22). The death of Jesus is essential for the salvation of humanity. However, the essence of his sacrifice is not just in the fact of his death, but in the character of the life that is given. The sacrifices and offerings of the law are replaced by the body of Jesus, who died because he came to do the will of God. (There is an echo here of the Gethsemane tradition, as there is clearly in 5.7–8.) The effective sacrifice is that of the one sinless and wholly obedient high priest, who does not have to sacrifice for himself, and so can sacrifice himself.

The author expresses his argument through the quotation and exposition of Ps. 40.6–8. His point could not be made in the Hebrew version, which reads 'Sacrifice and offering you did not desire, but ears you have dug for me', making the prophets' contrast between any offering of sacrifice and obedience to the word of God (cf. Isa. 1.12–20). The Septuagint translation, however, gave the more elegant verb 'prepared', and the author of Hebrews must have used a text in which the Greek noun *otia*, 'ears', had been read as *soma*, 'body'. This is one point at which it is clear that he writes in a Greek-speaking and -reading milieu, whether his readers are Greek-speaking Jews or educated Gentiles.

He is emphatic that the sacrifice of Jesus is single, unprecedented and unrepeatable: in his characteristic word, *ephapax*, 'once for all'. The offering of his obedient life was a unique event in time. Surprisingly, this passage is one of the rare occasions where the author refers back to his opening statement of the pre-existence of Christ (1.1–3), which stands in the Epistle in unresolved tension with the all-pervasive theme of Christ's full humanity. He must be totally identified with those for whom he offers his one effective sacrifice, but also he came into the world as God's 'appointed heir', committed to do his will. SL

Luke 1.39–45 (46–55)

There is a cartoon-like quality to the episodes in Luke's infancy narrative, and its immediacy and vitality may be lost if we move too quickly to view it as a documentary. Elizabeth and Mary are presented as larger-than-life characters in the one vivid encounter that Luke portrays at the beginning of Mary's three-month stay with Elizabeth. The episode is steeped in the atmosphere of the Jewish Scriptures. This gives a certain 'once upon a time' (cf. 'in those days', v. 39) ambience to the narrative, and it serves to show the continuity between the story of Israel and its God and the story that Luke will unfold of the ministries of John and Jesus. Yet this account does not only look backwards to the older story of which it is now a part. It also includes distinctive Lucan interests, which foreshadow and anticipate elements that will be prominent in the main part of his two-volume narrative. This episode, like the rest of the infancy narrative, is an overture that introduces themes yet to be developed.

Elizabeth and John are each filled with the Holy Spirit, a recurring Lucan interest. We are told this explicitly of Elizabeth, but it is implied of John when he too (1.41,

44, cf. 1.15) recognizes Jesus. Thus Luke also shows how prophecy and therefore God's design is being fulfilled in the events that he relates (cf. 1.45). Luke stresses the importance of Elizabeth and John in God's purposes, but already it is clear that John is subordinate to Jesus and Elizabeth to Mary; each older figure recognizes the greater importance of their younger counterparts (vv. 42, 44).

Elizabeth underlines the importance of Mary's accepting belief of God's word to her (1.45, cf. 1.38), yet Mary is not merely passive. She rushes to visit Elizabeth, presumably because the angel has told her of Elizabeth's part in God's unfolding drama (1.39, cf. 1.36). Mary is no wilting violet, and on her lips we hear the prophetic message of the radical and revolutionary nature of the rule of the God whose Son she carries.

Luke may have taken an existing hymn which he adapted to this context by the insertion of v. 48, but we cannot be sure. It is modelled on Hannah's song (1 Sam. 2), but it offers comfort for all who are lowly/humiliated/poor/dependent on God and not proud of their own resources and independence. God will continue to act in conformity with his action in the past – the implicit message of the echoes of Jewish Scripture, and the explicit point of vv. 54–55 – and he will do so in practical and material ways. These words of warning to those who are wealthy and powerful should not be robbed of their economic and political force. Nor should we minimize or obscure Luke's words of solace and hope to those whose poverty and oppression sustain the wealth and comfort that we enjoy – for now, at least. A hard edge is present in this hymn of praise.

The importance of the way in which individuals and communities use and share their material resources is a recurring theme in Luke and the early part of Acts. Here Luke presents his hearers with a reminder of the revolutionary nature of God's rule – past (vv. 50–55), present (for Mary) (vv. 48–49), and future (vv. 48b, 50). LH

Christmas Day and Evening of Christmas Eve

Set I

Isaiah 9.2–7; Titus 2.11–14; Luke 2.1–14 (15–20)

Isaiah 9.2–7

This passage illustrates how God's word in Scripture can prove relevant at different times, and in very varied circumstances. The many parallels to the 'royal psalms' show that this passage could have been used at the coronation of any of the Davidic kings. Such an occasion was seen as the dawn of a bright new epoch (v. 2, cf. 2 Sam. 23.4; Ps. 110.3). The joy of hope the occasion brought, like the joy of harvest or the division of the spoils of war (v. 3) finds echo in 1 Kings 1.39–40; Ps. 132.9. The overthrow of national enemies (vv. 4–5), the responsibility of the king (1 Sam. 8.19–20), is assured because of the promise of God to his 'son' (Pss. 2.8–9; 89.23). Indeed, at his accession the king was 'born', given birth as a son by God (v. 6, cf. Ps. 2.7). As Egyptian pharaohs at their accession were given a number of titles, so the king here is given four. He will govern in divinely given wisdom of counsel; he will be a god-like warrior; he will be a 'father' to the nation for a long period and, by his military prowess and just rule (v. 7), he will establish conditions of 'peace', that is both security from the nation's enemies and all that makes for fullness of life (cf. Ps. 72.1–4, 8–11, 16). Indeed, such conditions will endure 'for ever' (v. 7, cf. Ps. 72.5), as conventional a wish as 'O king, live for ever'.

This passage may, therefore, consist of a number of very general themes from the royal worship of the pre-exilic Jerusalem temple. Yet Isaiah may have composed it particularly for the accession of Hezekiah to the throne, in which case the 'darkness' and distress of the later part of ch. 8 (see especially v. 32, cf. 9.2) would have referred to the ravages caused by the Assyrians under Tiglath-Pileser III. Yet such times of darkness often returned. Job uses the same word as that in v. 2 to describe the darkness of the underworld and the despair of death (Job 10.21–22). Again and again the people of God would have felt the need for the birth of a great deliverer who would fill the conventional phrases of the enthronement ceremonies with new and real meaning, especially when the Davidic line proved a failure and came to an end. A passage like this would furnish 'messianic' hopes for the Jewish people after the exile. And Christians found in the birth, life, death and resurrection of Jesus the perfect fulfilment of all that is merely promised in this passage (Matt. 4.15–16). Nevertheless, at each level it reinforces the truth that, only when the king's sovereign rights are acknowledged, can people know the blessings of his reign.

The promise rests on God's 'zeal'. The word can denote the 'ardent' love of a lover (Song of Sol. 8.6) and God's burning concern for the well-being of his people (Zech. 1.14). RM

Titus 2.11–14

This passage is one of a small number of more doctrinal interludes in the largely pastoral, ethical and organizational topics that occupy the greater part of the Pastoral Epistles. This proportioning of the theological and practical themes is one factor that leads us to think of these writings as coming from the post-Pauline church world of the late first or early second century: practical concerns were now even more pressing for the Christian communities, and so was the need to find ways of developing cohesion in holding to basic Christian beliefs that could be succinctly stated.

It is hard to think of a more succinct statement of those beliefs than that presented here, with its mixture of doctrine and, immediately, its moral implications. And (v. 15) all is to be propagated with authority, the arrangements for which are of major importance for this writer, in the closely interwoven spheres of Church and household (1.5–9; 2.1–10; cf. 1 Tim. 3).

Nevertheless, despite the community concerns, the vision remains universal ('salvation to all', v. 11), even if God's practical goal has an Israel-like quality – the creation of a purified people (v. 14).

The vocabulary in which the doctrine is couched owes something to Scripture and something to the wider religious terminology of the day. 'Has appeared' (v. 11) and 'manifestation' (v. 13) belong to the same family of words: *epiphaneia* conjures up the drama of a visit by the deified emperor, with its excitement and hope of tangible benefits. All the more so with Christ. This idea of his appearance (however expressed) had tended to be associated with the hope of his return, but now the two statements refer to the first and the second comings, as if in balance. They are the brackets within which Christian life is lived.

'Saviour', though a scriptural word, is also characteristic of the imperial cult. It is a favourite with this writer to refer to both God and Christ. The translation of v. 13, it has to be said, presents problems. That commonly given ('our great God and Saviour, Jesus Christ'), which seems to affirm Christ's divinity, would be unique in this (and probably, in fact, any other New Testament) writer, and it is hard to imagine quite what might have been in his mind (he is not the most daring of theologians) – unless the context is indeed that of other cults, and Jesus Christ is being affirmed as *our* deity and saviour (as opposed to those worshipped by others): he, and he alone, is the centre of our full devotion. Less dramatically, the translation could and perhaps should be: 'the glory of the great God and of our saviour Jesus Christ'. It is God who sent Jesus as a supreme act of 'grace' (v. 11); and the writer's perspective appears plainly in 1 Tim. 2.5. LH

Luke 2.1–14 (15–20)

This passage, so beautifully crafted in Luke's narrative, certainly counts among the most familiar passages in the Bible. Dramatizations of the Christmas story as well as repeated readings make it a well-known text. People who know little or nothing about the Christian faith know about the shepherds and the angelic chorus. For that reason, the text presents a challenge to the preacher to hear and declare a fresh word that probes the familiar and yet moves beyond it.

What immediately emerges from the early portion of this story is the political context in which the birth of Jesus is recounted. We are told that Emperor Augustus had ordered an enrolment and that Quirinius was governor of Syria. Despite the problems surrounding the historical accuracy of this beginning (dealt with in most commentaries), the narrative setting cannot be ignored. It is not against the background of the reign of Herod, the local ruler who is known for his heavy-handed and brutal ways, that the story of Jesus' birth is told (as in Matthew's Gospel), but against the background of the Roman Empire.

The Emperor Octavian was a prominent figure, who solidified the somewhat divided loyalties of the various regions of the empire and ushered in the famous Pax Romana. In 27 BC, the Roman senate gave him the title 'the August One'. Poets wrote of his peaceful ideals and anticipated that his reign would signal a golden age based on virtue. Ancient monuments even ascribed to him the title 'saviour'. He represented a high and hopeful moment in Roman history.

Luke gives Octavian his familiar title and recognizes his authority by noting that 'all the world' (actually the Roman Empire) is encompassed by his decree. Often in ancient times the demand for a census evoked rebellion and opposition, but Luke records a dutiful response: 'All went to their own towns to be registered.' The mention of Augustus not only provides an indispensable time reference to help readers date the events that are being narrated, but also enables Luke to explain how Mary and Joseph, who lived in Nazareth, had a baby born in Bethlehem.

The introduction, however, provides a much more important function than this. It sets the stage for the birth of one who is Saviour, Christ the Lord. Octavian is not pictured as an evil, oppressive tyrant, a bloody beast 'uttering haughty and blasphemous words' (Rev. 13.5). The Roman state in Luke's narrative simply does not represent the enemy against which Christians must fight. The backdrop for Jesus' birth is rather a relatively humane and stable structure, the best of ancient governments, which led to dreams of a peaceful era and aspirations of a new and wonderful age. The decades between the time of Jesus' birth and the time of Luke's narrative, however, exposed the failed hopes and the doused aspirations. Octavian is succeeded by caesars who turn the imperial dreams into nightmares.

Against the horizon of disillusionment, we read of the birth of another ruler, from the lineage of David, whose meagre beginnings, on the surface, do not compare with the promise and hope of Augustus. All the world obeys the caesar, but Jesus' parents are rejected and relegated to a cattle stall. Yet the birth of Jesus is good news for all the people, ensuring a new and lasting promise of peace and goodwill.

The narrative does not present us with a confrontation between Augustus and Jesus, but with a contrast between vain expectations and true hope, between the disappointment that follows misplaced anticipations and the energy born of a divine promise, between the imposing but short-lived power of Caesar's rule and the humble manifestation of the eternal dominion of God, between the peace of Rome and the peace of Christ. The titles for Jesus, found later in the narrative (Luke 2.11) – Saviour, Christ and Lord – stand out starkly against the claims made for Augustus, and in the ensuing story become titles interpreted in fresh and surprising ways.

The setting for Luke's birth narrative clarifies for us the distinction between false hopes and true ones. Relatively humane, stable structures that contribute to the well-being of others often tend to promise more than they can deliver. Their very positive nature becomes seductive and generates impossible expectations. In contrast, Jesus is the anchor for reliable hope, for dependable promises, for anticipations that are more than fulfilled. CC

Set II
Isaiah 62.6–12; Titus 3.4–7; Luke 2.(1–7), 8–20

Isaiah 62.6–12

It is usually thought that chs. 56—66 come from the time shortly after some had returned from the Babylonian exile and were addressing the tasks of rebuilding city, temple and national life so poignantly mirrored in the book of Haggai. Some of the great promises of return in chs. 40—55 had, therefore, been fulfilled, but the reality fell painfully short of the kind of pictures of salvation promised there. So the words and imagery of chs. 40—55 are used a great deal in these chapters to reassure them and renew those hopes.

In the light of v. 1 it is probably the prophet and his circle who are called upon for such an active ministry of intercession in vv. 6–7. The idea of the prophet as 'watchman', looking, like the sentry on the walls of a besieged city, for the first signs of deliverance and proclaiming news to the people, is a familiar one (e.g. Ezek. 3.17; Isa. 21.6–12; 52.8, cf. 2 Sam. 18.24–27). Here the prophet calls for a more strenuous response to the situation than a resigned 'How long, O Lord?' It brings us face to face with the mystery of God's self-limitation in calling for active human participation in the accomplishment of his work, in both deeds and, as here, in prayer.

The response from God is as emphatic as could be imagined, reinforcing the promise of deliverance from the crippling economic hardship which comes from political subservience with an oath of the most solemn nature (vv. 8–9). The promise envisages the restoration of worship in the rebuilt temple as they praise God and know fellowship with him there (v. 9). The same link between economic prosperity and the centrality of God among them in the rebuilt temple is made by Haggai (Hag. 2.4–9).

Again active human participation is called for in a clear allusion to the promise of 40.3–5 that God would miraculously make a highway by which his exiled people could return home (v. 10). Here prophet and people are called on to make all ready for the great things God is going to do in their midst. Presumably, what is in mind is being ready by repentance and faith and doing all in their power to rebuild a new community. Again the mystery of divine sovereignty which yet makes use of human cooperation is stressed.

The promise of that divine sovereign initiative is that God himself will be present in power and grace among his people (he himself is described as their 'salvation' in v. 11). To know him *is* salvation, yet he always brings his 'reward' and 'recompense' with him, v. 11, cf. 40.10. Among the 'rewards' of fellowship with him is the giving of a new nature ('name', v. 12, cf. v. 2). His people will have been 'redeemed' from their bondage by their divine kinsman (cf. Lev. 25.25–28); they will be God's people because he has 'sought' them (cf. Ezek. 34.11–16) and they will live as God's chosen bride (cf. v. 4, and Eph. 5.25–27). RM

Titus 3.4–7

Like the other virtually formulaic, brief doctrinal passages in the Pastoral Epistles, these verses are a concise statement of basic Christian faith. Many of the characteristic words of these writings are here: 'appeared', 'saved', 'saviour'. Therefore much that was said about 2.11–14 (see p. 17) is equally relevant here.

But there is in these verses, in this surely post-Pauline writing, rather more Pauline vocabulary than in the other passage: notably in v. 7, where we are reminded of the language of Rom. 5.1f.; 8.17. Equally Pauline is the putting of the contrast between righteous works and God's mercy (v. 5). However, the linking of the mercy of God and baptism is unique. And this is the only reference to baptism in the Pastoral Epistles, perhaps rather surprisingly in view of their interest in the practicalities of Christian life.

'Rebirth' is not used elsewhere in the New Testament explicitly in relation to baptism, though a parallel idea of the utterly transformative meaning of the rite occurs in Romans 6.4, and in the closer parallel in John 3. It is akin to Paul's sense of Christ's coming as giving a new creation. The link between baptism and the Spirit is common early Christian teaching: cf. 1 Cor. 12.13 and numerous passages in Acts. The rite is far more than one's initiation into Christianity or the Church in a purely formal sense: it is a making new – an entry to the life of the new age, in the here and now. The Spirit is a recognized symptom of the presence already of the new state of affairs to which both Jewish and Christian hope looked and which Christian faith saw as now available as the fruit of Christ's saving life and death. It is one of the most powerful verbal means used in early Christianity to express the experience of radical newness and strength of fulfilment which were major features of the Christian community. LH

Luke 2.(1–7), 8–20

The birth of Jesus is the centre of Christmas. What one learns about Jesus from the narratives that relate his birth comes, however, from the actions and words of the other characters of Christmas – in Luke, from the shepherds, the angelic messenger, the heavenly chorus, the mysterious bystanders (2.18), and Mary; in Matthew, from repeated angelic messengers, Joseph, the wise men, Herod, the chief priests and scribes. Nowhere is that more evident than in the Lucan story, where a bare statement of the birth of Jesus is followed by the intriguing account of the nameless shepherds. They are traced from their location in the field tending their flock through their visit to Bethlehem and back to where they originated. From their actions and their interactions with the angelic messenger and the heavenly host, we learn about the character and significance of Jesus' birth.

We first meet the shepherds doing what shepherds are supposed to be doing – tending their flocks. They no doubt remind Luke's readers of the shepherding done once in these same regions by Jesus' famous ancestor, David. The routineness of these shepherds' lives is abruptly interrupted by the appearance of the angelic messenger. Their world, circumscribed at night by the wandering of the sheep, is exploded by the awesome presence of this one who brings news of Jesus' birth. The manifestation of the divine glory, the shepherds' fright, the announcement of the messenger disrupt their order and uniformity and set them on a journey to hear and see earth-changing events.

Three things we note about the intrusive announcement of the messenger. First, the good news includes great joy for 'all the people'. It is not merely the shepherds' small world that is changed by the word of Jesus' birth, but it is Israel's world. While Luke sets the story of the birth in the context of the Roman Empire (2.1–2), he has a primary interest in the destiny of Israel and 'the falling and the rising of many' for whom this baby is sent (v. 34). Jesus' relevance for the world, in fact, begins in the city of David as the fulfilment of Jewish expectations. It includes the acceptance of Jewish traditions (vv. 21, 22–40, 41–52), and only from this very particular origin does its universal character emerge.

Second, the announcement focuses on three astounding titles this baby is to carry – Saviour, Messiah and Lord. 'Saviour' has meaning in the narrative because original readers would recognize that the exalted Emperor Augustus had borne such a title. Unfortunately, the eager anticipations for a brighter, more peaceful day stirred by his rule were long since dashed by the brutality and weakness of his successors. Now a true and promise-fulfilling Saviour appears. 'Messiah' (or 'Christ') reminds us of Israel's hope for the anointed figure and God's grand design that he will inaugurate. 'Lord', interestingly, occurs four times in our passage, and in the other three instances is used for God (2.9 [twice], 15). It is inescapable in such a context, then, that divine associations be attached to Jesus (in v. 11).

Third, the angelic announcement designates the sign that will assure the shepherds that they have found 'a Saviour, who is the Messiah, the Lord'. But such a strange sign! Hardly fitting for one bearing such honoured titles! The babe 'wrapped in bands of cloth and lying in a manger', however, is only the beginning of the story of God's unusual ways in accomplishing the divine rule. Not by might or coercive tactics, but in submission and humbleness, Jesus fulfils his vocation.

Perhaps it is the perplexity caused by such a menial sign for such an exalted baby that evokes the immediate confirmation of the heavenly chorus, who join the angelic messenger in a doxology. God is praised for the birth of this child because the birth begins God's reign of peace on earth. The creatures of the heavenly world, in a context of praise, announce God's good plans for this world.

Having heard the heavenly witnesses, the shepherds now decide to go to Bethlehem and 'see' this revelation. Like other disciples who abruptly leave fishing boats and tax tables, they go 'with haste'. We are not told what happened to the flocks, apparently left in the fields. The shepherds' old world has been shattered by the appearance of the messenger, and now they are in search of a new one, one centred in the event that has occurred in Bethlehem.

When the shepherds find Mary, Joseph and Jesus, the narrator records that they report the message that had been made known to them about the baby. To whom did they give their report? To Mary and Joseph? Perhaps. Perhaps the shepherds in responding to the angelic messenger in fact become a confirmation to Mary and Joseph of the significance of this baby so unusually born. But there must have been a wider audience for the shepherds' report too, since 'all who heard it' were astonished – not believing or thoughtful or adoring, just 'amazed'. Apparently nothing spurred them to ask questions or pursue the matter further. In contrast, Mary clings to what has happened. She continues to ponder the events and the words (the Greek word is inclusive of both) of the shepherds' visit.

Finally, the shepherds go back to where they came from, apparently back to fields and to flocks, but not back to business as usual. What was told them by the angelic messenger has been confirmed. They have heard and seen for themselves. Their old world is gone, replaced by a new world. Whatever the structure and order of life before, their world now is centred in the praise and glorifying of God. The nights in the field will never be the same. CC

Set III
Isaiah 52.7–10; Hebrews 1.1–4 (5–12); John 1.1–14

Isaiah 52.7–10

The prophet predicts the certainty of coming deliverance for God's people in a graphic poem depicting the arrival of the messenger bearing news of victory to a besieged and beleaguered city. To share the suspense which precedes it and the intoxicating sense of relief which follows it we need only to read of David and his people anxiously waiting for news from the battlefield (2 Sam. 18.24–28).

First comes the single messenger, running from Babylon, the place of Israel's defeat and misery, appearing over the 'mountains', i.e. the Mount of Olives. At a distance it is impossible to say whether he brings good news or bad. Until he comes within hailing distance it is like watching a doctor coming in to tell us the result of a medical examination. Then the body language and shout tell that the news is good, victory has been gained (cf. 2 Sam. 18.28). God's victorious kingship over hostile forces has been established. The faith and hope expressed in their worship (Pss. 96.10; 97.1; 99.1) has been realized in fact.

Now the city watchmen take up the good news of the messenger (v. 8). In place of anxious hope they have now seen for themselves evidence of victory. 'Eye to eye' they see God returning to his city and his people, just as Job, who had 'heard of God with the hearing of the ear' could say 'but now my eye sees you' (Job 42.5).

The song of salvation, begun as the messenger's solo, then swollen by the concerted shouts of the watchmen, is taken up by the whole chorus of God's people. They are apostrophized as 'the waste places of Jerusalem' (v. 9) because they live in the ruins of their former buildings and among the shattered disillusionment of their former hopes. When God comes as saviour it is the 'waste places' of human suffering, sin and despair that are the first to be so transformed that they become the scene of praise and joy. The promise of the prophet that God would 'comfort' his people (40.1) has been fulfilled, and he has shown that, in their need and failure, they are still 'his' people as he takes on the role of nearest relative and 'redeems' them from their slavery (cf. Lev. 25.25–28).

God has taken his arm from his mantle and acted in power on behalf of his oppressed people (v. 10, cf. Ezek. 4.7). And this is no introverted, domestic matter within the small family of Israel only, but is accomplished on a universal scale. It is because he is the only God of all the earth, victorious over all other powers, that God can redeem his people and fulfil his purposes for all the nations through them (v. 10).

All is of God. Effective messengers and watchmen serve their people best by speaking of God and what he has achieved. RM

Hebrews 1.1–4 (5–12)

The document known as the Epistle to the Hebrews opens with none of the address and greetings that characterize the Pauline letters, but with a polished and highly rhetorical statement of the person and work of Christ; more like the text for a sermon or the proposition for an argument. Ideas are introduced that will be expounded later in the epistle: the continuity between the old and the new, as in chs. 11—12.1; the sacrificial work of Christ and his exaltation to heaven, as in chs. 8—10. God has spoken through 'a Son', and in 2.10–14 the author will describe him as a son among many brethren, fully identified with them. He will clearly affirm Jesus' humanity, but here at the outset needs to express the deeper significance of that individual human life. There are obvious comparisons to be made with the Prologue to the Gospel of John and both authors draw on the language of wisdom, as in Prov. 8; here most closely echoing Wisdom of Solomon 7.26.

Scholars disagree as to whether 'wisdom' in Jewish tradition was understood as a heavenly being, present with God at creation as his agent, or as a personification: a way of talking about the creative work of God himself; but here it hardly matters, for whatever is meant by the wisdom of God is now seen in the person of Christ.

The opening statement is followed by a series, or catena, of quotations, loosely linked by verbal echoes in a manner familiar in Jewish exegesis, and all taken to demonstrate the Son's superiority to angels. There is no need to employ the conspiracy theory of interpretation and to suspect a veiled attack on a contemporary deviant group who held Christ to be an angel, of whom there is no evidence at all. All the texts are ones that may have been used as messianic texts in Judaism and came early into Christian use, and so would have been familiar to the readers. There is some suggestion later in the epistle that the author was dealing with an educated audience who were, however, failing to grow in their faith (5.11–14). They need to be 'stretched' to explore the meanings of familiar texts, and the exposition of such texts as Ps. 110.4 will shape the course of his later argument. SL

John 1.1–14

Beyond the sentimentality and romance of Christmas, we encounter in the baby born at Bethlehem, so the passage tells us, nothing less than God's decision to become human.

One notable feature of the Prologue to the Fourth Gospel is the prominence of visual language (a particularly relevant feature for the Epiphany season). 'Light' and 'glory' are terms associated with the Word, and 'seeing' (alongside 'receiving' and 'believing') is the verb used for the perception of faith. Even before a statement of the incarnation, we read that the life found in the Word illuminates human experience, that the light continually shines in the darkness, and that the darkness has neither understood nor succeeded in extinguishing the light. (The Greek verb in 1.5 translated in the NRSV as 'overcome' has a double meaning: 'comprehend' and 'seize with hostile intent.' Perhaps an appropriate English word retaining the ambiguity would be 'grasp', or 'apprehend'.)

The mention of John the Baptist, who is a kind of lesser luminary or reflected light (5.35) and is contrasted with the true light, signals the movement from a pre-incarnate lumination to the historic advent of the light in Jesus. It is in this context that we understand that the coming of the light into the world 'enlightens everyone' (1.9). This universal reference has sometimes been taken to refer to the ancient notion that every individual possesses a spark of the divine, a measure of a universal conscience. The function of religion (any religion?) is to nurture the inextinguishable spark until it glows with understanding, so the argument goes. But such a reading hardly coheres with the evangelist's use of the image of light throughout the Gospel. Jesus claims in a specific way to be the light of the world (8.12), without whom people grope in the darkness (12.35). The coming of the light entails judgement, because it discloses that people prefer darkness to light (3.19). What seems to be implied in the Prologue is that all people, whether they believe it or not, live in a world illuminated by the light just as they live in a world created by the Word. What they are called to do is to trust the light, to walk in it, and thereby to become children of light (12.36).

Whether as a bolt of lightning in a dark sky, or as a distant beam toward which one moves, or as a dawn that chases the night, what light does is to push back darkness. The Prologue, however, gives no hint that the light has totally banished the darkness, that life now is a perpetual day. In fact, the story John tells reiterates the powerful opposition of the darkness in the ministry of Jesus and beyond. But the promise of the Prologue is that the darkness, despite its best efforts, including even a crucifixion, has not put out the light.

The last paragraph of the prologue has to be understood in terms of the many references to the book of Exodus, which it reflects. In a sense its background is the statement that 'no one has ever seen God' (1.18). Though in fact there are places in the Hebrew Bible where people 'see' God (e.g. Exod. 24.9–11; Isa. 6.1), the statement seems to recall the occasion where Moses, eager to behold the divine glory, is not allowed to view the face of God, only God's backside (Exod. 33.23). In contrast, now God is seen in 'the only Son'.

Furthermore, the seeing of the divine glory is made possible by the incarnation of the Word, who 'tabernacled among us'. The Greek verb translated in the NRSV (John 1.14) as 'lived' more specifically means 'tented' or 'tabernacled', and recalls the theme of God's dwelling with Israel, in the tabernacle of the wilderness wanderings and the temple at Jerusalem. In the humanity of Jesus, the Christian community has beheld the very divine glory Moses wished to see, that unique and specific presence of God that hovered over the tabernacle as a cloud by day and a fire by night.

Terms like 'light' and 'glory' tend toward abstractions and become very difficult to communicate in concrete language to a contemporary congregation. What, then, does it mean to 'see' God, to behold the divine glory? Two other words repeated in the Prologue help in the translation: grace and truth. To behold God is to be a recipient of wave after wave of the divine generosity (grace) and to experience God's faithfulness to the ancient promises (truth). 'Seeing' includes but goes beyond mere sense perception; it has to do with becoming children of God, with discovering the divine benevolence and reliability. Revelation in the Fourth Gospel has a strongly soteriological cast (17.3). CC

The First Sunday of Christmas

1 Samuel 2.18–20, 26; Colossians 3.12–17; Luke 2.41–52

1 Samuel 2.18–20, 26

It has to be frankly acknowledged that this reading does not easily fit in with either the Christmas season, or the Gospel (the visit of the 12-year-old Jesus to Jerusalem). The boy Samuel finds himself, probably from about the age of four onwards, at the sanctuary of Shiloh because his mother has dedicated him to God's service. This is because God has answered Hannah's prayer, and given her a son, thus removing from her what was considered to be the reproach of barrenness. These circumstances do not correspond with those of the Christmas story, nor those of the Gospel for the day.

It is a pity that vv. 22–25 are omitted from the reading, because they provide a possible way in to using the passage. They relate to the wickedness of the priest Eli's sons, including their immoral behaviour. Eli is also said to be very old. All this puts the situation of Samuel in the story into sharp relief. He is a child and a young adolescent growing up separated from his family save for a yearly visit (the little robe that his mother made and took to him each year must have cost many tears on both sides), and under the tutelage of an elderly priest whose sons are anything but a good influence. The story implies the isolation and the vulnerability of someone who is to become very important to Israel, as the threat from the Philistines to the nation's very existence becomes real.

The themes of separation and vulnerability come closest to the implications of the Christmas story. If Jesus, in his perfect humanity, was not aware of being separated from his heavenly family, he certainly experienced internal separation within his earthly family, as he followed his vocation, much to his family's distress. This is partly what today's Gospel is about; and he was certainly vulnerable, as the story of the Passion indicates. The story of Samuel does not provide superficial parallels with the New Testament. It is only as the narrative is probed more deeply (in a sermon rather than simply a reading!) that its value can be appreciated. JR

Colossians 3.12–17

The two final chapters of Colossians (like the latter parts of other Pauline letters) are largely devoted to moral teaching. Here, following the establishing of a doctrinal base in the 'risen' standing of Christian people and a list of vices which are, therefore, to be 'put to death' (v. 5), and then a statement, akin to others in Paul, of the multi-ethnic, multi-status composition of the community for whom 'Christ is all' (v. 11), we have an uncomplicated list of virtues, of the kind common in the literature of the time. Again, the list contains few surprises and is comparable to passages else-where. There are also few exegetical difficulties, and the passage invites reflection rather than head-scratching.

All the same, it is important to note the presence of a number of well-known features. The previous verses drew the familiar contrast between the new way of life and the old: 'in these you once walked' (v. 7), and put the whole ethical instruc-tion in an eschatological perspective: because of the prevalence of vice (sex, greed and idolatry), 'the wrath of God is coming' (v. 6).

Now the contrary virtues are headed by humility and its dependent social quality of forgiveness, which has God's forgiveness as its driving motive (cf. the Lord's Prayer). But love is the head of the moral pyramid, as in all the Gospels, as well as in Paul himself.

Then we have a practical note, referring to actual practice at Christian meetings: teaching, admonition and (in a reference virtually identical to Eph. 5.19–20, and therefore important in discussions of the connection between the two writings) music. Little can be said with certainty about the hymns referred to, though the New Testament is studded with possible examples, not least Col. 1.15–20 (see also Phil. 2.6–11; Eph. 5.14; and numerous passages in the Revelation of John). For the context of their use, 1 Cor. 14 provides the most vivid evidence. It must remain open whether 'the word of Christ' (v. 16) refers to something as precise as the tradition of his teaching and whether the giving of thanks (v. 17) refers to something as formal as the Eucharist: whether it does or not, the words 'to the Father through him' give a succinct statement of the structure and point of later eucharistic prayer. LH

Luke 2.41–52

Given the normal human curiosity about the youth of revered or honoured figures, it is perhaps surprising that the canonical Gospels contain only this single story about the youth of Jesus. The apocryphal Gospels supplement, of course, with astonishing stories about the boy Jesus striking down difficult playmates and raising them up again or shaping sparrows out of clay and bringing them to life. If Luke's story of the boy Jesus in the temple seems tame by comparison with those later legends, it nevertheless shares with them the desire to explain that Jesus' greatness could be seen already in his childhood. The unknown boy from Nazareth demonstrates such prodigious wisdom that he amazes the teachers in the temple precincts and bewilders his parents!

In its Lucan setting, the story does more than simply glorify Jesus, however. First, its setting in the temple continues the Lucan motif of Jesus' continuity with the tradi-tions of Israel. His parents' piety has already been demonstrated in their offering of 2.22–38 and in the narrator's note that they went to Jerusalem annually to celebrate the Passover. Here we find Jesus himself in the temple and engaged in discussion with Israel's teachers.

Second, the story anticipates the radical commitment that Jesus' teaching will later demand of his hearers. What the adult Jesus asks of his followers, the child Jesus here enacts. He concerns himself with the things that matter to the extent that fundamental family relations are treated as secondary matters. The meaning of the phrase the NRSV translates as 'in my Father's house' is quite ambiguous, as the commentaries on this passage will explain. Whatever the phrase means, it claims as first priority the connection of Jesus with the God who is indeed his father. This statement becomes even more impressive when we recall the high priority Jesus' contemporaries assigned to loyalty to family connections.

Third, in spite of the distance between Jesus and his parents that is implied by his question, 'Why were you searching for me?' and in spite of their inability to understand his behaviour, he demonstrates the appropriate obedience by returning to Nazareth with them. This feature of the text is closely linked with the first two, for the piety of Jesus' family and his own profound sense of connection to God are reflected in his obedience to the fifth commandment.

As long as we read this passage as a praiseworthy incident in the life of the young Jesus, it remains largely innocuous. If we change our lenses, however, and read it through the experience of Jesus' human parents, particularly Mary, it becomes much more troubling. In addition to the theme of Jesus' wisdom and devotion, another theme that appears here and continues throughout the Gospel is the inability of others to comprehend Jesus and his message. No one, not even Mary, fully understands who Jesus is or what his mission will involve.

The way in which Luke tells the story invites readers to consider it along with the parents, for the action of the story revolves around their experience. They leave Jerusalem, they travel, they discover that their child is missing, they begin a frantic search to find him, they eventually find him in the temple. It is difficult not to be moved by the fierce worry that must surely accompany such a journey.

The discovery of Jesus engaged in dialogue with the teachers of Israel may lead to astonishment, but it does not diminish the anxiety of his parents. The NRSV considerably understates the intensity of Mary's question, which betrays that she and Joseph have been in the grip of a terrible anguish. That it is Mary rather than Joseph who asks the question arouses the attention of interpreters, for in the Mediterranean culture of that era the father would be expected to take the initiative in confronting a son. One reason often given for the change here is that the scene itself concerns the Heavenly Father of Jesus, a point that might be confused were Joseph to speak. Throughout the infancy narrative, however, Luke draws attention to Mary and her responses to events (for example, 1.26–38, 46–56; 2.6–7, 19, 34). That he does so here also should not be surprising.

Two further comments by the narrator focus our attention on the human parents of Jesus, and especially Mary. The first comment (Luke 2.50) indicates that 'they did not understand what he said to them'. The second comment is that Mary 'treasured all these things in her heart' (v. 51), but this translation in the NRSV is somewhat misleading. Mary 'keeps' these things, much as Jacob kept events surrounding the troublesome Joseph (Gen. 37.11) or Daniel kept his visions (Dan. 7.28). These events perplex and trouble Mary, who turns them over again and again and again.

What Luke conveys here is something far more significant than a mere mental or emotional scrapbook of the infant Jesus. Despite Gabriel's announcement (or even because of it?), Mary does not understand what she sees and hears. In common with all other followers of Jesus, she must wait and see what will unfold, who he will become, and where his Father will lead him. She stands with the Church itself, trusting that this child comes from God, consenting to obedience, and straining to comprehend. BG

The Second Sunday of Christmas

Jeremiah 31.7–14 or Ecclesiasticus 24.1–12; Ephesians 1.3–14; John 1.(1–9), 10–18

Jeremiah 31.7–14

These are probably not the words of the prophet Jeremiah, but the work of a disciple whose outlook was similar to that of the author of Isa. 40—55. They were probably composed towards the end of the Babylonian exile, which lasted from 597 to 540 BC, and were meant as a comfort and challenge to those in exile. Where they were spoken/written and precisely to whom they were addressed is uncertain.

The opening words are either a command to the people to lead into the prayer 'Save, O Lord, your people', or, more likely, a declaration that God's victory is already accomplished, in which case a preferable translation would be 'the Lord has saved his people' (so NEB, REB).

God affirms that he is about to bring the exiles home, no matter how far away they might be. It is noteworthy that explicit mention is made of precisely those groups who would find the journey, mostly on foot, of some thousand miles (if only Babylon is envisaged) most arduous and forbidding: the blind, the lame, pregnant women and those giving birth. Their journey will be made possible because God will provide an even path (rather than a straight path) which is well provisioned with water. Behind this language is the image of the shepherd leading his flock, finding the best pasture, and paying particular attention to its weakest members (cf. Ezek. 34.16).

The description of the life of the returned community in Jerusalem is one which draws on those images that most adequately express a perfect existence in the harsh world of subsistence farming. 'Life shall become like a watered garden' (cf. the description of paradise in Gen. 2.10), and those things that sustain the necessities of life (grain, wine, oil, flocks and herds) will be abundantly blessed. The dancing of young women and the rejoicing of young and old men symbolize the peace (i.e. the lack of danger from enemies) that Jerusalem will enjoy.

Was this prophecy fulfilled? The answer must be 'no'. The actual restoration after 540 BC was nothing like what is envisaged here. Will it be fulfilled? The answer must again be 'no', at any rate at the level of its details, which concern the restoration of a peasant and not an industrial or technological society. What, then, is the value of the passage? Its value is that it is a sublime expression of the compassion of God: a God who, because he regards his people as his very offspring, can never be indifferent to their plight and their sufferings; a God who, because he has scattered, will gather his people. Then why has he scattered, or allowed his people to be scattered? The parent image partly answers this question. How can children grow up if they are always to be under parental control? The good news is that God will never give up on his people – including ourselves. JR

Ecclesiasticus 24.1–12

This poem, in which personified Wisdom speaks in the first person, draws upon other parts of the Old Testament, most notably Gen. 1 and Prov. 8.22–36; but it also contains original ideas. The opening introduction (vv. 1–2) sets the scene for Wisdom's oration. There is a twofold scenario. In v. 2 she is standing in the divine assembly, surrounded by God's angels and his heavenly armies (the stars). In v. 1 she is speaking to 'her people', i.e. Israel. How she combines these two stances is explained by the two parts of the passage.

The first part of Wisdom's speech in vv. 3–6 describes her privileged position in relation to God and the created order. That she 'came forth from the mouth of the Most High' has made Jewish interpretation identify her with the Law (Torah), and Christian interpretation identify her with the Logos (cf. John 1.1). 'Mist' in v. 3 translates the Greek, whereas the Hebrew version discovered in Cairo in the 1890s has a word meaning 'dark cloud'. This takes us closer to Gen. 1 as does the Hebrew word rendered as 'abyss' in v. 5, the same word translated as 'deep' in Gen. 1.2. The idea of 'covering the earth' in v. 3 is also similar to the spirit of God hovering over the waters in Gen. 1.2. Combined with allusions to the Genesis creation narrative is one from the exodus and wilderness wanderings traditions. The 'pillar of cloud' in v. 4 alludes to the symbol of the divine presence at Exod. 13.21 and elsewhere. The word 'alone' in v. 5 is important, because it excludes other deities from the governance of the universe and firmly anchors Greek ideas of wisdom (Sophia) into Israel's monotheistic faith.

The second part of the poem describes how universal Wisdom entered into a special relationship with Israel and Jerusalem. The idea that God chose Israel as the particular nation for which he would care is found in Deut. 32.8–9. Here, he cares for Israel through his surrogate, Wisdom. Initially, Wisdom is represented as ranging over the whole universe seeking a resting place (v. 7; and cf. again the hovering spirit of God in Gen. 1.2) until God commands her to go to Israel (the Jacob of v. 8) and Jerusalem. Three times in vv. 7–8 come words based upon the Hebrew verb *shakan*: 'where should I abide?', 'place for my tent', 'make your dwelling'. In later Judaism this verb is used for the noun *shekinah* denoting the divine presence, while in John 1.14 'dwelt among us' (*eskenosen*) uses the Greek verb that usually renders the Hebrew *shakan,* including here in the Septuagint. Thus does the poem nobly express the transcendence and imminence of the divine principle, embodied for Jews in the Law (Torah) and for Christians in the incarnation. JR

Ephesians 1.3–14

Paul customarily opens his letters with an expression of thanksgiving for God's action in the lives of the congregation he addresses. Ephesians, which was probably written by a disciple of Paul rather than by Paul himself, not only continues that practice but expands it. Virtually the whole of chs. 1—3 is taken up with expressions of praise and thanksgiving. Eph. 1.3 introduces this dominant mood of doxology with an ascription of praise to God for God's gifts to humankind. Since the word 'blessing' in Greek can refer both to an act of thanksgiving or praise and to an act of bestowing some gift on another, the play on the word in this verse sets the tone for what follows: God is to be blessed for God's blessings. The extent of these blessings comes to expression in the phrase 'every spiritual blessing in the heavenly places'. God's goodness takes every conceivable form.

Verses 4–14 detail the form of God's blessings and focus on God's choosing of the elect. First, the author points to the agelessness of God's election: 'He chose us in Christ before the foundation of the world.' This bit of eloquence need not be turned into a literal proposition about God's act of election. Instead, the author asserts that God's choosing has no beginning. Just as it is impossible to identify the beginning of God's Christ (John 1.1), so it is impossible to conceive of a time when God did not choose on behalf of humankind.

God's election creates a people who are 'holy and blameless before him'. Verse 5 elaborates this characterization of God's people. They become God's children through Jesus Christ, but always what happens is 'according to the good pleasure of his will'. Everything that has occurred comes as a result of God's will and results in 'the praise of his glorious grace that he freely bestowed on us in the Beloved'. In the face of God's eternal choice on behalf of humankind, in the face of God's revelation of his Son, Jesus Christ, in the face of God's grace, the only appropriate response is one of praise (v. 6).

Verses 7–14 continue the exposition of God's gifts to humankind – redemption, forgiveness, wisdom, faith. The exposition culminates with repeated references to the inheritance believers receive through Christ (vv. 11, 14). That inheritance carries with it the responsibility already articulated in v. 6, which is to praise God's glory. Primary among the Christian's responsibilities is the giving of praise to God. With v. 15, the writer moves from this general expression of thanksgiving for God's actions on behalf of humankind to particular expressions of thanks relevant to his context. He constantly keeps the Ephesians in his prayers, asking for them 'a spirit of wisdom and of revelation as you come to know [God]' (v. 17). The prayer continues in v. 18 with the petition that believers might be enlightened so that they know the hope to which they have been called and the riches that are part of God's inheritance. This mood of doxology continues throughout ch. 2 and most of ch. 3, as the author celebrates the nature of God's action in Christ Jesus.

For Christians in the West, these words may have an alien and perhaps even an exotic tone. They run counter to at least two of our most deeply held values. First, these verses insist over and over again that humankind is utterly dependent on God. To assert that God creates, God destines, God wills, God reveals, God accomplishes God's own plan means that human beings, in and of themselves, accomplish nothing. This assault on the Western sense of independence and autonomy poses not only a challenge, but also a significant opportunity for preaching.

The second way in which this text cuts against the grain of Christianity in a modern context derives from its insistence on the obligation to praise God. Our thoroughgoing pragmatism inclines us to respond to the claim that God has acted on our behalf with the question, 'What are we to *do*?' If we stand in God's debt, then we understand ourselves to be obligated to pay back the amount owed. The text, however, stipulates no repayment, for the debt can never be paid. Instead, the exhortation is to give God thanks and praise. To our way of thinking, this is no response at all, and yet it is fundamental to our existence as God's creatures. The reading of Ephesians should prompt us to recall the words of the Westminster Larger Catechism, that the chief end of human life is 'to glorify God, and fully to enjoy him for ever'. BG

John I.(1–9), 10–18

See Christmas Day, Set III, pp. 24–25.

The Epiphany

Isaiah 60.1–6; Ephesians 3.1–12; Matthew 2.1–12

Isaiah 60.1–6

This passage introduces a section (chs. 60—62, and especially 60.1–22) that announces the good news of deliverance for stricken Israel. The imperatives 'arise', 'shine', are feminine singular and so it is 'Zion' which is addressed, that is the community whose life is centred on the still poor and unreconstructed city. The future action of God is announced in a series of 'prophetic perfects'. It is seen as so certain that it can be described as having happened already.

They are to 'rise' from the lethargy of despair and to 'shine', but with the reflected light of God for it is his 'glory', that is, his manifested presence, which is 'rising' on them, ushering in a new age as the rising sun brings a new day. Three times in vv. 1 and 2 the words 'on you' are repeated, emphasizing that it is these very defeated, fearful people who are being summoned to reflect the light of God who comes among them, just as Moses' face shone with the reflected glory of God (Exod. 34.29–35, cf. 2 Cor. 3.18).

By contrast, the other nations are still in deep darkness (v. 2a). This might be an allusion to the 'darkness' which covered the face of the earth before God said 'Let there be light' at creation (Gen. 1.2–3). More likely, however, it is recalling the exodus story when God's presence ensured the Israelites had light by which to travel while the pursuing Egyptians were frustrated by darkness (Exod. 10.21–23). So, attracted by what they see of the miracle transforming Zion, these Gentile nations come to seek the source of that light for themselves (v. 3) so fulfilling the original promise to Abraham that 'all the families of the earth' would be blessed through him (Gen. 12.1–3).

Nor do these nations come empty-handed. They bring back all the dispersed Israelite exiles whom they have taken away captive (v. 4), a sight destined to bring such joy that, when the people see it, they will be radiant with the light of God's presence and power (v. 5, cf. Ps. 34.5, the only other instance of this word in the Old Testament) and their hearts will be enlarged to accommodate all their joy.

Further, the prophet pictures caravans of camels trekking across the desert bearing rich gifts of gold and frankincense, just as the Queen of Sheba brought tribute to Solomon, having heard of his great reputation (1 Kings 10.1–2). This inspired a continuing hope for the Davidic king (Ps. 72.15). Verse 6 here has probably also influenced the account in Matthew's Gospel of the coming of the wise men from the east bearing gifts (Matt. 2.1–11).

If all this sounds the note of nationalist chauvinism we have at least to remember that the Gentiles are attracted, not by Israel's splendour, but by the degree to which they reflect God's splendour (cf. Matt. 5.16). Further, the nations are envisaged as coming, not as servants of Israel, but as fellow worshippers in the temple (v. 6). RM

Ephesians 3.1–12

Following the first two chapters of Ephesians, with their extensive thanksgiving to God, in 3.1 the author takes up Paul's ministry in the context of God's mystery. Verses 1–3 characterize Paul's calling as his 'commission'. Verses 4–6 elaborate on the nature of God's mystery that is now revealed, and this section provides the most obvious entrance into a discussion of the Epiphany. In vv. 7–9, the focus is once again on Paul's ministry concerning that mystery, and in vv. 10–12 it is on the ministry of the Church as a whole.

The opening statement breaks off awkwardly after the identification of Paul as 'a prisoner for Christ Jesus for the sake of you Gentiles'. Verse 2 verifies Paul's calling as prisoner on behalf of the Gentiles by referring to the gift of God's grace that bestowed on him a 'commission' on behalf of Gentiles. Verse 3 makes specific the nature of this gift of grace, in that the mystery became known to Paul through revelation. In common with all believers, Paul's knowledge of God's action comes to him solely through God's own free gift.

Verse 4 returns to the term 'mystery', which is initially described only as a 'mystery of Christ'. The newness of the revelation of this mystery emerges in v. 5, which emphasizes that only in the present time has the mystery been revealed. This assertion stands in tension with statements elsewhere in the Pauline corpus regarding the witness of the prophets to God's action in Jesus Christ (e.g. Rom. 1.2; 16.26). What the author celebrates is the present revelation of God's mystery, and the contrast with the past helps to emphasize that fact but should not become a critique or rejection of past generations. Similarly, the second part of v. 5 identifies the 'holy apostles and prophets' as recipients of revelation, not because revelation confines itself to those individuals but because of their central role in proclamation.

Verse 6 identifies the 'mystery of Christ': 'the Gentiles have become fellow heirs, members of the same body, and sharers in the promise in Christ Jesus through the gospel'. Given the previous few verses, we might anticipate that the 'mystery' refers to the mystery of Jesus' advent. For this letter, however, the 'mystery of Christ' has a very specific connotation, namely, the inclusion of the Gentiles. Each word identifying the Gentiles in v. 6 begins with the prefix *syn*, 'together', emphasizing the oneness created through the mystery. We might convey this phrase in English as 'heirs together, a body together, sharers together'. For the writer of Ephesians, central to the 'mystery of Christ' is the oneness of Jew and Gentile.

The emphasis here on the social dimension of the gospel, the unification of human beings, needs specific attention. Certainly Ephesians does not limit the mystery to its social component, as if the only characteristic of the gospel is its impact on human relations. The extensive praise of God and of Jesus Christ in chs. 1 and 2 prevents us from reductionism. Nevertheless, here the radical oneness of Jew and Gentile who become one new humanity (2.15) becomes a necessary ingredient in the larger reconciliation of humankind to God (2.16). Any separation between 'vertical' and 'horizontal' dimensions of faith here stand exposed as inadequate.

Verses 7–9 return us to Paul's role with respect to the gospel. He, despite his own standing as 'the very least of all the saints', receives the gift of preaching among the Gentiles and, indeed, among all people (v. 9). Proclamation of the gospel comes not from Paul and his fellow apostles alone, however. Verse 10 identifies the role of the whole Church in proclamation. The Church, both through its verbal proclamation and through its actions, makes known God's wisdom. Here that wisdom is addressed to 'the rulers and authorities in the heavenly places'. The gospel addresses not only human beings but all of God's creation.

Verses 11–12 affirm once again the purpose of God in the proclamation of Paul and of the Church. God's purpose has its final goal in Christ Jesus our Lord, 'in whom we have access to God in boldness and confidence through faith in him'. These last terms connote more in Greek than the English translations can convey. To speak 'boldly' (*parresia*) is to speak without regard for the consequences, and to have 'access' (*prosagoge*) is to have, through Jesus Christ, a means of drawing near to God. In other words, the revelation, or epiphany, of Jesus Christ carries with it both the obligation of proclaiming the gospel and the strength needed for carrying out that obligation. BG

Matthew 2.1–12

The Book of Common Prayer explained Epiphany as the manifestation of Christ to the Gentiles, and this is certainly how Matthew understood his story of the wise men. He never describes them explicitly as Gentiles, but the way in which they are presented by Matthew indicates that this is how he meant them to be understood. Thus they ask where the child is who has been born king of the Jews, in contrast with the Jewish chief priests and scribes, who know the answer from the Scriptures; they say 'king of the Jews', whereas Jews usually referred to themselves as Israelites. Notice that Herod rephrases their title with 'the Messiah'.

The story presents a contrast between Gentile 'wise men' (astrologers, whom Matthew surely values as among the intellectual elite of their day, a plus mark for the Christian cause) worshipping the true king and a Jewish false king seeking his apparent rival's death. Antitheses of this kind are characteristic of Matthew's Gospel: destruction–life; wheat–weeds; good servants–bad servants; etc.

There is another point which confirms this view of the wise men. Matthew seems to have arranged his whole book as a diptych, with the beginning matching the end; e.g. 'God is with us' (1.23) and 'I am with you always' (28.20). Similarly, the coming of Gentiles in ch. 2 is matched at the end by the command to make disciples of all the nations (*ethne*, Gentiles). In one of the very few healing stories that Matthew adds to what he had received from Mark, the contrast is made between the faith of a Gentile and the faithlessness of Israel, and between the final salvation of Gentiles and the damnation of Jews (8.5–13).

The presence of this theme in Matthew's Gospel is extraordinary, and calls for some explanation. The book as a whole seems to come from a church or churches where the law of Moses was still regarded as authoritative (5.17–20). We might therefore have assumed that these 'Jewish Christians' would have disapproved of a mission to Gentiles. Moreover, the Gospel does contain the prohibition, 'Go nowhere among the Gentiles' (10.5f.). The Twelve are to preach to Israel, and to Israel alone (perhaps, however, just for the present, during Jesus' lifetime, with 28.20 providing for the rest of time). There remains, however, something of a puzzle about how Matthew quite held these two attitudes together; and we can also note his use from time to time of 'Gentiles' as a term of abuse or at least as an expression of superiority: 5.47; 6.32; 18.17: is that just an unthinking and unregenerate reflex?

Perhaps, like Paul, he was convinced of the rightness of preaching to Gentiles, by the bare fact that they had received the Spirit. And, also like Paul, by the fact that Jews, on the whole, were less likely to become Christian believers than Gentiles were. Perhaps, even as a Jew, he was on the 'liberal' wing that saw a positive future in God's purposes for at least some Gentiles.

Whatever the reason for it, Matthew's book contains both a high belief in the Jewish elements of Christianity and a conviction that these are to be made available to those who were not physically descended from Abraham. Though Jesus himself had few contacts with Gentiles, Matthew, like Paul before him, and like Luke and John later, believed that the mission to the Gentiles was according to the will of God. For him this must have been in many ways a costly belief to hold. JF

The Baptism of Christ

(The First Sunday of Epiphany)

Isaiah 43.1–7; Acts 8.14–17; Luke 3.15–17, 21–22

Isaiah 43.1–7

The lectionary does not reproduce the biblical words exactly, but omits 'But now' before 'Thus says the LORD'. This obscures the function of vv. 1–3a, which are probably an answer to an unrecorded complaint of the people that they have been abandoned by God. God replies that because he formed (created) the people in the first place, he will never abandon them. This first creation (at the exodus) was an act of redemption; it will not be the last such act. God knows his people by name, and this indicates a special relationship that will not be broken on God's side. The reference to waters, rivers and fire should not be taken literally. They indicate general dangers that will face the people as they make the journey back from their exile in Babylon to Jerusalem and Judah.

It may be necessary to rearrange the verses, so that v. 5a, 'Do not fear, for I am with you', precedes v. 3b, 'I give Egypt as your ransom'. We then have two assurances of redemption, each beginning with 'Do not fear' (cf. v. 1b). The language of 'ransom' in v. 3b raises the question of the person to whom the ransom is paid ('ransom' language in the New Testament raises similar problems!). In the Old Testament there is no one comparable to God to whom a ransom could be paid, and the word cannot, therefore, be taken literally. What is probably intended is the divine empowerment of the Persian ruler Cyrus (cf. 45.1), whose conquests will be the means whereby the exiles will be freed to return home. (Cyrus's successor Cambyses, in fact, conquered Egypt.) The exiles will be gathered from the four corners of the earth (another piece of poetic exaggeration) because they belong especially to God as his sons and daughters.

This passage is not about baptism, but about the importance of names; about the fact that when we use a person's name, especially a first name, a relationship of some kind is implied. Naming happens at baptism, and signifies God's knowledge of the one baptized and his commitment to that person. At the baptism of Christ, there is no naming, unless the divine voice saying, 'You are my Son' is considered to be such. What is of overwhelming importance is the inexhaustible commitment of God to all he knows by name. JR

Acts 8.14–17

The epiphany or manifestation of Christ is associated with the revelation of the Christ Child to the nations, represented by the Magi, but also with the revelation of his identity as Son of God by the voice from heaven at his baptism. This is the epiphany theme emphasized in the icons and ceremonies of the Eastern Orthodox Churches, and now recaptured and emphasized in the Western lectionary. The passage in Acts suggests the double association: the preaching of the apostles moves beyond Judaea to Samaria, in the first stage of the programme for which they were commissioned by the risen Christ in Acts 1.8, and the Samaritans are baptized. Samaria is a transitional point in the move to the Gentile world: its people shared the worship of the one God, but were regarded by their Jewish neighbours as doing so imperfectly, in their temple on Mount Gerizim, and were also regarded as a mixed-race people since the defeat and settlement of northern Israel by Assyria in 722 BC (2 Kings 17). In Luke's Gospel, Jesus shows a particular interest in Samaritans, and this is carried through into the mission of his disciples. It is the John who once suggested calling fire from heaven on to a Samaritan village (Luke 9.54) who now comes to lay hands on Samaritans.

The reason for Peter and John's journey is puzzling. It suggests that the baptism of the Samaritans by Philip was incomplete and that the Holy Spirit was given only with the laying on of hands by apostles; and this has therefore been read as the 'proof-text' for the practice of confirmation by bishops in the apostolic succession. Philip himself was not an apostle, but one of the 'deacons' chosen by the apostles in Acts 6; but his subsequent baptism of the Ethiopian eunuch in ch. 8 does not seem to need any further supplementation. In Acts 19.1–7 Paul lays hands on disciples who had been baptized but not received the Spirit, but their baptism was imperfect, based only on that of John the Baptist. Philip, like Paul, baptized 'in the name of the Lord Jesus'. Further, in Acts 10.44–48, the Holy Spirit comes to the household of Cornelius in advance even of Peter's baptizing them!

It is not possible to extract a consistent church order from the narratives of Acts. It may be that this reflects the fluid and exploratory situation of very early Christianity, before any such order emerged, but more probably the details of practice are secondary to the thrust of the narrative itself. The mission to the Samaritans is not an incidental occurrence or a private initiative: it is a necessary step forward in the movement of the gospel outward from Jerusalem, where the Church had begun with the descent of the Spirit at Pentecost and the preaching of the apostles. There may be a sense that Philip, the Hellenist with his Greek name, does not quite make the connection: but even without that extra nuance, the apostles from Jerusalem are there to affirm and so 'confirm' this advance; and not only they, but the Holy Spirit, active as much in Samaria as in Jerusalem. SL

Luke 3.15–17, 21–22

All the synoptic Gospels include the baptism of Jesus, and each of them connects Jesus' baptism with John the Baptist and also labours to show Jesus' superiority to John (presumably as a result of some challenge from disciples of John). Mark is content to have John assert his inferiority to the one who will follow him (Mark 1.7–8), but Matthew takes matters a bit farther, having John initially demur from the task of baptizing Jesus (Matt. 3.13–15). Luke takes matters yet a step farther, placing the notice of John's arrest and imprisonment just before Jesus' baptism (Luke 3.18–20) and announcing Jesus' baptism with no reference whatsoever to the name of the one who baptized him. Placing Jesus' baptism in the context of John's ministry suggests that Jesus is baptized as part of that ministry, but Luke provides no details. The Gospel of John does not include a story of Jesus' baptism by John, although John there functions as a powerful witness to Jesus.

If the Synoptics share a story of Jesus' baptism, they also connect that baptism closely with the Holy Spirit. John's prophetic announcement about the one who will follow him includes a reference to a future baptism with the Holy Spirit (Mark 1.8; Matt. 3.11; Luke 3.16; compare John 1.19–34), and Jesus' own baptism is marked by the descent of the Spirit (Mark 1.10; Matt. 3.16; Luke 3.22). These references to the activity of the Spirit are significant in all the Gospels, of course, but they take on a heightened significance in Luke because the Spirit has already been exceedingly active in the early chapters of Luke's Gospel.

Luke's story begins with an announcement of John the Baptist's birth, in which Gabriel proclaims that 'even before his birth he will be filled with the Holy Spirit' (1.15). In response to Mary's bewildered question about how she will bear a child, she learns that 'the Holy Spirit will come upon' her (1.35). Elizabeth suddenly breaks forth in praise of Mary at the instigation of the Spirit (1.41–42), and Simeon visits the temple at the precise moment when Mary and Joseph arrive with Jesus because the Spirit prompts him to do so (2.27). Small wonder that interpreters have sometimes referred to Luke-Acts as the 'book of the Holy Spirit'.

These early actions of the Holy Spirit have been the sort that readers would easily identify as gospel in the sense of 'good news'. Even if the experience of being overcome by the Holy Spirit may have terrified Mary or Elizabeth, readers will surely welcome these manifestations of God on behalf of God's people. In the proclamation of John the Baptist, however, a new element enters the picture: baptism 'with the Holy Spirit and fire' (3.16). John's description of this form of baptism sounds like anything but good news: 'His winnowing fork is in his hand, to clear his threshing floor and to gather the wheat into his granary; but the chaff he will burn with unquenchable fire' (3.17). To be sure, Luke also includes the more congenial motif of the Spirit's descent upon Jesus in a form like that of a dove and the heavenly declaration of Jesus as God's Son (3.22), but that provides little comfort for those who anticipate the 'winnowing fork' that is to follow!

Contemplating these and other Lucan references to the Holy Spirit can produce a multitude of bewildering questions. Is the descent of the Spirit on Jesus different from the Church's reception of the Spirit at Pentecost? How does the Spirit-inspired speech of John the Baptist or Elizabeth differ from that later granted to Peter or Paul? What exactly is baptism with the Holy Spirit, and how is it connected with water baptism, with church membership, with prophecy?

In this writer's judgement, attempts to produce a systematic statement of Luke's understanding of the Holy Spirit inevitably fail. The evidence simply does not lend itself to logical generalizations. Luke draws on language about the Holy Spirit in a variety of contexts, and he is more concerned with asserting the presence and activity of the Spirit than with charting the Spirit's moves.

In this particular passage, the first reference to the Spirit serves to reinforce the prophetic motif already introduced in the Magnificat and in the oracles of Simeon. The coming of Jesus Christ does not baptize the status quo; rather, it overthrows every power and undermines all that seems certain in the world's eyes. Many among Jesus' hearers will find this most unwelcome news. If Luke's is a Gospel of mercy, it is also very much a Gospel in the prophetic mode.

The second reference to the Spirit connects Jesus both with the Spirit and with God. In the complexity of Luke 3.21–22, we can see why the Church later employed trinitarian language to give voice to the relationship among the three, Father, Son and Spirit. For Luke, however, the scene ensures that Jesus' ministry itself derives from the Holy Spirit, that Jesus himself is God's Son.

The decision to exclude 3.18–20 from the reading for this Sunday is understandable, given the way in which John's arrest seems to intrude upon an otherwise clear move from the baptism practised by John to the baptism of Jesus. The inclusion of John's arrest is important, however, for it recalls that the price paid by those who act at the behest of the Spirit is often a high one. BG

The Second Sunday of Epiphany

Isaiah 62.1–5; 1 Corinthians 12.1–11; John 2.1–11

Isaiah 62.1–5

The opening words added by the lectionary to the biblical text, 'The LORD says this', create the impression that the passage is addressed by God to the exiled people. This may be correct, although the third-person language (e.g. 'that the mouth of the LORD will give', rather than 'that I will give' in v. 2) has led commentators to identify the speaker of at least vv. 2–5 as the prophet. The poetic language is very vivid. Jerusalem's vindication will be as noticeable as a dawn or a burning torch (dispelling darkness or shining at night?). The images then become royal. Kings were given new names at their coronation; yet it is not so much that Jerusalem will be or become royal, as that the restored city will be evidence of God's kingship – will be the crown and sceptre in the hand of God. The new names will indicate a change of status. The name 'forsaken' implies being abandoned by a husband, and 'desolate' implies barrenness. Their replacements express vividly the reversal of these states and lead naturally to the concluding verse, where the image of marriage is used to express the joy that God will have in regard to his people.

It is not known whether the passage is a promise of hope to people still in exile, or reassurance to those who have returned from exile and who find themselves in the midst of ruins and poverty. In material terms the promises were hardly ever fulfilled. They are part of the paradox that what God values and calls his own exists in an as yet unredeemed world, and does not always appear to be blessed, from a human standpoint. JR

1 Corinthians 12.1–11

1 Corinthians 12.1–11 forms an important part of the argument of Paul, which began in 11.2 and runs up to the end of 14.40. Many of the passages in this section of the Epistle are so well known that they are often read in isolation from those around them. 1 Corinthians 12.1–11 is no exception. Like its near neighbours in the Epistle, this passage makes most sense when read as a part of the overall argument of chs. 11—14. One of the biggest problems encountered by the Corinthian church is a breakdown of relationship due to a lack of respect one for another. The Corinthians seemed unable to honour the differences that existed between them whether on grounds of gender (11.2–16), wealth (11.17–34) or, as here, gifts of the Spirit (12.1–31). Paul urges the church to recognize their unity in the Spirit (12.13) and above all to love each other (13.1–13).

Paul begins this passage by acknowledging how easy it is to be swept away by matters of the Spirit. He reminds the Corinthians that before they were Christian they were carried away by idols that could not even speak. How, then, are they to identify 'things that come from the Spirit' (which may be a better way of taking *ton pneumatikon* than 'spiritual gifts') when people speak their message? Paul states that the test is quite simple: only those who can acknowledge the Lordship of Jesus speak by the Holy Spirit.

The use of the two phrases, 'Jesus is cursed' (*anathema*) and 'Jesus is Lord' (*Kurios*), is intriguing here. They are not natural opposites. Why then does Paul use them to argue such an important point? It is possible that they refer to the crucifixion and resurrection. Someone who had experienced the Holy Spirit, as the earliest disciples did at Pentecost, would be able to recognize that Jesus' resurrection and ascension into heaven followed his crucifixion and would now be able to say that Jesus is Lord. Someone who had not had such an experience (e.g. Jews encountered in the argument) would see just the crucifixion and so would consider Jesus' death to indicate that he remains cursed (Deut. 21.23 'anyone hung on a tree is under God's curse'). This is something that Paul explores in more depth in Gal. 3.13.

Paul moves from arguing for a single test to discern the activity of the Spirit of God to an acknowledgement that the manifestation of the Spirit will differ from person to person. At this point Paul begins to use a different word (something that is not apparent in the English translations). In v. 4 he uses the word *charisma*, instead of *pneumatikos* as in v. 1. This word stresses that these gifts are gifts of grace. Thus Paul indicates that these manifestations are not a natural extension of an experience of the Holy Spirit. An experience of the Holy Spirit causes one to say 'Jesus is Lord'; anything more is a gracious gift from God. Furthermore, while these manifestations are all different, they all originate from the same source; diversity comes from an original unity.

One of the most unusual features of this passage is the trinitarian reference that it contains. In vv. 4–6, Paul makes three consecutive statements concerning first the Spirit, then Christ and then God. These three parallel and consecutive statements are the earliest example of explicit trinitarian language in the New Testament. It is all too easy to read back into this passage later, complex trinitarian theology. As far as possible we must avoid this, though it is remarkable that when Paul has cause to explore the theme of unity and diversity in detail he does so with reference to the Spirit, the Lord and God.

Paul's primary emphasis in this passage is the unity out of which diversity may emerge. The problem of the Corinthian church is that they have lost sight of their original unity. So it is only after establishing the absolute unity that arises from the Spirit that he ends his discussion by looking in detail at the different gifts available: nine in total. This is not an exhaustive list as other gifts occur elsewhere in Pauline writings (Rom. 12.6–8; 1 Cor. 12.27–28; and Eph. 4.11) and tend to include more practical gifts such as giving and preaching. Paul concentrates here on the gifts present in the Corinthian setting, all of which have equal validity and none of which are to be disparaged.

Throughout this passage Paul constantly focuses the attention onto basics. Things that come from the Spirit can appear complex. Spiritual things can carry us away and there is a wide variety of ways in which the Spirit can be made manifest but at the heart of all of this lies one Spirit. The action of this Spirit can be discerned by the ability of the speaker to acknowledge the present reality of Jesus, not dead and cursed on a cross, but living and reigning in heaven. Diversity within the Church is only legitimate when it finds its roots in this simple truth. PG

John 2.1–11

John calls the great deeds of Jesus 'signs', directing our attention to their inner meaning, beyond their role as mere 'wonders'. So, in this Gospel, 'sign' is almost always a positive word (but see 4.48 where it is linked to 'wonders' in its disparaging sense, typical of the other Gospels). Here is the first of the succession of signs that occupy much of chs. 2—12 (which C. H. Dodd called John's 'Book of Signs'); and then the passion is perhaps to be seen as the greatest of all, to which, in various ways, the rest point. Here, that hint of the passion is to be found in the final verse: Jesus shows forth his 'glory', his God-given splendour that is seen in its highest degree in his death by crucifixion (e.g. 13.31f.).

We are given this story to read at this season of Epiphany, by centuries-old association, as a result of v. 11: Jesus 'manifested' his glory; and surely because of its theme of the widening of God's bounteous provision beyond the confines of Judaism (water), into the headier reaches of the new salvation in and through Jesus (wine). As in the scene at the cross (19.25–27), perhaps the (unnamed) mother of Jesus signifies Israel, from which Jesus springs (as indeed, therefore, does 'salvation', 4.42), even as he then transcends it. This transcending of old Israel explains what (despite various attempts at mollifying) remains the harsh candour of v. 4: in this Gospel particularly, the place of the old dispensation rarely avoids negativity; for Jesus, we remember, has in truth been at work from the very start (1.1–3). Hence, the 'glory' (i.e. his true nature and role in all its radiance) that Jesus displays here in this action is one with that which believers continue to 'behold' (1.14). He is 'light', and the light of glory is there to be seen, though of course not all perceive (v. 10). So the faith that is evoked (in the disciples, v. 11) by this act is not at all the cheap product of sheer amazement at so much wine so miraculously produced (the quantity is huge – like the abundance of grace in 1.16 [cf. v. 17] and of bread in 6.1–14: God's saving generosity is without bounds). It is rather the faith that binds his own to him and brings them into the new dispensation – whose character is woven into them in the supper discourse of chs. 13—17, words achieving life. In the Christian mystery, newness is always to the fore and the sense of it must not be lost. In the hierarchy of the signs, this, worked on inanimate matter rather than a human being, is sometimes seen as the 'lowest' (with the raising of Lazarus in ch. 11 as the topmost); but it contains in fact the whole gospel message, in its own idiom and manner. LH

The Third Sunday of Epiphany

Nehemiah 8.1–3, 5–6, 8–10; I Corinthians 12.12–31a; Luke 4.14–21

Nehemiah 8.1–3, 5–6, 8–10

This passage should really begin at 7.73b, with its important information that the events described happened in the seventh month which was, or was to become, the new year, and which was also the month in which the Feast of Booths was celebrated (see 8.13–18). Such is the tangled relationship between the books of Ezra and Nehemiah that it is usually accepted that Neh. 8 once formed part of an Ezra memoir, and that it was removed by an editor into Nehemiah material in order to provide a climax to the work of Ezra and Nehemiah. It is further broadly agreed that the reference to Nehemiah at 8.9 is an addition to the original text, designed to make the two men contemporaries. This is, in fact, the only occurrence of the two names together.

Several matters regarding the selection of the verses and the translation need to be pointed out. The use of the word 'book' is misleading since books, in the sense in which we understand them, would not be invented for another 600 years. 'Opened the book' (v. 5) should be taken to mean 'unrolled the scroll'. Second, by omitting the list of names in v. 4b, the selection gives the false impression that Ezra was standing alone on the platform. Those 'who could hear with understanding' (vv. 2, 3) were children old enough to be included in the gathering. The date of this event is tied to complex critical questions about the books of Ezra and Nehemiah. A setting in the latter part of the fifth century BC is a reasonable compromise.

A public reading of the law before all the people gathered together has several overtones. It is similar to covenant ceremonies where the conditions of the covenant were rehearsed (cf. Deut. 31.9–13 where a septennial reading of the Law during the Feast of Booths is commanded) and it is also reminiscent of the way in which laws were promulgated much later in Scandinavian countries (and still today in the Isle of Man). Within the narrative structure of Ezra/Nehemiah, the reading of the Law, which was part of the Pentateuch as we know it, had the effect of re-creating the community as a people brought into being and sustained by the God of Israel. The laws that were read set out the groundwork for relations between members of the community, and between the community and God. A sense of purpose and unity was discovered. The reaction of weeping (v. 9) can be understood in two ways. It can be seen as tears of joy for a renewed sense of communal belonging; it can be seen as tears of penitence as the words of the Law disclose to the people what they had failed to do. At the end of the passage, it is joy that predominates. 'The law of the LORD is perfect, reviving the soul . . . the precepts of the LORD are right, rejoicing the heart' (Ps. 19.7–8). JR

I Corinthians 12.12–31a

This passage continues Paul's exploration of the theme of unity and diversity within the community, which began at the start of ch. 12 and which reaches its climactic conclusion in Paul's hymn to love in ch. 13. In 1 Cor. 12.1–11 Paul addressed the question of the variety of spiritual gifts and the way in which they relate to each other. Here Paul takes the theme one step further by looking not at the gifts but at the people who practise them. Just as the spiritual gifts are diverse but equal, so also are the people who use them within the Church. Paul exhorts the Corinthians to recognize the genuine diversity that exists within the community and to support it in all its variety. In this passage he speaks both to the weak and to the strong, exhorting the weak to take a full and equal place within the community and encouraging the strong to include them in everything that they do.

Paul chooses a startling metaphor to argue this point: the Corinthian church is the body of Christ. The phrase the 'body of Christ' is now so familiar to us that it has lost its edge. It is important, however, to realize the impact of this image on Paul's first hearers. Paul wrote 1 Corinthians in the mid-50s AD, only 20 or so years after the death of Jesus. At this stage, there would still have been plenty of people alive who had seen the real, physical body of Christ, either before his death or after his resurrection (he says in 15.6 that more than 500 people saw Christ after he was raised from the dead). What Paul is saying here is that the body of the risen Christ is still to be seen but now it is apparent in the community of the Church. In other words the community has become the resurrection body of Christ. Each member of the community became a part of this body at baptism (12.13). What appears at first glance to be a simple metaphor that clarifies the point Paul is making is in reality a profound statement about the nature of the Church and its relationship to the risen Christ.

Paul's use of a body metaphor here is significant because of the connection with Christ: the Corinthians are not any old body; they are Christ's body. The body metaphor, however, is nothing new. It was used commonly in Greek literature to call for harmony and interdependence between people, particularly in a political setting. A particular example of this can be found in Plutarch's *Moralia* (478D) where he discusses how eyes, ears, hands and feet work together for the mutual benefit of a body. Paul takes this commonly used image and subverts it to demonstrate the radical nature of this new community 'in Christ'. Body imagery is used elsewhere in Greek literature to argue in favour of hierarchy: the body works well when everyone knows their place and keeps to it. Here, although there is a body hierarchy it is only superficial. Some parts of the body may seem to be more important than others but in effect all are equally important. Paul illustrates this point comically. He conjures up the image of a giant nose or a conversation between an eye and a hand to show that diversity is important (so that the body is not just a giant nose) and that each part is equally important (the eye and the hand need each other). Within the body of Christ any apparent hierarchy must be undermined by a recognition of the necessity of diversity and the equality of all.

Paul ends this passage by listing various roles within the Church, some of which he has mentioned earlier in ch. 12 (e.g. prophecy, 12.10) and others which he has not. Of particular note are the perhaps surprisingly mundane roles that the NRSV calls 'forms of assistance' and 'forms of leadership'. In fact these roles seem to refer to administrative support and strategic planning respectively. Alongside prophecy, speaking in tongues and healing, these gifts may seem out of place. Their inclusion, in fact, proves Paul's point. The whole range of abilities and gifts within the Church, from the most dramatic to the most mundane, are equally valuable for the effective working of the community, a community which is not just a collection of individuals but the manifestation of Christ's resurrection body on earth. PG

Luke 4.14–21

By contrast with the fanfare of the infancy narratives, complete with canticles of praise and an angel chorus, the bombast of John's preaching, and the dramatic confrontation with the devil, Luke's account of the beginning of Jesus' ministry sounds a rather quiet note. After all this prologue, Jesus goes home to Galilee, 'and a report about him spread through all the surrounding country' (Luke 4.14). The report apparently concerns his teaching and the praise it receives from 'everyone' (v. 15).

In one sense, vv. 14–15 merely provide a transition from the temptation scene to the synagogue scene. The point is to announce that Jesus is now at work and then to show what that work entails. These transitional verses serve an additional function, however, in that they suggest a positive and warm response to Jesus' teaching, a response that unravels even in the initial proclamation in Nazareth. The ominous note in Simeon's canticle cannot be forgotten (Luke 2.34–35).

The importance Luke attaches to the Nazareth scene is revealed in the care with which he constructs it. Apparently he begins with a brief story about Jesus' return home, a story that both Mark and Matthew place much later in the ministry (Mark 6.1–6; Matt. 13.54–58). He highlights the story by moving it to the beginning of Jesus' ministry and, more important, by the addition of the quotations from Isa. 61.1–2 and 58.6. The changes convert a short story of confrontation into a programmatic announcement that concerns both the nature of Jesus' ministry and the character of the Church that will follow from that ministry.

In a word, the ministry of Jesus is prophetic. That should surprise no reader who has followed Luke's story carefully. The prophetic theme announced here already appears in Mary's Magnificat, with its celebration of God's grace to the lowly and God's scorn for the proud and mighty. Although couched in different language, John the Baptist's preaching also anticipates the prophetic theme of Jesus' ministry with his warning about the judgement that accompanies the arrival of Jesus.

The quotations from Isaiah in 4.18–19 concentrate the prophetic theme on the person of Jesus. Those gathered in the synagogue may not yet understand that the quotation applies to Jesus himself, but the reader surely knows that the Spirit is indeed 'upon' Jesus and that he is one anointed to preach or, as the NRSV puts it, 'to bring good news'. The claim of Luke 4.21 certainly identifies the passage with present events, namely, with the ministry of Jesus.

What it means to 'bring good news to the poor' takes on specificity in the second half of v. 18 and in v. 19.

> to proclaim release to the captives
> and recovery of sight to the blind,
> to let the oppressed go free,
> to proclaim the year of the Lord's favour.

The language of liberation has become so commonplace in recent decades that we may not hear the urgency and the daring of this call. To declare that the captives and the oppressed should go free, and that this action results directly from the will of God, suggests already that the kingdom of God is at hand. Luke again and again calls up this theme with his stories of Jesus' inclusion of the outcasts and with later stories in Acts that portray the divine release of early Christian prisoners.

The 'recovery of sight' likewise figures large in Luke-Acts, for Jesus not only gives sight to the physically blind (Luke 18.35–43) but enables others to see what has been hidden (Luke 24.31). By the same token, those who thought they could see find themselves blinded (Acts 9.8–9), and still others refuse to see what is put before their eyes (Acts 28.26–27).

The 'year of the Lord's favour' or, more literally, 'the acceptable year of the Lord' (RSV) may refer to the jubilee year. If so, what Luke here signals is the claim that the gospel demands a certain attitude about possessions. Followers of Jesus will find that they are expected to share possessions with others. Luke reserves some of his harshest words for those who use money irresponsibly, especially for those who might use the gospel for financial gain.

The lection ends with v. 21. Verses 21–30 are the gospel reading for the following Sunday. To omit all discussion of these verses, however, simply distorts the passage. The response of the synagogue has only begun when all present stare at Jesus following his reading from Isaiah.

The worshippers are initially amazed and a bit perplexed by what they hear from the mouth of 'Joseph's son' (v. 22). He assists them by recalling two events from Israel's history. Elijah acted to save the widow at Zarephath instead of some Israelite widow, and Elisha healed the leprosy of Naaman the Syrian rather than that of another Israelite. The implication is clear to those who drive Jesus out of town and attempt to kill him: those who are included in the liberation of Jesus' ministry come from within *and from outside* Israel. It is not the theme of liberation per se that offends the good folk of Nazareth, but the awareness that liberation includes those outside their own circle. BG

The Fourth Sunday of Epiphany

Ezekiel 43.27—44.4; I Corinthians 13.1–13; Luke 2.22–40

Ezekiel 43.27—44.4

The 'glory' of God, that is, the divine presence that fills the temple, is an important factor in the structure of the book of Ezekiel. A vivid description of this glory is given in Ezek. 10, and at 11.22–23 the glory departs from the Jerusalem temple on account of the wickedness and idolatry practised within it. This same glory appears to Ezekiel in Babylon (ch.1), and then returns to the Jerusalem temple in the context of Ezekiel's vision of a restored city and temple (Ezek. 43.1–5).

The lectionary passage follows on from stipulations about sacrifices that, for seven days, will purify the altar in the restored temple. These are the 'these days' of v. 27, and they will enable the altar to be used for regular offerings. The implication that God will accept the people only after the offerings are resumed has to be set alongside the numerous passages in the Old Testament that say that God values sincerity of heart and the pursuit of justice more than animal and other sacrifices (cf. Isa. 1.11–17, Ps. 51.15–17). Without going into the complicated geography of the temple, the point of Ezek. 44.1–2 and the closed gate is that once the divine glory has used an entrance it remains inaccessible to humans. However, the prince (a future ruler) may have a special route and place reserved for him.

The passage ends with Ezekiel's guide (an angelic figure) leading him to see the divine glory. Bizarre as the descriptions of this glory in Ezekiel might seem, they convey something of the incomparability of God, before which humanity is as nothing. JR

I Corinthians 13.1–13

1 Corinthians 13 has to be one of the best known and best loved chapters of all Paul's Epistles. It is not hard to see why. In this chapter Paul utters what we might call a 'hymn to love'. In it he piles up phrase after phrase in praise of love within the Christian Church. The effect is a profound exploration of the kind of love to be found among those who are 'in Christ'. In the past, much has been made of the distinction between the various different words for love in the Greek language. Three words occur regularly: *eros* or erotic love; *philia* or sisterly and brotherly love; and *agape*, the word used here. One of the problems in working out what this word means is that, unlike *eros* and *philia*, *agape* is used relatively infrequently outside the New Testament and early Christian writings, though the verb connected to it is much more common. Ultimately, however, this should not cause us any difficulty. The whole point of this chapter is that Paul provides a definition of the word here which offers

a radical redefinition of what love is. Paul's use of this relatively rare word for love allows him to distinguish Christian love from those non-Christian notions of love that abounded in the Corinthian setting. It is defined by heavenly principles not earthly ones and is unlike any other type of love that the Corinthians have ever encountered before.

The chapter falls quite noticeably into three sections, vv. 1–3, 4–7 and 8–12 with a climactic summary statement in v. 13. Verses 1–3 emphasize the importance of (Christian) love, vv. 4–7 state the nature of it and vv. 8–12 the eternal permanence of this love. Paul moves smoothly from one section to the next, building on the foundations of its predecessor.

Verses 1–3 tells why love is important in the first place. Paul stresses this by looking at three areas which were highly prized by the Corinthian church: speaking in tongues, prophecy and generosity to the poor. The first two of these show why this passage is relevant here in 1 Corinthians. In the previous chapter Paul explored the diversity and equality of spiritual gifts. Two of these are speaking in tongues and prophecy. He then goes on, in ch. 14, to look at these two gifts in more depth determining how they should, and should not, be employed within the Christian community. Chapter 13, therefore, acts as a bridge between the general discussion of all spiritual gifts and the specific discussion of speaking in tongues and prophesying in ch. 14. Any practice of spiritual gifts, particularly these two, must begin and end with the radical, transforming love of which Paul speaks in this chapter.

At first glance it seems strange to include generosity to the poor alongside speaking in tongues and prophesying. Paul has not mentioned this as a spiritual gift in ch. 12, nor does he go on to discuss it in ch. 14. Paul does take this theme up again in chs. 16.1–4 when he reminds the Corinthians about the collection for the Jerusalem church. That collection, however, is a disciplined saving of extra money, earned during the month, for the church in Jerusalem, not an enthusiastic giving away of everything that one owns. Paul stresses the excess of the action here by adding 'if I hand over my body'. This could mean anything from placing yourself constantly at the service of others to selling your body into slavery to generate more money for the poor. The most likely explanation for Paul's silence about this action elsewhere is that it was not a matter of controversy for the Corinthians. This was something they all accepted as part of a Christian lifestyle. The only comment Paul made about it was that they should practise it with love.

Verses 4–7 explore what this love is. Paul defines the concept with a mixture of positive and negative statements about what love is and what love is not. The list begins with two positive statements, which are then contrasted with a string of negative ones. Many of these are qualities of which the Corinthians are themselves guilty. Love is not envious, unlike the Corinthians who have 'jealousy and quarrelling' among them (3.3). Love is not arrogant nor does it rejoice in wrongdoing, but this is something that Paul accuses the Corinthians of in 5.1–2. Love runs counter to all natural human reaction. Paul sums up his definition in v. 7 with a return to four positive statements, which he uses elsewhere (e.g. 1 Thess. 1.3) to summarize the task to which the Christian is called. This life-changing love bears, believes, hopes and endures.

In vv. 8–12 Paul moves from the effects of love on the behaviour and attitudes of individuals to the universal manifestation of it. This shift is particularly clear between the end of v. 7 and the beginning of v. 8. Verse 7 ends with love 'endures all things'. In other words Paul is saying that someone who loves with this kind of love will never give up no matter what happens. Verse 8 begins 'Love never ends', and goes on to contrast this with things that will end such as prophecies and tongues. So the love that endures all things does so because it is derived from this universal love that has no end. Human manifestations of it will match its endurance as well as its other qualities.

Paul ends this passage with his climactic statement about the three things that will remain when all else fails: faith, hope and love. This verse acts as a conclusion both to vv. 8–12 and to the whole chapter. Verses 8–12 began with a statement that love will not end, v. 13 ends with the positive version of this statement: love, together with faith and hope, remain. So this important verse draws together Paul's argument throughout the chapter. Love underpins and outlasts everything else. It is the greatest of all because, as v. 7 indicates, faith and hope grow out of love, whereas love does not necessarily grow out of either faith or hope. Love exists before and after everything else. PG

Luke 2.22–40

The narratives in Luke 1—2 evoke the atmosphere and world of old Israel, sometimes (as in the echoes of Sarah in the aged Elizabeth and in the near repeat of Hannah's song from 1 Sam. 2 in the Magnificat) very old Israel indeed. It is a literary old Israel, for Luke writes here in the style and vocabulary of the Septuagint. The evocation occurs also in the depiction of the characters – not just Elizabeth and Mary, but Zechariah and the rest; in the dominant temple scenario, and indeed in the nature of the episodes themselves. We are to understand that, new and decisive in God's purposes as Jesus is, he is no novelty or bolt from the blue. Even if his saving significance is for all, Israel can still be seen as 'thy people' (v. 32).

Simeon and Anna (Luke works in pairs of persons throughout these chapters) are typical of the venerable holy sages of Israel, and their great age ratifies their wisdom and their power to speak God's truth. And as through all Luke's history, they are Spirit-led. Paralleling Zechariah in relation to John, Simeon reminds us of Eli in relation to Samuel and Anna of Judith in the second-century BC tale of piety. Both are obscure figures, exemplifying the divine favouring of the poor and simple, as the Magnificat said. (In the figure of Anna, Luke may also have an eye on the status of Christian widows in his own day, as described and regulated in 1 Tim. 5.) They are in effect oracular persons, and Simeon's words are almost a catena of scriptural allusions. All this is more important to Luke than the precise details of the ritual which the parents of Jesus carry out and in fact he has not wholly understood the law's requirements. The 'presentation' of a new firstborn carried no visit to the temple and was distinct from the mother's 'purification' which entailed sacrifice: it is the latter which Luke is really describing.

It is hard to know whether Luke is keen to show Jesus as rooted in scriptural validation for reasons of doctrine (God's work is uninterrupted from start to finish) or, also perhaps, for reasons connected with his church situation in the later first century, when Jewish Christians were becoming more plainly a minority and needed reassurance, perhaps in the face of some Gentile-Christian intolerance: it is a message of balance and reconciliation that Acts is at pains to reiterate, notably in the council of Acts 15.

All the same, as the annunciation story and the shepherds' vision have already made clear, Jesus is the focus of faith and hope: the one who brings 'salvation', a word resonant for Jews and pagans alike, and virtually confined to Luke among the evangelists. Yet the child's purpose will only be carried out through suffering which Simeon also foresees. The suffering will also devastate Mary: in the image in v. 35 we have one more example of how Luke is the true originator of what would eventually flower as Marian devotion. LH

The Presentation of Christ

(2 February)

Malachi 3.1–5; Hebrews 2.14–18; Luke 2.22–40

Malachi 3.1–5

The book of Malachi, evidently dating from the late fourth century BC, was written or compiled within a society that contained sorcerers, adulterers, perjurers, and corrupt employers and landowners (cf. v. 5). This state of affairs, together with other unsatisfactory conditions, produces a series of charges and counter charges in the book, as God and the people engage in a dialogue of questions and answers. The passage in 3.1–5 is best seen as God's reply to what immediately precedes (2.17), where God takes objection to the view that he approves of, or is powerless to deal with, evil-doers.

The Hebrew of 'I am sending' implies that something is about to happen. A messenger or angel (the same word in Hebrew) will precede the coming of God to his temple. The function of the messenger is unclear. If it is to prepare the people for the divine coming, then why will it be necessary for God to refine and judge (vv. 2–5)? Perhaps the messenger's function will be to warn the people of the imminence of the divine judgement. At any rate, the divine coming will be painful for those who experience it. People may desire God, but will they be able to endure his judgement?

This judgement will begin with the temple and its worship (v. 3), with the place that ought to know better because it supposedly exists to mediate between the people and God; the place where the experts in prayer, sacrifice and holiness are supposed to be found. The judgement will then pass to the social sphere. A religion in which the cult is acceptable but which tolerates social injustice is an abomination to the Old Testament prophets. True religion is neither an acceptable cult without social justice nor social justice without a worthy cult. The two must go together because they belong together. People who fear God but are indifferent to their fellow human beings, especially those most socially disadvantaged, do not really fear God. People who are only humanitarian workers fail to recognize that the deepest instincts of human sympathy and compassion are God-given.

Although this reading is selected to go with the Gospel story of Christ's presentation in the temple 40 days after his birth (cf. Lev. 12.2–8) it is arguably the story of the cleansing of the temple (Mark 11.15–18) that comes closest to a fulfilment of this prophecy in the ministry of Jesus. JR

Hebrews 2.14–18

No writer in the New Testament was more dedicated to the sense of Jesus' identification with the human race, 'his brothers and sisters in every respect', than the author of Hebrews. In ch. 1, using a barrage of Scripture quotations, he had established his heavenly status as God's Son, occupying the role of God's 'wisdom' and above the angels, seated at God's right hand. But then the writer had shifted his gaze – to Jesus who, in the role foretold in Ps. 8, had become (to take the words in a convenient sense that the Greek version could bear) 'for a little while' below the angels, a human among humans (2.7). (In the Hebrew, the sense was spatial, not temporal.)

Yet in that place, he had a task that was unique: he was to bring 'many sons to glory', by being 'the pioneer of their salvation' (2.10) – an image found also in Acts 3.15 and 5.31. Again, scriptural texts demonstrated that Wagnerian hero-role: Ps. 22.22 and Isa. 8.17–18. It is made plain that his position in relation to the angels, temporarily put aside, was now incidental. Instead, his significance related to human beings, specifically 'the descendants of Abraham': this writing functions, it now emerges, within Jewish horizons, however wide some of its language.

The leadership role of Jesus prompts the first appearance of the image or analogy that comes to dominate the later chapters: that of the high priest who, human as he is, has the role of making 'expiation for the sins of the people', above all on the Day of Atonement. Whether the actual high priests of Jerusalem saw themselves quite thus is another question; here, it is their very identity with everybody else, in temptation and suffering, that qualifies them to perform their vital and sacred task. Humility and leadership are not incompatible. LH

Luke 2.22–40

See the Fourth Sunday of Epiphany, pp. 51–52.

The Fifth Sunday of Epiphany

Isaiah 6.1–8 (9–13); I Corinthians 15.1–11; Luke 5.1–11

Isaiah 6.1–8 (9–13)

Any inner or visionary experience usually comes to people only via the symbols and thought-forms of their world. If what they tell others about their experience is to make any sense, the account of what has happened to them must also draw upon available and shared symbols. This means that descriptions of what is ultimately indescribable are inevitably located in a particular place and expressed in particular language. In the case of the present passage, the prophet's experience is described in terms of the Jerusalem temple and royal symbolism of his times. He hears the divine beings praising God in his own language, Hebrew. That descriptions of encounters with the divine can transcend the particular symbolism and language in which they are expressed is indicated by the fact that the hymn of the seraphim has become a central part of Christian liturgy (it also features in Jewish liturgy) and is repeated daily in many languages. It must not be supposed, however, that such language can be taken literally, as though the heavenly hosts actually use Hebrew to praise God; or that God is actually attended by fiery creatures with six wings. All such language merely points to realities far beyond human understanding.

These opening observations are meant as a warning against too literal an understanding of the passage. We are not told that the prophet was in the temple; indeed he could not have been in the most holy part of it. And if the hem of God's robe filled the temple and the seraphim were above him, then the temple was merely a part of a much larger canvas of his vision. Only if we accept this are we in a position to consider some of the details of the temple and royal symbolism.

The opening words may be less concerned to date the vision to the death of King Uzziah (Azariah) in *c.* 734 BC, than to contrast the dead earthly king with the enthroned and eternal heavenly king. The world 'holy' repeated by the seraphim denotes a quality of being that somehow lays bare all human self-sufficiency and self-deceit. The traditional Hebrew vowelling of v. 3c yields the sense 'the fullness of the whole earth is his glory', which some modern commentators prefer. But God's 'glory' is his ineffable presence, especially in Ezekiel, which is why the usual rendering is that the earth is full of God's glory. This is not panentheism, but the claim that God ultimately rules the whole world. The prophet's response 'I am lost' can also be translated 'I am speechless'. Both possibilities have something to be said for them. The former expresses the prophet's feeling of complete worthlessness consequent upon his vision of God's majesty; the second indicates that one who is about to be given a prophetic task has nothing to say. However, part of the revelation of God's otherness is his gracious act of removing Isaiah's sense of unworthiness. The prophet overhears discussion in the divine court. Not for the last time in human experience, his confrontation with the living God leads to his willingness to respond immediately and unconditionally to his service. JR

I Corinthians 15.1–11

Paul reminds his hearers of the gospel that he proclaimed and they received. The introductory 'who', the balanced clauses, and some language untypical of Paul himself lead many to assume he is quoting in vv. 3–5 a very early credal confession of faith, which must go back close to the events themselves. He makes no mention of the empty tomb, or the women who discovered it, and understands his own vision of the risen Christ as comparable to those of the other male witnesses. His main concerns are to assert the reality of Christ's resurrection (which was presumably beyond dispute among believers) in order to provide a basis for insisting on belief in the future resurrection of believers, which some believers in Corinth were denying (v. 12). Unlike St Luke and the creeds that separate them, Paul saw Christ's resurrection and ours as part of the same divine mystery in which we are already caught up. He also insists on the unity of faith shared by all the witnesses, perhaps in opposition to factions in Corinth appealing to different leaders (ch. 1).

Paul also refers to the early appearance to Peter ('Simon' at Luke 24.34) and the later Gospels support an appearance to 'the Twelve' (presumably 11). An appearance to James the brother of the Lord is credible because it would help explain his subsequent leadership of the Jerusalem church. It is puzzling that Paul's strongest supporting argument, an appearance to over 500 'brethren' some of whom can still be interrogated now, some 25 years later, is otherwise unknown. This (and the differences from and between the Gospels) underlines the fragmentary character of the Easter traditions without weakening their certainty about the event itself. It should be emphasized that, like the incarnation and all divine events, the 'resurrection' is a mystery. It is expressed in the metaphorical language of being raised or got up, and elsewhere of exaltation, ascension or enthronement. Paul does not envisage a literal resuscitation – flesh and blood cannot inherit the kingdom of God (v. 54) – and as a divine event without analogy the resurrection of Jesus cannot be evaluated by historical methods. But it left traces that can be assessed by historians, notably the faith of the early Church and also the Gospel records of an empty tomb. It remains foundational for Christian faith – not as an isolated event, but as communicating and revealing God's vindication of Jesus who is the one and only foundation of faith (1 Cor. 3.11).

Which Scriptures this early creed has in mind in vv. 3 and 4 (e.g. Isa. 53 – cf. Rom. 4.25) is less important than the general conviction that the event of Christ fulfils Scripture as a whole. That Paul is content to repeat the early Jewish-Christian tradition interpreting Jesus' death as an atoning sacrifice should perhaps warn his successors against discarding older theological ideas, even if they like Paul himself place the emphasis elsewhere in communicating the gospel. We may also note that as speaking of the resurrection is speaking of God it is typically fused with speaking autobiographically (v. 9) – which to a believer means speaking of grace (v. 10), yet without false modesty. RM

Luke 5.1–11

Luke reserves his accounts of the calling of the disciples until Jesus' own ministry of teaching and healing has been established. Jesus' preceding ministry was conducted alone; now he calls on others to follow him and to join in his work.

Simon's response to Jesus offers a model for others to follow: first those who were with him on the lake, then those who will read or hear Luke's account. Simon does what Jesus asks, even though he might question the wisdom of his command (vv. 4–5). He appears to recognize the presence of God manifested in the miraculous catch of fish and realizes that it points to the authority of Jesus. Simon's call or commission can thus be compared to that of Isaiah of Jerusalem (Isa. 6.1–10). Simon is fearful and conscious of his own sinfulness in response to an epiphany of God, but is reassured and commissioned to go to others under the authority of the one who sends him.

Jesus' command to make fishers of men is addressed to Simon alone, but others who have sailed with him also obey. Luke thus introduces the prominent members of the Twelve: Simon, James and John. They have participated in a catch of fish under the authority of Jesus, which perhaps anticipates and represents the expansion of the Church through the outreach of those who will later preach under the authority of Jesus, even when he has gone.

Luke's statement that those who followed Jesus left everything (v. 11) is an example of Luke's insistence that their disposition towards possessions is symbolic of their response to God's call on their lives. The place of possessions in the life of those who follow Jesus is a recurring Lucan emphasis: the disciple's attitude to personal possessions is an expression of faith in practice, even if there is no uniformity in the way in which this faith is to be expressed. Possessions and wealth – and boat-owners may be thought of as running their own business – need not be evil, but Luke leaves no room for the Christian to be neutral about them.

Here the emphasis is on the centrality of putting God before wealth and material security. Simon, James and John see beyond the short-term gain of the marvellous catch to the one who has brought it about. Elsewhere Luke shows how this works in practice for a variety of individuals and circumstances. AG

The Sixth Sunday of Epiphany

Jeremiah 17.5–10; I Corinthians 15.12–20; Luke 6.17–26

Jeremiah 17.5–10

The interpretation of this passage depends initially on the translation of a rare Hebrew word *'ar'aar* in v. 6, which is rendered as 'shrub'. The shrub in question is usually identified as the Phoenician juniper (cf. REB) on the basis of its similar name in Arabic; but this is not a desert plant and it does not occur in the wilderness of Palestine as demanded by the present passage. A strong case can be made for the translation 'destitute'; for even if a shrub other than the juniper is supposed, the fact that it survives in the desert undermines the point being made in vv. 5–6, which is that it is impossible for humans to survive in a parched, uninhabited desert. Similarly, there is no hope of survival to those who only trust in human things. The contrasting verses, which are similar to Ps. 1.3, do not imply that those who trust God live lives entirely free from danger and anxiety. Troubles are hinted at in the references to heat and drought. The point is that their faith in God provides resources that enable them to face their troubles with hope and confidence.

The concluding verses can be taken as an explanation of what precedes. The reason why it is idle to trust in human resources alone is because the heart is devious and perverse. This does not necessarily mean that it is thoroughgoingly evil. Humans are capable of generous thoughts and actions; but their strength is limited, and their loyalty can break down. Human hopes are disappointed time and again. The fact that God tests the mind and searches the heart is part of the process of being like a tree planted beside the water. God's testing brings self-knowledge, and thus the knowledge of human limitations; but it also enables humans to trust in God's mercy. Even if a just distribution of rewards is not always apparent in the world, experience of God's mercy supports one's hope in an ultimate justice. JR

I Corinthians 15.12–20

1 Corinthians 15 is a ringing defence of resurrection. The longest of all the chapters of 1 Corinthians, it explores the topic from numerous different angles. The chapter begins with a defence of Jesus' resurrection (vv. 1–11), it then moves on in this passage to support the resurrection of the dead in general (vv. 12–34) before asking more practical questions about what resurrection will be like (vv. 35–58). This passage (vv. 12–20) responds to the Corinthians' doubts about resurrection and demonstrates why Paul was so concerned about their uncertainty on this topic. The passage implies that the Corinthians were not questioning Jesus' resurrection but their own. The implication of v. 12 ('how can some of you say that there is no

resurrection of the dead?') is that some of the Corinthians did not believe in life after death, or at any rate in resurrection. This is not an unusual question in this period; we know that there is an ongoing debate in both Jewish and Greek circles about what happened after death. It is likely that those in Corinth who said that there is no resurrection of the dead were simply reflecting one aspect of this complex discussion. What Paul demonstrates here, however, is that for those who are 'in Christ' resurrection from the dead is not a small, inconsequential doubt but the questioning of a fundamental part of belief.

The resurrection of the dead, he claims, is intertwined with the basic proclamation of the gospel: 'Christ died for our sins according to the Scriptures . . . was buried,' and 'was raised on the third day according to the Scriptures' (15.3–4, NIV). Jesus' resurrection is important in its own right but also because it demonstrates that personal resurrection will take place. The Corinthians must not believe one without the other. They cannot believe that Jesus has risen but that they will not, nor that they will rise but that Jesus did not. Jesus' resurrection and their own are inextricably linked, the one proving the validity of the other. In fact, Paul takes his argument even further than this. Resurrection is the linchpin of the whole of Christian faith. Anyone who denies that they will experience resurrection after they die, is denying faith in general: 'If there is no resurrection of the dead . . . your faith is futile' (v. 14). It is hard to imagine how Paul could have said this any more strongly than he does here. For him, this belief about life after death is part and parcel of Christian faith. If it does not exist, then Jesus did not rise from the dead and God is not who Paul has claimed him to be, that is the one who raised Jesus. Those who deny that they themselves will be raised from the dead at some point in the future are saying that Jesus is still dead and that God is not who Christians think he is.

In the course of his impassioned defence of general resurrection, Paul makes an important passing comment. If Christ has not been raised from the dead, then the Corinthians are still in their sins (15.17). This is an interesting point. A study of atonement theology can lead to an assumption that it is the death of Jesus alone that atones for sin. Paul's aside here indicates that this is not the case. If Jesus had died and remained dead the atoning power of his death would be invalid. It is the death and resurrection together that provide atonement for sin. If there is no resurrection and Jesus has not been raised, then the Corinthians are still in their sins.

In v. 19, Paul reaches the climax of his argument in favour of a belief in resurrection. Without it Christians are to be more pitied than anyone else: their good news has no substance, their faith is pointless, they are pathetic liars, sin continues unchanged and those who have died have perished. The Corinthians may think that in dispensing with a doctrine of life after death they are dispensing with an unimportant, marginal facet of faith; in fact they are cutting off the branch on which they are sitting. PG

Luke 6.17–26

Because Luke's 'Sermon on the Plain', from which this and the following two gospel lections are taken, has drawn less attention than Matthew's 'Sermon on the Mount', interpreters may not bring to the text quite the same exaggerated expectations that accompany reading of the Matthean version. Nevertheless, the temptation to see the sermon as providing us with direct access to 'Jesus' message' or 'Jesus' teachings' is serious. A careful reading of the passage, together with a comparison of Luke's version with that of Matthew, should confirm that both evangelists have shaped the material very much to address the needs of their own communities. That, after all, is a fundamental task of preaching.

In its Lucan setting, the sermon takes place just after Jesus calls the Twelve, here referred to as apostles (6.12–16), and in the context of a multitude of disciples who have come to hear Jesus and to be touched by him (6.17–19). When Jesus speaks, he addresses himself specifically to the disciples, to those who have committed themselves to follow him.

The Lucan version of the Beatitudes differs from the Matthean form in that Luke's is shorter, in the sense both that the list of beatitudes is shorter and also that each individual beatitude is more briefly expressed. In addition, of course, Luke differs from Matthew by including the accompanying list of 'woes' in vv. 24–26.

The care with which these beatitudes and woes are constructed emphasizes their importance. Each of the beatitudes is contrasted with a parallel woe as follows.

	Beatitude			*Woe*
v. 20	the poor		v. 24	the rich
v. 21	the hungry		v. 25	the full
v. 21	those who weep		v. 25	those who laugh
v. 22	those who are hated		v. 26	those of whom people speak well

'Blessed' are the poor, the hungry, the grieved, the hated. In Greek literature outside the Bible, this word (*makarios*) could carry connotations of happiness. In the Septuagint, however, to be 'blessed' is not so much to be subjectively happy as to be regarded as righteous, to be blessed in God's sight (see e.g. Deut. 33.29; Ps. 1.1; 40.4). Particularly in our contemporary context, with its preoccupation with the achievement of personal happiness, this distinction is an important one. The Septuagint likewise employs the 'woe' form to indicate God's displeasure and the grief that will follow from that displeasure (see e.g. Isa. 5.18–23, where the NRSV reads 'Ah').

The fourth beatitude warrants particular attention because it is more developed than any of the others. (That is not to say that the others are insignificant, especially since Luke's concerns with the poor and oppressed are clearly articulated as early as the Magnificat.) Even acknowledging all the problems with reading Luke's community situation off the pages of his Gospel, it is difficult not to read this lengthy promise of God's favour for those who are despised as a reflection of the context of Luke's church. Here, as in the Stephen speech in Acts 7, the treatment of Jesus' followers is likened to that of Israel's prophets (see Acts 7.51–53).

Running through the passage is a contrast between the present and the future. Those who 'are hungry now' will be filled in the future (Luke 6.21). Those who 'weep now' will laugh (v. 21). The 'rich', by contrast, have already received their consolation (v. 24). Those who are 'full now' will be hungry in the future, and those who 'are laughing now' will find their laughter turned to mourning (v. 25).

Along with this contrast between the present and the future runs a contrast between human assessment and the assessment of God. In three of the beatitudes and their corresponding woes, this contrast is implicit rather than explicit; by human standards, the poor, the hungry, and the sorrowful are anything but the possessors of God's kingdom. In the fourth beatitude, however, this contrast becomes explicit. Those who are rejected by human beings have a great reward 'in heaven'. Luke's use of that phrase elsewhere strongly suggests that it is a circumlocution for 'from God'. Rather than a place, 'heaven' refers to God's own assessment, God's judgement (see e.g. 15.7, 18, 21).

An initial reading of the Lucan Beatitudes might prompt us to accuse Luke of a 'pie in the sky by and by' attitude; that is, he encourages people to endure their present suffering by holding out hope for rewards sometime in the indefinite future. When we take into account both the time element ('now' versus the future) and the issue of divine versus human assessment, however, something more complex emerges from this passage. A crude paraphrase might be, 'Things are not always what they seem.' Those who seem to be prospering may not be, not in God's sight. Those who seem to be suffering may be blessed, at least in God's sight. Paul puts it somewhat differently in 1 Cor. 1.25: 'God's foolishness is wiser than human wisdom, and God's weakness is stronger than human strength.' BG

The Seventh Sunday of Epiphany

Genesis 45.3–11, 15; I Corinthians 15.35–38, 42–50; Luke 6.27–38

Genesis 45.3–11, 15

This is in many ways the climax of the story of Joseph in Egypt. Despite the unpromising circumstances of his arrival there he has prospered and has become the pharaoh's right-hand man. (It is interesting to note that whereas in Exodus the pharaoh is pictured as a vain and ineffective despot, here the portrayal is much more sympathetic. Speculation in either case as to who the actual historical ruler may have been is not very rewarding; they are both literary products.) Back in Canaan, meanwhile, Jacob and his remaining family, now augmented by another brother, Benjamin, are suffering the effects of famine. A visit to Egypt in search of provisions brought them under suspicion and one brother, Simeon, was left as a hostage. Only if they bring with them Jacob's youngest son Benjamin will Simeon be released and more provisions made available. Benjamin is allowed to accompany his brothers on the next journey despite his father's misgivings, but the drama is heightened when Joseph orders him to be arrested on a trumped-up charge. Will the brothers abandon him to his fate, as they had done with Joseph himself years before? Ch. 44 had ended with a declaration of loyalty by Judah, to his father and to his young brother.

Joseph is persuaded that the brothers' attitude had changed, and our reading is the happy reconciliation. Joseph is not modest in setting out his own position ('father to Pharaoh', v. 8, is not a title that Egyptians would have recognized), but the main points are that the immediate crisis of famine is averted, and the long-term reunion of the family can now be envisaged. For the moment there is no talk of return to Canaan; from this story we might suppose that the extended family is to settle in Egypt permanently. We know, however, that this episode in the story is part of a larger whole. It is being told as a preliminary to the account of the exodus; indeed it may have been composed deliberately to reconcile two traditions of the people's origins, one speaking of migration from Mesopotamia, the other of exodus from Egypt. Whatever we decide about that, this episode deserves to be taken at its immediate level, of a reconciliation seen by believers as the direct result of God's planning (vv. 7–8a). RC

I Corinthians 15.35–38, 42–50

The question of resurrection which Paul is dealing with in ch. 15 has more and more ramifications and he takes them one by one. It is not entirely clear what his articulate Corinthian Christians exactly had in their minds on the matter. We have only Paul's side of the conversation and have to guess at theirs. They were certainly sceptical about 'resurrection', which, because of Jesus, Paul saw as vital to the gospel (vv. 3–8). But quite what did they mean? Was it that they believed in the survival of the 'soul' after death, or that, in their hyper-religiosity, they thought of themselves as already in the resurrection-state? After all if Paul had taught them about baptism along the lines of what he was to write in Rom. 6.3–11 it was not an improbable conclusion to draw (cf., later, Col. 3.1). The first would mean that their scepticism related to our having anything like a bodily future; they were thinking in the Greek as against the Jewish mode. In favour of the second hypothesis is their strange practice of being baptized on behalf of their dead (v. 29), which Paul does not actually condemn: they would only do this if they wanted their loved ones to share, without delay, their own transformed state. Paul's objection to this is in line with his criticism of their conceit about being ever-so 'wise' (chs. 1–4) and about their wonderfully exciting spiritual gifts (chs. 12–14). Steady on, he says, you have not yet arrived and your 'full fulfilment' still lies ahead. Christ is the first fruits (v. 20): the harvest (i.e. you!) is not yet here. After all, we should reflect, if these people had no belief in 'resurrection' in any sense, could they have responded in the first place to Paul's Christ-gospel, to which his resurrection was integral, even if their way of seeing resurrection was, we might say, ethereal, even ecstatic, in tendency?

Then the question naturally comes: 'All right, we have a future still ahead of us, and you insist that it is "bodily", but what on earth can you mean by "bodily"?' Whether they found Paul's answer satisfactory we cannot tell. He seems to haver between a full-blown 'resurrection-of-the-body' doctrine and a 'survival-of-the-soul' view (roughly, between Jewish and Greek tendencies; Paul was a man of two cultures). Yes, he says, you will indeed still be 'bodily', but it will be not a physical body, such as you now have, but one made of 'spirit'. There will be a transformation, as he goes on to explain (vv. 51–54). Perhaps we may put it by saying that essentially this future is not some kind of natural property of the self but purely a gift of God, with its own special and appropriate 'glory'. 'Spirit' betokens the divine. Paul presumably believed that Christ's risen self was 'spiritual' in this sense, i.e. transformed into a wholly different state (vv. 35–38); a fusion of continuity and discontinuity in relation to his earthly life. But, whatever we may make of the detail, the essential point is that our future, whatever it is, is not a matter of right but of gift. Like all life, it comes from God alone. LH

Luke 6.27–38

To love an enemy is simply impossible, for an enemy is by definition someone hated rather than loved. An enemy who is loved is no longer an enemy. So great is the contradiction implicit in the opening words of this passage that Christians, perhaps inevitably, resort to any available means to wrest the passage into some manageable form. The Pelagians of every generation will insist that enemies can be loved if only people will try harder. Others will opt for a more spiritualized interpretation of what it means to 'love' an enemy. Still others will attempt to bury the demand beneath a mound of references to ancient attitudes toward the enemy.

Nothing will reduce the demand of this passage, but attention to the context and the larger argument may help us to understand it. Luke 6.27 marks a transition in the Sermon on the Plain, away from the beatitudes and woes and toward specific concerns regarding treatment of the enemy. The opening of v. 27 ('But I say to you that listen') recalls the earlier setting of the sermon ('They had come to hear him', 6.18) and anticipates the closing of the sermon (6.47). Jesus addresses the disciples, those who are committed to hearing even what they cannot fully comprehend.

The topic of one's treatment of enemies resumes the concern of vv. 22–23 of the Beatitudes and probably again reflects Luke's knowledge of Christians who are in fact experiencing rejection because of their discipleship. How would the Christian community respond to those who ostracized them for their faith? The response to this question in vv. 27–36 (vv. 37–38 take up a different topic) moves from demand (vv. 27–31) to explanation (vv. 32–34) and finally to the theological basis for the demand (vv. 35–36).

'Love your enemies, do good to those who hate you, bless those who curse you, pray for those who abuse you.' The active, verbal character of these demands is crucial. 'Love' in this passage is less a noun, a characteristic, an emotional state, than it is an action. While it may be impossible to *feel* love for the enemy, it is not impossible to *act* in certain ways, even for those whom experience has shown to be the most entrenched of opponents. What Jesus means by the love of enemies becomes clear in the three verbal demands that follow and that explicate the initial demand: 'Do good', 'bless', 'pray'.

Several concrete examples provide additional clarity about what it means to love the enemy. A disciple who is struck should offer the other cheek; a disciple whose coat is taken should offer the next layer of clothing as well; no beggar should be turned away; no one who takes away possessions should be asked to return them. With the exception of the first, all these specific examples concern possessions, not surprising given Luke's emphasis elsewhere on the handling of possessions as profoundly revealing of one's capacity for discipleship.

The series of demands culminates in the so-called Golden Rule. As the commentaries will amply illustrate, this principle is well known in antiquity in a variety of forms. Searching for something unique to Jesus' formulation that somehow makes it superior to other formulations is beside the point. What v. 31 offers in this context is a general principle, probably one that was familiar to Luke's audience, that would help to explain how to go about the difficult task of loving the enemy.

At the end of v. 31, however, that demand still cries out for an explanation. Why should it be the case that disciples of Jesus must love their enemies? Significantly, no promise is made that this action will convert the enemy into a friend, will modify the enemy's behaviour, or even alter one's own feelings toward that enemy! Instead, Jesus explores the established alternative behaviour of equitable exchange – loving only those who love in return (vv. 32–34).

Loving only those who love us is not a credit (literally, a 'grace'), for 'even sinners' can do that. Again, at least in v. 34, the specific example concerns the treatment of possessions. Why lend only to those who will lend in return? 'Even sinners' can do that. Here, of course 'sinners' refers to those outside the Christian community, not to the theological conviction that all people remain sinners. Even those who are the enemies of the faith can act with a minimal kind of equity, returning tit for tat. Surely disciples of Jesus should hold themselves to a higher standard.

With vv. 35–36 we come to the final restatement of this demand and then the underlying reason: 'Your reward will be great, and you will be children of the Most High; for he is kind to the ungrateful and the wicked. Be merciful, just as your Father is merciful.' All of this is demanded by virtue of God's own graciousness and mercy. Christians behave lovingly to their enemies not as a ploy to out-manoeuvre them, not even because they anticipate a reward (although the language of reward is used here), but finally because God is a God of mercy. God is kind even to the undeserving, and that kindness must be found also in the lives of God's children.

With vv. 37–38, the sermon takes up yet another topic, that of behaviour within the fellowship of disciples. Here again, however, the implied standard is that of God's own behaviour. Judgement and condemnation should be withheld, for God will not judge or condemn. The example of measurement, such as the measurement of the marketplace, provides a final reminder that God's measure is not justice, but mercy. BG

The Second Sunday Before Lent

Genesis 2.4b–9, 15–25; Revelation 4; Luke 8.22–25

Genesis 2.4b–9, 15–25

This passage contains so many important themes that a whole series of sermons would be needed to do it justice! It is often called a second creation story; that this is incorrect is clear from the opening words. The passage presupposes the existence of the created world and tells of the origins of various things within it. This does not prevent the duplication of the account of the creation of human kind, however, which is here based upon a folk etymology – the similar sound of the words in Hebrew for 'man' (Hebrew *'adam*) and 'earth' (*'adamah*). The combination of earth and divine breath (the Hebrew is *neshamah, not* the more common word for spirit, *ruach*) indicates that human life is entirely dependent upon God, and that it is not something 'natural', and apart from God. The account of man being given the garden to care for has often been the basis for a theology of work, although this needs careful handling. The Israelite slaves in Egypt had work, which was hardly ennobling. Verses 15–16 look forward to the story of disobedience in ch. 3, which is a separate, and vast, subject.

Because of the interpretation of this passage in 1 Tim. 2.11–13, in which the prior creation of Adam to Eve is used as an argument for male superiority, vv. 18–23 have been closely scrutinized by feminist scholars. It is probably going too far beyond the evidence to claim that the *'adam* is an androgynous creature and that 'man' in the biological sense only comes into being once 'woman' is separated from the *'adam*. It is doubtful that this is what the presumed original readers were expected to understand. A sounder approach is to say that the 1 Timothy passage reflects the social situation of its time, and that it does not provide an authoritative, and for all times binding, interpretation of the passage. What Gen. 2 does emphasize is the mutuality and complementarity of the sexes – a harmony that will be shattered in ch. 3. The final verses (24–25) have been used to argue that heterosexual mono-gamous marriage is a 'creation ordinance' and the only form of sexual relationship acceptable to God. Some nineteenth-century scholars saw them as evidence for ma-trilocal marriage, that is, a married man living with his wife's rather than his own kin. In fact, the verses say no more than that humans reach a stage in life where they cease to be dependent upon their parents, and enter into new relationships with their attendant loyalties and responsibilities. The closing words about the nakedness of the human couple are a reminder that the story is set in beginning time, a time different from that of the Hebrew readers/hearers, who did not practise nakedness. JR

Revelation 4

After recording the letters to the seven churches, John is caught up to heaven to be shown what is to come: the 'apocalypse proper', following the pattern of Dan. 7—12 and Jewish apocalyptic books like 2 Esdras and 1 Enoch. Between the trials of the present and the tribulations of the future, however, he is given a vision of the eternal God. The divine name received by Moses in Exod. 3.14 was translated in the Septuagint, the Greek Old Testament, as 'he who is', and John glosses this to comprehend past and future. His imagery of God enthroned draws primarily, though not slavishly, on Ezek. 1, a passage that became central to Jewish *merkavah*, 'throne', mysticism; and John's vision may have its origin in part in mystical experience, like that which Paul describes in 2 Cor. 12.2–3. The four living creatures come from Ezekiel, where their movement suggests the four winds of heaven and the four corners of the earth. Irenaeus of Lyons drew on these ideas when making the four creatures the symbols of the evangelists and arguing the necessity of four Gospels to reflect the divine ordering of earth and heaven. There is no obvious source for the 24 elders, save the general idea of the divine council or court of angels (e.g. 1 Kings 2.19; Isa. 6.2). One suggestion is that the number represents the patriarchs and apostles, founders of the old and new peoples of God. It would be surprising to find human figures in John's heaven at this point, since elsewhere only the martyrs are seen there (6.9–11; 7.9, 13–14); but possibly they might be their angelic counterparts, like the 'angels of the churches' in the seven letters.

The living creatures and the elders join in antiphonal song. John's vision is a matter of hearing as well as seeing, as music features strongly throughout. There is indeed more music in the Apocalypse than in the whole of the rest of the New Testament – though it is essentially the music of heaven, not necessarily reflecting the music of the church communities on earth. The creatures' song echoes that of the seraphim in Isaiah's vision of God enthroned in heaven (Isa. 6.3), the *Trisagion*. That of the elders, with its opening acclamation, 'worthy art thou' and list of attributes (cf. Rev. 5.12, addressed to the Lamb) has no Old Testament background, but may instead derive from forms of ritual and ceremonial in honour of the Roman emperor. These have been associated particularly with the Emperor Domitian, who desired to be addressed as 'Our Lord and our God' and in whose reign Revelation has traditionally been set. The great enemies of God's people, the dragon and the beast, will claim human worship (4.4): but here at the opening of John's vision it is clear to whom worship, in every form, is properly addressed. SL

Luke 8.22–25

Luke now opens a new section of the Galilean ministry with the first of a series of three miracles. Each emphasizes the power of Jesus. Jesus has just spoken of the need to do the word of God (v. 21); now by his word he stills the winds and waves and brings to safety his disciples. The miracle depends not on the faith of the disciples (which is absent) but on the authority of Jesus.

Luke's focus is christological. Although the disciples call Jesus master, their amazement at his mastery of nature and their question as to who he really is reveals that they still have much to learn. Fear and amazement have not yet given way to faith. Perhaps Luke's concern is to show them and those who encounter Jesus through the eyes and ears of the first disciples that Jesus has the same dominion over the seas and waters as Yahweh: cf. Pss. 18.16; 29.3–4; 65.7; 89.9; 104.6–7; 106.9; 107.23–32. If so, then Jesus' control over the waters may also symbolize his control over the forces of evil.

Certainly Jesus' rebuke of the waters (v. 24) recalls his earlier exorcisms (4.35, 41), and the stilling of the storm is followed immediately by the account of the exorcism of the demoniac called Legion. Thus each story helps to interpret the other: Jesus overcomes chaotic forces through a spoken command leading to the return of calm and a sense of fear and wonder among those who have witnessed his power. Sudden storms on the Sea of Galilee are well known; the ferocity of this storm, enough to terrify even seasoned sailors, serves as a foil to the extent of Jesus' majestic power, as do the huge number of the demons expelled from Legion and destroyed with the Gadarene swine.

Luke indicates that Jesus, like Yahweh, is to be known to his disciples as their saviour and deliverer no matter what the circumstances: no opposing power can resist his word of command. AG

The Sunday Next Before Lent

Exodus 34.29–35; 2 Corinthians 3.12—4.2; Luke 9.28b–36 (37–43)

Exodus 34.29–35

This passage has been chosen because it is referred to in the second reading, 2 Cor. 3.12—4.2. It raises some fascinating questions. At first sight, the passage is not logical. The shining face of Moses, the result of his being in the divine presence, makes the Israelites afraid to come near to him. However, they do so on being called by Moses. Having finished speaking to them, Moses covers his face with a veil or mask. This is removed when he again draws near to the divine presence. The oddity is that one would expect Moses to have put on the covering *before* he spoke to the people and not after he had finished speaking, and the AV tried to overcome the problem by translating v. 33: 'And till Moses had done speaking with them, he put a vail [*sic*] on his face.' Various explanations have been put forward to explain why Moses put on the covering only *after* he had finished speaking: that it was to cover up the fact that the brightness would fade; or that it was to prevent the Israelites from being normally frightened by the brightness, except that when Moses conveyed to them the words he had received from God, they saw the brightness and thus took heed of the words. The passage implies that Moses must always have worn the covering, although there is no hint of this anywhere else in the narratives, nor is there any evidence that Israelite priests wore veils or masks to indicate their status, and that this passage is the justification for this practice. While the motif of a priestly covering or mask may have been borrowed from the practice of neighbouring peoples, the purpose of the passage is to emphasize the incomparability of God and the special status of Moses as his chosen lawgiver. An interesting sideline on the passage is that the Hebrew verbal stem *qrn* could mean 'to shine' or it can be connected with *qeren* meaning 'horn'. The Latin version took the Hebrew to mean that Moses had horns, which is why many great artists represented him as a horned figure. JR

2 Corinthians 3.12—4.2

This passage continues a theme begun by Paul earlier in the chapter. In v. 4 Paul declares his confidence, which he has through Christ towards God, and his competence, which comes from God, as a minister of a new covenant. It is this new covenant that Paul turns his attention towards in the rest of the chapter. He contrasts the new covenant sharply with the old. The new covenant is associated with Christ and the Spirit as opposed to the old covenant, which is associated with Moses. The difference between them, he declares, is one of glory. The glory experienced by those who received the old covenant faded rapidly, whereas those who experience the new covenant encounter permanent, resplendent glory. Verses 12–18 conclude Paul's argument on this and only really make sense in the light of vv. 7–11 where Paul sets up the contrast between the glory of the two covenants.

In v. 12 Paul begins to make greater use of the story in Exod. 34.29–35 that he refers to briefly in v. 7. This is the account of Moses' encounters with God on Mount Sinai. The story in Exodus recounts that Moses descended from Sinai with such a shining face that Moses and the people were afraid. Moses, nevertheless, summoned them to him to hear his message, after which he covered his face until the next time that he ascended the mountain to meet with God. The reason that Paul gives for Moses' wearing a veil after he came down from the mountain is so that the people of Israel might be prevented from seeing the glory fading from his face (v. 13). Moses' veil was designed to keep the full impact of the glory, that they beheld, in their minds until the next time that Moses ascended the mountain to meet with God.

The next step in Paul's argument is confusing. He moves straight from describing Moses' veil to saying that, as a result of Moses' veil, a veil lies over the minds of the people of Israel whenever they read the commandments of the old covenant. It is not entirely clear why Paul makes this step nor what he means by it. The most likely explanation is that he is saying that the people of Israel became more used to the veil than they were to the glory of God. What became fixed in their minds was not the fullness of the glory of God, as Moses had intended, but the veil that prevented them observing the glory fading. They became more interested in something that prevented them from seeing, than they were in something that they actually saw.

Paul's point is that in the new covenant a veil is never necessary because the glory of God never fades. The glory of the Lord is constantly available to all members of the new covenant. Each one of them is being transformed into the likeness of Christ so that when they look in a mirror they see not themselves but the glory of the Lord. It is no longer necessary to journey to a mountaintop to experience God's glory, it is present and can be beheld in each member of the new covenant. God's glory is no longer available just to one special person who then passes this on to others; it is equally available to all the people of God.

This passage ends (4.1–2) with a return to the point at which Paul began his argument in ch. 3. It is clear throughout this Epistle that Paul is being called upon by the Corinthians to defend his ministry. In 3.1–6 he begins to do so by referring to the nature of the new covenant, which is one of spirit not of letter. In the intervening verses Paul has laid out a vision of an inclusive community that encounters the full and permanent glory of God, not in a single special person, but in each and every member of this new covenant. So, Paul says at the start of ch. 4, in the light of this he does not lose heart. He feels able to commend himself to those who are a part of this covenant. This glory-laden, inclusive community of God that he has just outlined in ch. 3 will recognize what he says to be true. PG

Luke 9.28b–36 (37–43)

Jesus' true identity has not yet been fully understood by those in Luke's narrative, and Luke seeks now to heighten the christological understanding of his audience. The focus is on Jesus' identity and his place in the purpose of God. Peter has just declared Jesus to be the Messiah (9.20), but this incident reveals that he does not yet appreciate what this means.

Luke's account of the transfiguration is closely related to what has gone before. Jesus has just spoken of glory to come (9.26), and such glory is manifested now on the mountain (9.31–32). If the decision to remove from this reading the strong and specific connective at v. 28a – 'about eight days after these sayings' – is intended to obscure this link, then it would appear to be perverse. Luke seems insistent that glory will come only through the cross. Jesus' glory is revealed only after he has spoken of the costly way of the cross, the way that he will take and which he calls his disciples to follow. Conversely, it is in the context of glory that Moses and Elijah speak of Jesus' impending exodus at Jerusalem (v. 31). Thus Luke provides his audience with a framework in which to understand the narrative of his journey to Jerusalem and death. God is in control, and Jesus is to fulfil his will (v. 31; cf. 9.51; 24.44).

Prayer is a key Lucan interest, and Jesus' own private prayer often precedes significant events. The mountain (v. 28b) is a place of prayer, somewhere Jesus goes for communion with his Father (cf. 6.12; 22.39–40). Just as prayer preceded another heavenly voice when God addressed Jesus as his Son (3.21–22), so prayer now precedes the words of acclamation addressed to the disciples (9.34–35). The disciples hear who Jesus is – for they are told explicitly – in case (or because) they have not understood what they have seen.

These words are also an implicit rebuke to Peter. His wish to build three tents may represent misunderstanding on a number of levels. The offer of three tents may suggest that he sees Jesus, Moses and Elijah as on a par; but Moses and Elijah speak of Jesus, and God tells Peter to listen to his Son. Jesus' pre-eminence is thus asserted. Peter may also wish to capture and domesticate the presence of God's glory as if it could be contained in a dwelling (cf. Acts 7.48–50). Perhaps most importantly, his offer may indicate a failure to understand the necessity of Jesus' journey to Jerusalem. Peter wishes to linger at the place where God's presence has been experienced, but Moses and Elijah indicate that Jesus must go to Jerusalem, where he will accomplish his departure (v. 31, cf. 9.51; 19.28). Peter offers an obstacle to the divine purpose that Jesus is to fulfil.

What has been revealed to the disciples is not yet for public consumption (v. 36). But when Jesus descends from the mountain, back to the level of human suffering, God's majesty is nevertheless apparent in his compassion for a father and his only child (vv. 37–43). AG

Ash Wednesday

*Joel 2.1–2, 12–17 or Isaiah 58.1–12; 2 Corinthians 5.20b—6.10;
Matthew 6.1–6, 16–21 or John 8.1–11*

Joel 2.1–2, 12–17

The book of Joel appears to have been occasioned by a devastating plague of locusts round about the year 400 BC. These locusts and the havoc they have wrought are explicitly described in 1.4–7, one effect of the plague being that some of the regular offerings in the temple have been interrupted (1.13). While ch. 1 describes the threat to the land of Judah, ch. 2 envisages the plague approaching Jerusalem itself. The city is put on a war footing with the blowing of the trumpet, and the sky darkened by the dense cloud of the flying locusts, seems to be a portent of the coming day of the Lord (v. 2), an event that prophetic tradition had come to associate with judgement. Just as the locusts were unstoppable by any human agency, so nothing could forestall the day of the Lord.

In the verses omitted from the reading (vv. 3–11) the oncoming unnatural army is described in vivid and terrifying poetic images, leading to frightened reactions from heaven and earth, and sun, moon and stars (v. 10). Such phenomena elsewhere accompany descriptions of God's coming in judgement, and the army of locusts is seen as one commanded by God (v. 11).

In the face of this terror, God offers respite. If the people return to God, if they proclaim a solemn fast, and if they pray to God to spare them, he may alter their fortunes for good. The book, from 2.18 onwards, implies that the times of prayer and fasting have been noted by God, who now promises his blessing on the land.

This material prompts two questions. Was the plague averted as a result of the prayer and fasting? If it was, did the people remain faithful once the danger was over, or was theirs a temporary piety prompted more by the instinct of self-preservation than a genuine desire for repentance?

The closest point of contact between the text and modern readers lies in the fact that, when confronted by overwhelming forces of nature, humankind becomes aware of its limitations and seeks help from the divine. If we can learn to live our lives as what we really are – creatures with limits to our strength, our intellect and, ultimately to our lives – we may be able to achieve the kind of genuine dependence upon God that is not generated solely by emergencies, special occasions or self-interest. JR

Isaiah 58.1–12

At the heart of this passage is the complaint of the people in v. 3a that God is failing to act in their present distress. Verses 1–2 state God's call to the prophet to go to the heart of their need – their sin. He is to speak with the vehemence and urgency that is the hallmark of all authentic prophecy (for the voice like a trumpet, cf. Hos. 8.1, and for the task of showing the people their true need, cf. Mic. 3.8).

In this case the clarity and insistence are all the more necessary because the people are armour-plated in a complacency built on the fervour of their religious and devotional activity (vv. 2–3). The fact that only fasting is mentioned and not sacrifices suggests that the temple is not yet rebuilt (cf. v. 12). Probably this dates the oracle early after the return in 538 BC, before the rebuilding instigated by Haggai and Zechariah in 520 BC.

Fasting was practised in times of crisis and was regarded as a sign of humility before God and dependence on him in times of crisis (cf. Joel. 1.14; Jer. 36.9). It appears to have been constantly repeated during the time of the exile, for people came to Jerusalem to ask if they should continue this practice of 'many years' now that Zechariah assures them the new age is dawning (Zech. 7.3).

The prophet gives two reasons why their fasting is ineffectual. The first is that it is self-regarding (v. 3). The words may mean that they are more concerned with their own business interests than the rights of others but, possibly, that they have been looking more for religious 'kicks' than true relationship with God.

The second is that it is a cloak for their failure to live in the way God requires (cf. Isa. 1.10–17). Verses 3b–4 describe their internecine strife and their exploitation of those dependent on them.

Verses 6–8 contain one of the finest descriptions of true religion to be found anywhere in the Old Testament. The practice of fasting is not rejected, but a true spirit behind it is expressed only when it is backed by concern for 'doing' righteousness (cf. v. 2), especially for the poor and 'little people' of society.

It is when they truly express such an attitude towards God (a relationship always affecting and being affected by the attitude shown towards other people) that God will arise as light for them (cf. 60.1) and heal them (cf. 57.18–19). Indeed, their need is for inner healing rather than change of circumstances. For then, even as they travel like Israel earlier through their own wilderness, they will find God's presence guiding them just as their fathers did (v. 8, cf. Exod. 14.19–20). Restoration is promised in the expansion of vv. 9b-12 but, meanwhile, it is those who keep faith in the dark times who are the real 'builders' of any community (v. 12). RM

2 Corinthians 5.20b—6.10

Contemporary Christians sometimes look back to the early days in the Church's life with rose-tinted glasses. That period seems to have been inhabited by believers who were filled with zeal, who knew the necessity of evangelism, who had the advantages of a new and innocent faith. Read with care, Paul's letters reveal another side to the story, one in which there are conflicts, struggles and misunderstandings. In the present passage, Paul pleads with baptized Christians, people whom he elsewhere characterizes as being 'in Christ' and belonging to the 'body of Christ', to become reconciled to God. The need for reconciliation is inherent in the Christian faith – it is not a symptom of degeneracy in the latter days of the Church's life.

Set against the other texts assigned for Ash Wednesday (e.g. Ps. 51) and other reflections on the need for reconciliation between God and humankind, 2 Cor. 5 sounds a distinctive note. Here human beings do not cry out to God for forgiveness and reconciliation, for it is God who seeks reconciliation. In the sending of Jesus Christ, God acts to reconcile the world to God (5.20a). Paul characterizes the gospel itself as God's making an appeal to human beings to be reconciled to God (5.20; 6.1). Consistent with Paul's comments elsewhere (Rom. 1.18–32), the point he makes here is that it is not God who must be appeased because of human actions; but human beings, who have turned away from God in rebellion, must accept God's appeal and be reconciled. Even in the face of the intransigence of human sin, it is God who takes the initiative to correct the situation; human beings have only to receive God's appeal.

The urgency of the appeal for this reception comes to the fore in 6.1–2. Without accepting God's reconciliation, the Corinthians will have accepted 'the grace of God in vain'. Moreover, the right time for this reconciliation is now: 'Now is the acceptable time; see, now is the day of salvation!' This comment about time lays before the Corinthians the eschatological claim of the gospel. As in 5.16 ('from now on'), Paul insists that the Christ-event makes this appeal urgent. There is also, however, a very specific urgency that affects the Corinthian community. It is time – or past time – for them to lay aside their differences and hear in full the reconciling plea of God made through the apostles. Time is 'at hand' (NRSV 'near'), both for the created order as a whole and for the Corinthians in particular.

Throughout the text, Paul asserts that it is God who brings about this reconciliation, but he also points to the role of Christ. God reconciles the world 'in Christ', that is, by means of Christ. Specifically, God 'made him to be sin who knew no sin' (5.21). To say that Christ 'knew no sin', consistent with Paul's understanding of sin as a state of rebelliousness against God, means that Christ was obedient to God, that Christ submitted to God's will. That God 'made him to be sin' suggests, in keeping with Rom. 8.3 and Gal. 3.13, that Christ's death on the cross had redemptive significance. Through it human beings are enabled to 'become the righteousness of God' (2 Cor. 5.21b); in Christ's death the reconciling act of God becomes concrete.

Paul's eloquent plea for reconciliation stands connected to comments on the ministry that he and his co-workers are exercising among the Corinthians. Throughout this entire portion of the letter (1.1—7.16), in fact, the focus is on both the nature of the gospel and the nature of the Christian ministry. That dual focus exists not simply because Paul is once more defending himself against his critics (although he certainly is defending himself!), but because the ministry can be understood rightly only where the gospel itself is understood rightly. Paul's ministry, like his gospel, has to do with reconciling human beings to God. In 6.3–10 he expands on that role, insisting that he and his colleagues have taken every measure that might enhance the faith and growth of believers in Corinth. Ironically, he begins his itemization of the things that commend him with a list of things that would certainly not impress many readers of a résumé or letter of recommendation – afflictions, hardships, calamities, beatings, imprisonments . . . For those who see the gospel as a means of being delivered *from* difficulties rather than *into* difficulties, Paul's commendation of the ministry will have a very negative sound. As earlier in the letter, he insists on the contrast between how the apostles are viewed by the world and how they stand before God. If the world, with its standards of measure, regards them as impostors, unknown, dying, punished, those assessments matter not at all. Before God, the apostles know that they are in fact true, well known, alive and rejoicing.

This aspect of the passage makes powerful grist for reflection for those engaged in Christian ministry today, but it is equally relevant for all Christians, especially on Ash Wednesday. The reconciliation God brings about in Jesus Christ obliges not only ordained ministers but all Christians to proclaim the outrageous, universal, reconciling love of God. BG

Matthew 6.1–6, 16–21

It was perhaps not very respectful towards the author of this Gospel to omit from this lection the Lord's Prayer that is at its centre, but at least we can be led to focus on a particular aspect of Matthew's teaching, here and elsewhere: his use of financial language in his exposition of the good news. That use is down-to-earth: for example, the noun 'reward' (coming four times in our passage) can mean payment for work done, and the corresponding verb can mean to pay workers for what they have done (e.g. 20.8, where both words occur). In the whole section, 6.1–21, Matthew presents Jesus as an accountant advising clients to invest in long-term securities rather than in those that mature sooner, and to do without interest payments in the meantime.

For all our love of money – or perhaps because of it and of our feelings of guilt about it – we find this way of thinking embarrassing when it is applied to God. Should not our love for him be pure? ('Not with the hope of gaining aught, not seeking a reward . . .') Matthew appears not to have thought so. His characteristic emphasis on reward can be seen by comparing the frequency with which he and the other evangelists use the noun: Matthew 10 times, Mark once, Luke three times, John once. He has created problems for moral theologians.

But there is another aspect of Matthew's language that must be borne in mind. In vv. 4, 6 and 18, he refers to God as 'your Father' (see also 7.7–11). God's rewards are presents; there is no need to think of them as payments for work done. In Matthew, the language of commerce gives way to that of family. We are not employees in a faceless business, but sons and daughters of a father. It is a sad fact that 'paternalism' became a term of abuse in the late nineteenth century. No New

Testament writer calls God 'father' more than Matthew, normally with a possessive 'my', 'your' or 'our'.

Matthew believed that to love God was the greatest and first commandment (22.34–40). There is some evidence that in Judaism at the time of Jesus there were reckoned to be three pious acts through which one fulfilled this command: almsgiving, prayer and fasting (see e.g. Tobit 12.8). If they are performed in order to acquire a good reputation in the sight of others, then they lose their reality as deeds of love *for God*. Matthew is very clear on this aspect of the matter. But there is more to it than that. If they are done in order to receive payment from God, they cease to be acts *of love* for God. There is a saying from the Jewish fathers: be not like servants who serve the master on condition of receiving a gift, but be like servants who serve the master not on condition of receiving. It is entirely the result of God's love that he repays according to their work (Ps. 62.12, quoted, in its darker aspect, at Matt. 16.27; see also 20.1–16).

Matthew has not, therefore, transferred the language of payments and earnings to the relationship between God and his family without transforming it. It is a happy fact that God's love for his creatures expresses itself in gifts, embarrassing though we find such excessive generosity. JF

John 8.1–11

It is dispiriting (but perhaps not wholly surprising) that this passage has traditionally been known as 'the pericope concerning *adultery*', when so many readers have been glad to find it the story about Jesus' generous forgiveness and his shaming of the censorious. It has indeed been the comfort of sinners and the banner of the liberally minded, even though there are always those to wag a cautionary finger with the final words: 'go, and do not sin again'. But from a pastoral point of view, it has been a prime model, leaving its mark notably on the practice of sacramental confession. And, in another dimension, who can forget, once having seen it, Guercino's picture in the Dulwich Picture Gallery, with the look of piteous contempt on the face of Jesus as he confronts the woman's tormentors? As the word goes, it says it all.

From a more academic point of view, however, the story is remarkable for a quite different reason. It is unique in the Gospel tradition in being demonstrably an example of what form criticism has seen as the earlier stage of all the stories. It truly is a floater and came to rest in this location in the Gospel of John only late and, as it were, by accident. The oldest manuscripts do not have it at all, while others put it after 7.36, and still others place it at various locations in the Gospel of Luke. Indeed, it has often been felt that in ethos and tendency this is a Luke-type story, with its loving generosity of spirit. It certainly has no Johannine 'feel'.

Yet if its floating character presses us to dub this story apocryphal, that seems unsatisfactory, for it has none of the magical features which tend to characterize those episodes from the life of Jesus to be found in the later apocryphal Gospels. Quite the contrary: it is among the most believable (as well as welcome) episodes in the entire canon. It is not surprising that critics have put forward the case for its authenticity as a genuine memory from Jesus' life. After all, if Jesus' teaching and behaviour left a special mark, must it not have been precisely for striking, generous and unusual acts of this kind? It was an inspired move that the designers of the lectionary gave it to be read on Ash Wednesday.

Guercino also painted a picture of the scene in the garden on Easter Day. He used the same man as model and dressed him in the same clothes. I do not know whether he was making a deliberate point about the identity, the sameness, of Jesus across all divides of time, place and state; but in any case we can ponder the point. And in another way, the presence of this story in the still-read canon (even by the skin of its teeth – it might so easily have slipped into oblivion) speaks of the eternal freshness of the truth of its winning message. LH

The First Sunday of Lent

Deuteronomy 26.1–11; Romans 10.8b–13; Luke 4.1–13

Deuteronomy 26.1–11

Verses 6–9 contain what was once called Israel's 'small creed', a summary of the main events of the nation's history of salvation, beginning with Jacob (the 'wandering Aramean' or, to cite other renderings, a 'homeless Aramean' [REB], a 'Syrian ready to perish' [RV]). The lack of reference to Abraham or to the Sinai lawgiving in the 'creed' was taken as evidence that the 'creed' was early and that the missing themes had not been incorporated in the completed story. If these verses can be called a creed (they are no longer thought to be early and incomplete) it is because they lay emphasis upon divine actions which reveal God's character. This character is that of a liberator from oppression and a creator of freedom and human responsibility.

Creeds ought not to remain things of the mind, but should govern action; and this is certainly the case here. The 'creed' is to be recited when the land yields its first fruits, and these are taken to the sanctuary to be offered before God in thankfulness. The land does not belong to the Israelites to do whatever they want with it. It is a gift from God, as the contrast between the homeless, wandering ancestor and the settled offerer makes clear, together with what God did to reverse the parlous situation that faced the ancestor and his descendants. Thus it is no accident that the offerer is commanded to share his bounty with the Levites (priests who have no land for producing food) and aliens. The latter may have included foreigners, but even also Israelites separated from their kin, and thus dependent on the generosity of others.

The whole passage is an excellent example of the fact that a theology of creation must rest upon a theology of redemption. The created order does not unambiguously point to a benign creator. Such belief only comes from meeting God in his redemptive acts, which then carry the obligation that the created order must be treated as something needing liberation from oppression. JR

Romans 10.8b–13

The season of Lent always brings the Church back to the basics, to issues that are bedrock and essential. It is no time for marginal matters that linger about the periphery, but is for those topics and experiences that lie close to the heartbeat of the faith. The texts of Lent force us to reflect on where we as communities and individuals stand in relation to the centre, and then they invite a process of self-examination, repentance, forgiveness and new life.

The epistle reading for today confronts us with some fundamental affirmations that define who we are and, by implication, who we are not. Identifying the lesson as fundamental, however, by no means implies that the passage is simple and without problems. Commentators enter the complex argument of Rom. 9—11 with care, because it concerns not only Christian basics but Israel's rejection of the gospel and Paul's agonizing but hopeful prophecy of Israel's destiny. Any comments about Israel must take into account the optimistic conclusion of this section (11.25–36).

Romans 10.1–17 focuses on Israel's predicament. Its rejection of the Messiah stems not from its lack of religious zeal but from its failure to grasp that the Torah points to Christ, the Torah's very goal and completion (10.4). Its ignorance of this peculiar expression of divine grace ('the righteousness that comes from God') leaves Israel futilely seeking to initiate a relationship with God on its own (10.3).

Then the text underscores the affirmation of 10.4 by declaring that the Torah (in this case Deut. 30.12–14) really witnesses to Christ (10.6–10). With a midrashic form of exegesis, the case is made that Christ's coming and his inclusion of non-Jews as well as Jews into the community of the 'saved' does not represent a change in God's intentions, a plan B that goes into effect when plan A won't work. Rather, in Jesus, God is faithful to the original promise made to Israel. The message that is near to Israel in the Torah is the same as the message that is near now in the gospel. Deuteronomy 30.14 (cited in Rom. 10.8a) finds its fulfilment in the two confessions of Rom. 10.9 – Jesus is Lord and God raised him from the dead. (Interestingly, the link is made by correlating three terms – 'word', 'lips', and 'heart'). Whereas the Jews saw in the Torah an instrument by which to justify themselves before God, Paul sees in it a pointer to Christ, in whom God fulfils the promise.

Verses 11–13 draw out three further implications of God's action in Christ – believers can count on God ('No one ... will be put to shame'); Jews and non-Jews are brought together in the community of the 'saved' on the same footing; and the acceptance of both is rooted in the amazing generosity of God.

What does the preacher do with this passage? Its complexity threatens its use. There are at least three directions in which one might move with a sermon during Lent. First, there is the basic recitation of what we believe – Jesus is Lord, and God is the one who raised him from the dead. These two creeds fill out Israel's otherwise unfinished story (found in Deut. 26.1–11) and show God as faithful to the promises made. Both creeds also carry challenging overtones. Other pretenders to lordship are excluded; other answers to the riddle of death are rejected.

Second, the text provides an opportunity to reaffirm the basic Pauline message of grace, to say again that our relationship to God is rooted in the divine benevolence and not in our self-sufficiency. It is often here that the Jews are mistakenly used as a foil against which to contrast grace, as if they knew (and know) nothing of God's mercy. Such a notion grossly distorts the plight of the Jews and often leaves Christians somehow feeling superior simply because they are not Jews. Paul is sensitive to the temptation and later warns his Gentile readers about becoming proud in their situation vis-à-vis Israel (11.17–20). Grace is meant to evoke awe, not arrogance.

Third, the text invites us to reaffirm the breadth and inclusiveness of God's people

(10.12–13). Throughout Romans, pride of place has gone to the Jew (1.16; 9.4–5), but ultimately grace makes all sinners equal: 'There is no distinction', 'the same Lord is Lord of all', 'everyone who calls on the name of the Lord shall be saved'. The chosen people are defined no longer in terms of the Torah, but in terms of Christ.

On the one hand, we rejoice at such inclusiveness. As outsiders we are brought into God's family and made full participants. On the other hand, we sometimes wonder at God's decision to be gracious to so many. Like Jonah pouting over the inclusion of the Ninevites and the elder son offended at his father's generosity to his prodigal brother, we find grace puzzling, if not offensive. Our reaction unfortunately exposes our failure to comprehend the richness of God's mercy.

So in struggling in Rom. 9—11 with the situation of his kinsfolk, Paul presents us with the ABCs of our faith, more than enough for our Lenten reflection. CC

Luke 4.1–13

Luke's account of the temptation of Jesus is a bridge between earlier chapters which establish Jesus' identity and later chapters which relate his public ministry. It is primarily christological in focus. (Only secondarily, if at all, is Jesus presented as a model for the believer facing temptation. Jesus' overcoming of temptation is unique, an integral part of who he is and what he is called to do.) Jesus' obedience under trial, established before his public ministry begins, will undo the disobedience of Adam, and his faithful sojourn in the wilderness will undo the disobedience of Israel. Israel sought to put God to the test; Jesus submits to be tested himself (v. 12, cf. Deut. 6.16). Jesus' sonship will emerge as one of simple but faithful obedience.

Luke's narrative links with his preceding account of Jesus' identity. He is full of the Holy Spirit (a distinctively Lucan phrase), as befits one who is conceived by the Spirit (1.35), anticipated as the one who will baptize with the Holy Spirit (3.16), and publicly and visibly given the Spirit when endorsed as God's Son (3.22). Yet the Spirit of whom Jesus is full is the Spirit by whom he is led into the wilderness. It is God who leads Jesus into this period of trial, not the devil. The specific temptations narrated are only part of a longer (v. 2) and comprehensive (v. 13) trial.

If it is not clear to those who heard God's voice (3.22) that Jesus is God's Son in a way that others are not, then this seems clear from the genealogy. Jesus is not descended from Joseph (3.23). Rather, like Adam (3.38), his life comes directly from God. Thus it is the nature rather than the fact of Jesus' identity as God's Son that the devil sets out to challenge, seeking to cause Jesus to reinterpret and pervert his role by exploiting it for personal gain. This is the question underlying each of the devil's tests: will Jesus be a faithful and obedient son, unlike Adam, God's first disobedient son?

The link with Israel, also God's son (Exod. 4.2–23), and his trial/testing in the wilderness (v. 1, cf. Deut. 8.2; Exod. 16.4) for 40 days (v. 2) adds a further dimension to the implicit comparison with Adam. Jesus will be tested to see not only if he will adhere to the God-given constraints of his position (v. 3, cf. Gen. 2.16–17), but also if he will keep God's commands and understand that one does not live by bread alone, but by every word that comes from the mouth of the Lord (v. 4, cf. Deut. 8.3).

Three times the devil tests Jesus by asking him to seize power to be used for his own personal benefit. Three times Jesus chooses to serve not self but God. Luke places the Jerusalem temptation in the third and climactic position. Jerusalem is Jesus' goal in the third Gospel (9.51; 19.28 etc.), but Jesus will be exalted there and enter his glory (24.47) not by forcing God's hand now (4.9–11) but by conforming to God's will (22.42). He will go the way of the cross. AG

The Second Sunday of Lent

Genesis 15.1–12, 17–18; Philippians 3.17—4.1; Luke 13.31–35

Genesis 15.1–12, 17–18

Read in the context of Gen. 12—25, this passage indicates how difficult it was for the founding ancestor of the Hebrews to accept that God would grant him posterity. Already in 12.2, Abram has been given the divine assurance that he will be the ancestor of a great nation. Although nothing is known about adoption practice in ancient Israel, it is implied here that the childless Abram has adopted a slave to be his heir. God assures him in a vision (the great Jewish commentator Maimonides (*c*.1135–1204) argued from this passage that *all* divine communications and miracles in the Bible occurred in visions) that he will have a son and that his descendants will be as numerous as the visible stars at night. Abram is still not convinced, and seeks further reassurance. This comes by way of a mysterious dream in which he sees a flaming torch and smoking fire-pot pass between the pieces of sacrificial animal that Abram has cut in two. The origin of the symbolism probably comes from the Hebrew idiom, where 'to make a covenant' means literally 'to cut a covenant'. What this meant in practice is indicated in Jer. 34.18: 'And those who transgressed my covenant . . . that they made before me, I will make like the calf when they cut it in two and passed between its parts.' What is implied is a ceremony in which the parties to a covenant accept that they will share a similar fate to the animals that have been cut in two, if they break the terms of the covenant. The parties involved would appear to have walked between the parts of the severed animal(s). In the case of Gen. 15, the divine presence is represented by the fire-pot and the torch, and the whole dream or vision is the strongest possible confirmation that God will be true to his promise.

Strange as the story is, it reflects the fact that receiving, especially receiving things from God, is far from easy for many humans. The giver is in a superior position, the receiver in an inferior one, or so it appears; and human pride prefers to be in a superior position. At the same time, there are nagging human doubts, especially if things seem to be too good to be true. Abram needs more reassurances than this passage indicates. It invites modern users to reflect on their attitude to giving and receiving, especially where God is involved. JR

Philippians 3.17—4.1

Paul's letter to the Philippian church is notable for the succinct way in which he makes points explored much more fully elsewhere, both (fortunately for us) in his other surviving writings and, presumably, in the teaching he had given to those whom he had gathered into the community 'in Christ'.

Characteristically, he unites the ethical and the doctrinal. Outsiders – and we cannot tell for sure how far specific people are in mind (but see v. 18) – are devoted to the fulfilment of their own worldly interests and desires. But why does this make them, precisely and rather dramatically, 'enemies of the cross of Christ'? Perhaps because they disregard the priorities – self-giving, total generosity, even with life itself– that brought Christ to such a fate.

The Christian perspective is the precise opposite. We have the word *politeuma* – which is variously rendered (and 'commonwealth' is not the most helpful word). 'Citizenship' is a bit formally political; the word can mean something close to the modern 'ethnic minority'. In a Mediterranean city, especially a formal Roman colony like Philippi, Jews, Romans and others might feel themselves both of the city, yet also belonging to their own smaller grouping: Paul perhaps especially, in contrast-cum-similarity to the Jews in the place, who seem to have sniped at the Christians as like them but also different (Paul's familiar predicament). So let us say that Paul means that the Christians' real sphere of social life is not, ultimately, within the busy community of Philippi or its equivalent, but 'heaven', the 'place' of God. We may appear to be living in London or Paris, but in reality we belong elsewhere, with God and the life that stems from him, and which he so graciously pours out. And even more, it is a life marked by expectancy: what we have already is not all. Jesus will return to change us, by sheer unmerited gift, to his own heavenly state. Such a destiny is quite enough to keep us firm – in the meantime. It took the Gospel of John to help us to see that life in Christ can be, truly and satisfactorily, of indefinite duration, here and now without diminution of its reality.

Note that 'saviour' is not a word otherwise used by Paul to refer to Jesus, though it is common in the secondary Pauline writings, especially the Pastoral Letters. When Paul uses the verb, 'save', it usually refers to the final act of God, when all is wound up and God's purpose fulfilled, and this is the setting of Jesus' role here. Here, that role includes the transformation of 'bodies', which is explored in such detail in 1 Cor. 15. We shall be there, not as of right but by God's gift; and not merely continuing as we are ('surviving', as we put it, commonly aspiring no further) but, more excitingly, in a quite new state, modelled on Christ himself. Finally, Paul is proud of his converts: they are like the garland (4.1) one received for winning at the city games. He would be happy to do a lap of honour. The use of football and athletics in sermon illustrations has a distinguished pedigree. LH

Luke 13.31–35

Here Luke offers a succinct summary of the central section of his Gospel, Jesus' journey to Jerusalem (cf. 9.51; 13.22; 19.28, 41). This journey gives Jesus an opportunity to teach, and it underlines the centrality of Jerusalem in the third Gospel. Luke conveys a sense of continuing and inexorable movement, for Jesus' journey is rooted not in his own desires but in the purpose of God. It is necessary for him to go to Jerusalem (v. 33).

It is unclear and probably unimportant whether these Pharisees are friendly or hostile. Their message allows Jesus to reflect on his destiny, and his reply to Herod makes clear that he journeys to Jerusalem to fulfil the will of God, not to escape any plot of Herod. Jesus is not concerned to avoid his death at the hands of Herod; he is under a higher authority, which means that he must continue on his journey.

The reference to the third day cannot but resonate with a Christian audience. We are reminded that Jesus' goal is resurrection (cf. 9.22; perhaps also 2.46). This is the accomplishment of his course, the end for which he strives, the goal of all his work. Yet it is closely related to his exorcisms and healings, the substance of his ministry (together with his teaching, although that is not here made explicit) in Galilee and on his way to Jerusalem.

Luke's first volume begins and ends in Jerusalem. But the portrait of the city here is not a flattering one. Jesus shows compassion for the city, echoing feminine images of God as a bird who shelters her young under her wings (v. 34, cf. Deut. 32.11; Ps. 91.4). The characterization of the city as one which repeatedly rejects those whom God sends to it does not preclude Jesus' compassion for Jerusalem, and his apparent prediction of her demise (Luke 13.35a) is clearly made in sorrow rather than in anger. The fact that Jesus will be killed not only in Jerusalem but through Jerusalem adds further poignancy to his lament for the city.

These words, probably an allusion to Jer. 22.5, are ambiguous in the present context. It is unclear whether the 'house' of Luke 13.35 is the city, the temple or the people (household) of Jerusalem, nor whether it is rejected/abandoned/forsaken or merely left. Jesus will be acclaimed as the one who comes in the name of the Lord (19.38) – but it will be by the whole multitude of the disciples (19.37), not by the people of Jerusalem (cf. 23.13, 18, 27–31). Jerusalem's judgement is therefore inevitable, the consequence of its failure to see who Jesus is and to respond to him accordingly. This hard message may not be conducive to acceptance in modern ears, but it should come as no surprise in the unfolding development of Luke's narrative. John's message was one of wrath to come, and the very hour at which Jesus spoke of Jerusalem's fate (13.31) was one in which he had spoken of many who would fail to enter the narrow door (13.24) and many who would be thrown out of the kingdom of God (13.28). AG

The Third Sunday of Lent

Isaiah 55.1–9; I Corinthians 10.1–13; Luke 13.1–9

Isaiah 55.1–9

It may be obvious to modern Western readers that public resources of water should be freely available to all thirsty people. This is not obvious in the Middle East where water is scarce, and where traditional sources of water may be jealously guarded and defended. The invitation to everyone who is thirsty to come to the water must therefore be seen in this light. The thirsty are also likely to be the hungry, and they, people without money, are invited to buy and eat. The invitation then spirals higher to embrace wine and milk, which are not priced.

The sequel, in which people are chided for spending money on what is not bread, makes it clear that water, food, wine and milk are not to be taken literally in this passage, although this point should not be developed in the direction of supposing that only 'spiritual' and not practical things are being spoken of. There probably is a contrast between at least two types of religion implied in these words. There is religion that involves payment and gives little in return (which was probably how the prophet thought of idolatry) and religion that depends upon the gracious and free gift of the God of Israel. Yet, as the paradox of buying food when one has no money implies, the gifts of God are not free, the cost being borne by him.

The second part of the passage moves to practicalities, and at the same time brings more surprises. God promises to make an everlasting covenant with his people, based upon his love for David. Yet its scope is not restricted to Israel. David was not a leader of the people (singular) but a leader of peoples. There are echoes here of royal ideology found, in certain psalms such as Ps. 2.8 'ask of me, and I will make the nations your heritage'; but whereas this royal ideology may have the sense of Israelite rule and thus domination over other nations, the emphasis in the present passage is different. The nations will gladly accept any invitation to be included in the covenant; indeed Israel may be knocked over in the rush to join (cf. v. 5)! This will be because of the graciousness of God made apparent in what he does for Israel, but his purpose will be to show that that graciousness is intended for everyone.

These verses bring to a conclusion that part of Isaiah that began with ch. 40, and the idea of the active word of God forms a narrative arch between 40.8 and 55.11. Whether the Israelites knew that rain and snow return to the atmosphere in the form of vapour is unlikely. The Old Testament view of these things is that God has storehouses of snow and hail (cf. Job 38.22) and that water is kept in the heavens in waterskins (Job 38.37). Presumably these were not thought of as unlimited supplies; rather, such things as rain and snow were divine messengers that were sent to do specific tasks before returning to report to God. God's word is then to be seen in these terms.

What is God's word and how does it return to him? The prophets employed a mode of speaking that has been called the 'messenger formula', which was used when kings sent messages to each other. The king would speak his message in the presence of an ambassador, and the latter would then travel to the court of the king for whom the message was intended, and repeat the message verbatim. When prophets used the formula 'thus says the LORD' they were implying that they were uttering a message that they had heard God speak. This may help us to make sense of the mechanics of vv. 10–11, the two verses that follow our reading. Their main point is that all the words that have been spoken in chs. 40—55 will be fulfilled as surely as rain and snow help plants to grow. JR

I Corinthians 10.1–13

The lesson from the Epistle for today presents the readers with an extended warning and a promise. On the one hand, the Corinthians are faced with the failings of the Israelites of old, and thereby are called themselves to avoid the practice of idolatry (actually sharing in the cultic meals in the pagan temples). A confidence about their own status in no way guarantees immunity; idolatrous behaviour will inevitably lead to disaster. On the other hand, the readers are reminded of the faithful God, who has not abandoned the chosen ones and who always provides a means to cope with the testing.

The structure of the passage is significant. The first paragraph (10.1–5) lists four miraculous events enjoyed by the Israelites at the time of the exodus: the leadership of the cloud, the crossing of the Red Sea, manna from heaven and water from the rock. Together they function as something like 'sacraments' for the Israelites – like baptism and the Eucharist. All the people (and the 'all' is stressed) are distinguished by the special attention given by God. Yet their privileged position in no way assures them of automatic protection from the divine displeasure when their behaviour warrants it. 'They were struck down in the wilderness' (10.5). The paragraph reads like a Christian midrash on the story of the exodus.

The second paragraph details four particular occasions (10.6–12) when 'some' of the people failed and were appropriately judged by God for their failings: idolatry (Exod. 32.1–6), sexual immorality (Num. 25.1–9), putting Christ to the test (Num. 21.4–7) and complaining (Num. 14.1–38; 16.41). The reports of these incidents serve as warnings for the readers that they not be caught in the same temptations and so be judged. They are to learn from the experience of Israel, especially if and when they think themselves 'above' judgement and immune to the divine displeasure. The homily on Israel is meant to teach the readers a lesson.

The concluding verse (10.13) offers a word of comfort to those addressed by the warnings of the previous 12 verses. God has not forgotten people caught in intense testing (the Greek word can mean either 'testing' or 'temptation'). The divine provision is stated in three ways: a protection from its being too much, an escape from it (*ekbasis*), and the sustenance to endure it.

At the heart of the gospel lies an unconditional word of acceptance – God's love for the unlovely. It is a message needing to be heard time and again. Yet the repetition of the good news often breeds indifference, arrogance, and presumptuousness. In familiar categories, grace gets cheapened, and God gets treated like a doting parent who can never say no and can never resist indulging the weaknesses of the children. Israel at times thought like this. Apparently the Corinthians were in danger of the same delusion. Their privileged position and the fact that they enjoyed an active sacramental life dulled their sensitivities and led them to suppose that a little idolatry here and a little idolatry there would hardly bother God. A reminder of Israel's story is meant to get their attention and prod a reflection on their own present.

But the good news is not compromised by the warnings against false security. In fact, warnings can become good news when they shake us from a stupor and alert us to danger. A smoke alarm is good news when a fire breaks out. We can be grateful for the lessons drawn from Israel's story, and now from the Corinthians' story, that prod us to change.

In this light, the familiar 10.13 does not need to be taken as a caveat to the warnings, as if the warnings are only idle threats that a kindly God would never carry out. Rather, 10.13 can be taken as a promise. Testings are common to human experience, but because God is faithful, God can be counted on to keep the testings from exceeding our strength to bear them and to provide for us an escape hatch. Implicit in the verse is a recognition of humans' need for help from beyond themselves.

Though 10.14 is beyond the bounds of the passage, its presence is noteworthy ('Therefore . . . flee from the worship of idols'). The reassurance about God's faithfulness and the news about God's providing a way out do not relieve individuals and communities from the imperative of the first commandment. In fact, they become yet another reason to abandon our idols, to leave behind the alluring deities created by human hands, whether they be ancient or modern. cc

Luke 13.1–9

Parables and sayings of eschatological judgement (Luke 12.35–59) provide the context 'at that very time' (13.1) when Jesus is told of the death of the Galileans killed by Pilate. These teachings are the context in which he offers his warnings to repent (vv. 3, 5) and the related parable of the fig tree. Jesus is not diverted by the interruption to his teaching, but uses it to teach further about the judgement of God.

Apparently implicit in the report of the death of the Galileans is the suggestion that they were sinners who had met the sort of end of which Jesus has just spoken. Perhaps there is an element of Jerusalemite snobbery in pointing to Galileans as sinners. If so, Jesus deflects it with a counter-example of the sudden and unexpected death of dwellers in Jerusalem. But this report of a Roman official putting to death Galilean pilgrims in Jerusalem may in fact anticipate the sudden and cruel death that will be the fate of another Galilean pilgrim at the hands of Pilate. Luke foreshadows what is to happen to Jesus, and Jesus' denial that neither these Galileans nor Jerusalemites were punished as sinners perhaps anticipates and refutes any charge that his own appalling death at the hands of Pilate was the result of the judgement of God upon him.

Modern readers, at least in the affluent West where death is kept usually at a comfortable distance, may naturally see in this discussion a debate about the problem of evil, suffering and injustice. Luke's ancient audience may have been more matter-of-fact about death, aware that it was an ever-present part of everyday life. Those who report the death of the Galileans suggest that they were more sinful than themselves and therefore deserving of God's judgement. Jesus' reply suggests rather that the ever-present possibility of sudden death should cause those aware of the possibility of imminent judgement to consider their own lives rather than seeing others as more sinful than themselves (vv. 3, 5). There is yet time to produce good fruit, but it will not last for ever. Thus Jesus suggests that it is the patient mercy and forbearance of God that means that so far they have escaped the judgement of God, not the relative sanctity that they claim for themselves.

The parable of the fig tree therefore offers a mixture of judgement and hope, and the fate of those killed by a brutal dictator or a collapsing building sheds little light on questions of theodicy. Such questions are not unimportant, but their answers may be beyond our reach. Yet each of us has the chance to take responsibility for our own sinfulness and to repent in the period in which God withholds his judgement. That time may end at a time and in a manner that we do not expect; Luke warns his audience to examine themselves, not the others. AG

The Fourth Sunday of Lent

Joshua 5.9–12; 2 Corinthians 5.16–21; Luke 15.1–3, 11b–32

Joshua 5.9–12

The immediate prelude to this passage is not, as the words added to the Bible in the lectionary imply, the crossing of the River Jordan, but the circumcising of the nation. According to Josh. 5.6–9 no circumcising had been done during the wanderings in the wilderness. With the arrival of the people in the promised land it is time for the ending of slavery and the hope of freedom to be celebrated by various ceremonies. The first is the circumcision of the nation. When this has been completed and the people have healed, Joshua speaks the words with which the lectionary passage begins. There is a pun in Hebrew on the name Gilgal and the verb *galal*, meaning 'to roll'. Presumably Israelites who, in later generations, asked why Gilgal was so named were told that it was here that the disgrace (the forced labour) of Egypt was finally and officially abolished; when the nation set foot in its own land and was freed from the enslavement in Egypt and the anxieties of the wanderings in the wilderness.

Three other events mark the passage from slavery to freedom: the observance of the Passover for the first time in the promised land, the eating of what had been produced in the promised land, and the cessation of the manna that God had provided in the wilderness. If the passage is to mean anything to modern congregations, it is probably by explaining the connection between liberation, and how it is marked and celebrated. What ceremonies, if any, powerfully indicate to Christian worshippers that, to refer to the epistle, in Christ 'everything has become new?' JR

2 Corinthians 5.16–21

Every now and again Paul gives us a glimpse of the cosmic extent of his understanding of Christian theology. This is one of those occasions. In this passage Paul sets out his vision of a new creation which came into being through Christ's death and resurrection. Through these events the world has turned on its axis and will never be the same again. What makes this passage so profound, however, is that in the same breath as he is describing the cosmic impact of Christ's death, Paul also describes the intimately personal impact of that event. Paul's vision takes in the whole world and each individual person at one and the same time.

He begins by setting out the nature of this new creation. It is to be sharply distinguished from the old creation. The old creation was a creation of 'flesh' (the NRSV 'human' does not quite do justice to the contrast here), whereas the new creation is a creation of 'spirit'. The language of creation reminds of the references to Adam that we find elsewhere in Paul (e.g. Rom. 5.14; 1 Cor. 15.22). At the time of Adam the old world of flesh was created and all who lived after him were influenced by his deeds. At the death of Christ, however, a new creation came into being, which has reversed the effects of that first creation. The world is now a very different place, characterized by the things of the spirit and by reconciliation. What Paul is describing here is an eschatological event occurring not at some far distant point in the future but 'from now on' (v. 16). The new order has already begun.

The result of this new creation is that everything and everyone is seen in a new light, not the old light of the flesh but the new light of the spirit. This seeing afresh stretches even to Christ himself. Here we find an answer to one of the great conundrums of the Pauline Epistles. One of the remarkable features of the Pauline writings is that very few of the events of Jesus' life are mentioned. Here we find an explanation for this. Paul believes that, in the new order brought about by Jesus' death and resurrection, the things of the flesh are much less important than the things of the spirit. Those who live in the new creation see things in a new perspective, the perspective of the risen and ascended Christ, not of the earthly Christ.

One of the slightly confusing elements of this passage is that Paul moves seamlessly from the personal to the cosmic and back again. Consequently it is often hard to work out whether he is referring to the state of the world as it is now or the state of the individual. The confusion between the two, however, is part of Paul's point here. The world itself changed irrevocably at Christ's death. In this passage Paul is encouraging each Corinthian Christian to join in with that change rather than clinging to the old creation, represented by the things of the flesh, which has passed away. The world is now in a situation of perfect reconciliation with God. Each individual is invited to join in with that reconciliation and to be reconciled to God. The task of each person who is a member of this new order is to act as an ambassador to draw others into reconciliation with God in alignment with the new created order.

One of the key issues of this passage is how Paul saw God's action of reconciliation taking place. The language of v. 19 is unclear. Was God reconciling the world in or through Christ, or was it that God was in Christ reconciling the world? In other words did the reconciliation take place through the agency of Christ or was it because all the fullness of God dwelt in Christ (as in Col. 1.19) that the reconciliation could take place? Both answers are fully possible within the broader Pauline theology and it is entirely possible that Paul left the meaning deliberately ambiguous here.

Paul ends this passage with a bold statement. At the heart of the new creation lies a paradox. The new creation was made possible by a switch in status between Christ and the rest of humanity. Christ became sin so that humanity could become 'the righteousness of God'. Here we see the profundity of Paul's claim. Christ's action did not simply allow humanity to become righteous but to become God's own righteousness. This righteousness is characterized by faithfulness in relationship and loyalty to the covenant. A humanity that portrays these most God-like of characteristics is truly a new and wonderful creation. PG

Luke 15.1–3, 11b–32

'There was a man who had two sons.' Even in these days of rampant biblical illiteracy, many in the congregation will recognize the so-called 'parable of the prodigal son' immediately from its opening sentence. The astonishing theological implications, the penetrating psychological insights and centuries of representations and retellings make this among the most familiar of biblical passages. That very familiarity may prompt preachers to turn to other readings or to seek to wrench some new insight from the parable, but this parable can stand on its own. Simply to tell it once more is to preach the gospel afresh.

While the parable is commonly referred to as the 'parable of the prodigal son', some refer to it as the 'parable of the lost son', in keeping with the parables of the lost sheep (15.3–7) and the lost coin (15.8–10) that precede it. Still others refer to it as the 'parable of the loving father', reflecting both the opening words of the parable itself and the dominant motif of the father's generosity to his sons. Whatever title we use, this parable concerns three people ('a man who had two sons'), all of whom are involved in matters of recognition and non-recognition.

The younger son initiates the action in the parable. For reasons that remain unstated, he asks that his father give him the property that he stands to inherit on the father's death. Attempts to clarify the legal details of this situation are not terribly successful, given our limited knowledge of first-century Palestinian practice. Clearly the younger son could expect to receive a fraction of what the elder son would receive.

Heedless of the advice of Ecclus. 33.20–22, the father accedes to the son's request. The son then leaves for a 'distant country' and squanders his inheritance. Because of the assumptions often made about his behaviour, it is worth noticing that Jesus says only that the son was engaged in 'dissolute (*asotos*) living', which simply refers to inappropriate or undisciplined habits. Later on, the *elder* son accuses him of spending the father's money 'with prostitutes' (v. 30), but that charge should be read with some suspicion, since the elder son is scarcely a neutral observer of his brother's habits! What concerns Jesus is that the young man runs out of money and finds himself in a position utterly abhorrent to Jews, that of tending pigs.

Verse 17 marks the turning point in the younger brother's story: 'He came to himself.' The Greek expression has connotations very like those in contemporary English. What prompts this recognition is irrelevant, for what is important is that the son recognizes his situation. As a hired hand in his father's household, he would be better off than he is at present.

The younger son's recognition of his situation stems from a perception about his own plight. It is crucial to see, however, that the father's recognition stems, not from the son's recognition (or from his repentance), but from the sheer joy of seeing his 'lost' son once more. The father, essentially absent from the story since v. 12, suddenly becomes the primary actor; he sees, he is filled with compassion, he runs, he embraces, he kisses. Before the son can complete his own confession of recognition, he calls for the best clothing and the best food and initiates a magnificent celebration. Both father and son are found.

Contemporary readers enjoy this moment in the parable, for we identify with the relief of the son and the joy of the father. What that enjoyment overlooks is that the father has acted with an exuberance that would merit scorn from his neighbours. The wise and dignified patriarch ought not run to meet anyone. Certainly he ought to enquire about this son's behaviour, to ascertain his intent, to hear his confession before extending forgiveness. At the very least, the neighbours will mutter about cheap grace.

The older son does more than mutter, of course. For him there is no recognition scene. He does not run to meet his brother or even assent to his father's generosity. Instead, this 'loyal' son gives voice to the complaint of all 'good' children everywhere. He has worked, not as a hired hand, but as a slave. Never has he received even a goat for celebrating with his friends. But the 'bad' child has been rewarded simply for coming home, when no other option was left to him anyway.

How to respond to the older son, who has indeed done everything right and never been rewarded for his goodness? Two options come to mind. The father might agree with the son's assessment and offer him his own fatted calf and grand celebration, humouring him into acceptance. Or the father might defend himself and scold the son for his selfishness, enjoining him to put aside such legalistic measurements.

Perhaps the most poignant movement of the father in the story is in relation to this good, loyal older son. When the son refuses to enter the celebration, the father takes the initiative to find him and plead with him (v. 28). When the son makes his case, the father does not disagree or belittle. He restates his own recognition but with these words of introduction: 'Son, you are always with me, and all that is mine is yours' (v. 31). The generosity lavished on the son who was lost outside the household is now extended also to the son who is lost within the household. The father's love knows no limitations. BG

Mothering Sunday

Exodus 2.1–10 or 1 Samuel 1.20–28; 2 Corinthians 1.3–7 or Colossians 3.12–17;
Luke 2.33–35 or John 19.25b–27

Exodus 2.1–10

The name 'Moses' is probably part of an Egyptian name, as found in the name of Pharaoh Thutmose(s), and connected with the verb *msy* 'to be born' and the noun *mes* 'child'. It is remarkable that the greatest founder of the Israelite nation should have a partly Egyptian name, and it suggests that Moses is not an invented figure.

In the present passage, however, the Egyptian name has been forgotten, even if Moses' Egyptian origins have not. The end of the story, in which Moses' name is explained as 'I drew him out of the water' depends on the similarity of the name Moses (Hebrew *moshê*) and the Hebrew verb *mashah* 'to draw (out)'. A further implication is that the story of Moses' preservation (the passage must be set in the context of the pharaoh's order that all Hebrew baby boys must be killed) belongs more to the realm of folk tale than that of fact. Stories from elsewhere in the world about the miraculous preservation of a future ruler while a child have been cited, including the close parallel relating to Sargon of Akkad, whose mother laid him in a basket of rushes.

But if it is correct to see the story as an instance of the genre of the miraculous deliverance of the future ruler when a child, what must not be overlooked is the realistic and resourceful human female side of the story. The bonds between the mother and her child, and between the child and his sister, are so strong that they lead to bold and imaginative action. Moreover, such is the nature of human sympathy, especially that evoked by a helpless baby, that when the pharaoh's daughter discovers the child, she deliberately overlooks the facts both that he is 'foreign' and that helping the child will involve disobeying her father's expressed decree. Far more instances of brave and self-sacrificing action by mothers on behalf of their own and other children must exist than parallels to the story of the delivered future ruler!

The function of this passage in the story of Moses is to explain how the future deliverer of the Israelite nation grew up in the Egyptian court. Its deeper message is that God works through the emotions and the determined and resourceful action of women, especially mothers. JR

1 Samuel 1.20–28

Motherhood and childhood as understood today in the West is a comparatively modern invention. In ancient Israel, as in the rest of the ancient world, women were expected, along with tackling arduous routine daily tasks such as fetching water, to bear as many children as possible, preferably males. They could expect to be constantly pregnant and childbearing and rearing from the time of their marriage, at 13 or 14, until they were around 40.

A barren woman was an economic liability as well as a failure in the eyes of her family and society. Perhaps the reason why Elkanah had two wives (1 Sam. 1.2) was because he could not afford economically and for social reasons to have one wife who bore him no children. Peninnah may therefore have been a second wife, who was married when Hannah produced no offspring. The tender way in which Hannah's husband treated her (1 Sam. 1.5, 8) needs also to be understood against the harsh realities of life in ancient Israel.

The birth of the son to Hannah, therefore, did more than remove a social stigma. Although we are not told whether Hannah had other children after the birth of Samuel, the possibility must be entertained.

Hannah's decision to dedicate her precious son to the service of God at Shiloh indicates how heavy the burden of her barrenness had been, and how important to her its ending was. She probably suckled her son, as was normal, for two or three years before bringing him to Shiloh, years that she would have relished in the circumstances. The offerings that accompanied the bringing of the child to Shiloh were lavish. A three-year-old bull would be an especially valuable animal.

The purpose of the narrative is to prepare readers for the remarkable career that the boy born in response to the divine answering of prayer will have. Modern readers will sympathize with pressures placed upon Hannah to conform to the social and economic expectations of women of her day. Such pressures are not unknown in today's world, where people are not accepted for what they are, but for how they measure up to norms of career, motherhood or physical beauty. God, fortunately, sees things differently. JR

2 Corinthians 1.3–7

In literary form, the passage follows a convention of the time, normal in Paul's writings, whereby a letter's opening greeting is followed by some form of thanksgiving. Here (alone, but see 1 Pet. 1.3f. and the dubiously Pauline Eph. 1.3f.), he uses a Jewish variant: a 'blessing' (*berakah*) – 'Blessed be God who . . .'

The content is dominated by two groups of words, which engage in an elaborate, interwoven dance: comfort or encourage, encouragement (*parakaleo*, *paraklesis*); and affliction, suffer, sufferings (*thlibo*, *thlipsis*, *pascho*, *pathemata*). The effect is clearest if the passage is read aloud, as, certainly, it was meant to be. The very repetition would have made it memorable. The first group is one of Paul's favourites (65 occurrences, but chiefly in this letter). As the Gospel of John shows, the theme and the linkage caught on (via the related *parakletos*). In Paul himself, it is a powerful word, to which the English 'comfort' scarcely does justice.

'Affliction' and 'sufferings' make the natural counterweight. And of course the pattern corresponds to the fundamental one of death-resurrection, founded in the pattern of Christ, that is so pervasive in Paul (see e.g. 4.7—5.5). And God, father of Jesus, is praised for the assurance that comfort (encouragement, strengthening) will prevail. As the pattern is that of Christ, so it is also ours, for we live 'in him'. What is more, the life and its pattern are mutual, with Paul on the one hand and his converts on the other as partners to the roots of their existence. In relation to this Christian community, Paul had ample reason to hold on doggedly to this fact of life. LH

Colossians 3.12–17

The two final chapters of Colossians (like the latter parts of other Pauline letters) are largely devoted to moral teaching. Here, following the establishing of a doctrinal base in the 'risen' standing of Christian people and a list of vices which are, therefore, to be 'put to death' (v. 5), and then a statement, akin to others in Paul, of the multi-ethnic, multi-status composition of the community for whom 'Christ is all' (v. 11), we have an uncomplicated list of virtues, of the kind common in the literature of the time. Again, the list contains few surprises and is comparable to passages elsewhere. There are also few exegetical difficulties, and the passage invites reflection rather than head-scratching.

All the same, it is important to note the presence of a number of well-known features. The previous verses drew the familiar contrast between the new way of life and the old: 'in these you once walked' (v. 7), and put the whole ethical instruction in an eschatological perspective: because of the prevalence of vice (sex, greed and idolatry), 'the wrath of God is coming' (v. 6).

Now the contrary virtues are headed by humility and its dependent social quality of forgiveness, which has God's forgiveness as its driving motive (cf. the Lord's Prayer). But love is the head of the moral pyramid, as in all the Gospels, as well as in Paul himself.

Then we have a practical note, referring to actual practice at Christian meetings: teaching, admonition and (in a reference virtually identical to Eph. 5.19–20, and therefore important in discussions of the connection between the two writings) music. Little can be said with certainty about the hymns referred to, though the New Testament is studded with possible examples, not least Col. 1.15–20 (see also Phil. 2.6–11; Eph. 5.14; and numerous passages in the Revelation of John). For the context of their use, 1 Cor. 14 provides the most vivid evidence. It must remain open whether 'the word of Christ' (v. 16) refers to something as precise as the tradition of his teaching and whether the giving of thanks (v. 17) refers to something as formal as the Eucharist: whether it does or not, the words 'to the Father through him' give a succinct statement of the structure and point of later eucharistic prayer. LH

Luke 2.33–35

For the passage from which this is a brief extract, see pp. 51–52. It is a detail which, though pregnant and moving, is easily passed over in the flow of Luke's Gospel. It is a vignette, whose place in Christian life and imagination lay ahead, in the Middle

Ages and since, and in the artistic and devotional tradition rather than the academic; also more Catholic than Protestant. It is one of the roots of Marian devotion, in particular that which centres on Mary as the suffering mother, forever alongside her Son, with his death implicitly yet cryptically foretold from the start by Simeon, and her involvement at the end and afterwards foreshadowed in these ominous words.

Their significance for Luke and his narrative remains mysterious. In one sense, however, this is not so: Luke is the effective founder of the 'cult' (however understood) of Mary; the first Christian writer to make her a Christian heroine, with a clear and emphatic role (yet almost in her own right) in the coming of Jesus. And this particular aspect, that is, her being associated with Jesus' suffering, now foreshadowed for the first time, is new. It is hard not to read it without the interposing of innumerable medieval and renaissance paintings of Mary's place in the dying of Jesus and its aftermath. This is already (but surely anachronistically?) the Mary of the *pietà*.

If however we stick to Luke's own context, there is more to be said, or at any rate there is an adjustment of perspective. Simeon, prophet-like, utters two oracles, first the Nunc Dimittis, with its general assurance of universal salvation now at hand, and now, in vv. 34–35, a more specific statement of Jesus' own part and his mother's association with his fate. The word rendered 'thoughts' is usually used, in the New Testament, in a pejorative sense: it is judgement that Jesus will bring, the 'fall' as well as the 'rise' of 'many in Israel'. He will be the instrument of God's sundering of his people into the genuine and the false, a common idea in apocalyptic and not here elaborated. It is in line with the frequent quoting of Isa. 6.9, making intelligible the rejection of Jesus by his own people. The passage occurs significantly, in relation to Paul's apostolate, in Acts 28.26. So the theme can be said to bracket Luke's work as a whole. The reference to the sword is obscure – despite numerous attempts to interpret it down the centuries. In any case, with its centring on death and division, this is a sobering reading for the normally rather cheerful atmosphere of Mothering Sunday, though even so it has its own realism. LH

John 19.25b–27

Since early days Christians have been touched by Jesus' tender love for his mother as he hangs dying on the cross. Traditionally in the words, 'Woman, behold your son', he is seen as commending his mother to the care of the disciple whom he specially loves, knowing that he – her firstborn – can no longer provide for her. In fact, this passage is about much more than this. Jesus is creating a new relationship: Mary is given a new 'son', and the beloved disciple a new 'mother'.

Many questions have been raised about this passage. Why does John alone mention the beloved disciple at the cross? According to Mark, when Jesus was arrested, all the (male) disciples 'forsook him and fled'. Only women watched Jesus' crucifixion, looking on 'from afar' (Mark 15.40). Would the Romans have permitted Mary to come near enough to hear Jesus' words? Does John envisage two, three or four women present? (Probably four.) Why do John and Mark have only one name in common (Mary Magdalene)? These questions are helpfully discussed by Raymond Brown in his massive book *The Death of the Messiah* (New York: Doubleday, 1994). For the evangelists, the women who follow Jesus to the cross, and are first at his tomb on Easter morning, seem to be models of loyalty and faithfulness (though the silence of the women in Mark 16.8 remains a mystery).

Mary is not mentioned by name; Jesus simply addresses her as 'woman' (cf. John 2.4). Nor is 'the disciple whom Jesus loved' named; it is only church tradition which identifies this figure with the apostle John. This curious 'anonymity', combined with the Fourth Gospel's love of deeper meanings, has led scholars to suggest allegorical or symbolic interpretations. One suggestion is that in these verses the dying Jesus is creating a new family – a new community. The 'woman' Mary has been interpreted as the Church, the 'mother' of believers. The beloved disciple is often seen as representing the ideal follower(s) of Jesus. Some see the scene as representing Jesus' natural family, hitherto unbelievers (cf. John 7.5), becoming part of his spiritual family. Others see Mary as representing Israel, or rather part of Israel, coming to faith in Christ.

This is a difficult text on which to preach for Mothering Sunday, when our thoughts are turned to families, and gratitude to our parents (especially mothers). If we stress Jesus' love for his mother, we rely on our pious sense of what must have been the case. If we interpret this text symbolically of Israel and the Church it may seem irrelevant to the occasion, and even anti-Jewish. Although Jesus in the Gospels enjoins respect and care for parents (Mark 7.10), he does little to support traditional 'family values' (see John 2.4; Mark 3.31–35; Luke 2.49; 11.27f.); rather he stresses the priority of discipleship over family ties (e.g. Matt. 10.37; Mark 10.29; Luke 14.26). Maybe we could focus imaginatively on Mary and what it must have been like for her to be the mother of Jesus. RE

The Fifth Sunday of Lent

Isaiah 43.16–21; Philippians 3.4b–14; John 12.1–8

Isaiah 43.16–21

At first sight, the logic of the larger context of this passage is confusing, if not contradictory. While it begins with a call to forget former things (v. 18), it then seems to dig up the past as God complains that the people did not bring him the appointed sacrifices (vv. 22–24). A further difficulty is that elsewhere in the Old Testament and Isaiah (cf. 1.12–15; 66.3) there seems to be a repudiation of the idea that God requires sacrifices. These difficulties can be overcome if we assume that vv. 22–4 are a divine reply to a complaint of the people (cf. v. 26, not included in the reading, which mentions a disputation). The complaint is that the sacrifices and offerings *were* duly made, but that in spite of this Jacob was given to destruction and Israel to reviling (v. 28). In reply, God says in effect that even if the sacrifices and offerings were made according to the letter, they were not made according to the spirit. What the people actually brought before God was their sins and iniquities (v. 24b), for which their insincere offerings effected no forgiveness. In this context, v. 23b is at first sight confusing, because God appears to be saying that *he* did not make offerings to *Israel*! It is almost impossible to reproduce the subtlety and wordplay of the Hebrew here. REB has: 'I did not exact grain-offerings from you, or weary you with demands for frankincense', which reads more logically.

There is a second part to the divine response to the people's complaint about their plight, and this is that, all along, they have misunderstood the nature of their relationship with God. They have sought, through their offerings, to make him indebted to them; he, however, is the incomparable one (cf. v. 25a) who forgives sins and blots out the past. They must learn to be thankful for his mercy.

This thought returns us to the beginning of the passage, because whatever else forgiveness is about, it is about facing a future which is no longer encumbered by the past. The people are to set out on a new journey, one in which the desert provides not dangers from wild animals and lack of water, but new opportunities and the protection of the God who has formed a people for himself (v. 21). This journey can be thought of physically, as applied to the return of exiles from Babylon to Judah in the sixth century BC, or as representative of the spiritual journey of a forgiven people; that is, a people always facing a future unencumbered by the past. JR

Philippians 3.4b–14

In the verses that immediately precede this reading, Paul issues a warning against 'the dogs', the 'evil workers', 'those who mutilate the flesh'. Scholars debate a number of details about the group Paul has in mind, but it appears that its adherents insist on circumcision for Gentile Christians and boast about their connections with Israel (see Phil. 3.2–4a).

This lection constitutes part of Paul's response to this group. He begins with the claim that he has more reason than they for 'confidence in the flesh' (v. 4). Verses 5–6 form a kind of curriculum vitae, beginning with aspects of Paul's life that were decided by virtue of his birth. He was 'circumcised on the eighth day, a member of the people of Israel, of the tribe of Benjamin, a Hebrew born of Hebrews' (v. 5). The second half of the list includes matters over which Paul did have a choice: 'as to the law, a Pharisee; as to zeal, a persecutor of the church; as to righteousness under the law, blameless' (vv. 5–6). He himself made decisions to pursue and maintain these behaviours.

The picture these phrases create contradicts the general impression many people have, in large part a legacy of Augustine and Luther, that the 'pre-Christian' Paul was riddled with guilt over his inability to live as the law demanded. On the contrary, Paul presents himself as an accomplished Jew who had been deeply involved in the best part of his tradition and who defended that tradition zealously. (The reference to persecuting the Church does not necessarily contradict this picture, since Paul's persecution may well have been social and economic harassment, which he saw as part of protecting his people.)

The break between v. 6 and v. 7 is dramatic. Without ever even hinting at a vision or a light or a 'road to Damascus', Paul marks the change conventionally referred to as his 'conversion': 'whatever gains I had, these I have come to regard as loss because of Christ.' Again contrary to the general impression of Paul, he does not depict his call or conversion as the solution to a problem, the release from some deep moral or psychological or spiritual crisis. Quite the opposite! 'Because of Christ', all these accomplishments became for him simply 'loss'.

Verse 8 restates this assertion more strongly. It was the 'surpassing value of knowing Christ Jesus' that led to the radical transformation of Paul's values. He now regards them as 'rubbish'. At this point the NRSV is somewhat euphemistic in its translation; the monographic word 'dung' is much to be preferred. Even the best that Paul had accomplished he came to regard as nothing more than garbage because of the revelation of Jesus Christ.

What Paul means by 'knowing Christ Jesus' becomes more clear in the remainder of the lection. First, it means being 'in him' (v. 9), the connection with Christ and all believers that elsewhere Paul terms 'the body of Christ'. Second, it means leaving aside the righteousness of one's own accomplishments in favour of the righteousness that 'comes through faith in Christ' (v. 9). No longer can Paul speak or act or think as if his work is his own alone, or as if his work acquired for him standing before God. The righteousness Paul now seeks is God's own. That righteousness finally ends in the resurrection itself (v. 10).

Despite the significant change Paul has experienced, he is careful to acknowledge that he has not yet arrived at the goal. The goal itself appears to be of two sorts. First, he identifies 'the resurrection from the dead' as his goal; that is, he aims at being with Christ following his own death (see 1.23). The second goal is spiritual maturity, but that goal is somewhat obscured by the NRSV. Translated more literally, v. 12 opens with the words, 'Not that I have already received this or already been made mature.' Paul acknowledges that he has not yet achieved the goal he would set for himself.

He continues to pursue that goal 'because Christ Jesus has made me his own'. The English translation here needs to be more forceful as in 'because I have been overtaken by Christ Jesus'. Paul's understanding is that he was seized or captured by Christ, not that he initiated the relationship, or that he earned it somehow. Because of that seizure, which Paul now understands to have been a gift of grace, he continues to strive toward what lies ahead.

Paul's interpretation of his own conversion is highly suggestive for contemporary reflection on what it means to proclaim the gospel. Unlike many traditional approaches to evangelistic preaching, which offer the gospel as the answer to problems in people's lives, Paul understands the gospel to be just the opposite. It gave him no answers to problems, but instead it disturbed his answers and sent him in search of a new 'solution', a new understanding. More precisely, it thrust a new understanding on him, an understanding that required radical reassessment of past, present and future. BG

John 12.1–8

Both Matthew and Mark include in their Gospels stories that parallel this one (Matt. 26.6–13; Mark 14.3–9; compare also Luke 7.36–40), and for them also the event is closely connected with the impending passion and death of Jesus. With his customary eye for detail, John has taken particular care to locate the anointing of Jesus between the raising of Lazarus and the death of Jesus.

The story begins with the chronological note that this episode occurred 'six days before the Passover' (v. 1). Since the narrator has just referred to the nearness of the Passover in the preceding scene (11.55–57), the time reference here seems superfluous. In that preceding scene, however, people are speculating as to whether Jesus will dare to go to Jerusalem for the festival, for the officials have arranged to arrest Jesus if he in fact comes for the Passover.

The story also begins by connecting this episode with the resurrection of Lazarus. It takes place in 'Bethany, the home of Lazarus, whom he had raised from the dead' (v. 1). Verses 2–3 again refer to Lazarus and to the presence and activity of Mary and Martha. Neither Matthew nor Mark identifies the woman who anoints Jesus, and it can scarcely be accidental that John so carefully names the three individuals whose presence is significant in ch. 11. The raising of Lazarus is a pivotal event in John's Gospel, one to which it is impossible to remain neutral. It prompts belief on the part of some (11.45), but it also prompts the decision by others that Jesus must be put to death (11.46–57).

The response of Mary to the restoration of her brother's life can be gauged by the extravagance of her act in v. 3. She 'took a pound of costly perfume made of pure nard, anointed Jesus' feet, and wiped them with her hair'. Even before Judas' calculating remark about the value of this perfume, first-century readers would know that this large quantity of high-quality perfume was remarkably valuable. That its fragrance filled the entire house (v. 3b) further affirms its costliness and the luxuriousness of Mary's act.

What first-century readers would find extremely odd in this story is that Mary anoints the feet of Jesus rather than his head, as is the case in Mark 14.3 and Matt. 26.7. She then wipes his feet with her hair, which results in the dissipation of the very costly perfume she has just poured out on to his feet! Two possibilities for interpreting this gesture both seem plausible. First, in John 13.1–20, Jesus washes the feet of the disciples, dries them, and then instructs them that they are to do the same for one another. Mary's gesture of anointing the feet of Jesus and wiping them with her hair may anticipate symbolically this act of service. Second, anointing the feet may also anticipate the anointing for burial that Jesus refers to in v. 7.

Judas' response, of course, addresses the money involved rather than the part anointed. In the parallels to this story, the question about the value of the ointment seems to reflect a straightforward concern about priorities. Here, by contrast, the question covers the sinister purposes of Judas. Had the perfume been sold, he was the one who stood to benefit from the money thus acquired. The narrator elsewhere explains that Judas' betrayal of Jesus comes about as a result of the devil's intervention, and this comment gives specificity to that claim (see 6.70–71; 13.2, 27).

Jesus' response comes on two fronts: first, a defence of the action of Mary, and second, a rebuttal to Judas' feigned concern for the poor. The claim that Mary bought the perfume 'so that she might keep it for the day of my burial' is a little unclear. Had Mary consciously intended such usage for the perfume, she would not have used it at this dinner. Jesus probably refers to the unanticipated function of Mary's action. The day of his burial is now quite close, and Mary's action foreshadows the anointing needed then.

More familiar, of course, is the saying that concludes the lection: 'You always have the poor with you, but you do not always have me.' Removed from its narrative context, as it too often is, this saying seems almost callous. 'You always have the poor' is not, however, a statement about the social attitudes that ought to govern the Church's behaviour. Instead, it contrasts the presence of the poor with the impending absence of Jesus. The Johannine Jesus frequently refers to his return to the Father, to the imminence of his departure, to conditions that will obtain in his absence. Given that feature of the Fourth Gospel, this statement is but a forceful reminder that Jesus will be present only for a brief time.

The irony within this passage is striking. Judas speaks for the poor, at least he does on the surface. We might even characterize his words as reflecting prophetic concern for the outcast and marginalized. Mary, by contrast, appears to engage in a frivolous, wasteful act. It is Mary, however, who is the real prophet in this story, for she is the one who knows what the hour is and where the crisis occurs. BG

Palm Sunday

(Liturgy of the Passion)

Isaiah 50.4–9a; Philippians 2.5–11; Luke 22.14—23.56 or Luke 23.1–49

Isaiah 50.4–9a

Although the word 'servant' does not appear in this passage, its close similarity to 49.1–6 has led most to see it as the third of the so-called 'servant songs'. It is the most intensely personal and individual of them all. While in the others the servant could well depict 'Israel' in one way or another, as well, perhaps, as an individual or group who see themselves as embodying the calling of 'servant Israel', this seems like the outpouring of someone who sees himself in the prophetic tradition of such figures as Jeremiah, called, through many setbacks and much persecution, to summon 'servant Israel' to fulfil their true destiny. One commentator entitled this passage 'the Gethsemane of the Servant'.

Among the strongly individualistic features are the repeated mention of parts of the body – tongue, ears, back, cheeks, beard and face – a forceful reminder that God uses real human beings for his purposes. His word always has to become 'flesh'.

Before he can teach others the servant has himself to be 'taught', a word which appears twice in v. 4. It can come to mean 'those who have been instructed' and who are therefore 'skilled' or 'learned' (see, in various ways, NRSV, NEB, REB, NIV). Yet the verse speaks of daily listening to God and receiving his word, so that the second use of it is indubitably passive. Anyone who speaks for God and who hopes to teach others must be lifelong and perpetual learners themselves. Only then are they able to perform God's purposes in human lives, such as sustaining those who are 'weary', God's own mission (cf. Isa. 40.30–31).

The sense of failure expressed in 49.4 is now reinforced by open and physical opposition (vv. 5–6), whether from fellow-Israelites because of his conviction that God has purposes for foreigners (for an opposed point of view see 45.9–13), or from Babylonian officials for his conviction that their power would wane (e.g. 43.14).

Yet, just as faithfulness through failure was a necessary prerequisite for the discharge of his mission (49.5–6), so persecution is an inescapable part of the 'learning' process for God's servant. Through such experiences his own faith is renewed as, in a courtroom metaphor, he becomes convinced that God will not desert him. He will be given the strength necessary for his task, his 'face set like flint' (v. 7, cf. Ezek. 3.8–9). Taught by God through his constantly renewed communion with him and by experience of his strength through persecution and rejection, he sees his mission in its true perspective. It is God's purpose that, ultimately, shall prevail (vv. 8–9). It is a lesson that was also learned by Paul through similar persecution (Rom. 8.31). RM

Philippians 2.5–11

It is usually held that though Paul's purpose in the wider passage is to urge the virtue of humility, these verses represent a separable unit, theological in character. Over the past 80 years in particular, it has become common to see them as an early Christian hymn, probably antedating Paul's use of it here in what may be his last extant letter. It may be seen to fall most naturally into three strophes (concerning Christ's pre-existent status, his self-abasement to earthly life and to death, and his subsequent exaltation to universal lordship). Thus, the passage may be taken as perhaps the oldest summary statement of Christian faith available to us, certainly in anything like poetic or imaginative form. If that is right, then its 'advanced character', in the common assessment of doctrinal terms, is all the more striking; for it seems to state a christological doctrine that is of the same order and ambitious profundity as that of the Johannine prologue.

There is dispute over the most likely sources of parts of the doctrine here stated and almost every word has its difficulties. It may be that Jesus is seen in terms of an amalgam of not wholly consistent Jewish images, with both speculation about Adam and 'wisdom' theology (like that in the Wisdom of Solomon) being prime contributors. The overall doctrine is of both the comprehensiveness of Jesus' significance and the cosmic scope of his achievement. In that way, the words are a striking example of that early Christian manner of laying hold of every possible Jewish idea and symbol and applying them to Jesus.

The final verses are the least problematic, appearing to draw on Isa. 45.23 and Ps. 110.1, that most common of all early Christian proof-texts, backing the idea of Jesus as 'lord', yet to God's glory. The background of the first part (vv. 6–8) is less clear, but the model for Jesus may best be seen as Adam; only, unlike him, Jesus accepts willingly his allotted place in God's purpose (no grasping at or retaining of equality with God), and even accepts the degradation of the cross. The two 'moves' in Jesus' drama are expressed with great vividness, even theatricality, and there is no missing the strength of the claims being made for Christ, though it is doubtful whether the 'form' of God in v. 6 carries, in context, the idea of 'divinity'; it is probably derived from the Gen. 1 picture of man as made in the image of God. So Jesus is seen as succeeding where Adam (and all of us, his progeny) failed – a doctrine used by Paul in Rom. 5 and 1 Cor. 15. Even if the comparison is less with Adam than with 'wisdom' as developed in Jewish thought, the picture is no less striking and the teaching no less powerful in its claim: Jesus' place is, for always, by God's side, his co-regent. All the more remarkable then is his foray into the world where death awaited him; and all the stronger his claim on allegiance and worship. LH

Luke 22.14—23.56

Luke's passion narrative is based on that of Mark, but it has so many extra elements or points of difference that it is often suggested that he had access to an additional source, which he has incorporated into what he inherited from his predecessor. But the special Lucan elements are mostly so characteristic of his interests and favourite themes, as found in both Gospel and Acts, that it is perhaps more likely that much is owed to his own way of seeing the story of Jesus and what it tells us of God, his purposes and the way of life to which he calls us.

The sayings of Jesus from the cross illustrate this strikingly. Mark had Jesus utter only the mysterious and problematic words from Psalm 22.1, 'My God, my God, why hast thou forsaken me?' Matthew took this over, but Luke drops it. Instead, he gives us three utterances by Jesus: first, the prayer for the forgiveness of those who torment him (23.34); second, the words of comfort and assurance to the penitent thief, whose turning only Luke describes to us (23.43); and third, Jesus' devout self-commendation to God in his dying moments (23.46). Each of these sayings represents a thoroughly Lucan motif. The first and third are in fact reproduced at the dying of Stephen, first witness to Jesus who paid with his life (Acts 7.59, 60); moreover, the aspect of the first whereby the Jews who put Jesus to death are said to have acted in ignorance, and may therefore be exonerated, reappears in Acts 3.17 and 13.27. Luke shows both Jesus and his early followers stretching out a forgiving hand to old Israel, eschewing enmity; perhaps it was a message that his own churches at the end of the first century needed to hear. We may suppose that Luke wishes us to learn a positive and holy way of death from Jesus' quoting of Psalm 31.6: 'Into thy hands I commend my spirit.' And the words to the thief, giving assurance of Jesus' companionship in paradise, are typical of his willing outreach to sinners, especially in Luke's depiction of him: compare 7.36–50; 19.1–10. In other words, Jesus dies in a manner which Luke sees as exemplary for us all, as well as typical of his gracious life. Jesus dies as he had lived. In his time of extremity, there is no varying.

The response to his dying on the part of the centurion is again subtly and significantly different from Mark's 'Truly this man was son of God': 'Certainly this man was righteous'. The word *dikaios* is taken in the RSV to mean 'innocent'. If that is correct, Luke is shifting the emphasis from a point of belief to a point of apologetic (which in fact echoes the words of Pilate [e.g. 23.22] and indeed of all figures of Roman authority in Acts); Jesus, like his followers, merited no persecution, which came from malevolent Jews (and they themselves did not realize the meaning of their actions). But perhaps Luke echoes the wording of Wisdom of Solomon 2.12–20, where the righteous man, who is indeed God's son, is shamefully persecuted.

Other aspects of Luke's passion move in similar directions. By contrast with the utter isolation of Jesus in Mark, here we have his suffering greeted with mourning and compassion – not just by the centurion but also by the women of Jerusalem (23.27–30), to whom Jesus responds, characteristically, with comfort. Again, his love finds ready expression. Similarly, in Luke, Jesus heals (his final, typical act of this kind) the man whose ear was severed by Peter (22.51); just as he also evokes Peter's penitence for his denial (22.61), like the father of the erring son in the parable (15.11–24). In fact, Peter's coming restoration for the apostolic mission (as indeed that of all the disciples) is already assured by Jesus' words at the supper, which, like all Jesus' meals in Luke, is the scene of his beneficent teaching (22.28–

32). Even Judas' end is not depicted as a well-deserved punishment, as Matthew implies in 27.3–10, but more as a horrible accident (Acts 1.18–20). Similarly, Jesus has pity on his disciples in Gethsemane. In Mark, they are shown as callous; here, they sleep 'out of grief' (22.45). For Luke, Jesus dies as he lived, a model of God's love and saving compassion for his people. LH

Maundy Thursday

Exodus 12.1–4 (5–10), 11–14; I Corinthians 11.23–26; John 13.1–17, 31b–35

Exodus 12.1–4 (5–10), 11–14

The account of the institution of the Passover raises at least three difficulties for modern readers. The first is why it was necessary for the blood daubed on the door-posts to be a sign to God, indicating which houses should not be afflicted by the firstborn plague. After all, elsewhere in the plagues narratives God was able to exempt the Israelites from plagues that affected the Egyptians (cf. Exod. 9.22–26), so why was it not possible for the final plague? The second difficulty is the moral one of believing in a God who apparently puts to death the innocent children of the whole people, when only its ruler is in dispute with Israel. It needs further to be noted that there is a tension in the prescriptions between daubing the blood, which is essential in the Egyptian context, and consuming the lamb, which becomes the central part of the rite after the deuteronomic reform (cf. Deut. 16.1–8).

In order to explain these difficulties various theories of the origin of the rites have been proposed, such as that the blood of a lamb was daubed on their tents by herds-men moving from winter to spring pasturage, in order to ward off misfortune; or the death of the firstborn has been explained in terms of the custom of dedicating all firstborn male humans and animals to God (cf. Exod. 13.1). It has also been pointed out that, whatever its origins, the Passover became connected with the barley harvest, at which unleavened bread marked the transition from bread made with the old grain to that made with the new.

Little of this will be of assistance to modern congregations and preachers, and a certain amount of idealizing will be unavoidable if the passage is to be used creatively. A possible starting point is the deuteronomistic observance (Deut. 16.1–8), in which the emphasis is placed upon sharing the meal in remembrance of deliverance which has affected those in every subsequent generation. This deliver-ance was as much political as spiritual, in that it freed people from slavery. Such deliverance was not achieved without cost and struggle, and it is an unfortunate fact of life that the innocent, including children, are caught up in and become the victims of human strife. However, the redemption of Israel from slavery is intended to bring benefits to all the nations, including Egypt. If Israel is not a light to the nations in the manner in which it establishes and practises mercy and compassion among its citizens, the Egyptians will have paid a heavy price in vain; and the Old Testament, in its narratives of the wilderness wanderings, is unsparing in its con-demnation of the attitude of the very generation that was freed from slavery. The path of redemption is never easy, as the whole passage indicates. JR

I Corinthians 11.23–26

These lines concerning the sharing of bread and wine are so familiar to most Christian ministers that the act of reading the text may seem superfluous. As the 'words of institution' they are known by heart and can be recited verbatim. And, indeed, that intimate knowledge of this passage is consistent with the way in which Paul introduces it. When he writes, 'For I received from the Lord what I also handed on to you', he uses technical language for the transmission of tradition, and the Church's intimate knowledge of this passage continues that understanding of it.

The tradition itself contains the simple and direct words that connect the ordinary sharing of bread and wine with the death of Jesus and its significance for humankind. The bread signifies the body of Jesus, broken in death. The cup signifies the blood of Jesus, poured out in death. Through that death comes a new covenant, and through participation in the meal comes the remembrance of Jesus. The word remembrance (*anamnesis*) appears in both the statement regarding the bread and the statement regarding the wine, suggesting that the Lord's Supper is vitally connected with the Church's memory of Jesus. What the exact nature of that remembrance is becomes clearer in 1 Cor. 11.26.

With v. 26 Paul no longer cites the traditional words of Jesus, but offers his own interpretation of the Supper: 'For as often as you eat this bread and drink the cup, you proclaim the Lord's death until he comes.' Two crucial points emerge here. First, Paul asserts that the very act of the meal *is* an act of proclamation. In the celebration of the Lord's Supper itself, the Church engages in the preaching of the gospel. Protestant exegetes, uncomfortable with the omission of the verbal act of proclamation in this passage, long rejected this point by attempting to argue that Paul means that preaching *accompanies* every celebration of the Supper. If understood that way, however, the verse simply tells the Corinthians what they already know (preaching accompanies the meal) and adds nothing at all to the passage. Verse 26, in fact, culminates Paul's discussion of the meal by explaining its significance. The Lord's Supper is not just another meal, the eating of which is a matter of indifference; this celebration is itself a proclamation of the gospel of Jesus Christ.

The second point Paul makes in this verse comes in the final words, 'You proclaim the Lord's death until he comes.' The Lord's Supper is a very particular kind of proclamation – a proclamation of Jesus' death. A different kind of celebration, perhaps a celebration of Jesus' miracle of multiplying the bread and the fish, might proclaim Jesus' life and teaching. Even the Lord's Supper might be understood as a celebration of the person of Jesus as a divine messenger. Building on the words of institution with their emphasis on the coming death of Jesus, Paul forcefully articulates his view that the Lord's Supper proclaims Jesus' death. Unless the final phrase, 'until he comes', merely denotes the time at which celebration of the Lord's Supper will come to an end ('you keep proclaiming in this way until Jesus returns'), what it does is to convey the eschatological context in which the Church lives and works. The Church proclaims Jesus' *death* within the context of a confident expectation that he will come again in God's final triumph.

In this passage Paul has a very sharp point to make with Christians at Corinth, who are preoccupied with factions, with competing claims about the gospel, and with what appear to be class struggles. Paul's comments about their celebration of the Lord's Supper do not make the situation entirely clear to us, but it appears that they have followed the customs of the day, according to which the hosts of the meal served the choicer foods to their social peers and the less desirable foods to Christians of lower social or economic status. The activity of eating and drinking, and the struggle over that activity, have dominated the celebration of the meal. Paul's response to that situation is to recall forcefully the nature of the Lord's Supper. This is not another social occasion. It is *in and of itself* the proclamation of Jesus' death. Because it is a proclamation, Christians must treat it as such. Whatever conflicts there are about eating and drinking, they belong outside and apart from this occasion.

As earlier in the letter, Paul emphasizes the proclamation of Jesus' death as central to the gospel itself (see 1 Cor. 1.18–25; 2.1–2). Over against the Corinthians' apparent conviction of their own triumph over death, their own accomplishments and spiritual power, Paul asserts the weakness of Jesus, whose faithfulness to God led to his death, and Paul insists that the Church lives in the tension between that death and the ultimate triumph of the resurrection.

In the context of the Church's observance of Maundy Thursday, this passage recalls again the death of Jesus. That recollection is no mere commemoration, as occurs with the recollection of an anniversary or a birthday. The remembrance, especially in the Lord's Supper, serves to proclaim the death of Jesus Christ once again, as the Church continues to live between that death and God's final triumph. BG

John 13.1–17, 31b–35

Maundy Thursday derives its name from Latin *mandatum*, 'command', referring to the 'new commandment' given by Jesus at the Last Supper. The command to love is rooted in Old Testament teaching (cf. Deut. 6.4f.; Lev. 19.18), texts combined by Jesus in his famous 'summary' of the Law (Mark 12.29–31 par.). In the Johannine writings this teaching is given new impetus as it is grounded in Christ's own love for his disciples, and the Father's love for the Son and for all who obey his word (cf. John 13.34f.; 14.21; 15.9–13; 1 John 4.7–21). It is especially poignant that Jesus gives this command after washing the disciples' feet as an example of humility and love, and before giving up his life for others.

The footwashing is unique to John's Gospel, and there has been much speculation why it replaces Jesus' sharing of the bread and the cup in John's narrative of the Last Supper. The evangelist must have included it because it was important to him and perhaps his community. What does it mean for him?

Most obviously Jesus washes the disciples' feet as an example of humble service. In the ancient world, where people walked the fields and dusty streets in open sandals or with bare feet, footwashing was a normal preliminary before meals. Washing someone else's feet was a menial task, done by 'inferiors' for 'superiors'. It was performed for guests by slaves (usually women), by children for parents, wives for husbands, and sometimes by devoted students for their teachers. It was unheard of for a teacher to wash his pupils' feet. Yet this is what Jesus does, as an 'acted parable' or visual aid, to show those closest to him that their role must be not that of 'lords', but of servants. The teaching is exactly the same as given in Luke's narrative of the Last Supper (22.27), when Jesus rebukes his disciples for disputing over who is the greatest with the words, 'I am among you as one who serves (*ho diakonon*)'.

Yet the footwashing in John is more than a moral example. It comes at a turning point in the Gospel, as the evangelist moves from his account of Jesus' self-revelation through 'signs' and personal encounters to his 'hour', when the time has come for him to be 'glorified' (cf. 13.1, 31f.). The verbs which John uses to describe Jesus' laying aside his garments and resuming them are the same distinctive terms as were earlier used for his laying down his life on the cross and taking it up in resurrection (10.11, 15, 17f.). The footwashing illustrates Jesus' loving 'his own' to the end and prefigures his death: cf. Mark 10.45, 'the Son of Man came not to be served but to serve, and to give his life a ransom for many'. Like Peter, we have to learn to accept Christ's 'washing' of our feet, so that we may share in his work of service and reconciliation. Do we have here a neglected sacrament? RE

Good Friday

Isaiah 52.13—53.12; Hebrews 10.16–25 or Hebrews 4.14–16; 5.7–9; John 18.1—19.42

Isaiah 52.13—53.12

This final 'servant song' is undoubtedly one of the greatest passages in the Old Testament and yet, with its densely packed thought and highly symbolic poetic language and imagery, one of the most difficult to interpret. The text presents many difficulties, perhaps evidence of the problems scribes and others have found in understanding it in the course of its transmission. Commentaries discuss these in detail. Yet the grand sweep of thought is clear, speaking in the sublimest language of the deepest mysteries of God's dealings with human beings.

It opens (52.13–15) and closes (53.11b–12) with words of God about his servant. The body of the song is spoken by an unidentified group in the first person plural commenting on the action rather like the chorus in a Greek tragedy. Like the psalms of lament and prophetic passages, especially in Jeremiah, it depicts the servant's suffering, yet contains assurance of God's triumphant vindication of him.

God's opening words about his servant (52.13–15, cf. 42.1) and closing speech (53.11b–12) confirm that his role will be to bring surprised joy to the nations. Indeed, by his 'knowledge' (which he gains from his own relationship with God, cf. 50.4) he will, like a sacrificial victim, cover their sins and bring them into a right relationship with God. Thus his ministry will be triumphantly vindicated as he believed (50.8–9).

The human speakers describe the suffering of the servant which so disfigured him (53.1–3); realize that he suffered as a sacrificial victim for their sins which they now freely confess (vv. 4–6); speak of his suffering and death (vv. 7–9), but, finally, see his vindication by God (vv. 10–11a.).

Who are these speakers? They may be the Gentile kings now telling of that which before they had never heard or known (52.13b). In that case the 'suffering servant' must be Israel, who suffered innocently at their hands. Yet, by his glorious redemption of his 'servant' Israel, God has so revealed his glory that all nations come to recognize and know him (43.8–13). Or the speakers may be fellow Israelites who, having failed in their mission to be God's witness to the nations, need someone or some group who, by their faithfulness to God and suffering for his sake, bring them back to an awareness of him. In their renewed recognition of God and relationship with him the servant's ministry is vindicated.

As poetry and profound theology the symbol of the 'suffering servant' can operate at many levels, finding, as Christians believe, its supreme embodiment in Jesus. What it does show is the extraordinary power of vicarious suffering. Just as we are born into life by the pain of our mothers, advance to understanding by the dedication of our teachers, and appreciate music, literature and art through the gifts of others, so God's love reaches us through those who are ready to pay the price of being its agents. RM

Hebrews 10.16–25

Hebrews is composed of an alternation of exegetical passages, often worked out with skill and ingenuity, followed by consequent ('therefore', v. 19) exhortation, sometimes, as here, developing the scriptural material in new, but characteristic ways. The theme of the new covenant, familiar from the words over the cup at the Last Supper, appears in the suggestive text in Jer. 31.31–34, which has been quoted in full in 8.8–12 and provides a leitmotif for chs. 8—10. There, the focus was on the word 'covenant', with its dual sense as the treaty-like bond between God and his people, and a will which only comes into force with the testator's death (see the word-play in 9.15f. – not easy to render into English). Here, it is on the more pervasive concern of this writer: the removal of sin, once by means of endlessly repeated animal sacrifices, now by the once-for-all death of Jesus.

By the time he wrote (surely after AD 70), the offering of beasts in the Jerusalem temple had ceased – in any case, he shows no interest in the rituals in practice, only in the provisions he finds in the Pentateuch. In that sense, his method is bookish. These he exploits here – yet further: this has been his subject from ch. 8. Detail after liturgical detail has been taken up and shown to be absorbed or fulfilled in some aspect of the death of Jesus, who occupies the roles of both high priest and victim in the ritual of the Day of Atonement. It is fruitless to seek tidy logic here. The pattern works by a concentration of images, even more than Johannine in its intensity. The symbolism of the entry into the Holy of Holies, seen as the counterpart of heaven, leads to a movement straight from Jesus' death to his heavenly arrival (cf. 12.2); there is no room in this scheme for his resurrection.

Then, our share in this great result awaits us, assured by the purifying water, presumably in baptism, here seen as the counterpart of liturgical purificatory washings in the old Law. Finally, there is a practical note: Christians must meet together, at least for the sake of mutual encouragement, as the future consummation approaches. SL

Hebrews 4.14–16; 5.7–9

As at Christmas, so on Good Friday a passage from Hebrews serves to affirm the full humanity of Jesus: like us in weakness, in temptation and in despair. The reference to Jesus' 'loud crying and tears' cannot fail to recall the Gospel story of Gethsemane, especially in the Lucan version which emphasizes Jesus' mental and physical anguish. His prayer was to the God who was able to save him from death, and the author states firmly that 'he was heard' – yet he died. It was not that his prayer went unheard: prayer can be answered by 'no' as well as 'yes'; but here the author probably means us to understand that Jesus' prayer was answered with the assurance that this death was not only inevitable but necessary; an answer that Jesus accepted: 'thy will be done'. Jesus was heard because of his *eulabeia*, a word the English versions find difficult to translate in this context (e.g. 'godly fear', RSV, and 'reverent submission', NRSV). It has to do with awe in the presence of God, not naked human fear, and reflects the fact that Jesus faced his suffering in prayer. There is a similar problem with the translation of the first clause of the following verse: some translations opt for the concessive 'Although he was a Son ...' so that the process of learning obedience seems a contradiction of Jesus' real role and status but a part of his emptying himself of his divinity; but it could be read as causative: it is precisely *because* Jesus is son among many children of God (2.10–14), and fully human, that obedience through suffering is his lot. (The same ambiguity is found in the 'christological hymn' of Phil. 2.) Again: he 'learned obedience' can be understood as describing how Jesus, through the repeated experience of testing learned how to obey, or that he learned obedience in the sense of discovering the full extent of the demand, what it really means to obey. And so he was made 'perfect': a term frequent in and characteristic of Hebrews, with connotations of completeness and so effectiveness. Because both Jesus' identification with humanity and his obedience to God were complete, they effect salvation, enabling us to approach the throne of God as Jesus did, and find it the source of mercy and grace in time of need. He is the great high priest, fully identified with those whom he represents, offering the only fully effective sacrifice, the sacrifice of himself, and so opening up access to God. SL

John 18.1—19.42

The four evangelists describe the story of Jesus' passion in different ways. Each has episodes or details lacking in the others, and each his own theological slant. Whereas Mark stresses Jesus' humanity and suffering, culminating in his great cry of dereliction from the cross, 'My God, my God, why have you forsaken me?' (15.34), in Luke Jesus dies calmly, fully trusting in God: 'Father, into your hands I commend my spirit' (23.46). Matthew alone mentions the legions of angels that Jesus could have called to his aid (26.53).

John's special emphasis is on the *kingship* of Jesus, and his 'autonomy' throughout his arrest, 'trials', mocking and crucifixion. John has no account of the 'agony in the garden', nor of Judas' kiss of betrayal. Jesus identifies himself to those who had come to arrest him with the words, '*Ego eimi*' ('I am [he]'), and his opponents all fall to the ground in awe. Jesus himself tells them to let his followers go free. He carries his own cross.

In the dialogue with Pilate Jesus' true kingship is a recurrent theme: Jesus makes it clear that he was born to be king, but that his kingship is not 'of this world'. Both Pilate (18.39; cf. 19.14) and the crowd (19.3) refer to him as 'King of the Jews', and Jesus dies with these words affixed to the cross – words which Pilate refuses to change, in spite of protests. Throughout all this runs the irony that what Jesus is called in mockery he is in reality, 'the King of Israel' (cf. 1.49) – and much more!

Most remarkable of all is perhaps Jesus' final 'word' from the cross, 'It is accomplished' (19.30): he has completed the work that God gave him to do.

Behind all four passion narratives lies the theme of fulfilment of Scripture, sometimes explicit (e.g. Mark 14.27; John 19.24, 37), sometimes implicit. In 19.28 Jesus' words 'I thirst' may allude to Ps. 22.15; cf. Ps. 69.21. Many commentators note the irony that the source of 'living water' (4.14; 7.37) now needs to be given a drink. But Jesus' 'thirst' in John is probably more than physical (this is not to minimize his agony). Jesus' 'food' was to do the will of him who sent him (4.34); now he has to drink the 'cup' the Father has given him (18.11).

After his death, blood and water flow from Jesus' side (in John alone). Some interpret this as showing that Jesus truly had died (perhaps from a rupture of the heart, which can produce such apparent effects); more probably the blood and water symbolize the spiritual cleansing and new life effected for believers through Jesus' death. The unbroken bones, the hyssop (19.29), and the flow of blood all point to a sacrificial understanding of Jesus' death (cf. 1.29, 36). Only John describes the role of Nicodemus in anointing Jesus' body. The huge quantities of myrrh and aloes (19.39) perhaps hint at a *royal* burial. RE

Easter Day

Isaiah 65.17–25; 1 Corinthians 15.19–26 or Acts 10.34–43; John 20.1–18 or Luke 24.1–12

Isaiah 65.17–25

This passage looks forward to a future in which the created order will be renewed, and when everything that mars the present world will be set aside. The city of Jerusalem is the place in which these hopes will be realized, but it is implied that the blessings spoken of will be universally enjoyed. The first ill to be removed will be weeping and cries of distress (v. 19). These can have many causes, including mourning the dead, caring for someone in great pain and receiving news of the death of a family member in battle. These causes will be done away with. Next, there will be no deaths in infancy and everyone will enjoy a long lifespan. This indicates that death will be present in the restored world, but not the kind of death experienced in the present world. It will hold no fears nor be accompanied by suffering. Verses 21–23 mention the unfairness of a world in which people profit from the labours of others, while those who perform the labours get nothing. This situation will be reversed. Because the hindrances will be removed that prevent God from carrying out his ideal will, prayers will be answered before they are even uttered. Finally, the vegetarian creation of Gen. 1.30 will return. Animals will not prey on each other. There will be no 'nature red in tooth and claw'.

In what sense, if at all, has the resurrection of Christ brought about this hope? Obviously, the world remains untransformed, and 2,000 years of Christian belief and practice have not removed the things that mar it. Perhaps the resurrection is like the leaven put in the dough. Its workings are not obvious, but the completion of these workings will produce a new state of affairs. Meanwhile, the vision of a renewed world gives hope and direction to all for whom the unfairness of the present world is a source of shame and despair. JR

1 Corinthians 15.19–26

In 1 Cor. 15.19–26, Paul reaches the climax of his passionate argument about resurrection. This is no abstract discussion about a point of doctrine but a down-to-earth, immensely relevant refutation of the Corinthian doubt that the dead will be raised. In the previous passage (vv. 12–18), Paul has stated negatively why a belief about resurrection is essential: if the dead will not be raised, then Jesus is still dead and Christianity is useless (vv. 13–17). Here he states the positive reasons for believing this: Jesus *has* been raised and this proves that everyone else will be raised as well. One of the most important features of this passage is that in it Paul outlines the practical relevance of Eastertide. At Easter we celebrate what happened to

Jesus but, this passage tells us, as a result we also celebrate what will happen to us. Paul holds up Jesus' resurrection here as a foretaste of things to come. Easter is a celebration of the triumph of life over death, begun by Jesus and continued at some point in the future by us.

Paul uses the metaphor of 'first fruits' to set up his argument here: 'Christ has indeed been raised from the dead, the firstfruits of those who have fallen asleep' (v. 20, NIV). This is an image resonant with meaning. First fruits are, as their name suggests, prior in time to the rest of the harvest. They also promise more of the same. The fact that the crop has begun to produce such fruit indicates that more of the same can be expected in the future. This is an important feature that Paul goes on to expand in what follows. The significance of Jesus' resurrection is not just that he was the first person to be raised from death to new life but that he is representative, he is the same type of being as those who will be raised in the future. It is worth noting here that Jesus is the first person to experience this kind of resurrection from the dead to new life; other examples of people coming back to life after they have died (such as the son of the widow of Zarephath, 1 Kings 17.17–24, or Lazarus, John 11.1–44) are examples not of resurrection but of revivification. The difference is that the others will die again and Jesus will not.

Paul picks up the representative aspect of Jesus' resurrection in 1 Cor. 15.21–23. Here Adam and Christ represent the fate of human beings. This is an argument that Paul uses again in Rom. 5.12–21, though there it appears in a much more complex form than here. The significance of what Paul is saying is that through Adam's actions death entered the world. Since Adam represents the whole of the human race, anyone who follows after him will have the same fate as Adam, i.e. death. Jesus, however, also represents humanity and through his actions the possibility of resurrection from that death is now opened up. Anyone who follows after him will experience resurrection from the dead. Jesus' humanity makes him the new Adam par excellence.

Jesus' resurrection is not only significant for what it cancels out from the past; it is also important for what it augurs for the future. In vv. 23–26, Paul establishes that the resurrection has inaugurated a new age. This age will continue until the resurrection of the rest of humanity, the handing over of the kingdom to God and the utter destruction of death. Jesus' resurrection promises the completion of all these things. These events have a strict order but could not even have begun to take place until the first event of resurrection had occurred. The language that Paul uses here is resonant of the apocalyptic tradition. In apocalyptic texts the climactic intervention by God into the world and the subsequent resurrection of the dead is expected to occur during the end times. For Paul, Jesus' resurrection signals that these events have begun to happen. Those of us who live in this era must understand what is happening and what this promises for the future.

The language of apocalyptic that Paul uses here is alien to many people today. Language that refers to battles between powers, the destruction of death, even the resurrection of the dead is not something that sits comfortably with our modern culture. Nevertheless it is important to recognize that this is language with which

Paul himself is very comfortable and which he uses regularly in his writings to describe the effects of living a life 'in Christ'. For Paul, the resurrection has issued in a new way of being and he speaks of this in cosmic terms. The effects of the resurrection mean that nothing will be the same again. We might not use the same language, imagery or cosmology but the message that, post-Easter, the world is now a place infused with new life and hope is surely one of the utmost contemporary relevance. PG

Acts 10.34–43

Peter's speech to the gathering at the house of Cornelius has roughly the same contents as the other major speeches by Peter in the early chapters of Acts, and indeed that by Paul in Acts 13 (though its reference to Jesus going about 'doing good', v. 38, is unique). This similarity of pattern has led to at least two not wholly consistent conclusions: that the speeches represent a standard pattern of Christian missionary preaching in the early decades, a pattern which may even be seen as one of the ancestors of the later baptismal creeds (a connection with the rite is discernible in some of the Acts episodes, including this one, v. 47f.); and that they are so similar (and the likelihood of shorthand records so remote) that, probably like all the Acts speeches, they are Lucan compositions, whatever they may or may not owe to memory and tradition – so following the practice of writers of the day. This second idea can be strengthened: the speeches are imbued with peculiarly Lucan themes and patterns, the present example being no exception. Note the universal scope of the message (v. 34), though its roots are in Israel (v. 36); the perception of Jesus as a doer of good, a fine description of especially Luke's characterization of Jesus; the post-resurrection meals with the chosen witnesses (v. 41, cf. Luke 24.35); the command to preach (v. 42, cf. Luke 24.48; Acts 1.8); Jesus as future judge (v. 42; Luke 21.36). The speeches contain what Luke saw as the core of the faith.

Cornelius is important as representing a real step forward in the mission. As promised in Acts 1.8, the preaching began in Judea, then moved to Samaria. But Cornelius is a Gentile, though one who is 'devout' and fears God (v. 2). He is one of a number of such people in Acts – a group for whose existence in at least some of the cities of the empire there is now other evidence and who may seem to be natural subjects for successful Christian evangelism: Gentiles who frequented the synagogue and valued its religious and moral teaching, but for whom conversion to Judaism seemed a step too far. Such people were perhaps social misfits of one kind or another (recent immigrants, upwardly mobile freedmen, independent-minded women, cf. Lydia in 16.14), and to whom the blessings of the Christian message may well have been both intelligible (for its roots in Judaism and in Scripture) and peculiarly attractive. It offered a spiritual home. With Cornelius the centurion (he invites comparison, like other Acts characters, with one in Luke's Gospel, the centurion in 7.1–10), the mission is on the verge of the wider move to the (fully) Gentile world. That will occupy Paul and others from chs. 13—20, and indeed implicitly to the end of the book, where Paul carries on the work even from his place of rather loose custody in Rome, 'openly and unhindered'. LH

John 20.1–18

Today's Gospel tells one of the best-loved resurrection stories. It is carefully constructed, beginning with Mary Magdalene's arrival at the tomb (vv. 1f.). Next, two male disciples discover the empty grave-clothes: one 'sees and believes' (vv. 3–10). They both go home. Then we return to Mary at the tomb (vv. 11–18).

John's account shares many elements with the other Gospels. In all, the first people to visit the grave are women (though their number and names vary). They find the stone rolled back, and see an angel/angels (or a man/men in white). There are, however, differences. In Mark, the women run off and tell nobody (16.8; the following verses are an addition). In Matthew, but not Luke, Jesus appears to the women and they cling to his feet (28.9). Some texts of Luke 24.12 have Peter go to the tomb, but only John has Peter and the 'beloved disciple' run there together. The 'beloved disciple' appears to be a model of faith (but why does he just return home with Peter?).

In 20.1, 11–18, John focuses on just one woman at the tomb. Mary comes while it is still dark. It has been suggested that the darkness may symbolize the disciples' desolation. In the course of our narrative she moves from bewilderment to faith. At first she stands outside the tomb, weeping. Even after the angels have spoken to her, she still assumes the body has been removed. She takes Jesus for the gardener, surmising that he was responsible for its removal (what an irony!). But when he addresses her by name (cf. 10.3, 14), she recognizes him as her 'Teacher'. After he tells her of his ascent to the Father, she acknowledges him as 'Lord'. Entrusted with his message for his 'brothers' (the disciples), she truly becomes the *apostola apostolorum*.

John's account is so personal and moving that it is tempting simply to let it warm our hearts. Yet thinking people are bound to ask 'What really happened?' The resurrection is not the sort of event that can be verified from historical evidence, and the Gospel-writers themselves seem to understand it differently. Luke, with his descriptions of Jesus eating with the disciples (24.30, 41–44), stresses its seeming physicality. Matthew, with his great earthquake and opening of the tombs (27.52–54; 28.2) heightens the miraculous. John's attitude is more ambiguous. Is his careful description of the grave-clothes and napkin (v. 7) designed merely to show that the body had not been stolen (robbers would not have left them folded)? Or does John want us to understand that the risen Jesus passed *through* them (cf. his passing through closed doors in 20.19)?

We are not likely ever (in this world) to discover exactly what took place. The main point is that the first Christians firmly believed that something stupendous happened. God vindicated Jesus. Witnesses saw him alive (cf. 1 Cor. 15.5–8). The disciples were transformed and the Church was born. Can we share in their gladness and trust, and let the risen Christ transform our lives? RE

Luke 24.1–12

Luke's first story in his Easter sequence is (unless all Synoptic theory is groundless) based on Mark 16.1–8. But how different it is. One could say that it was a cheerful adaptation of Mark's mysterious and awesome account, that raised as many questions as it answered. But 'cheerful' is too superficial a word, though confidence and joyfulness do characterize a great deal of Luke's writing: the Christian evangelist has a great deal to be joyful and confident about. These qualities are rooted in what God has achieved through and in Jesus, from start to finish – from the ground-laying for his birth in ch. 1 to his resurrection and its sequel in ch. 24 (with Acts lying ahead).

What changes has he made? Like Mark (but unlike Matthew), he tells us that the women's purpose was to anoint Jesus' body, for which we learnt of the preparations at the end of the previous chapter, described there quite fully. Corresponding to the women of Jerusalem who (in Luke alone) had wept for Jesus along the *via dolorosa* in 23.27–31, and not unlike the holy women who dominate the birth narratives in chs. 1–2, the women who come to the tomb are a kind of pious chorus, a devoted escort alongside Jesus in life and death (cf. also 8.1–3). The stark solitude of Jesus in Mark is mitigated. And their piety is emphasized: the women had waited, in order to keep the sabbath, 'according to the commandment'. As in 2.21–40, for example, Luke holds to the proprieties of Judaism.

Mark gave us a young man at the tomb, Matthew a single angel, increasing the drama and the apocalyptic status of what is happening. Luke sees 'two men', but clearly they are to be taken as angels (see 24.23), reminding us of the 'two men' at the transfiguration (9.30), Moses and Elijah, appearing from heaven, and indeed of the ascension scene (Acts 1.10) as well as the crowd of angels at Jesus' birth. Angels (often described as 'men' in the Old Testament, but then emerging as more than that, e.g. Gen. 18 and Judg. 13) betoken huge importance for the occasion concerned – in the purpose of God. It is a moment for go-betweens, so that we might not mistake the weight of what is before us. Like the disciples at the transfiguration, the women respond with appropriate awed reverence.

Here, the women have no worry over the stone entrance to the tomb (contrast Mark 16.3): as in both Mark and Matthew, it has been moved, though, unlike Matthew, Luke does not tell us how. Luke's most daring amendment to Mark is his shift in the reference to Galilee: it is not the place the disciples are to go to but simply the place where Jesus had foretold his coming resurrection (9.22). This of course clears the way for Luke's second volume, Acts, where all centres on Jerusalem as the scene of the Church's origins and first mission (and Galilee scarcely figures, only at 9.31).

More serious in doctrinal importance, however, is his removal of the puzzling elements of fear and (even more) of silence in Mark. Matthew had (sensibly) introduced joy alongside the fear. Luke says nothing of the women's mood, but their silence is removed and the tale is told, which surely makes sense of the narrative as a whole. Only now do we hear their names. As in Mark it is unclear whether Mary who is mother to James is also mother to Jesus and it is hard to know why Luke would not be clear: see Acts 1.14, and then the role of James, brother of Jesus, as Acts unfolds. Joanna had appeared at 8.3, among the women who served Jesus in Galilee. The news was not believed (it was only women who gave it?), and it took the Emmaus walkers to carry conviction (see 24.22–23), together with a visit to the tomb by Peter (v. 34). This is mentioned in v. 12, and of course parallels that in John 20.3–10, where the description is fuller and the beloved disciple is also present. The manuscript evidence for v. 12's being part of the original text is dubious, and it may have come in from knowledge of John 20 or to foreshadow v. 34. We have here a story of great beauty, but Luke's masterpiece (and centrepiece) on the resurrection still lies just ahead (vv. 13–35). LH

The Second Sunday of Easter

Exodus 14.10–31; 15.20–21 or Acts 5.27–32; Revelation 1.4–8; John 20.19–31

Exodus 14.10–31; 15.20–21

Where the sea was that the Israelites crossed and what exactly happened are questions that cannot be answered. This has not deterred commentators from attempting answers, however, even though the outcomes have often been less than satisfactory. Take, for example, the suggestion that the wind that held back the sea and dried the seabed was an actual wind that the Israelites were able to take advantage of. Even if we have never personally experienced hurricanes, we shall have seen sufficient evidence on television of their effect to know that a wind strong enough to part the sea would have been devastating for any humans and animals anywhere near it. Another, more plausible, suggestion is that the Israelites took advantage of tidal conditions to cross a strip of land at Lake Sirbonis not unlike the causeways at Lindisfarne or Mont St Michel, and that the incoming tide then swept away the pursuing Egyptians.

Most attempts to find a natural explanation for the Red Sea crossing only make it abundantly clear that the narrative as we have it goes out of its way to emphasize the supernatural. Further, similarities between Exod. 14 and 'holy war' narratives in books such as Joshua and Judges have been pointed out. Typical features of such narratives are the command not to be afraid (v. 13, cf. Josh. 10.25), the promise that God will accomplish the victory, and the fact that Israel's contribution to the outcome is little or nothing. Also, it is God who throws the enemy into panic (v. 24, cf. Josh. 10.10; Judg. 4.15).

What this means is that Exod. 14 is similar to narratives in Joshua and Judges and elsewhere, that present God as a God of war fighting on behalf of his people, and giving them victories that involve the deaths of their enemies. That this is a problem for modern readers goes without saying; but several points need to be made. First, narratives of this kind belong to rhetoric rather than reality and have parallels with other literature in the ancient Near East. Second, such narratives belong to later rather than earlier strata of the Old Testament. They are not evidence for primitive or barbaric practices in an early state of Israelite development, but functioned story-wise in the way that the violence contained in modern literature, film and television function in modern society. Third, a human race that has perpetrated the horrors of the wars of the modern era cannot afford to be morally superior. The purpose of Exod. 14 is to say, however problematically, that Israel owes its existence and freedom entirely to God. That it also includes a strong statement of the people's unwillingness to believe that this is possible, that slavery is preferable to freedom, should also not be overlooked. JR

Acts 5.27–32

In a second appearance before the high priest and the council of the Jews, Peter and his companions reaffirm their faith in Jesus' death and resurrection. (The core of their statement is the same as that in speeches in the preceding chapters, cf. 2.22–24, 32–33; 3.13–15; and 4.10–12, which has been argued to reflect a common pattern in early apostolic preaching.) Responsibility for the death of Jesus is placed squarely on the shoulders of the Jews, as they recognize; their perception that 'you are determined to bring this man's blood on us' chillingly recalls the words of the crowd in Matthew's passion narrative: 'his blood be on us and on our children' (Matt. 27.25). There is no indication here of the participation of the Romans in the course of events (contrast Acts 2.23; 3.13); even their mode of execution, crucifixion, is translated into the language of Jewish capital punishment, taken from Deut. 21.22–23. Paul also makes that association, in Gal. 3.13, and draws from it an interpretation of the saving effect of the death of Jesus: dying under the curse of the Law pronounced on 'he who hangs on a tree', Jesus bears the curse of the Law for us and so redeems us from it. Luke does not seem to attach any comparable theological value to the death of Jesus as such; his pattern is one of human action and divine reversal: 'you killed him . . . God raised him' (so also Acts 2.23–24; 3.15; 4.10). Resurrection is, however, not just reversal but exaltation, and in that act God gives Jesus new authority.

In view of the Jewish context of the apostles' statement, it is surprising that the titles expressing Jesus' authority are more obviously Hellenistic in background. *Archegos* (as meaning 'prince') and 'saviour' are found as titles for Hellenistic and Roman rulers, but might serve as equivalents to 'Messiah' for non-Jewish readers. The former term is only otherwise found in the New Testament in Acts 3.15; Heb. 2.10 and 12.2; from its root *arche*, beginning, it can also mean 'founder' or 'pioneer'. Thus in Hebrews Jesus is the one who leads the way, or goes ahead (Heb. 10.19–20), as for Paul he is the 'first fruits of those who have died', whom his own will follow (1 Cor. 15.20, 23). For Luke, the risen and exalted Jesus marks a new beginning, a new knowledge of God for his people expressed in the mutual relationship of repentance and forgiveness. This is what John the Baptist came to preach at the beginning of the gospel (Luke 3.3), and what the apostles in turn were sent out by the risen Jesus to proclaim at the end (24.47). Here, with their preaching under threat, they reaffirm their own authority, as witnesses to the events of Jesus, obedient to God rather than to men, and empowered by the Holy Spirit. SL

Revelation 1.4–8

In his opening address to his readers in the seven churches of Asia, John proclaims Christ as the one who died, was raised, is present in authority, and who will come again. He is the 'faithful witness', *martus*, in his death. John characteristically describes as witnesses those who have been put to death (e.g. Rev. 2.13; 12.11;

17.6), lending the Greek word a distinctive meaning and giving the English 'martyr'. The martyrs have a special place in John's vision. As in Acts the first martyr, Stephen, dies in clear imitation of Christ (Acts 7.55–60), so in the Apocalypse the martyrs follow him in witness through death and into life. He is the 'firstborn of the dead', whose resurrection guarantees that of others (cf. Paul on Christ as the 'first fruits of those who have died', 1 Cor. 15.20; and also Acts 5.31, Jesus the *Archegos*). At the end of his vision John sees the resurrection of the dead (Rev. 20.12) and the new age in which there will be no more death (21.4), but the martyrs anticipate this, and are already in heaven beneath the throne of God (6.9).

The risen Jesus holds present authority as 'the ruler of the kings of the earth', the Davidic king-messiah of Ps. 89.27; and is about to be universally revealed on the clouds of heaven like Daniel's Son of Man (Dan. 7.13). This Christ-figure is, however, one with the man Jesus: and therefore exercises his rule because of his death and resurrection. When the conquering Lion of the tribe of Judah is proclaimed in heaven, John will see the slaughtered Lamb (Rev. 5.5–6).

Supreme power, of course, belongs to God 'the Almighty': one rendering in the Greek Old Testament of the Hebrew *Yahweh Sabaoth*. The divine name revealed to Moses in Exod. 3.14 was translated into Greek as 'He who is', and John develops this into a ringing statement of God's eternity. God is past, present and future; but so also is Christ. As 'the faithful witness' who died *he was*; as 'the firstborn of the dead' and 'him who loves us', *he is*; and *he is to come*, still as the one who was 'pierced' (an allusion to Zech. 12.10). This is more than analogy. At many points the Apocalypse clearly suggests the divinity of Christ, and in its conclusion John will hear the living Jesus apply to himself the language used here of God, Alpha and Omega (Rev. 22.3). Following the conversion of the Emperor Constantine, a distinctive symbol for Christ in the Christian Roman Empire was the *chi-rho* monogram, often combined with those Greek letters *alpha* and *omega*. The authority of the risen Christ is a sharing in the power of God – and this is also experienced by his followers. Those whom he has freed from sin (a variant reads 'washed', perhaps in allusion to 7.14) become a kingdom of priests: the description of Israel as God's redeemed people in Exod. 19.6; also applied to the Church in 1 Pet. 2.5.

God and Christ are joined in the opening greeting of v. 4, as is a third subject, the 'seven spirits' before the throne of God, seen there and in 4.5 as 'the spirits of God'. In 3.1 it is the living Christ who has the seven spirits, and in 5.6 they are 'the eyes of the Lamb'. This interchange is another mark of the relationship between Christ and God. It is comparable to the description of the Spirit as the Paraclete in the Gospel of John: in 14.16–17 to be sent by the Father after Jesus has gone away, but in 16.7 to be sent by Jesus himself. In both Johannine writings, to different degrees and in different expression, there is the 'raw material' for later trinitarian definition. SL

John 20.19–31

The resurrection appearances in the Gospels serve two main functions: first, they witness to the fact that Jesus is alive; and second, they enable the risen Christ to instruct and commission the disciples. Today's gospel describes two separate appearances of Jesus, followed by a brief conclusion to the Gospel (ch. 21 is believed by most scholars to be an appendix).

In vv. 19–23 Jesus appears to the assembled disciples in a house on Easter Day itself. Functionally, this corresponds to the appearance described in Luke 24.36–49. Jesus greets the disciples, identifies himself to them, and equips them for mission. There are striking links with John's supper discourses. There, Jesus promised to 'come' to the disciples (14.18), which is what he now does (20.19). He said he was giving his 'peace' to them (14.27); he does so now (20.19f.). In his 'high-priestly' prayer he spoke (proleptically) of his sending them out (17.18); he does so now authoritatively (20.21).

Of particular interest is his 'breathing' on them in fulfilment of his promise to send them the Holy Spirit or Paraclete (20.22). The 'insufflation' (as it is often called) is a creative and effective act of symbolism, reminiscent of Gen. 2.7 where the Lord creates humankind and breathes into Adam the breath of life (cf. Ezek. 37.9; in the Greek text the same verb, *emphysao*, is used in all three passages). While some have seen this as only a foretaste of what is to happen at Pentecost, this can hardly be anything other than the Johannine *equivalent of* Pentecost. There is absolutely no need to read John with Lucan spectacles and to presuppose that this dramatic gift of the Spirit is merely a preliminary to an event fifty days later.

The commission which accompanies the insufflation parallels the 'great commission' in Matt. 28.18–20, and that narrated indirectly in Luke 24.47. What is surprising is the strong focus on the forgiveness and retention of sins, without any mention of preaching or baptizing. The saying recalls Matt. 16.19 and 18.18, and may ultimately derive from Isa. 22.22. While some have seen this as conveying 'power' to one group within the Church (e.g. bishops and priests) to declare sins forgiven, more probably it should be seen as addressed to the disciples as representatives of the whole ecclesial community.

Verses 24f. prepare the reader for the fact that Thomas was not present on this occasion. The appearance a week later is unique to John's Gospel. Theologically its main function is to illustrate the nature of resurrection faith. Thomas says that he will believe only when he can see and touch Jesus' wounds. Yet when Jesus invites Thomas to touch him, he acknowledges Jesus as his 'Lord and God' without this physical assurance. The blessing that follows on those who have not seen and yet have faith is for all future believers. Has Thomas outshone even the 'beloved disciple' in his faith? RE

The Third Sunday of Easter

Zephaniah 3.14–20 or Acts 9.1–6 (7–20); Revelation 5.11–14; John 21.1–19

Zephaniah 3.14–20

The prophet Zephaniah is generally assumed to have been active in the early part of the reign of Josiah (640–609; cf. Zeph. 1.1). His prophecies in chs. 1 and 2 and beginning of ch. 3 speak of the coming day of the Lord and the judgement that will bring, not only upon Judah and Jerusalem, but also upon surrounding peoples such as those in Gaza, Ashkelon, Moab and Ammon. At 3.8 the mood changes to one of future promise; and although it is possible that Zephaniah is responsible for some of the material in 3.8–20, the concluding verses, especially from v. 16, seem to presuppose the situation of the Babylonian exile, with its language about dealing with Jerusalem's oppressors, gathering its people and bringing them home.

Verses 14–15 have been likened to language that could have been used at a coronation. The hopes and expectations that such an occasion would arouse are related, however, not to an earthly king but to the presence of God among his people, among them not for judgement (as in the opening chapters of Zephaniah) but for salvation. The theme of God being with, or in the midst of his people is a powerful one in the Old Testament (cf. Ps. 46. 5, 7, 11). The name Emmanuel – God with us – (cf. Isa. 7.14) is an important instance.

In vv. 16–17, 'holy war' themes appear, in the command to Jerusalem not to fear (cf. the notes on the Second Sunday of Easter), and in the description of God as a warrior who gives victory. Another important theme that is present is the idea that the exile brought shame and reproach upon the people in the eyes of the other nations and, by implication, upon the God of Israel. This situation will be reversed. Israel will receive renown and praise from the other nations when God ends its captivity and restores its fortunes.

However, it would be wrong to read the passage purely in military terms. No doubt the fortunes of war, and matters such as victory and defeat, were important to the Old Testament writers; but the prophetic tradition is not interested in Israel for its own sake, but as the people that will enable the nations to desire and embrace God's rule of justice and peace. The eirenic promises of restoration imply the prior punishment, judgement and purification, so strongly stated in the preceding chapters. JR

Acts 9.1–6 (7–20)

Luke's story of Paul's conversion is one of radical transformation, from persecutor to proclaimer of the gospel. There is no hint of any preparation, no seeds of doubt sown from his presence at the stoning of Stephen, no prolonged depression and agonizing like that of the other classic converts, Augustine and John Wesley. It was a once-for-all event, brought about by the direct intervention of God in his life. Paul would have recognized this account of his experience: it is the way he refers to it in Gal. 1.11–16. In another way, however, he would have difficulties with Luke's presentation. For Luke, what Paul experiences is a vision, with flashing light and the voice of an invisible speaker. It is very different from the Easter experience of the disciples at the end of Luke's Gospel, who walk, talk and eat with a Jesus whom they can recognize. And it must be different. For Luke, the 40-day period between Easter Sunday and the ascension is a unique and unrepeatable time. Only those who have been part of it can be witnesses to the resurrection and truly be called 'apostles' (Acts 1.21–25). For all that Paul is Luke's great hero, his conversion is post-ascension; his knowledge of Jesus necessarily different in kind. Paul would reject this interpretation. For him, the risen Lord appeared to him as to the others, and it is what made him an apostle. He might be last, he might be least, but his testimony is the same (1 Cor. 15.3–11).

The Paul of the Epistles might also have difficulty with the role of Ananias in Luke's account of the conversion. It is Ananias who hears in his own vision that Paul is to be the Lord's chosen messenger to the Gentiles, and in Acts 22.12–16 he passes this charge on to Paul. Paul himself is insistent that his commission to the Gentiles was inherent in his call from God (Gal. 1.15–16), and that his gospel was wholly unmediated. This is basic to his sense of his apostolic authority. There is really no way of reconciling Luke and Paul, save to say that they have different interests and emphases in giving their accounts.

There are three accounts of Paul's conversion in Acts (cf. 22.3–11; 26.9–18). They differ in narrative detail, but agree in the central words of the vision, 'I am Jesus whom you are persecuting'. Jesus is now present in his Church, and identified with its suffering. Thus Stephen died, in imitation of Christ, and thus Paul too will make his journey to Jerusalem. Paul never quotes those words, but he draws from his conversion experience the discovery that Christ is 'in him' and he 'in Christ' (Gal. 2.20; Phil. 3.9–11), and his theology of the Church as 'the body of Christ' (Rom. 12.4–5; 1 Cor. 12.12–13) might also be seen to be a working-out of that first revelation.

Luke records that the disciples of Jesus were first called 'Christians' in Antioch (Acts 11.26). Here they are those who belong to 'the Way'. This term, which recurs in Acts but not clearly elsewhere in the New Testament, might represent a very early understanding of the community as following the way of life and light, in contrast to that of death and darkness, drawn from the Jewish 'Two Ways' theme found in the Qumran *Manual of Discipline* and inherited in the early Christian writings, the *Didache* and *Epistle of Barnabas*. It might otherwise denote the followers of Jesus as the eschatological community: those who 'prepare the Way of the Lord' in answer to the call of John the Baptist. Alternatively, it might represent Luke's own understanding of the Church. A characteristic theme of his Gospel is the journey of Jesus, with his face set to go to Jerusalem (9.51); now it is for his disciples, in the power of his risen presence, to go on their journey from Jerusalem to the ends of the earth. SL

Revelation 5.11–14

This reading forms the culmination of the scene that begins in Rev. 4.1 with John's vision of the court of heaven, and the lection itself will scarcely make sense without attention to the preceding context. John witnesses the splendour of the divine throne itself, the glorious court that surrounds the throne, and the multitude that offers ceaseless praise to God (4.2–11; note the many references in Revelation to this heavenly throne; e.g. 1.4; 3.21; 6.16; 7.9–11; 20.4). He then sees the scroll held by 'the one seated on the throne' (5.1), a scroll that not only explains the final events of human history but whose opening will actually set those events in motion (see 6.1 and the following depiction of the opening of the seals).

Only one thing is lacking, and that is the agent who is worthy to open the scroll. One of the elders announces that there is one who can open the scroll: 'the Lion of the tribe of Judah, the Root of David' (5.5). When John looks, however, he sees not a lion at all but a 'Lamb standing as if it had been slaughtered' (v. 6). The Lamb receives the scroll from the hand of God, and then the heavenly court breaks forth in song, praising the Lamb and acknowledging its worthiness to open the scroll (vv. 7–10).

At this climactic point in the vision, the lection proper opens. Verses 11–14 can best be characterized as a great crescendo, for the crowd of singers swells throughout and the praise escalates in scope. In the first song to the Lamb, those who sing are the 'four living creatures and the twenty-four elders' (v. 8). In v. 11, this throng has grown to include 'many angels' and 'the living creatures and the elders', so that the numbers are now 'myriads of myriads and thousands of thousands'. By the conclusion of the singing, however, 'every creature in heaven and on earth and under the earth and in the sea' has joined in this majestic praise (v. 13).

This crescendo is no mere literary flourish, however. The vast numbers of singers in this passage recall the vast numbers of the heavenly court also imagined in Dan. 7.10; 1 Enoch 14.22; 40.1; and in Heb. 12.22. Moreover, the apocalyptist is surely aware that the court of the Roman emperor likewise comprised large numbers of people from an array of social classes, and that the emperors were often acknowledged with songs and chants. By ascribing those same features here to the God Christians worship rather than to the Roman emperor, the apocalyptist challenges the fundamental power assumptions of the state.

The intense crescendo of vv. 11–14 relies both on the singers and on the content of their hymns. The hymns of vv. 9–10 and 12 address the Lamb alone, as the hymns of 4.8 and 11 address God alone. With v. 13, however, the singers address their praise 'to the one seated on the throne and to the Lamb'. What belongs to God also belongs to the Lamb. It is anachronistic to read trinitarian thought into this passage, as some interpreters have done, but the elevation of the Lamb is striking.

Here also the hymn concludes with the words 'for ever and ever' and is followed by the amen of the four living creatures (v. 14). The heavenly court, unlike those known on earth, will have no end.

Central to the passage is its praise of the 'Lamb that was slaughtered' (v. 12). Here we encounter both a central figure in Revelation (see e.g. 6.1, 16; 7.9, 10, 14, 17; 12.11; 13.8; 14.1, 4, 10; 15.3; 21.9, 14, 22, 23, 27) and a much-disputed historical problem. Does the presentation of Jesus as a lamb stem from the paschal imagery of Exod. 12 (see 1 Cor. 5.7; 1 Pet. 1.19) or perhaps from the 'lamb . . . led to the slaughter' of Isa. 53.7, or even the apocalyptic image of the sheep or ram in 1 Enoch 89.42; 90.9 (cf. Dan. 8.20–21)?

Whatever the origin of the imagery, its ironic thrust in this passage is clear. The messianic figure (the 'Lion of the tribe of Judah', the 'Root of David') is none other than a lamb, and a lamb who has been slaughtered. It is that Lamb who is worthy, not only to open the seals of the scroll (v. 9), but to receive 'power and wealth and wisdom and might and honour and glory and blessing' (v. 12). The sheer diversity of the gifts ascribed to the Lamb is astonishing. They include the political and economic realms and form a profound challenge to the authorities that suppose themselves to be rulers of the world.

Elisabeth Schüssler Fiorenza has rightly observed that a question fundamental to the book of Revelation is, 'Who is the true Lord of this world?' (*Revelation: Vision of a Just World*; Minneapolis: Fortress, 1991, p. 58). That question is not only important for understanding the seemingly bizarre visions of Revelation, but for understanding their appropriateness for the Easter season. Employing a variety of forms and drawing on a large array of sources, early Christians consistently asserted that the resurrection confirmed irrefutably the power of God over all creation and in every time and place. The implication of that power for the supposed power of Rome emerges more clearly in Revelation than elsewhere in the New Testament, as the apocalyptist unabashedly declares that God's sovereignty means the end of human power. BG

John 21.1–19

This final chapter of the Gospel of John is commonly seen as an appendix (though no manuscript suggests the book ever circulated without it), because the last verses of ch. 20 obviously make an ending. But there is nothing to convince us that it comes from a different hand, and it is best seen as rounding off the Gospel by dealing with a few outstanding questions that seemed important to the author; and some of them affected other evangelists too.

So, there is the question whether there was any appearance of Jesus in Galilee (cf. the promise evidenced in Mark 14.28; 16.7 and fulfilled only at Matt. 28.16–20), which would (we may suppose) sanctify Galilean Christianity when Jerusalem was (or, by the end of the century, had been) plainly the Church's physical centre. Luke was grudging on this matter, mentioning the church in Galilee only at Acts 9.31.

It is often suggested that, by knowledge of the written source or of such a tradition, John drew for the opening story, vv. 1–14, on the episode in Luke 5.1–11;

there are indeed striking similarities. In any case, the story resembles in various ways others among the resurrection stories themselves: failure initially to recognize Jesus afflicted also the walkers to Emmaus (Luke 24.31) – Jesus was the same yet strangely different; eating together also reminds us of Luke 24.36–43, with fish again on the menu (as indeed in the earlier feeding stories). Here, however, the fish are in profusion, and commentaries will suggest possible explanations of the 153 in v. 11; perhaps they presage, somehow, the Church's universal harvest of souls.

The final section (vv. 15–19), which is distinct, stands with other, rather different passages as a way of authorizing Peter's restoration (and then undoubted leading position in the Church) after the earlier denial: cf. Matt. 16.17–19; Luke 22.61; and of course implicitly his prominence in Acts 1—15. Yet he does not oust the Johannine preference for 'the disciple whom Jesus loved', who first recognized Jesus and whose role is recognized in the chapter's final verses (John 21.20–25) – and who is possibly identified, enigmatically, in the figure of Nathanael, that unusual Johannine disciple (v. 2; cf. 1.45–48). In this chapter alone, the beloved disciple does seem to become more of an individual, less a symbol of the true and full following of Jesus, closest to him. Yet love for Jesus is not his monopoly and is firmly confirmed as found in Peter too.

This is a chapter which is then of initial interest much more to its original audience than to later readers, who may focus only on intriguing titbits of possible church history. There is, however, a message in the mysterious reality yet ungraspability of the risen Jesus, who alone knows where rescue is to be found and then himself provides it (vv. 12–13). LH

The Fourth Sunday of Easter

Genesis 7.1–5, 11–18; 8.6–18; 9.8–13 or Acts 9.36–43; Revelation 7.9–17; John 10.22–30

Genesis 7.1–5, 11–18; 8.6–18; 9.8–13

Within the narrative structure of Gen. 1—11 the story of the flood is important because it is the dividing line between the original creation of Gen. 1 and the creation of our experience, in Gen. 9. The former creation is a vegetarian creation, as indicated by Gen. 1.30, that is to say, it is a world without 'nature red in tooth and claw', apart from one destructive element: the human race.

The flood as described in Gen. 7 is an undoing of creation. Creation in the Old Testament is a matter of order, of the restraining and ordering of forces which, when unleashed, can overwhelm and destroy the world. Thus the references to the fountains of the deep bursting forth and the windows of heaven being opened (v. 11) indicate that God has relaxed the forces that restrain the destructive power of nature (cf. Job 38.8, 10–11 'who shut in the sea with doors . . . and prescribed bounds for it . . . and said "Thus far shall you come" ').

Part of the order of creation is also the moral order, and the Old Testament is clear that the disruption of the moral order can affect the natural order; which is why God brings the flood upon the earth; to destroy the destructive creature, humanity, whose evil undermines the created order.

Noah and his family and the animals that enter the ark are the nucleus of a new world in the post-flood era. We are not told in what respect Noah is righteous; but the fact that he is, and that God can use this righteousness to preserve the human race that otherwise deserves extinction, is an important theme in the passage.

The story of the flood is one that provokes many reactions, from those who contend that Leonard Woolley found evidence of a flood at Ur (he did not; what he found had been caused by wind!) to those who are ever looking for, and claiming to have found, the ark.

Since 1872 it has been known that the biblical story of the flood is only one of numerous such stories from the ancient Near East, whose heroes are known variously as Ziasudra, Atra-hasis and Ut-napishtim. Flooding in the Tigris–Euphrates region of ancient Mesopotamia could have devastating results; whether there was a universal flood is less likely. Who would survive to tell us about it? Comparison with the other ancient flood stories shows how much more profound the one contained in the Old Testament is, as part of the larger narrative of Gen. 1—11, which boldly asserts both that God is the creator of the world, and that the world he originally made, the vegetarian world, is not the world of our experience. JR

Acts 9.36–43

The apostles' witness to the risen Jesus is a matter of deed as well as word, and in this follows the pattern of his own ministry. The story of Peter's raising of Tabitha clearly recalls in main theme and in detail Jesus' raising of Jairus' daughter (Luke 8.49–56). Both stories, in turn, echo Jewish tradition in the stories of Elijah's raising of the son of the widow of Zarephath (1 Kings 17.17–24) and Elisha's of the son of the Shunammite woman (2 Kings 4.32–37). The continuity of the Church with both Jesus and Israel is important for Luke.

In the context of his narrative, other themes are also present. Peter is called to Joppa, a port city with a very mixed population, to a woman who, though presumably Jewish, has an Aramaic name with a Greek equivalent (both mean 'gazelle'); and he then goes to lodge with Simon the tanner, a man whose occupation, dealing as it does with the carcasses of dead animals, rendered him unclean in the eyes of strict Jews. These are hints of what is to follow. Peter will be going on to Caesarea to answer the call of the Gentile Cornelius and to learn that 'What God has made clean, you must not call profane' (Acts 10.15). Earlier in ch. 9, Paul entered Luke's narrative, and for a while stories of Peter and Paul will alternate. Both will preach to Gentiles, and in similar terms; both heal; both raise the dead (Paul in 20.9–12). The parallels between the two are an important demonstration of Luke's theme of the unity and unanimity of the Church (as in 4.32), whether he is accurately describing the earliest community, portraying a golden age that never was, or papering over cracks painfully exposed in Paul's letters.

The raising of Tabitha immediately follows the healing of Aeneas in 9.32–35. Both in the Gospel and in Acts Luke often provides male/female sequences (e.g. the parables of Luke 13.18–21 and 15.4–10, and the pairings of Dionysius and Damaris at Athens in Acts 17.34 and, less happily, Ananias and Sapphira in 5.1–10). Women play a prominent part generally in his narrative both in the Gospel and Acts and this probably reflects their presence in the churches of the Hellenistic cities that he knew. Widows, as a vulnerable group in society, are the objects of charity in Acts 6.1, and the seven male 'deacons' are selected to meet their needs. Here it is the woman Tabitha who is 'devoted to good works and acts of charity', providing clothing for the widows who mourn her loss. She is not called 'deacon' like Paul's friend and benefactress Phoebe in Rom. 16.1, but 'disciple', in the correct feminine form of the noun, found only here in the New Testament. SL

Revelation 7.9–17

Who are the great multitude seen in heaven? One answer is to contrast them with the 144,000 sealed from the tribes of Israel in the preceding verses: those were drawn from the Jews and these are from the Gentiles. Another way is to note the alternation of 'hearing' and 'seeing' in vv. 4 and 9, as in Rev. 5.5–6, where the seer 'hears' about a lion and 'sees' a lamb: they are not two but one. So the 144,000 and the great multitude may be one group: God's true chosen people, drawn alike from all the nations of the world. Perhaps more importantly, however, they are martyrs. In the seer's vision the martys have a special place: they have been seen already under the altar of heaven in ch. 6; and for them alone is the first resurrection of ch. 20. In a situation where Christians experience active persecution, or have cause to anticipate that it will come (which seems to be the case with the book of Revelation), it is natural that those who share with Christ in suffering and death, who have 'washed their robes . . . in the blood of the Lamb', are seen to have a special status as his closest followers or witnesses – and it seems to have been the author of Revelation who extended the meaning of the Greek word *martus*, 'witness', to mean specifically witness in death, as in 2.13. In the modern West it is more common for Christians to experience indifference than active hostility, and the role of the martyr may seem a matter of past history, but modern martyrs are rightly commemorated in the new statues at the west end of Westminster Abbey, and Christians continue to suffer for their faith, not least in the Asia Minor of the book of Revelation and in the Holy Land itself.

The vision of the great multitude is punctuated with song. Here the martyrs proclaim the salvation of God and the Lamb, and their acclamation is confirmed by the *Amen* of all the inhabitants of heaven: the songs of humanity and of heaven are joined. Outbursts of song are characteristic of the Apocalypse: sometimes they seem to echo the psalms, but more often to be new compositions. It is possible that they represent hymns used in the early Christian communities (e.g. Col. 3.16), but perhaps more probable that they are the free composition of the poet-seer himself. Certainly they express his high Christology: salvation belongs both to God and to the Lamb; God is seated on the throne, but the Lamb is at the centre of the throne. SL

John 10.22–30

Questions and requests are always important. Who makes them, how and when they are made, and what response is sought often tell us a great deal about the seeker. Certainly in the narratives of the Gospels the nature of both the questions and requests put to Jesus and the character of the ones making them determine the responses given. Some are sincerely posed, some seek to entrap Jesus, whereas others, whether honest or devious, expose mistaken assumptions that make a straightforward response impossible.

The request of the Jews, 'How long will you keep us in suspense? If you are the Messiah, tell us plainly' (John 10.24), is hard to categorize. A literal translation of the initial question ('How long are you taking away our life?') could suggest a threatened, defensive posture of the Jews. Is it sincere or hostile? While readers of John's narrative have come to recognize 'the Jews' not as a designation for the Jewish people as a whole but only for religious leaders who oppose Jesus and regularly provoke antagonistic debate, the previous passage relates a division among this group in which some predictably react negatively to Jesus and others at least are curious (10.19–21). From which group do the question and request come?

Whether the questioners are genuine or adversarial, in either case the request demands an unambiguous answer to a straightforward question ('If you are the Messiah, tell us plainly'). Jesus is asked to declare himself in categories that are firmly in place in the ideology of those making the request. 'Do you or do you not fit our criteria for Messiahship? Tell us without equivocation.'

Jesus' reply reminds us that an understanding of who he is cannot be simply a matter of deciding whether Jesus measures up to some preconceived notion of how a divine figure *ought* to act. Jesus eludes prior categories, totally redefines even those cherished titles drawn from Israel's past (for example, Messiah, Son of Man, Son of God). It is no different with our contemporary categories – superstar, healer, guarantor of happiness, peace-giver. Jesus transcends and transforms them all.

There is another problem with the Jews' request. They seem to assume that a decision about the Messiah is merely a matter of processing information. If Jesus will provide the data, they can arrive at a reasoned conclusion. Jesus' response throws that sort of logic into a cocked hat ('You do not believe, because you do not belong to my sheep', v. 26).

Knowledge of the Messiah has to do with a reorientation of the knower, a change of location from one community to another – a persistent theme of John's Gospel. Nicodemus came with his knowledge, and it was not all bad ('We know that you are a teacher who has come from God'), only to be told that he had to be born from above (3.2–3). Knowing the Messiah involves a radical conversion, a movement from one fold to another. The Jews, for whatever reason, demand a straightforward answer, but they discover the issue is far more complex and demanding than that.

Reorientation and relocation are not all. There are promises made, tender promises of protection and security (10.27–29). Referring back to the earlier section of the chapter (vv. 1–18), believers are called 'my sheep' and receive a divine commitment that they cannot be separated from the care of the Shepherd. The threat of those who might seek to 'snatch' them from Jesus'/the Father's hand apparently also follows from references earlier in the chapter to thieves, bandits and wolves (vv. 8–10, 11–12). Such preservation comes at the cost of the Shepherd's life. (Interpreters will note the very ambiguous textual problem in v. 29, which leads to differing translations and varying nuanced readings. A critical commentary can shed light on the textual problem.)

Jesus' focus on the works that he does must not be misunderstood (v. 25). The works testify to Jesus not because they are extraordinary and attention-getting – which of course they *are* (changing water to wine, healing the official's son, feeding the multitudes) – and not because they offer conclusive proof of his Messiahship, but because they are the Father's works. Jesus' hand protecting the sheep is no less than the Father's hand (vv. 28–29). As the following section explains, the works are critical 'so that you may know and understand that the Father is in me and I am in the Father' (v. 38). The works witness to the coincidence of the activity of Father and Son, taking us close to the heart of John's Christology.

The concluding verse of the lection (v. 30), which has led to much speculation through the centuries (some of it idle and highly conjectural), spells out the implication of Jesus' works. In context, it is not a statement about the metaphysical connection between two persons of the Trinity, but an affirmation about the functional unity between Jesus and the Father. Moreover, in the narrative the urgency of the confession is highlighted, since it proves highly offensive to the audience and places Jesus at great risk (vv. 31, 39). cc

The Fifth Sunday of Easter

Acts 11.1–18 or Baruch 3.9–15, 32–36; 4.1–4 or Genesis 22.1–18; Revelation 21.1–6; John 13.31–35

Acts 11.1–18

Peter's vision at Joppa and his experience at the house of the centurion Cornelius in Caesarea had convinced him that it was right to baptize Gentiles; now he has to convince Jewish Christians in Jerusalem. Their complaint is, in fact, not that he baptized Gentiles, but that he ate with them, as he must have done while he stayed on with Cornelius' household for several days. Perhaps it was thought at some stage that Jews and Gentiles could share the same Christian faith while continuing to live as separate communities. Another approach would be to argue that Gentiles, in becoming Christians, must become Jews as well, and accept circumcision: this will be the argument at the 'Council of Jerusalem' in Acts 15. Peter's answer to his critics takes the form of retelling his and Cornelius' stories, with minor differences in detail, and he will allude to this again at the council. Luke uses the technique of recapitulation to underline the importance of an event: he does the same with the story of Paul's conversion, told in ch. 9, and retold in chs. 22 and 26. In those accounts Paul is called to take the gospel to the Gentiles; here it is Peter. It is important for Luke's theme of the unity of the Church that the two leading figures in his story act in parallel and with unanimity. Paul tells a different story: he regards himself as the apostle to the Gentiles, while Peter is 'apostle to the circumcised', and tells how he criticized Peter's timorous going back on his former practice of eating with Gentiles (Gal. 2.7–14). It is uncertain if Luke knew of this dispute between the two; if so, he has 'papered over the cracks' in their relationship in the interests of his larger theme.

Peter's account here has an interesting trinitarian dimension: it is God the Creator who has made all creatures clean (and therefore by implication the Jewish food laws were always misguided); it is the risen Lord who speaks to Peter in his vision (as he spoke to Paul in Acts 9.5); and it is the Spirit who takes the initiative in empowering the Gentile household. In concluding his speech, Peter goes further than the narrative of the preceding chapter. He makes the link between what has happened to Cornelius and his household and what happened to himself and his hearers and critics at Pentecost. For both, there was the same fulfilment of the promise of Jesus, the same gift of the Spirit by God, the same belief in the Lord Jesus, and the same prospect of life. In this new dispensation the former Jew/Gentile distinctions cannot stand; the argument is unanswerable. SL

Baruch 3.9–15, 32–36; 4.1–4

Baruch is a pseudepigraphic work; that is, one ascribed fictitiously to an ancient author, in this particular case, Jeremiah's secretary Baruch (cf. Jer. 32.12). There were good reasons for the author to conceal his identity, because he probably wrote in Hebrew in the period 164–62 BC, during the struggle of the Jews with the Seleucids, the Greek rulers of Syria. The Hebrew has not survived; the translation is based on a Greek text. Adopting the identity of Baruch, he was able to use the time and conditions of the Babylonian exile to describe his own times and, here, to exhort his readers to greater obedience to God.

The opening words are reminiscent of the *Shemaʿ*, the prayer that begins 'Hear, O Israel', at Deut. 6.4, and that became a test of Jewish loyalty. The phrases 'land of your enemies' and 'foreign country' in v. 10 are a poignant description of the Jews' own land under foreign rule. Their present plight is attributed to their having forsaken God, and they are encouraged to seek wisdom. Wisdom is the subject of the pronoun 'her' in v. 15, and in the continuation of the entreaty for the search for wisdom in vv. 32–6 there are strong overtones of Job 28 and 38. The verb translated as 'found' in v. 32 has the sense of 'probe' or 'examine', and indicates divine approval following examination. The next verses describe the incomparability of God. The implication is that one (wisdom) approved by such an incomparable God must be eminently worthy of special attention, especially as access to her has been singularly granted to Israel (v. 36). The concluding verses explicitly link wisdom with the Torah; that is, the Law, commandments and promises of God (cf. Ps. 119). It is Israel's great privilege to enjoy a special relationship with the incomparable creator of the universe. This should give courage and hope under the suffering being endured at the hands of an alien people. JR

Genesis 22.1–18

This is the story of the *aqedah*, the 'binding' of Isaac, and at several levels it is one of the most powerful passages within the whole Bible. In one sense it is, or should be, a cause of profound difficulty. What would the present-day media make of a story of a father who set out to kill his son on the grounds that he had been commanded by God to do so? Religious believers in both the Jewish and the Christian tradition seem sometimes not to realize how utterly offensive this story would be in 'real-life' terms. It is a story told to illustrate a particular set of beliefs, and must be treated as such.

Let us first consider the character of the story. Perhaps the first thing to strike us is the extraordinary economy with which it is told. No mention is made of Sarah, Isaac's mother; no picture is given of any agonizing self-doubt on the part of Abraham. He hears a call which he takes to be from God, and without a word and without delay ('early in the morning') he obeys. He realizes that the 'young men' must suspect nothing of what is to take place, and so he deliberately misleads them ('we will come back to you'), as of course he also misleads his son ('God will provide the lamb'). Isaac is old enough and strong enough to carry the wood of the burnt offering to a place 'far away', yet he does nothing to resist his father's murderous intentions.

In these ways the story retains its intensely dramatic qualities. But it is clearly not handed down simply as a story; it has a message to convey, of an immensely difficult kind. It is a demand that God's perceived requirements must be given an absolute priority over and above the normal demands of other human beings, even of one's own family. There is a sense, of course, in which the Christian story of the death of Jesus as being part of God's plan offers a parallel, but the tension is there eased because there were human agents who crucified Jesus. Here the potential killer is the young man's own father, who has been told that the victim is to be the one through whom his own line is to continue. (We recall that Abraham has sent away his other son, Ishmael, in the previous chapter, and we have no suspicion yet that Abraham is to have several more children [Gen. 25.1–2].) Here is a word picture that envisages that God's demands take such precedence that it would be wrong to 'withhold your son, your only son' if that was the sacrifice demanded.

Later tradition has made much of this story. Apart from the Christian parallel already noted, the link between the otherwise unknown 'land of Moriah' and the site of the Jerusalem temple is hinted at later in the Old Testament (2 Chron. 3.1), and has played an important part in the traditions of both Judaism and Islam. The present-day visitor to Jerusalem is still likely to be assured that the 'rock' that gives its name to the Dome of the Rock is the place where Abraham all but sacrificed his son: Muslims believe that the son was probably Ishmael. RC

Revelation 21.1–6

At the end of his vision John sees the new creation and the union of heaven and earth. All that separated God and humanity in the present age, all the rebellion and conflict that called for judgement has been overcome. There is no more sea, because the sea is a powerful symbol of the forces in the old creation unsubdued by God. In the beginning, in Gen. 1.1, the Spirit of God moved over the waters of chaos, and it was from the sea that John saw the beast emerge to launch his attack upon the saints (Rev. 13.1, 7). In the Old Testament the myth of the primordial sea (which may itself be an adaptation of earlier Near Eastern creation myths of the battle between god and monster, as in Ps. 74.13–14) may be merged with the tradition of the exodus, so that the story of deliverance becomes a story of new creation (Isa. 51.9–10). The essential characteristic of this new age is the presence of God with his people, with no distance and no barriers remaining. His 'tabernacle' will be with them, as the tent of God's glorious presence travelled with Israel during their wilderness wanderings (Exod. 40.34–38); and the new covenant between God and his people is established, in the terms foretold by Jeremiah (Jer. 31.31–33).

With God's victory won, there is no room for the sorrow and pain that have haunted so much of John's vision, and in the presence of the eternal God who is Alpha and Omega there is no room for death, for he gives from the water of life.

John's vision is like that of Paul, for whom death is the 'last enemy', to be swallowed up in victory in the great transformation of the mortal into the immortal at the last trumpet (1 Cor. 15.26, 51–55). Paul's and John's visions are of the new age of the future, in which they both believed, but both passages are now used at funerals, expressing a hope for the individual believer at death. There is justification for this use, for John's hope for the new age is anticipated earlier in his vision. In Rev. 6.9–11 the martyrs have been seen already waiting under the altar in heaven; in 7.9–17 the great multitude of those who have come through the great ordeal already stand before the throne, and their tears are wiped away; in 14.1–4 the Lamb's army have already been redeemed from the earth to be with him always. This hope for life, whether on individual death or in the new age to come, is grounded in belief in the resurrection of Jesus. For Paul, the risen Christ is the 'first fruits' of the dead (1 Cor. 15.20, 23); and at the opening of his vision, John had already seen him among his churches, the living one who was dead and is alive and who now holds the keys of death (Rev. 1.17–18). SL

John 13.31–35

It may seem a bit strange to be directed during the Easter season to texts that are set in the last few moments of Jesus' life. One would think them more appropriate for Lent than for Easter. In John's Gospel, however, Jesus' farewell conversations with the disciples immediately before the crucifixion regularly speak of his 'departure', a term that includes his death, resurrection and return to the Father. The language is typical of John's Gospel, where the incarnation is depicted as a journey from the Father to the world and back to the Father (for example, 13.1). Thus today's selection is particularly apt for the season between Easter and Pentecost.

First, we must observe the context. The verses preceding the assigned lesson recount Jesus' prediction of Judas' betrayal, concluding with his departure from the group and the poignant observation, 'And it was night.' The verses following the lesson relate Jesus' prediction about Peter's denials. Between these two dark and foreboding brackets comes the declaration of Jesus' glorification (v. 31).

The irony should not be lost. At the darkest moment in the narrative, when the anticipation of human failure seems certain because colleagues are conspiring to undermine their leader, the announcement is made of Jesus' glorification. His moment of exaltation, honour and praise is set against the backdrop of betrayal and denials.

But the prominent 'now' of v. 31 has a double reference. On the one hand, Jesus' glorification comes at a time of incredible disloyalty and faithlessness. On the other hand, it is the right moment, the moment of fulfilment, the time for returning to the Father (v. 1). Nothing has been left undone or incomplete; as Jesus' last words from the cross will put it, 'It is finished' (19.30). The betrayal and denials do not deter or thwart the divine intention.

Second, we observe the mutuality between God and the Son of Man in the moment of glorification. The language of vv. 31b–32, in fact, is awkward in its effort to draw the two together in this climactic event. God's glory is made known as the Father is glorified in the Son and as the Son is glorified in the Father. John's characteristic Christology emerges here (as in the Gospel lesson for last Sunday: 'The Father and I are one', 10.30), a functional unity in which the actions of the Son are no less than the actions of God, and vice versa.

The awkwardness underscores that Jesus is the full revelation of God, particularly at this moment of death and departure. The anticipated actions of Judas, Peter, the religious authorities, Caiaphas, Pilate and the soldiers only serve as a foil for the *real* action, namely, the reciprocal disclosure of the identity of Son and Father.

Third, there is an appropriate word for the disciples who are faced with the impossibility of following Jesus at his departure: 'I give you a new commandment, that you love one another' (v. 34). The pain of separation is addressed with a reminder about their mutual relationships in the community of faith. But if the commandment is a reminder (see Lev. 19.18), then why is it called 'new'? What distinguishes it from the many other places in the Bible where people are told to love one another?

Two features of the commandment make it 'new'. First, a new and unparalleled model for love has been given the disciples. 'Just as I have loved you, you also should love one another.' Jesus, who had loved his own in the world and was returning to the Father, 'loved them to the end' (John 13.1) or, as it might be translated, 'loved them to the uttermost' (see 15.13). In Jesus the disciples have a concrete, living expression of what love is. Love can no longer be trivialized or reduced to an emotion or debated over as if it were a philosophical virtue under scrutiny. Jesus now becomes the distinctive definition of love.

Second, Jesus' love for the disciples not only provides a new paradigm; it also inaugurates a new era. The Johannine eschatology is tilted heavily in a 'realized' rather than a futuristic direction. While one can speak of continuity with the past and hope for the future, the present moment is the decisive one. Jesus' coming opens up a radically new and different situation, in which the life of the age to come ('eternal life') is no longer only to be awaited as a future possibility (e.g. 17.3). As the writer of 1 John put it, 'I am writing you a new commandment that is true in him and in you, because the darkness is passing away and the true light is already shining' (1 John 2.8).

At the centre of the new era is the community established by Jesus, the intimate (though at times unfaithful) family, whom he affectionately addresses as 'little children' (John 13.33). What holds the family together and makes it stand out above all the rest is the love members have for one another – dramatic, persistent love like the love Jesus has for them.

It troubles interpreters sometimes that the command Jesus left is not a command to love the world or to love one's enemies, but to love one another. In other places the Johannine narrative expresses the divine concern for the world (3.16) and directs the disciples to engage it (20.21), but here Jesus' concern is for the community itself. He makes love the distinguishing mark of the Church, that characteristic of its life by which even outsiders can discern its authenticity.

Needless to say, this text lays a heavy challenge before the contemporary Church to evidence in the world a unique quality of life and action. Lest that become too burdensome a challenge, the Church needs also to be reminded that it is itself the object of unconditional love ('Just as I have loved you . . .'). CC

The Sixth Sunday of Easter

Acts 16.9–15 or Ezekiel 37.1–14; Revelation 21.10, 22—22.5; John 14.23–29 or John 5.1–9

Acts 16.9–15

The move from Asia Minor to European Greece is an important geographical advance in the progress of the gospel and, as usual, this is seen to be a matter not of human decision, but of divine direction (cf. 16.6–7). The story is now told in terms of what 'we' did: Luke could be using a first-hand diary source, or be writing as an eyewitness and companion of Paul. It has even been suggested that he was himself the 'man from Macedonia' who sought Paul's help, and that his pride in his native city is shown in the exaggerated status he gives to the city of Philippi! A city that had 'colony' status was one whose citizens also enjoyed the rights of Roman citizens, and was often established by a settlement of retired soldiers from the Roman army (Roman Philippi was so settled after the defeat of Brutus and Cassius by Octavian and Mark Antony). The maltreatment of Paul the Roman citizen in Philippi is all the more inexcusable in a place where such rights were familiar (vv. 22, 37–38).

Even in this very Hellenistic world, Paul retains his Jewish instincts, seeking out a place of prayer on the sabbath. This may have been an informal, outdoor gathering rather than a synagogue building. There is no mention of the presence of men, ten of whom were needed formally to hold a synagogue service, but it is anyway typical of Luke that women should be given prominence. Although it was a man from Macedonia who brought Paul to the region, it is a woman who is his first convert there. As often, a prior attraction to the synagogue provides a bridge for Gentile conversion to Christianity: Lydia (or 'the Lydian woman', for her home city of Thyatira is in the region of Lydia in the province of Asia), like Cornelius in ch. 10, is a 'God-fearer'. Far from conforming to the stereotype of a Greek woman as enclosed and male-dominated, she is independent, head of her own household; mobile, travelling between Asia and Greece; and involved in a lucrative trade in luxury goods (purple fabric dye, obtained from shellfish along the Asia Minor and Levantine coasts, was highly prized in antiquity). Lydia belongs to the same economic and social class as Paul's friend Priscilla (18.2–3), and in giving him hospitality provides a precedent for similarly independent benefactresses like Phoebe (Rom. 16.1) and Nympha (Col. 4.15). The prominence of women in earliest Christianity is often noted, and it is sometimes suggested that they responded to a new social status offered them in Paul's statement of equality: 'there is no longer male and female; for all of you are one in Christ Jesus' (Gal. 3.28). This is too simplistic. There were already women in the Hellenistic world who enjoyed social freedom: women like Lydia responded to something deeper in the gospel message. SL

Ezekiel 37.1–14

Although notions of life after death were rudimentary in sixth-century Israel, for a person not to be properly buried at death was considered to be a calamity. An individual's shallow grave was thought to be connected with Sheol, or the grave to which all the dead went, where they then existed in a shadowy, even lifeless way. People denied even this decency were more unfortunate; in a sense their lives had not been allowed to be completed.

These shared notions are the necessary background to Ezekiel's vision of the valley of dry bones. What he sees is evidently the aftermath of the battle, whose slain have been left unburied. Their flesh has been picked off by animals or carrion birds, leaving only the bones, which have become quite dry in the heat of the sun. A more hopeless scene could not be depicted, which is why the prophet gives the only possible human answer to the question 'Can these bones live?' which is, in effect, only you, God, know the answer to this question. The rest of the vision needs little elucidation, as the bones are reconnected, covered with skin and finally reanimated. The scattered, dried-up bones become a company of living individuals.

The passage is an excellent illustration of the different senses of the Hebrew word *ruach*, which is translated here as breath (v. 6), wind(s) (v. 9) and spirit (v. 14). Although in Gen. 2.7 a different Hebrew word (*neshamah*) is used for the breath that God breathes into Adam, Ezek. 37 well illustrates the Old Testament view that the difference between a living person and a dead one is that the former breathes (i.e. has *ruach*, breath) and that this phenomenon is to be related to the power of the wind, which humans cannot control, but which can have such obvious effects in the physical world. From this it is a short step to the idea of the Spirit of God as empowering individuals to do brave or noble deeds, or activities such as justice, music or artistic creation.

It has been plausibly questioned whether the application of the vision to exiled Israel (vv. 11–14) is a later expansion of the vision. The idea of bringing people from their graves does not exactly correspond with bringing to life unburied and scattered bones; and bringing people back to their land (v. 12) is no part of the vision. Whatever the original meaning of the vision, it was certainly appropriate for the restoration of Israel from exile; but that was within the world of human history. The original vision may have an eschatological dimension, that is, it may look forward to a new creation of humanity, one wrought by God after human action has produced the misery and hopelessness of a valley of dry bones. JR

Revelation 21.10, 22—22.5

John now describes in more detail the new Jerusalem, which he sees in his vision of the future, the new heaven and earth. The imagery clearly derives from the vision of the new city that is the subject of the last chapters of Ezekiel (40—48) and expresses that prophet's hope for the future restoration of his exiled people; but it is significantly adapted. Ezekiel's city is a real, if idealized, city: he looks for the restoration of a real Jerusalem in the land of Israel. John's city is the bride, the wife of the Lamb: the city is not a place but a community, the people of God who are also the people of Christ, united to 'him who loves us' (Rev. 1.5). John blends the image of Ezekiel's city with other prophets' image of Israel as the unfaithful bride of Yahweh (Hos. 2; Isa. 1.21; Jer. 2.20; the image drawn on also in Eph. 5.25–32). This is the Church as it will be: not the suffering and imperfect seven churches addressed in the opening letters of Revelation, but redeemed, purified and transfigured.

Ezekiel's city is dominated by its new temple, whose layout and rituals are described in great detail. John's city simply has no temple. There is no special place of meeting with God, for God and the Lamb are everywhere present: they *are* the temple. There is no need for a place for sacrifices, for there are no sacrifices in the presence of the Lamb who has been slain (Rev. 5.6). The gate to Ezekiel's city was shut, except for limited periods (Ezek. 44.1–2; 46.1); the gates of John's city are never shut: it is quite literally an 'open city' with access always available. Finally, Ezekiel's vision was essentially and exclusively a vision for Israel. No foreigners are admitted, save those who are resident aliens in Israel (44.9; 47.21). John's vision is universal: the nations will walk in the city's perpetual light, and with the leaves of the trees by its river they will be healed. Revelation often seems full of hatred, as the beleaguered minority anticipates the fall of the oppressive 'great city' (e.g. Rev. 18), but at the end there is a wide and generous hope.

It is interesting that John can deal so freely with Ezekiel's vision, using the image but radically changing some of its key elements: perhaps his sense of his own vision as new prophecy (so 1.3; 22.7, 18–19) gives him the authority to interpret and where necessary to overturn the old. There are also striking parallels with other Johannine writings: in the Gospel Jesus foresees replacing the temple of Jerusalem with 'the temple of his body' (John 2.19–21); and as here God and the Lamb give the city its light, so Jesus proclaims 'I am the light of the world' (John 8.12; 9.5; cf. 1 John 1.5–7). SL

John 14.23–29

In the Supper Discourses (John 13—17), the evangelist brings Jesus in from the world-scene, on which he has been so amazingly at work, to the enclosed community of 'his own'. Meticulously, and under many kinds of terminology and imagery, Jesus here lays out the conditions of life in the Church that is to be – indeed, already is, as the evangelist writes.

It is, most notably, a community in which Jesus, though 'absent', is also still 'present'. He goes to the Father (v. 28) but also is 'coming to you'. His continuing presence can be spoken of in terms of the Spirit (v. 26), which is less a substitute for Jesus than Jesus in a new but wholly recognizable form. So, of course, the community possesses Jesus' 'peace', his full and saving presence.

What is more, Jesus is so much one with the Father that this presence of Jesus is equally the presence of God. And presence is a strong idea: 'home' says NRSV

(v. 23). We may say 'permanent location', and 'abiding place' is the Johannine idiom.

It is worth noting that, in an important sense, the community is therefore a place of conservation and not innovation: it preserves what Jesus gave. It is not its business to have bright new thoughts and the Spirit is not to be seen as their agent (v. 26). Rather, they will maintain, by the Spirit's agency, what Jesus taught; and to keep that teaching is to keep God's 'word' (v. 24). We may discern here perhaps deliberate resistance in our writer to what were felt to be regrettable tendencies to novelty. The paradox is, of course, that to make his point, the evangelist uses a form of Christian discourse hitherto unknown, with its own character and vocabulary. Room for reflection here!

In these chapters then, we have 'realized eschatology' at its most powerful and uncompromising; and no space is left for anxious speculation about a 'second coming' of Jesus (though it made a brief appearance in chs. 5 and 6). What serious need could there be for that? What do these Christians lack in the present that has been given to them?

'The Father is greater than I' (v. 28) had a big future ahead of it, becoming the leading Arian proof-text in the fourth century. But that was not in the evangelist's mind. He was simply concerned to say that in Jesus and his people what was involved was nothing less than the totality of deity. LH

John 5.1–9

In one way, in the context of the Gospels as a whole, this story is not remarkable. It is in fact one of the points where the contents of the Gospel of John join hands most obviously with the Synoptics: there are many such objection-causing healings by Jesus on the sabbath (e.g. Mark 3.1–6; Luke 13.10–17; and cf. in content Mark 2.1–12). In general shape, as a healing story, told neat, without discussion included within it, it is paralleled in this Gospel only by that about the nobleman's son (4.46–54). And the suggestion is that John started with a stock of such stories (just like those in the other Gospels), then developed many of them (see John 9; 11) by making complex conversations out of them and the themes they suggested. Unlike that preceding story, however, this one is followed by an extensive discourse by Jesus (with interruptions) on the theme of his carrying out his Father's 'works', and indeed extending them. In doing such a 'work' as this, Jesus continues God's own creative activity, which, implicitly, overrules or transcends the sabbath, the divinely enjoined pause in work. Creation has the priority when threatened or impeded by need – such as that of the man who has lain impotently by the pool for virtually a lifetime. Like the similar Synoptic stories, there is a brazen defiance about Jesus' act, and it shows up the small-minded punctiliousness of those who would say, Could he not wait another few hours? God's creative and saving work will not wait; life will be remade. In Christ, a new world-order has come to birth.

Jeremias taught us that archaeology supported the architectural detail of this story (the pool and the five porticoes, v. 1), and so we were to pay greater respect than perhaps we thought right to the historicity of John's narrative. That is interesting, but should not distract from the message which, uniquely among sabbath stories in the Gospels, is brought out in the teaching by Jesus in the rest of the chapter. He does the 'works' of the Father and acts solely as his agent, as the giver of life. LH

Ascension Day

Daniel 7.9–14 or Acts 1.1–11; Ephesians 1.15–23; Luke 24.44–53

Daniel 7.9–14

The prescribed passage is the climax of the vision, written in Aramaic, in which the seer sees four beasts emerging from the sea (a symbol of chaos). Each beast, representing an empire, is more terrible than the one that precedes it, and on the head of the fourth beast there appears a little horn that displaces three horns, and which has eyes and a mouth.

With the beginning of the set passage, the scene switches from the source of the chaos and the destruction wrought by the beasts that emerge from it to a judgement scene on earth. The plural 'thrones' implies that there will be a panel of judges; but the dominating feature is the Ancient One (Aramaic, 'One ancient of days' i.e. years). The figure of white clothing and pure wool hair is meant to denote eternity and wisdom, and certainly not senility. The wheels of the throne are reminiscent of those of Ezek. 1, and the fire symbolizes purity and holiness. The fact that the beasts are only partially destroyed, even if their dominion is taken away, is an attempt to account for the persistence of evil in the world even after the judgement.

The climax is reached in v. 13 with the coming on the clouds of heaven of the 'one like a human being' (Aramaic, 'like a son of a human'). That this figure is in some sense 'heavenly' is indicated by his coming on the clouds of heaven, and by the qualifier 'like'. He is thus best thought of as an angelic figure. However, in the explanation of the vision in vv. 19–27, the dominion is given to 'the people of the holy ones of the Most High' (v. 27) in language almost identical with that of v. 14. These 'holy ones' are evidently those Israelites who have been persecuted and martyred by the little horn, usually taken to be Antiochus IV (175–164 BC) who banned Judaism from 168/7 to 164.

How can the persecuted ones be the same as the 'one like a human being'? This is the language of vision and symbols in which precision may not always be possible. The angelic figure may be a personification or may be a kind of heavenly guardian of the persecuted ones.

The fundamental message of the vision, however, is that the evil personified by the beasts, and embodied partly in the actions of desperate rulers, is ultimately subject to divine judgement. It is overcome not by greater, similar force, but by faithfulness to goodness and truth, which may lead to persecution and death. The dominion that is therefore given to the 'one like a human being' or the holy ones, is not based upon human ideas of power, but the experience of those who have drunk deeply from the well of suffering. JR

Acts 1.1–11

In the Lucan narrative of God's saving activity in Jesus Christ (the Gospel) and in the Holy Spirit (Acts), the story of Jesus' ascension marks the end of Jesus' post-resurrection appearances to his disciples and the prelude to the sending of the Spirit, thereby marking a transition point from Easter to Pentecost. In the liturgical tradition of the Church, Ascension is all of that and more, for it also has become a festival of the exaltation of the risen Christ.

The Acts lection for this day consists of two main components. The first (Acts 1.1–5) serves not only as an introduction to the entire book of Acts and thus to the work of the Holy Spirit in the life of the young Church, but also – in a more immediate sense – as an introduction to the Ascension miracle. The second part (vv. 6–11) is the account of the miracle itself. In both these sections, however, the primary emphasis is on the coming of the Holy Spirit.

Verses 1–5, after a brief statement of purpose (vv. 1–2) which parallels Luke 1.1–4, set forth a terse summary of the events of the 40 days following Easter, a time when Jesus 'presented himself alive to [the disciples] by many convincing proofs' (v. 3). It is perhaps assumed by Luke that 'Theophilus' has heard of these appearances of the risen Christ, since no effort is expended to provide the details of these encounters, other than what is offered in Luke 24. Following Jesus' order to the band of his faithful followers to remain in Jerusalem (Acts 1.4), he delivers the promise of God, namely, that God's Spirit is soon to be made evident in fresh ways. This coming of the Spirit is explained in baptismal terms: whereas water was the baptismal medium of old, 'you will be baptized with the Holy Spirit not many days from now' (v. 5).

The second part of our text (vv. 6–11) repeats this emphasis on the coming of the Spirit, but in a different context. Here this gracious and decisive gift of God's Spirit is compared to the political hopes the disciples had vested in the Messiah. Their question about the restoration of the kingdom to Israel (v. 6) betrays that not even the events of Easter and the succeeding 40 days had disabused them of a comfortable stereotype, that is, that God's Messiah would reinstitute the political fortunes of the old Davidic monarchy. Jesus deflects their question (v. 7) and refocuses their attention on the marvellous display of God's power and love that they are soon to see. It is not the restoration of the kingdom of Israel that will energize you, Jesus says in effect. Rather, 'You will receive power when the Holy Spirit has come upon you' (v. 8a). Thus vv. 5 and 8 lift before the reader an announcement from God that is not to be overlooked: the age of the Spirit is about to dawn.

Then Jesus is elevated beyond the limits of their physical senses, and 'two men in white robes' (compare Luke 24.4) gently chide the disciples for vacant gazing, even as they promise Jesus' second coming (Acts 1.9–11).

While the liturgical tradition of the Church has tended to make the ascension of Jesus into a festival to his glory and power, the emphasis in the biblical tradition is elsewhere. Not only is the ascension rarely mentioned in the New Testament (compare Luke 24.51 and Mark 16.19), but the interest in Acts 1 appears to be less in what is happening to Jesus than in what is about to happen in the lives of the earliest Christians. Twice in this brief passage the declaration is made that the Holy Spirit is about to infuse the life of the Church in new ways. Not that the Spirit was unknown before this. The 'Spirit of God' was the phrase that from very early times had been applied to special expressions of God's guiding and redemptive presence in human life (note, for example, 1 Sam. 11.6, and compare it to 1 Sam. 16.14). But the import of Acts 1.5 and 8 is that a new dimension to the Spirit's work is about to become evident. It is as different from what has gone before as the Spirit is different from the ordinary water of baptism. It is as different from what has gone before as the transcendent kingdom of God (v. 3) is different from the political kingdom of David and his descendants.

Just how the Spirit finds expression the disciples are not told. That is a matter of suspense, which will not be resolved until Pentecost (Acts 2). In the interim, they (and the disciples in every age) are to 'be my witnesses in Jerusalem, in all Judea and Samaria, and to the ends of the earth' (1.8). It will become clear only later that in this very activity of witnessing they will provide the channels for the Spirit's power and grace.

So in the New Testament perspective, Ascension is an interim time, a period – not unlike Advent – between promise and fulfilment. The disciples of Christ are called to live faithful and obedient lives and to remember that the wonder of God's love and presence revealed so radically in the cross and the open tomb still has in store fresh surprises of joy. The disciples of Christ are called to witness, little realizing how the Spirit lurks to transform all that they do into magnificent occasions for the outpouring of God's love. In this manner Ascension points to Pentecost and to all the marvellous ways of the Holy Spirit of God. BG

Ephesians 1.15–23

Like the earlier part of this opening chapter of Ephesians (1.3–14), in the original these verses are, grammatically, a single sentence. Both are statements of high rhetorical complexity and, to the modern ear, liable to be moving or even mesmerizing (rather than soberly illuminating) in their effect. The passage is such a baffling combination of Pauline phraseology and loftier-than-Pauline style that the suggestion is made that, in whole or at least in part, Ephesians is made up of liturgical forms – the prayers or hymns of Pauline Christians. The Jewish 'blessing' form of vv. 3–14 fits such a theory particularly well (though it is also found at the start of letters, even semi-artificial, literary ones).

Related to this is the still unsettled question of authorship. It can be maintained that the differences from Paul's genuine letters (long sentences, same words in different senses) are explicable on grounds of difference of purpose: this is less Paul the ethical pastor and teacher than Paul the preacher and worshipper; but the fact that Ephesians is little short of a catena of phrases from the genuine letters makes many see it as the work of a Pauline inheritor (like the Pastoral Epistles).

For our purposes the question is important chiefly as the ideas come up for consideration. Perhaps most interesting is the teaching in vv. 22–23, where Christ, very plainly in heaven (v. 20), is head of the Church, seen as his body, and now no longer in its various local manifestations but as universal in the fullest and most lofty sense. That is, there is both linkage and differentiation between Ephesians and undoubted Paul. In the more intense 'body of Christ' teaching of 1 Cor. 12, the Church and Christ are more thoroughly identified and fused: he and his people are a single entity, they in him. For all the high-flown language, the distinction here drawn makes the language of Ephesians look like a second-generation development, whereby the Church, of course dependent on Christ, nevertheless can be distinguished in its own right as a phenomenon in this world, while Christ reigns from above. It is close to the doctrine of Luke in Acts (for all its extravagance of expression), where the Church proceeds under the awesomely heavenly (and so now in effect distant?) Jesus.

Again like Luke, the writer distinguishes between the resurrection and ascension of Christ – helping, unwittingly, to warrant the Christian calendar of later years. Earlier, you could not sensibly make a distinction.

Nevertheless, Christians must themselves pray for heavenly insight: 'wisdom' and 'revelation' and 'enlightened' (vv. 17f.) are vibrant words in the piety of the time. And the cosmic perspective, as elsewhere, leans heavily on common early Christian proof-texts, Pss. 110.1 and 8.4, already part of Paul's stock-in-trade. Finally, 'fullness', part of an obscure final phrase, is again less innocent than it may seem: it was the sort of word probably to make the susceptible spine tingle, pointing the hearer to what we would see as proto-Gnostic connections, and lifting hearts to heaven. LH

Luke 24.44–53

The final verses of the Gospel of Luke are characteristic of the evangelist's picture of things and especially of his beliefs about the person and role of Jesus. On the one hand, he works with a division of history into the time of Israel, known in the Scriptures, the time of Jesus, and then the time of the Spirit-powered mission of the Church; but on the other hand, he is careful to show how the three phases interact, with the second and third 'emerging' from what preceded. So, though the Jerusalem temple had gone by the time of writing and though Jesus had foreseen its end, there is no gloating over this in Luke. Rather, he looks back to it almost fondly as the focal point of events surrounding Jesus' birth and upbringing and has shown Jesus grieving at the prospect of its fall; and here, at the end, it remains the holy place to which the disciples return to praise God at the close of resurrection day (and the motif will continue in Acts). Thus Jesus is in continuity with God's whole providential work and is, of course, its fore-ordained climax. Notice that to the formal 'law and prophets', Luke adds 'and the psalms' as giving the divine testimony to Jesus: it is a good addition for, in Luke as elsewhere, very many of the scriptural allusions and quotations come from the Psalter: it was a prime source of christological reflection and vehicle of communal self-understanding. This may be, in part at least, because scrolls of the psalms were more readily available than copies of some other parts of the old Scriptures; but many passages offered themselves, as it were on a plate, for Christian interpretation. The reference here to fulfilment is the second in the chapter: see also v. 27, in the Emmaus story. For Luke, the risen Jesus is at pains to root his work in sacred prophecy.

The passage also looks forward to the Church's mission, in effect to Luke's second volume, the book of Acts, where the horizon is no less than 'all nations', as indeed it has been since the beginning of the Gospel: see, for example, Simeon's words in 2.32 and the extension (by comparison with Mark) of the quotation from Isa. 40 in 3.4–6 to include the words, 'and all flesh shall see the salvation of God'.

Is Jesus' withdrawal in v. 51 a first shot at an account of the ascension, later rewritten and reframed, when Luke turned to write Acts? Or had he already planned his second volume, and is the idea here that Jesus withdrew at the end of this day, then manifested himself for the sacred period of 40 days (compare the temptation in ch. 4 and Israel's wilderness period) before his final bodily depart- ure? It depends whether you think Luke had his whole narrative in view from the start – and there are many indications that he had. As generally in Luke, the ending is thoroughly up-beat and full of confidence in the Jesus-given future. LH

The Seventh Sunday of Easter

(Sunday after Ascension Day)

Acts 16.16–34 or Ezekiel 36.24–28; Revelation 22.12–14, 16–17, 20–21;
John 17.20–26

Acts 16.16–34

This passage tells two stories of deliverance, from demonic and from human power. After Lydia, the independent woman, Paul's next encounter in Philippi is with a slave-girl controlled both by her masters, who exploit her talent – or her affliction – for their own gain, and also by an evil spirit. Luke calls it a 'python spirit' and says that it 'prophesied', using a verb never used for Jewish or Christian prophecy. The famous classical oracle at Delphi delivered its message through a woman known as 'the Pythia', perhaps speaking in a state of trance or ecstasy, and Paul's contemporary Plutarch, a priest of Delphi, records that in his day other speakers took the name 'Python' in claiming to be the mouthpieces of Apollo. In the only exorcism story in Acts, Paul delivers the girl from the spirit's power. His own deliverance is from prison, where he has been consigned by human authority. The account follows a pattern familiar in ancient story telling from Euripides' *Bacchae* onwards, but Luke highlights dramatic detail like the darkness of the innermost cell, where sound not sight reveals the presence of those held (it is reminiscent of Shakespeare's chilling account of the prisoner Barnardine in *Measure for Measure*: 'He is coming, sir, he is coming; I hear his straw rustle').

The stories reflect the variety in the social phenomenon of slavery in the Roman world. The slave-girl is a mere possession of her masters, 'a living tool', in the words of Aristotle. They have no interest in her cure: for them she is now damaged goods. Their concern, like the silversmiths of Ephesus in 19.23–27, is with their loss of profit. Pliny, governor of Bithynia at the beginning of the second century, and faced with Christians denounced to him by their fellow-citizens, would observe that the sale of fodder for sacrificial animals had dropped off as a result of their presence. Christianity is bad for business. The girl's owners want it quashed. Appealing to the status of the city of Philippi as a colony, whose citizens were also citizens of Rome itself, they get Paul and Silas before the magistrates by accusing them of introducing un-Roman customs and, ironically, secure the subjection of Paul, himself a Roman citizen, to treatment from which citizens should be exempt (16.37; this may be one of the beatings to which Paul refers in 2 Cor. 11.25). The Philippian jailer would also have been a slave: a 'public slave', owned by the city and doing a responsible job for it. He had some privileges: he would have been paid a wage, could probably contract a legal marriage and, as here, is able to have his own house; but his instant impulse to suicide shows how fragile his life is in the event of failure.

Both episodes would have suggested important associations for Luke's readers. In the first there are clear parallels with occasions in the Gospels where spirits recognize Jesus (Luke 4.31–36; 8.27–29). Like Jesus, Paul exorcizes; but importantly he does so 'in the name of Jesus'. The apostles do not just continue the mission of Jesus by doing as he did, but act in the power of his living presence. In the second, there is another parallel between Peter and Paul: Paul is miraculously delivered from prison in Philippi as Peter was in Jerusalem. The similar experiences of the two demonstrate the unity of the Church.

The jailer's household is baptized by Paul as was Lydia's, and that of Cornelius by Peter (Acts 10.48; cf. Paul's reference to household baptism in 1 Cor. 1.16). The household presumably included children (cf. 1 Cor. 7.14), so this has been taken as a precedent for infant baptism. Unlike Lydia, there is no suggestion that the Philippian jailer has been a God-fearer, and so crossed to Christianity by the 'bridge' of Judaism. His new faith involves a radical break from his Gentile past. When he asks, 'What must I do to be saved?' Paul's answer is as unequivocal as Peter's statement in Acts 4.12. SL

Ezekiel 36.24–28

This promise of the restoration of the people after the Babylonian exile tackles a fascinating problem in a way that raises further questions. Given that, from the moment of their deliverance from slavery in Egypt, the Israelites showed themselves to be selfish and distrustful of God's actions on their behalf, the crucial question becomes 'How can the people of God live truly according to this calling?'

God's promise is that he will cleanse his people, replace the heart of stone with one of flesh, and put a new spirit within them. Whether the translation 'make you follow my statutes' is right, is a question that must be addressed. As it stands, it suggests a degree of compulsion that will rob the people of freedom and, in any case, make the statutes and ordinances of God redundant. This is a reason for taking the Hebrew, which is literally 'I will do (or make) that you walk in my statutes' to mean that God will create the ideal conditions for his people to follow his statutes, not that he will turn them into compliant robots.

The theme of creating the right conditions to make possible the service of God is important, because in restored Israel after the exile, as in today's world, the right conditions never existed. This is also true for any Christian interpretation of the passage which sees it as a prophecy of the giving of the Holy Spirit after the resurrection. It cannot be said of the churches that they are any nearer to exhibiting the ideal nature of the people of God than was the case with ancient Israel, in spite of the churches' claim to have the Holy Spirit. The question 'How can the people of God live truly according to his calling?' remains unresolved within the constraints of the world as we know it. JR

Revelation 22.12–14, 16–17, 20–21

The concluding lines of Revelation consist of a string of several independent sayings that reiterate some major emphases of the book as a whole and formally close the work. Beginning with Rev. 22.12, the risen Jesus speaks, first and last, about the imminence of his return (vv. 12–13, 20), about the judgement his return will necessitate (vv. 14–15), about the testimony for the churches in the words of Revelation (v. 16), the call to salvation (v. 17), and the warnings about tampering with the book (vv. 18–19). While it is difficult to discern any organized movement through the passage, the general themes are evident.

Pre-eminent in this passage is the promise that Jesus will soon return. The notion of the imminence of the *parousia* appears earlier in the book (1.1; 2.16, 25; 3.11), but here references come often and with urgency (22.6, 7, 12, 20). The return of Jesus poses a threat for some, those who persist in sin and in opposition to Jesus himself. But for the Church, that promise is hope itself. Both urgency and perhaps a note of poignancy sound at the book's close, as the community responds to 'Surely I am coming soon', with 'Amen. Come, Lord Jesus!' First Corinthians closes with the same cry (16.22; there in Aramaic rather than Greek), suggesting that this urgent hope for Jesus' return was shared across several Christian communities; the cry itself may have a fixed place in the eucharistic liturgy (see 1 Cor. 11.26).

In Rev. 22.12, Jesus announces what will be one result of his coming: 'My reward is with me, to repay according to everyone's work.' The lectionary omits vv. 15 and 18–19, presumably because of their harsh statements concerning the judgement that will constitute Jesus' repayment for the works of some. Understandably, the preacher needs to approach these verses with particular care, so that the sermon does not serve only to engender fear or worsen guilt. Deleting these verses, however, deletes a crucial piece of the apocalyptist's world view, namely, dualism.

Throughout Revelation, as is the case with most apocalyptic writings, the author clearly divides the inhabitants of the world (indeed, of the cosmos) into the good and the bad. There can be no confusion about who sides with Babylon and who sides with the Lamb. Explaining this dualistic mentality is notoriously difficult, especially since it appears in so much ancient literature (and in many contemporary controversies as well!). In the context of a writing like Revelation, it functions to reinforce the community's boundaries and to encourage faithful behaviour. Such dualism also reinforces Revelation's insistence that God will finally triumph, for those who are aligned with the Lamb will both persevere and be rescued from the trials ahead.

For those who are aligned with the Lamb, the words of v. 17 form a call to perseverance, patience, and also hope and joy: 'Come.' It is not simply that Jesus must come for his own, but his own must be ready for his coming. Let 'everyone who is thirsty come' and 'take the water of life as a gift' (see 22.1). Those who stand with the enemies of the Lamb may yet cross over, although the overwhelming evidence of Revelation is that the apocalyptist holds out little hope for such conversion (see e.g. 22.11).

In part because of this impending judgement, Revelation concludes with an insistence on its own reliability. Throughout the book, assertions such as 'I am the Alpha and the Omega, the first and the last, the beginning and the end' (v. 13; see 1.8, 17; 21.6) have served to guarantee the trustworthiness of the visions and their interpretation. Here that reliability extends to the book itself, which is to be made available rather than sealed up (22.10), and which is not to be altered in any way (vv. 18–19). Particularly the warnings about altering the words of the book would be well known to John's audience, for various sorts of ancient writings carried warnings about their completeness and integrity.

Understanding the apocalyptist's work in this concluding section is one thing; preaching it is quite another matter. The urgency that pervades Revelation here comes to a head, and as it does contemporary preachers and teachers inevitably face the question of how to interpret such urgency some 2,000 years later. Especially in those Christian communities that live under oppression, the cry of v. 20 may be vivid and heartfelt, but what do we say in light of the delay? And what do we say to those (perhaps including some of us) who find the language of Revelation too wild even to consider?

When all is said and done, apocalyptic literature is not about predictions of time and events, but about the certainty that the God who stands before the beginning of history also stands beyond its ending. The evil that torments the cosmos, whether in human or metahuman form, may rule for a while, as Rome did and as other empires of varying sorts have since that time. But evil will not finally win, and God's people will finally be vindicated.

In the context of Eastertide, this distinction between urgency and certainty becomes especially important. The power of God evident in the risen Lord guarantees the future and total reign of God. Varying strands of the New Testament verbalize that certainty in different ways. Paul logically deduces the connection between the two and then envisages God's final triumph (1 Cor. 15). Mark depicts it in terms of the traditional hope for the return of the Son of Man (e.g. Mark 8.38—9.1). Revelation imagines the future in terms both vivid and foreign, but the underlying certainty remains the same. BG

John 17.20–26

The passage contains the charter of the ecumenical movement that began, substantially, first among Protestant churches, in the early twentieth century, with its slogan: 'that they all may be one' (oddly, given its wide-flung aim, often put in Latin, *ut omnes unum sint*). But the author of the Gospel of John did not have such post-Reformation church predicaments in mind when he wrote this passage, but was operating at a deeper, less ecclesiastical level; though what he wrote did carry its own kind of implications for life. At John 10.30, Jesus announces his unity (of act and purpose rather than abstract 'being') with the Father: 'the Father and I are one'. In the Supper Discourses (chs. 13—17), this way of stating the relationship of Father and Son is, like many others, extended – it is almost systematic – to include

the disciples and so all believers. In the enclosure of the supper room, itself symbolizing the Church as the community of Jesus' 'own', the mantle is verbally spread over
them. 'Oneness' is to be among their guiding features – along with doing Jesus'
'works' as he does those of the Father, being 'sent' just as he is sent by the Father,
loving one another as the Father loves the Son. The use of 'glory' in a similar way
(v. 24) carries the pattern to the most transcendent level.

   In other words, to be 'saved' is nothing less than to be incorporated into the divine
life. This is expressed most intensely and intimately of all by the language of mutual
indwelling with which ch. 17 ends. So Johannine mysticism reaches its sublime
end, bringing what has gone before to its culmination. It is of course a doctrine to
make much of church life at all levels slink away ashamed at its triviality and mis-
directed energy. LH

Day of Pentecost

Acts 2.1–21 or Genesis 11.1–9; Romans 8.14–17; John 14.8–17 (25–27)

Acts 2.1–21

New life – sudden, unmerited, irresistible new life! That is the reality the Pentecost narrative in Acts 2 broadcasts, and the text transmits the story in the most expansive way imaginable. All the stops on this great literary organ are employed: a heavenly sound like a rushing wind, descending fire, patterns of transformed speech, and the like. It is as if not even the most lavish use of human language is capable of capturing the experiences of the day, and that is undoubtedly one of the emotions the text wishes to convey.

It is not accidental, of course, that the birth of the Church, this great 'harvest' of souls, should occur on this important festival. The Feast of Pentecost, or Weeks, as it is known in the Old Testament, marked the end of the celebration of the spring harvest, a liturgical cycle that began at Passover and during which devout Israelite families praised God for God's grace and bounty. It also was the beginning of a period, lasting until the autumnal Festival of Booths (or Tabernacles), in which the first fruits of the field were sacrificed to Yahweh. And among at least some Jews the Feast of Weeks was a time of covenant renewal, as the following text from the Book of Jubilees (*c.* 150 BC) makes clear:

> Therefore, it is ordained and written in the heavenly tablets that they should observe the feast of Shebuot (Weeks) in this month, once per year, in order to renew the covenant in all (respects), year by year. (*Jub.* 1.17; trans. O. S. Wintermute in James H. Charlesworth, ed., *The Old Testament Pseudepigrapha*; Garden City, NY: Doubleday & Co., 1985, vol. 2, p. 67.)

Pentecost/Weeks is thus a pregnant moment in the life of the people of God and in the relationship between that people and God. Or to put the matter more graphically, but also more accurately, Pentecost is the moment when gestation ceases and birthing occurs. Thus, it is both an end and a beginning, the leaving behind of that which is past, the launching forth into that which is only now beginning to be. Pentecost therefore is not a time of completion. It is moving forward into new dimensions of being, whose basic forms are clear, but whose fulfilment has yet to be realized.

Those who follow the cycle of lectionary texts (or, for that matter, those who simply read the book of Acts) have been prepared for this moment. Twice, in connection with Jesus' ascension, the coming of the Spirit has been promised: 'You will receive power when the Holy Spirit has come upon you' (Acts 1.8; compare 1.5). That promise is now realized in a manner far surpassing the expectations of even the most faithful disciples. New life for the Church! New life for individuals within the Church! New life through the Spirit of God! That is the meaning of Pentecost.

No one present is excluded from this display of God's grace. Unlike other important moments in the history of God's mighty acts of salvation – the transfiguration (Mark 9.2–13), for example, where only the inner few are witnesses to the work of God's Spirit – everyone is included at Pentecost. The tongues of fire rest upon 'each' (Acts 2.3) of the disciples, and a moment later the crowd comes surging forward because 'each one' (v. 6) has heard the disciples speaking in his or her native tongue. In order that not even the least astute reader may miss the inclusiveness of the moment, the list of place names that begins in v. 9 traces a wide sweep through the world of the Greco-Roman Diaspora. That which happens at Pentecost is thus no inner mystical experience, but an outpouring of God's energy that touches every life present.

Yet not everyone responded to the winds and fires of new life, at least not in positive ways. Some mocked (v. 13) and, in their unwillingness to believe the freshness of God's initiatives, reacted with stale words (compare 1 Sam. 1.14) as they confused Spirit-induced joy with alcohol-induced inebriation. Perhaps it was the very extravagant expression of the Spirit's presence that drove them to conclude: 'This cannot be what it seems to be!' Yet what it seemed to be is precisely what it was. God's Spirit unleashed! New life – sudden, unmerited, irresistible new life! We may hope that those who mocked were among those who, on hearing Peter's sermon, were 'cut to the heart' (v. 37).

Peter's sermon begins – and this day's lection ends – with a quotation (vv. 17–21) from the prophet Joel (Joel 2.28–32a), and nothing could be more symptomatic of the nature of Pentecost than the transmutation of this text. That which in the prophet's discourse appears prominently as a forecast of destruction and death has become on Peter's tongue a declaration of new life. For Joel the signs of the outpouring of the Spirit are a prelude to disaster (see especially Joel 2.32b, c) but for Peter these wonders have been fulfilled in Jesus Christ, himself the greatest of God's wonders (Acts 2.22), and their purpose, *Christ's* purpose, is nothing less than the redemption of humankind. Again the Spirit has invaded human life in ways that shatter old expectations. It is not death that is the aim of the Spirit's visitation, but new life – sudden, unmerited, irresistible new life! 'Everyone who calls on the name of the Lord shall be saved' (v. 21). BG

Genesis 11.1–9

It is commonly, and wrongly, supposed that the giving of the Holy Spirit to the disciples on the Day of Pentecost is a reversal of the story of the Tower of Babel. There is no hint of this in Acts 2.1–21, and in any case the two passages do not complement each other. Genesis 11.1–9 is an account of the desire of humans to usurp the place of God. This leads to them being scattered, and then separated from each other by the barriers of language. While the different languages claimed in Acts to have been spoken by the disciples on the Day of Pentecost, met the different language needs of the listeners, these were Jews from the diaspora. The dividing of the human race into nations is not reversed on the Day of Pentecost.

In context, Gen. 11.1–9 is one of a series of stories set in 'beginning time' in which humans attempt to undermine the moral order. In Gen. 4 Cain murders his brother Abel; in ch. 6 the human race has become so wicked that the earth is destroyed by the flood. But the post-flood generation is no better, and the attempt of the people of Babel is an alarming parable of what happens when the human race tries to dispense with God and govern the world without him. The saying 'nothing that they propose to do will now be impossible for them' (v. 6) sounds chillingly modern in a world in which human technological achievements threaten the very existence of the planet and its inhabitants. In short, connecting the passage with Acts 2 runs the danger of trivializing its profound insights into the effects of a human ambition that tries to usurp the place of God. JR

Romans 8.14–17

Trinity Sunday speaks of God by speaking of what it means to be a believer. That requires reference to the revelation of God in Christ and the believer's integral relationship with him and in him, but also to God as Spirit, the metaphor of wind expressing the unseen power of God at work in the human spirit, guiding the moral life and evoking passionate prayer. Later theological reflection on God as Trinity led the fourth-century Church to define doctrinally this mystery of the divine life and the relationships into which believers are drawn and caught up. Paul's sober comments are plainly rooted in experience but they rise into the rhetoric that has helped shape subsequent Christian experience. This is the raw material of a doctrine that is vacuous without that experience of life in Christ, the Lord who is Spirit (cf. vv. 9–11; 2 Cor. 3.17).

Romans 8, on being a Christian (that is, life in Christ, or in the Spirit) can be pondered in the different sections of the chapter. As usual Paul unfolds his thinking by way of contrasts, here between 'flesh' and Spirit; that is, dislocated human existence and the divine power that has invaded and is transforming it. His vocabulary is apt to mislead because he uses common words in an almost technical way. 'Flesh' is not the sensuous part of human nature, and has little to do with sex in Paul's usage. It refers to the human realm, created by God but overcome by hostile forces, which obstruct the development of authentic human lives. It is finite, physical and weak, but the tragedy of its weakness is that it has fallen under the control of powers opposed to God. Its natural decay therefore carries more sinister overtones. Death is an enemy with a sting (1 Cor. 15.54–56) until the victory of Christ's resurrection breaks its power and allows the Christian to speak with St Francis of 'thou most kind and gentle death'.

This chapter celebrates God's action in Christ to redeem the desperate situation and create truly human lives lived in the perfect freedom of service and dependence on God. God's initiative (v. 3) evokes human response. Those who have been transferred into the new age by baptism (6.3) have received the Spirit, but they continue to live in this dislocated world and need to be reminded to live by the norms of God's new age, not by the old self-centredness and self-indulgence, labelled by Paul 'flesh'; that is, human existence under the power of 'sin' leading to 'death'.

The motivation to live the new life comes from the knowledge of who and what and where we are, and where we are going as people 'in Christ Jesus' (v. 1), liberated by 'the law of the Spirit of life in Christ Jesus' (v. 2). We are placed in a new relationship to God – that of sons and daughters – through our faith-based, baptism-placed, Spirit-graced relationship with Christ Jesus our Lord, the Son of God. The Spirit is God's power experienced as guiding the moral life and assuring believers of that relationship with God. It (or s/he) finds voice in the prayer of believers who know they are children of God, and therefore heirs. The filial metaphor describes a present relationship, but it also implies a legal status and so speaks too of future benefits. The son and heir's knowledge of the heavenly Father, mediated by the Spirit and based on the faith-relationship with Christ (cf. Gal. 2.20) gives certainty about God's fatherly character and promise of a beautiful future. This carries believers through the sufferings of the present time (v. 18), which they shall pass through in his company. RM

John 14.8–17 (25–27)

The liturgical calendar during this season is organized according to the sequence of events in the two New Testament books of Luke and Acts. Thus Good Friday, Easter, several Sundays in the Easter season, Ascension and Pentecost follow one another in an orderly fashion. The fact that the term 'Pentecost' is used at all and that Acts 2 is a suggested reading for each of the years of the lectionary cycle indicates the dependency on the schema of Luke-Acts.

The primary theme for this Sunday – the Holy Spirit – is, however, treated differently in other New Testament writings, less dramatically perhaps than the mysterious happenings of Acts 2, but no less profoundly. 'Gospel of the Spirit', a label often put on John, is symptomatic of an extensive consideration of the Spirit in that Gospel, and particularly as a topic of Jesus' teaching throughout his ministry. 'Pentecost' happens not after a period of 50 days after Easter, but on Easter evening. John helps us to think of the Spirit in ways other than sheer excitement or emotional agitation.

In John, especially instructive are the five passages found in the farewell discourses where the terms 'Advocate' and 'Spirit of truth' are used, and where Jesus anticipates the coming of the Spirit immediately following his departure (John 14.16–17, 25–26; 15.26– 27; 16.7–11, 13–15). Two of those passages are included in the Gospel lesson for today, and another is recommended for next Sunday (Trinity Sunday).

Four features of the Spirit stand out in the selection from John 14. First is the term *parakletos,* rendered by the NRSV as 'Advocate'. This represents a perhaps unfortunate change from the RSV 'Counsellor', since 'Advocate' highlights the legal overtones of the term (as in 1 John 2.1), prominent only in John 16.7–11. The text itself defines *parakletos* by adding 'to be with you for ever' (14.16). The Spirit as *parakletos* is

God's powerful and nurturing presence, given to the disciples in the wake of Jesus' departure.

Specifically, the disciples are faced with Jesus' words, 'If you love me, you will keep my commandments' (14.15). How are they to live in such a way that their affection for Jesus does not degenerate into sentimentality, but expresses itself in concrete deeds of mercy and in faithful obedience? Without his physical presence, how are they to cope with the forces arraigned against them, and no regress to what they were before he entered their lives? The answer is the Counsellor, whose sustaining influence has no termination.

Second, we encounter in 14.17 the term 'Spirit of truth', which recurs later in 15.26 and 16.13. The Spirit teaches. The Spirit enables the community to remember its link with Jesus.

The phrase is a promise that embodies both a threat and a hope. On the one hand, the Spirit will keep the Church's feet to the fire when it wanders into accommodating paths in search of an easier way. The 'Spirit of *truth*' (emphasis added) forces a reality check, prodding, needling, cajoling the community to embrace its distinctiveness as the people of God. The Spirit does not make things easier, only harder. On the other hand, the words Jesus taught contain commitments about resurrection, life, a secure dwelling place, a meaningful present and a hopeful tomorrow. The Spirit prevents the Church from forgetting that it has a future and helps it translate the message of Jesus so that the future is not simply endless time but rich with promise.

Third, the Spirit is sent by the Father – a divine gift. Twice in these five passages in John, the Father is specified as the sender (14.16, 26), and twice Jesus is the sender (15.26; 16.7). The stress is not coincidental. All the stratagems in the world cannot entice or force the Spirit's hand. No manipulation of a group, no set form of prayer, no upstretched hands. The promise to the Church of God's presence always remains at God's initiative, and yet it is a promise of *God,* and one on which the Church can rely.

Finally, the Spirit distinguishes the disciples from the world. The Church becomes a peculiar community, set apart by being indwelt by the Spirit. That carries some interesting implications. For one thing, the Church cannot take its cues for its life and mission from the culture, as if the culture posed all the right questions. As the text puts it, 'the world cannot receive' the Spirit, 'because it neither sees him nor knows him' (14.17). Without taking a superior stance toward the world (after all, the Spirit is a gift), the Church follows a script that seems to the world no more than an impossible jumble of letters.

For another thing, the peace that the Church seeks and receives is distinctive (14.27). All those 'peaceful' scenes thrust at us by the advertisers, enticing as they may be, turn out to be mirages, false promises that haunt us in the seeking. The peace given the Church is nothing other than the promise of the divine presence, the assurance of people not orphaned and destitute.

The Gospel of John confronts us with sobering and penetrating words for Pentecost. cc

Trinity Sunday

Proverbs 8.1–4, 22–31; Romans 5.1–5; John 16.12–15

Proverbs 8.1–4, 22–31

For ancient Israelites the natural world was not benign. The sentence passed on the man in Gen. 3.17–19 promises him toil and sweat in producing the food necessary for survival, and famine plays its part in the stories of Abraham, Joseph and Ruth, to name but three. The claim here, that Wisdom was present with God when he created the world, is a claim both that there is a rational basis to an otherwise ambiguous world, and that this rational principle is accessible to humankind.

As an alternative account of the creation to that in Gen. 1—2, our passage is a useful reminder that none of the biblical creation narratives can be made to conform to modern scientific accounts of the origin of the universe. There is no 'big bang' here; rather, there is a charming picture of God with a female companion (Wisdom is feminine in Hebrew) perhaps helping him (the meaning of the word translated as 'master worker' in v. 30 is uncertain) but certainly playing (rather than 'rejoicing' cf. v. 30b–31a) with the created order as though with new toys. There are resonances with the Genesis creation stories. The word translated 'depths' in v. 24 is the same word that is rendered 'deep' in Gen. 1.2, and it recurs in Prov. 8 in vv. 27 and 28. The idea that one of the purposes of creation is to ascribe limits, essentially to the sea (cf. v. 29), is implicit in Gen. 1 (and cf. Job 38.8–11) in that these limits are removed when God brings a flood upon the earth (Gen. 7.11).

Scholarly speculation has naturally focused upon the origin of the figure of Wisdom, with possible candidates being the Egyptian idea of *maat* 'justice' and the Greek figure of *Sophia*. The passage also undoubtedly comes from a later period in the growth of the Old Testament, when there was a felt need for an intermediate figure between a transcendent God and humankind. It may also have been necessary to counteract the challenge presented to Judaism by Greek philosophy.

Granted all this, the passage injects a marvellously light touch into the process of creation. It shows us a designer enjoying the work in company with someone who expresses her approval of what is done by playing with it. There is no 'first cause' or 'unmoved mover' here; and the presence of Wisdom and her especial delight in the human race ensure that the creation is far more than a machine that is left to run on its own once it has been made. The figure of Wisdom personifies God's unwearying care for the created order, and for the well-being of the human animal that is so destructive of what God has made. This is one reason why Jewish interpretation has connected Wisdom with the Torah, God's revealed law for every facet of the life of his people, and why Christian interpretation has made a connection with the divine Logos, the Word made flesh. JR

Romans 5.1–5

In Rom. 5, Paul begins to explore the nature of the new life of those who have been 'justified by faith'. The letter earlier affirms with relentless power the sinfulness of all human beings (1.18—3.20) and then the radical intervention of God in the event of Jesus Christ (3.21–31). Now the topic shifts to the consequences of that event for human beings: 'We have peace with God through our Lord Jesus Christ' (v. 1); 'we boast in our hope' (v. 2); and 'God's love has been poured into our hearts' (v. 5).

In contemporary English, the word 'peace' is used in a variety of ways, some of which are quite subjective and individualistic, such as 'being at peace' with oneself or feeling 'peaceful'. In its biblical context, however, 'peace with God' primarily connotes an objective sense of peace, the peace that comes when conflict is at an end (see e.g. Pss. 72.7; 147.14). Given Paul's earlier portrayal of sin as the entrenched human denial of God or rebellion against God (Rom. 1.18–32), peace with God connotes recognition that such rebellion is at an end.

In addition to peace, justification produces the 'hope of sharing the glory of God' (v. 2). Paul traces the birth of hope ('suffering produces endurance, and endurance produces character, and character produces hope', vv. 3–4); as he does so it becomes clear that he uses hope in a sense far different from the flabby and trivial hopes for pleasant weather or a hearty supper. 'Hope' for Paul is not the equivalent of desire or wish. To the contrary, hope refers to confidence, trust, conviction. The 'hope of sharing the glory of God' is Christian certainty that God's glory will be shared with all.

Hope 'does not disappoint' because 'God's love has been poured into our hearts' (v. 5). Although grammatically the phrase 'God's love' may refer either to human love of God or to God's love of humankind, in this passage Paul almost certainly has the second meaning in mind, as is clear from his comment on God's love in 5.8. In fact, Paul does not often use the vocabulary of 'love', apart from references to the beloved in the churches (see e.g. Rom. 1.7; 16.5; 1 Cor. 4.14; Phil. 2.12). When he does speak of God's love, it is, as here, in connection with the action of sending Jesus Christ on behalf of humankind (as in Gal. 2.20).

Those who are justified, then, have peace, hope and love. For these gifts and in these gifts they may boast. That may seem an odd assertion from the man who elsewhere writes that 'boasting is excluded' (Rom. 3.27; cf. Rom. 2.17; 1 Cor. 1.29; 5.6). But here Paul does not contradict himself, for the problem is not boasting in and of itself, as if boasting were simply a matter of bad taste or flawed manners. The criterion for discerning whether boasting is or is not acceptable is the basis on which it is done. People who boast in their own accomplishments (or what they believe to be their own accomplishments) stand condemned, but those who boast in God or in the things made possible by God are praised.

It is important to notice that peace, hope and love are already, even now, present within the community: 'We *have* peace with God' (Rom. 5.1, emphasis added). Given Paul's experience with the Corinthians, who mistakenly assumed that the gifts of resurrection were already theirs, he was wary of asserting too much about the present (as in Rom. 6.5: 'We *will* certainly be united with him in a resurrection like his', emphasis added). Does 5.1–5 assign too much to the present possession of believers?

We might answer that question in the affirmative, except for the powerful statements of agency that drive this passage and ground them firmly in God's action rather than in human accomplishment. To begin with, the peace that believers have with God comes 'through our Lord Jesus Christ, through whom we have obtained access to this grace in which we stand' (vv. 1–2). Later, it is God's glory that enables Christian hope (v. 2). Finally, God's love comes into the human heart 'through the Holy Spirit that has been given to us'. If believers have peace, hope and love, it is because and only because of the action of God in Jesus Christ and the sustaining power of the Holy Spirit.

Read in connection with Trinity Sunday, these references to God, Christ and the Spirit take on a particular significance. In common with other New Testament writers, Paul does not talk about the Trinity as such. The later christological controversies that prompted sustained reflection on the Trinity lay far ahead. Instead, Paul and other New Testament writers search for language with which to express the experience and convictions of early Christians. As a result, their comments do not always yield themselves to a systematic framework.

In this passage as elsewhere, the members of what would later be called the Trinity provide the basis for Christian existence. Christians live in peace with God because of Jesus Christ. Christians know the love of God because the Holy Spirit has poured out that love to them. Christians boast in God's glory, which they know through Christ and the Spirit. If Christians today find talk about the Trinity abstract and remote, for Paul it is as close as life itself.

(For additional commentary on this passage, see the Third Sunday in Lent for Year A.) BG

John 16.12–15

The gospel lesson today includes the final Paraclete saying embedded in the farewell discourse of John's Gospel. Last Sunday, with the celebration of Pentecost, the focus was on the first two of the sayings (14.8–17, 25–27), and the Day of Pentecost in Year B of the lectionary cycle highlights the third, fourth and fifth sayings (15.26– 27; 16.4b–15). Since each of the passages uses common terms for the Spirit and all are set in a common context, there is a natural overlapping in the interpretations. Clearly the focus of the final saying is the role of the Spirit as ongoing teacher in the life of the Church.

So much to say and so little time in which to say it is the universal problem when goodbyes are exchanged. A particular problem arises for Jesus in the farewell to his friends. He is the revelation of God, and the events immediately on the horizon – crucifixion, resurrection and departure – cannot possibly be grasped by the disciples ahead of time. The incidents are not just ordinary occurrences, but fundamental to who Jesus is and what he has come to do.

There are implications to be faced about what Jesus has already said and done. The book of Acts recites the story of the growing comprehension of the believing community about the reception of Gentiles into the Church, including even the 'conversion' of Peter as he encounters the centurion Cornelius (Acts 10—11). The Church has much to learn. 'I still have many things to say to you' (John 16.12) puts the Christian community in a learning mode, and the Spirit is the divinely appointed teacher.

'He will guide you into all the truth . . . he will declare to you the things that are to come' (16.13). Those are rather extravagant claims, but claims for a community that has extravagant needs. While the inclusive scope of the text ('all the truth', 'the things that are to come') may be open to being misconstrued, it should certainly not be underestimated. 'The things that are to come' no doubt includes both eschatological events and the immediate circumstances the community faces as it seeks to live out its calling. If what the Church needs is not new information but fresh discernment, better focused eyes with which to read the signs of the times and the relevance of its message, then the Spirit is a timely gift.

In technical language, the Spirit is the critical hermeneutic for the Church. The Spirit is the indispensable reality for the community as it seeks to interpret its tradition and its context. The Spirit enables the Church to be a community of both memory and hope. The Spirit 'brings forth fresh light from the Word' and enlivens it for its readers. If the Spirit is not operative in its vision, to enable the understanding of its sacred text and to expose the true situation of the world, then the Church is left to its own distorted sight.

How can the Church be sure? How can it discern what is right and what is wrong? How can it determine which of the many voices speaking is the voice of the Spirit? Does it go with every new fad? The Johannine community itself had problems with contesting claims that finally resulted in schism. The warning is appropriate: 'Beloved, do not believe every spirit, but test the spirits to see whether they are from God; for many false prophets have gone out into the world' (1 John 4.1). Not every new burst of energy, not every spurt of growth, not every surge in attendance is necessarily to be identified with the Spirit's activity, and not every speaker mouthing biblical phrases represents the voice of God.

The text offers something of a test in depicting a decisive characteristic of the Spirit: 'He will glorify me, because he will take what is mine and declare it to you' (16.14). No new revelation is offered as an addenda to Christ. As one commentator puts it, 'Pneumatology is subordinated to christology' (Charles H. Talbert, *Reading John: A Literary and Theological Commentary on the Fourth Gospel and the Johannine Epistles*; New York: Crossroad, 1992, p. 219). The Spirit quickens the community's sensitivity to the revelation already given in Jesus rather than uncovering unheard-of data. What does not cohere with what Jesus taught and did cannot have come from the Spirit of truth.

The Spirit's role, then, is self-effacing, in that the attention falls somewhere else – on a deepened appreciation of the Christ-event. Maybe this explains the difficulty the Church often has had in talking about the Spirit. To discern the

Spirit rightly pushes one inevitably to reflect on the One about whom the Spirit bears witness.

For Trinity Sunday, this fifth Paraclete saying speaks primarily to the relationship between Son and Spirit. The final verse mentions also the Father (16.15), and in the broader perspective of John's Gospel refers to the mutuality shared in the Godhead. cc

Corpus Christi/Thanksgiving for Holy Communion

Genesis 14.18–20; I Corinthians 11.23–26; John 6.51–58

Genesis 14.18–20

Chapter 14 has long been regarded as an erratic block in the Genesis story. It seems to describe a situation in which the leading rulers of the known world all converged on the area of the Dead Sea. In the story Abraham is introduced at a late stage and is envisaged as a warrior, with an extensive retinue, engaged in battles with large-scale enemy coalitions. This is a very different picture from the family story of surrounding chapters. The older source-critics were quite unable to assign this chapter to any of their preferred sources. Most modern scholars regard the chapter as a late addition to the main Genesis material, perhaps aimed at drawing out Abraham's connection with Jerusalem (assuming that 'Salem' here is a short form of Jerusalem), but no consensus has been reached.

Within this larger context the verses of our reading pose their own problems. Many have taken them to be an entirely separate unit, unconnected with the remainder of the chapter. Nothing is known of Melchizedek in historical terms; he is presented here both as king and as 'priest of El Elyon' ('God Most High'). This became a name applied to Yahweh, especially in the Psalms (cf. Pss. 7.17; 91.1). Whether this was the name of an originally Canaanite deity or simply one mode of describing Israel's own God remains unclear.

Melchizedek became an important symbolic figure within later traditions. He is mentioned at Ps. 110.4 as the typical priest, and is also mentioned in the Dead Sea Scrolls. The theme of Melchizedek as the true priest is taken further in the Epistle to the Hebrews, where Jesus is credited with priestly status 'according to the order of Melchizedek' (Heb. 6.20), and the links between Melchizedek and Jesus are imaginatively developed in the following chapter.

In Christian liturgical tradition these verses have played another important part, because the 'bread and wine' (v. 18) have been seen as prefiguring the eucharistic elements. Overall, one may say that this is one of those passages that will prove frustrating for those who wish to have a clear historical account, of the kind that can be backed up by reliable supporting evidence. By contrast it will be a delight for those who treasure literary allusions and traditions and are not greatly concerned about historical details. RC

I Corinthians 11.23–26

See Maundy Thursday pp. 107–108.

John 6.51–58

With its frequent use of material things as signs and symbols of the spiritual, John's Gospel has been seen as the 'most sacramental' of all. On the other hand, some scholars deny that its author even knew the sacraments, or suppose him to be anti-sacramental. It is true that John gives no account of Jesus' baptism (some would say that he suppresses it), and that he omits 'the institution of the Eucharist' from the Last Supper; but other parts of his narrative seem to reflect on the sacramental life of the Church.

One such passage is set for today's Gospel. It comes at the end of the 'bread of life discourse', following Jesus' miraculous feeding of a large crowd. John has already interpreted the miracle as a sign that Jesus is the prophet like Moses (6.14; cf. Deut. 18.15–18), as a feeding of the people far surpassing the manna (6.26–32; cf. Exod. 16.4, 15), and as showing Jesus not just as *giver* of living bread, but as the bread itself (6.32–35, 41, 48). This 'bread' is freely available to all who come in faith to him (6.35, 40, 47). Believers *have* 'eternal life', i.e. they experience the joy of God's presence associated with the age to come (6.51a–b).

At 6.51c the interpretation takes a new turn. The 'bread' is interpreted as Jesus' flesh, given for the life of the world. Now, only those who 'eat' Jesus' flesh and 'drink' his blood have life in them. A sacramental allusion seems inescapable. But how does this relate to the idea expressed earlier, that it is those who have faith who receive eternal life? Some scholars find the tension so great that they attribute vv. 51c–58 to an 'ecclesiastical redactor'. Others see these verses as the climax of the whole of 6.1–58.

The main thought seems to be that the Lord's Supper or Holy Communion is a means of sustaining and feeding the faithful (v. 55). Through it we assimilate into ourselves Christ's very self; we become one with him as he abides in us and we in him (v. 56). We already have eternal life, and Jesus will raise us up on the last day (v. 54). Note that these verses do not speak of Jesus' sacramental *body*, but rather of his *flesh* (Greek: *sarx*, the word used of the incarnation in 1.14). Conceivably this passage was added (whether by the evangelist or another) to correct people with problems over a 'fleshly' understanding of the incarnation or Eucharist (cf. the views attributed by Ignatius to the 'docetists'). Observe the strong introductory words, 'Truly, truly, I say to you . . .' (v. 53), and the divisive effect of this teaching. It is a shame, however, to read vv. 51c–58 merely as polemic, and certainly wrong to interpret them too rigidly. Seen in the context of the bread of life discourse, they offer an understanding of the Eucharist as an important part of a wider pattern by which Jesus Christ, the Word of God, nurtures and sustains his people. RE

Proper 3

(Sunday between 22 and 28 May inclusive, if after Trinity Sunday)

Ecclesiasticus 27.4–7 or Isaiah 55.10–13; 1 Corinthians 15.15–58; Luke 6.39–49

Ecclesiasticus 27.4–7

The main problem of interpretation of this reading is whether it is about a person's speech or a person's actions. The Greek word, *logismos*, which is connected in the lectionary translation with speaking in v. 4 has more exactly to do with reasoning, reckoning and debating, which is why the REB translates it: 'Start an argument'. In two passages the Greek Bible uses *logismos* to render the Hebrew word *heshbon* (Eccles. 7.25; 9.10) and it is this word that is found in the Hebrew remains of the book in both verses 4 and 5 of the present passage. A case can be made for translating *heshbon* in connection with trade, which is the subject of the opening verses of Ecclus. 27. If this is correct, it puts the passage in a different light. What exposes a person's character is not what is said, but what is done in trade, because trade gives an opportunity to make money by dishonest means. The writer of Ecclesiasticus is not enthusiastic about engaging in commerce precisely because of its potential for corruption (see 26.29—27.2).

If it is accepted that the passage is about speaking, a more robust translation is needed to do justice to the passage. The REB toughens up 'speaking' by referring to argument and debate. The AV rendering of v. 4 is also much tougher than what appears in the lectionary: 'As when a man sifteth with a sieve, the refuse remaineth; so the filth of a man in his talk.' However, the interpretation of vv. 4–5 in terms of the temptations of trade makes better sense of the passage as well as providing a way in to linking it to today's world. JR

Isaiah 55.10–13

These verses bring to a conclusion that part of Isaiah that began with ch. 40, and the idea of the active word of God forms a narrative arch between 40.8 and 55.11. Whether the Israelites knew that rain and snow return to the atmosphere in the form of vapour is unlikely. The Old Testament view of these things is that God has storehouses of snow and hail (cf. Job 38.22) and that water is kept in the heavens in waterskins (Job 38.37). Presumably these were not thought of as unlimited supplies; rather, such things as rain and snow were divine messengers that were sent to do specific tasks before returning to report to God. God's word is then to be seen in these terms.

What is God's word and how does it return to him? The prophets employed a mode of speaking that has been called the 'messenger formula', which was used when kings sent messages to each other. The king would speak his message in the presence of an ambassador, and the latter would then travel to the court of the king for whom the message was intended, and repeat the message verbatim. When prophets used the formula 'thus says the Lord' they were implying that they were uttering a message that they had heard God speak. This may help us to make sense of the mechanics of vv. 10–11. Their main point is that all the words that have been spoken in chs. 40—55 will be fulfilled as surely as rain and snow help plants to grow.

The final verses (12–13) envisage the return of exiles from Babylon to Jerusalem towards the end of the sixth century BC. The ending of exile has been the main preoccupation of these chapters since 40.2. It has been recognized, however, that the prophet thought of the ending of exile and the return as an event that would transform the created order. Already in 40.3–5 a 'coming' of God is envisaged that will fill valleys and remove mountains, and in 55.12–13 it is promised the earth will no longer produce thorns and briars. The language about mountains and hills bursting into song is similar to that in Ps. 98.8, where it is God's coming to judge the world that is being celebrated.

God's promises in Isa. 40—55 were fulfilled in the sense that the power of Babylon was broken and the exiles were free to return home. The transformation of the created order did not take place, and subsequent prophecy had to wrestle with the fact that life in the restored community often fell well below the hope that the return had excited. JR

I Corinthians 15.51–58

The last of the four epistolary selections from 1 Cor. 15 brings the chapter to a climax, both in a grand word of celebration at the defeat of death and in a pointed exhortation for life in the present. The powerful rhetoric of the passage becomes obvious in its frequent reading at funeral and memorial services, where commentary often detracts from the confident, triumphant affirmation made in the text. Precisely because it is a 'mystery' revealed, a secret made known, the resurrection defies logical explanation.

Three motifs dominate the passage. First is the vivid insistence on transformation, a theme begun in 15.35–50. While the 'here and now' is linked to the 'there and then' by a continuity (a 'body'), it is no natural evolution from one to the other. The resurrection entails something brand new.

Two verbs, both repeated in the paragraph, describe the transformation. One is 'change', a strong verb that in some contexts can even be translated 'exchange' (Rom. 1.23). 'We will all be changed' (1 Cor. 15.51, 52). The resurrection of the dead, then, is not to be compared to the evolution of the caterpillar into the butterfly nor to the maturation of the unruly child into the responsible adult. Death brings an abrupt break that necessitates a new beginning.

The second verb describing the transformation is 'put on', as in dressing. Something not there previously is donned, specifically the robes of imperishability and immortality (15.53–54). They become the promised attire given at the resurrection to distinguish those who inherit the kingdom of God. This heavy stress on transformation no doubt has a particular relevance to some of the intended readers of this letter, who apparently assume that they have already arrived, that baptism has ushered them into a heavenly existence on earth. The insistence on future transformation for them provides quite a jolt.

Another way to treat this transformation is to note that death means the end of perishability and mortality. All in our present existence that marks our aging, degeneration and decline, all evidence of sin's impact in our world, its threat and devastation, will be done away with. The *via negativa* is a characteristically apocalyptic way of referring to the future (Rev. 21.4, 22–27).

The second prominent motif in the passage is the defeat of death. Quotations from Isa. 25.8 and Hos. 13.14 are loosely drawn together in 1 Cor. 15.54–55 to express confidence about the future. So certain is the demise of 'the last enemy' (15.26) that even now death can be mocked with taunting questions (15.55).

It is striking that death is not thought of here, as it is other places in the Bible, as a natural phenomenon, the result of the winding down of our physical forces. Death comes as the venom of sin, empowered by the law, and any doing away with death must include also the defeat of sin. (Verse 56 sounds as if it belongs in Rom. 5 or 7 rather than 1 Corinthians!) This has happened in the death and resurrection of Jesus, depicted here as the victory God has given us and the ground for celebrating ahead of time.

This brings the argument of 1 Cor. 15 back to where it started in the beginning, namely, with the tradition about Jesus (15.3–5). Talk about the future, even confident claims and the language of goading contempt, is rooted in what has already happened – the death and resurrection of Jesus, who is the first fruits for all who belong to Christ.

The third powerful motif in the passage is the final exhortation (15.58), a consequence of all that has gone before. The readers, addressed as 'beloved' brothers and sisters, are urged to face the present in the light of the future. A resurrection faith is depicted, through the imperatives, as an existence that is paradoxically sturdy and immovable amid the winds of change, and at the same time growing in the work of the Lord. Though not specific, the language seems to call for stability and persistence in the life and ministry of the community.

Throughout 1 Cor. 15, the phrase 'in vain' (translating two different Greek words) occurs. In 15.2 a caveat is raised about the readers' faith: 'unless you have come to believe in vain'. For Paul himself, God's grace had not turned out 'in vain' (15.10), but for the Corinthians who deny the future resurrection both his preaching and their faith will have been 'in vain' (15.14). The final clause of 15.58, however, concludes the chapter on an encouraging note. It anticipates that the readers' faith will not continue to depend on a fully 'realized' resurrection, subject to the vicissitudes of experience and certain to turn up empty, but will ultimately trust in the certainty of God's future. 'You know that in the Lord your labour is not in vain.' BG

Luke 6.39–49

In this final lection from the Lucan Sermon on the Plain, Jesus turns his attention specifically to the behaviour of disciples toward others in the community of faith. (The concluding section of the sermon actually begins with Luke 6.37, but vv. 37–38 are assigned as part of the reading for the Seventh Sunday of Epiphany.) The variety of sayings and the shifts in the analogies make the passage seem a hodgepodge, but it is united by the conviction that behaviour and character cannot be separated. What one does stems inevitably from what one is. What one is necessarily reveals itself in what one does.

Verses 39–42 introduce this theme by means of sayings that address the issue of appropriate self-criticism and integrity. A person who attempts to correct another's flaws without understanding his or her own is not sufficiently self-aware. If judgement ought not to be levelled at others within the community, it can and must be brought to bear on one's own behaviour (vv. 37–38).

Significantly, the analogies employed in vv. 39–42 have to do with seeing. The blind person cannot see to lead another blind person down the road. The one whose own eye contains a log cannot possibly see well enough to correct another's vision. Luke's fondness for imagery related to light and to sight comes into play here (see e.g. Luke 1.79; 4.18; Acts 9.8–9, 17–18). Given contemporary – and justifiable – sensitivity to the needs of the blind for independence, preachers will want to treat the saying about the blind leading the blind with some care, perhaps connecting it with the larger Lucan concern for the gospel as the giving of light and for the right kind of vision.

In the middle of these sayings about sight, Luke 6.40 stands somewhat isolated: 'A disciple is not above the teacher, but everyone who is fully qualified will be like the teacher.' Clearly here Jesus addresses the nature of the Christian community as a teaching community. Its teachers remain disciples or students of Jesus, so that they never rise 'above the teacher'. Nevertheless, their behaviour must be like his own. The implicit warning here about the significance of Christian teaching and the responsibility of those who teach is serious indeed.

With v. 43, the analogies change from those related to sight to those related to agriculture, and the topic shifts slightly from that of integrity to the more underlying issue of general character. Just as it is obvious that good trees do not yield bad fruit, so it ought to be obvious that the 'produce' of a good person will be good and that of an evil person will be evil.

Verses 46–49 make explicit what has been implicit in vv. 43–45. The one who hears, really hears, the words of Jesus will necessarily act on those words. By doing so, that person erects a house that will withstand any storm that comes. The one who hears but does not act builds a house with no foundation at all, subject to destruction by any storm. The consequences envisioned in v. 49 are severe: 'Great was the ruin of that house.' If Luke shies away from explicitly eschatological language here, the implication is nevertheless clear. Those who do not follow Jesus' teaching are subject to the wrath of God in some final and devastating manner.

Verses 46–47 form a kind of challenge that brings to a culmination not simply this section, but all of the sermon. The one who calls Jesus 'Lord' must also behave as Jesus teaches. To come to Jesus, as the multitude does in v. 17, is not enough. Nor is it enough to listen to Jesus' teaching. Being present and listening must end in action, in obedience.

In one sense the concerns of this passage seem quite contemporary. One recent trend in ethics has emphasized the importance of character in shaping ethical behaviour. Rather than being preoccupied with instructing people in how to behave in given situations or with providing rules of behaviour, the argument runs, we need to work toward the shaping of character.

Of course, the roots for this emphasis on character are ancient. Luke's Sermon on the Plain does not so much provide new instruction about character as it reflects what would have been found in any Greco-Roman moralist. The good person inevitably acts in ways that are appropriate and fair-minded and just. In that sense, Luke's congregation would hear nothing particularly new or unique.

What does make the sermon distinctively Christian is the way Luke grounds the appeal he makes. *Christian* character stems from the awareness that Jesus is indeed Lord (v. 46) and from the overwhelming experience of the mercy of God (v. 36). What is being served here by a 'good' character (by the healthy tree) is not the city-state, the corporation or even the family. Instead, the Christian serves the one named 'Lord'.

In connection with this larger sense of the Christian character, v. 48 cries out for an allegorical interpretation along the lines of Eph. 2.20, in which Christ is the corner-stone and the apostles and prophets become the foundation. The analogy does not work, of course, as is clear immediately in Luke from the difficulty that arises when we read that the man in the story himself 'laid the foundation'. Nevertheless, in some profound sense the sermon recalls that it is God's own action in Jesus Christ that enables the development of a character that will act in accord with Jesus' will. BG

Proper 4

(Sunday between 29 May and 4 June inclusive, if after Trinity Sunday)

I Kings 18.20–21 (22–29), 30–39 or I Kings 8.22–30, 41–43; Galatians 1.1–12; Luke 7.1b–10

I Kings 18.20–21 (22–29), 30–39

The books of Kings are rightly so called, in that they are structured around accounts of the kings (and one queen, Athaliah), who ruled Judah and Israel during the tenth to the sixth centuries BC. Scholars debate how reliable this material is in historical terms, but that need not be a major concern in these notes.

The Old Testament readings for the next six weeks come from some of the most vivid stories in the whole Bible. Only extracts are appointed to be read, but if at all possible you should make time to read these extracts in their larger context – most of the biblical chapters are self-contained. The central characters are not kings, but two prophetic figures, Elijah and Elisha. But it is also stressed, from the first introduction of Elijah at 17.1 onwards, that the words and actions of these two prophets must be seen against the background of their usually stormy relation with the king of the time. That king in most of the stories was Ahab, pictured both in this block of material (1 Kings 16.30) and elsewhere (e.g. 2 Kings 21.3, 13) as the model of what a king should not be. At just one point he is presented more favourably (1 Kings 21.27–29, not included in the lectionary passages). It is striking that Ahab is the first king of Israel to be specifically mentioned in non-biblical sources, from which we would judge that he was competent and successful. We are reminded that our stories have a particular agenda to pursue.

The present chapter has two interwoven themes: a devastating drought, which has reduced the land to desolation; and false worship introduced by Ahab's wife Jezebel, who came from Sidon. Drought was a recurrent risk in Palestine, but for the writer this drought reflected the LORD's anger concerning false worship. A contest is to be held to see which God has control over the elements: Yahweh the God of Israel, or Baal, with his large entourage of prophets. In vv. 22–29 the tone is mocking; the Baal prophets work themselves up into a frenzy in their attempt to gain their god's attention, the aim, implied though never explicitly stated, being to bring rain. It is important to recognize the element of mockery; it would be unwise to treat this as a balanced picture of how Baal prophets always acted.

The last part of our passage brings out a deliberate contrast. Usually in the books of Kings any practice of sacrificial worship other than at Jerusalem is condemned, but the status of Elijah allows an exception, just as in the story itself the power of Yahweh overrides commonsense precautions. Precious supplies of water were poured into the trench. And then, at Elijah's simple entreaty, a vivid contrast with the desperate efforts of the Baal prophets, fire comes, and consumes everything – even the water (v. 38)! The set reading ends before the bloody conclusion is reached, with the slaughter of the Baal prophets. The remainder of the chapter tells of the arrival of the long-awaited rain, presaged by the phrase which has passed into English usage, the sight of a cloud 'no bigger than a man's hand' (v. 44). RC

I Kings 8. 22–30, 41–43

1 Kings 8 is a very long chapter. The three previous chapters have described the construction of the temple in Jerusalem. Now it is completed, and our reading picks up two themes. The first, in the bracketed verses, describes the actual dedication of the temple. In 2 Sam. 7 there is a tension between the understanding of God as being associated with a small movable shrine, the ark, and the construction of a fixed dwelling-place. The tension is said to be removed when the ark is brought into the temple; in fact nothing more is known about the ark. The temple and its ideology now becomes dominant. That is where 'the glory of the LORD', pictured as if it were a material substance, was to be located.

The required part of today's reading, however, takes the construction of the temple for granted, and is concerned with the prayer uttered by Solomon at its dedication. Notice first that the prayer is spoken by Solomon himself, not by any minion. Kingship was itself regarded as a religious office, and the temple was a royal building; some have even called it a royal chapel. (It may be helpful to remember that its dimensions were quite modest; it would be wrong to envisage anything comparable in scale with the great cathedrals of Christendom.)

The whole of Solomon's prayer touches on many points, but in the selection made for this reading the particular emphasis is on the tension within the idea of a God who cannot be contained in heaven, even the highest heaven, and who yet has a special care for a particular people. So vv. 22–26 stress that Solomon is regarded as the heir to the promise made to David, which is found in 2 Sam. 7. But in vv. 27–30 there is a wider perspective. While there is a special concern for the house where God's 'name' dwells (this idea of the 'name' signifying the divine presence is found often in this chapter), God's presence is not to be confined to the temple.

This is a tension that is perhaps even more acute in the modern world, and it is good for Christians to reflect on their understanding of a God whom they regard as both special to Christianity and also as the unique ruler of the whole universe. An example of what this kind of tension may mean concludes the reading. The conviction is expressed that foreigners may wish to join with Israel in the worship of this God; their prayers too are to be welcomed and accepted. It hardly needs to be emphasized that here is another issue that is of fundamental importance for all those who adhere to the great monotheistic faiths – Judaism, Christianity, Islam – in the contemporary world. RC

Galatians 1.1–12

With this passage Paul begins one of his most agitated letters to a church community. Paul's strength of feeling is clear even in the first few verses. On one level, the letter begins as we would expect, with a salutation from Paul to the church ('Paul, an apostle . . . to the churches of Galatia: Grace to you and peace'). On another level, however, this opening is far from usual. Paul omits entirely the small complimentary phrases describing the church that we find elsewhere. For example, in 1 Cor. 1.2 the church is described by Paul, among other things, as 'sanctified in Christ Jesus' and 'called to be saints'. Here the community is simply addressed as the churches of Galatia. Also missing is the section of thanksgiving in which Paul praises God for the people to whom he writes (see e.g. 1 Cor. 1.4: 'I give thanks to my God always for you . . .'). In this opening section we get a clear insight into Paul's anxiety about the Christian community in Galatia. The reason for Paul's agitation becomes apparent almost immediately. The Galatians have begun to doubt Paul's ministry and, even more importantly, the gospel he preached to them. This letter is a defence of the gospel that Paul announced to the Galatians and also of his right to preach it.

This passage begins and ends with a direct reference to Paul's relationship with Jesus. In Gal. 1.1 he defines the title 'apostle' by which he introduces himself ('Paul, an apostle'). The reason he can use such a title is not because he has been sent from any human being nor through any human agency but because he has been sent through Jesus Christ and God the Father. In the same way Paul has not derived the gospel that he preaches from any human source but directly as a result of a revelation of Jesus Christ (v. 12). This direct encounter with Christ is what defines the whole of Paul's ministry and is what gives him the confidence to speak in the way that he does. There is no doubt in Paul's mind that his ministry and message come directly from Christ himself. This is important for understanding Paul. He can come across as arrogant and irascible, refusing to hear anyone's viewpoint other than his own. Take for example in this passage v. 9, where he says, 'If anyone proclaims to you a gospel contrary to what you received, let that one be accursed!' What may be seen as arrogance is here revealed to be supreme confidence instilled by his encounter with the risen Christ.

Passages such as this give us an insight into one of the key questions facing the early Christian community. The issue of authority was vital for the early Church and Paul encounters it even more keenly than its other leaders. In the earliest communities authority was given to eyewitnesses of Jesus and most of all to the disciples themselves. Paul was neither a disciple nor even an eyewitness. In many cases the communities to whom Paul ministered questioned his authority, and we cannot blame them for doing so. In this passage Paul addresses this issue head on. Both his authority and his message come from Christ himself. Paul's response to his opponents provides a lesson on the true nature of Christian authority, which lies not in human beings or institutions but with Christ.

Although on the surface this passage, and the rest of the Epistle, are a defence of

Paul's authority in the early Church, something even more important is going on. What really troubles Paul is not their rejection of him but their desertion of 'the one who called you in the grace of Christ' (v. 6), that is God himself. Paul makes very clear that the choice for the Galatians is not a choice of two gospels, Paul's gospel and a different one, but a choice of loyalty to God or desertion of God. For Paul the choice is as stark as that. There simply is not another gospel, no matter who announces it. The reason for his confidence is, as we noted above, his encounter with the risen Christ. It is this encounter, and nothing else, that forms the bedrock of the Christianity that we still follow. PG

Luke 7.1b–10

There is first a question that affects the tone of the story: concerning the identity of the person healed. What was his level in society? The story of the centurion's servant, as it is called, has a parallel in Matthew (8.5–13). There, however, the word used for the sick one is *pais* rather than *doulos* ('slave'); it can mean 'child' as easily as 'servant' (though the centurion uses 'slave' in his demonstration of his authority in Matt. 8.9). If Luke knew Matthew, he may have been led by this latter verse to take the sick man himself to be the centurion's slave. In John's very similar story (4.46–54), the one healed is unequivocally a son. In either case, it is clear that the sick person is valued, whether it is for his own sake or for his usefulness.

But Luke's version gets its special slant and context from v. 5: the centurion has donated a synagogue in the town of Capernaum, perhaps the one excavated in recent years, sometimes referred to confidently as 'the centurion's synagogue'. For a mere centurion (not a high-ranking officer) to make such a gift would involve generosity of heroic proportions. So, though there are cases of similar donations in the period by (high-class) Gentile benefactors, it may be that Luke's interest is that we should see this man in a special light: as a kind of God-fearer, that is, a Gentile with an attraction towards Judaism, its morality, piety and writings. He would then be a first instance of a category of person that Luke attends to in Acts: notably in the centurion Cornelius in Acts 10 – also giver of alms, to the Jews of Caesarea – and Lydia (Acts 16.14). What is more, Luke is keen, at all available points (from Pilate onwards), to show Romans as well disposed not only to Judaism but even more towards Jesus – which the centurion in our passage has every reason to become. Maybe Luke wanted to reassure possible Roman converts to Christian allegiance or perhaps to encourage other Christians who might be fearful of Roman authority. But more specifically, Luke is keen to see members of the border-line category of persons, the God-fearers, between Jewish and Gentile in allegiance, as coming under Jesus' aegis. It is not unlikely that they were particularly attracted by the Christian mission in Luke's day: the Church offered them an equality of membership that Judaism could not. In our present passage, Jesus himself may be seen as the practical benefactor to such a one, though the man's response of 'faith' (v. 9) is, in the story, limited to being a belief in Jesus' healing power. But to the reader, such faith would represent something much more far-reaching. The centurion represents, already in Jesus' lifetime, one of Luke's steps towards the mission to all humankind – a foretaste of God's universal purpose of salvation through Jesus (cf. 2.32), of which Luke will demonstrate the realization, stage by stage, as Acts unfolds. LH

Proper 5

(Sunday between 5 and 11 June inclusive, if after Trinity Sunday)

I Kings 17.8–16 (17–24) or I Kings 17.17–24; Galatians 1.11–24; Luke 7.11–17

I Kings 17.8–16 (17–24)

Last week's reading follows today's passage, which can be seen as establishing Elijah's credentials. He had been introduced in v. 1 of this chapter without explanation as someone with direct access to the king, and one whose words are fulfilled: he announces a drought. Just as Jezebel was attempting to bring the alien power of Baal from Sidon into Yahweh's land, so Elijah is here commanded to show Yahweh's power in Sidon.

Verses 17–24 in many ways are a separate episode within the larger story. In the preceding verses the boy whose death is here described had been saved from starvation, along with his mother. Even when the woman is lamenting his death, she does not blame Elijah but regrets that he should have been required to bring her sin to remembrance. The writer seems to take it for granted that the woman's sin might have led to the son's death.

All this is preliminary; God's power, and the way it can be manifested through the prophet's actions, are demonstrated in the resuscitation of the child. Later tradition has sometimes used this story as an example illustrative of belief in a future life, but that issue is not actually raised here. The child is brought back to life and – though we hear nothing more of him – we are clearly meant to suppose that he then lived a normal life and died in full age. (Presumably the same is true of the widow's son at Nain in today's Gospel reading, which is largely based on this story.) The important issue that our story-teller wishes to bring out is the recognition by the woman – a widow and a foreigner, and thus among the least esteemed in that patriarchal world – of the power of the God of Israel at work through Elijah. In this first chapter Elijah's credentials are established, and it is not surprising that he became regarded in later Old Testament books as *the* typical prophetic figure (Mal. 4.5), and ranked along with Moses in the story of Jesus' transfiguration in the New Testament (Mark 9.4–5). RC

Galatians 1.11–24

Many a student essay has set out to reconcile or dovetail the autobiographical details in this passage and the beginning of ch. 2 with the narrative of Acts, and the exercise is no doubt salutary. But what lies behind the historical problem is more important still: that is, Paul's purpose in telling this tale, alongside Luke's design in the book of Acts. It seems undeniable that, for good Christian reasons, Luke was out to give the highest place to Christian harmony and essential agreement and, in that cause, to present Paul as one at heart with the mother church in Jerusalem. From Luke's distance, towards the end of the first century, and perhaps from a good desire to see these heroes as all exemplary, this is how things should be seen. For Paul, in the midst, they felt different, and other considerations loomed large.

His mission, even in remote Galatia, was under attack from the headquarters church in Jerusalem and its supporters, for he admitted Gentile converts, as it seemed, on the cheap and in defiance of the true nature of the Jesus-movement. It was, after all, undeniably a movement Jewish in roots and in character: to join it was to become a Jesus-following Jew. But Paul believed otherwise. His call by Jesus, intense in power and intimacy, was to 'preach him among the Gentiles' (v. 16). and it bypassed all other considerations. Yet Paul's Jewish credentials were impeccable (v. 14) – he was no maverick, no ignoramus. It was simply that the Jesus he had opposed had turned him round – a full 180 degrees. His revolutionary call was itself reminiscent of that of a prophet of old.

Yet it is not hard to see how deviant and even self-obsessed he must have seemed. No negligible figure, he had nevertheless let three years go by before visiting those he had formerly harried – Peter, James and the rest. And it seems that, once they met, their relations were good: it says much for the leaders' discernment and generosity of soul. He spent a fortnight consulting Peter (v. 18) ('visit' is too weak a word for *historesai*); perhaps this was when he learnt something of Jesus' life and teaching (cf. 1 Cor. 7.10; 9.14; 11.23–25). But it must be admitted that what we see is a small fruit of a fortnight's talk. Paul's shape of mind led him to 'major' almost wholly on the central gospel facts of Jesus' death and resurrection.

It is a story of great emotional complexity, putting us in mind of recurrent problems of how to deal with whirlwind figures who might after all have gospel truth on their side. We may surely feel how fortunate it was that the damping down of Paul was, apparently, not sought at first and, for a range of reasons, unsuccessful; though at times his mission got through by the skin of the teeth. LH

Luke 7.11–17

As elsewhere in the Gospels, stories intensify in character as one leads to another. So now the servant of 7.1–10 becomes a son, sickness becomes death, and the centurion gives way to a widow, with her life's support now removed. Widows in ancient society were among the most vulnerable of beings. Here, as elsewhere, Jesus meets crying need by the power of his commanding word. We note that here nobody asks Jesus to act and nobody involved is said to have 'faith' to elicit his sovereign deed. His sheer presence is enough and his power is given freely.

The story reminds us of those of both Elijah and Elisha (1 Kings 17.9, 17–24; 2 Kings 4.32–37), where the dead children of widows are raised. So the prophets' mantle descends now on the Messiah, as the transfiguration will soon make abundantly clear (Luke 9.28–36). This raising from the dead is in Luke alone, accompanying that of Jairus' daughter in 8.40–56, derived from Mark. So it fortifies this theme as John was to do even more impressively in the case of Lazarus (John 11.1–44).

In Christian reading and preaching, these stories come across partly as items alongside other stories of Jesus' bringing in of the kingdom (which exorcism is said specially to exemplify, Luke 11.20), and our story serves as part of the evidence that Jesus presents to the disciples of John the Baptist in the following episode (7.22). They also come across, necessarily, as foreshadowing Jesus' own rising from the dead, foretold in 9.22 and referred to, more obscurely, in 13.32 and 16.31: so we are led to look towards the culmination of his messianic mission. LH

Proper 6

(Sunday between 12 and 18 June inclusive, if after Trinity Sunday)

I Kings 21.1b–10 (11–14), 15–21a or 2 Samuel 11.26—12.10, 13–15; Galatians 2.15–21;
Luke 7.36—8.3

I Kings 21.1b–10 (11–14), 15–21a

Elijah is not mentioned in 1 Kings 20, and parts of ch. 19 form next week's reading, but here we have one of the most powerful illustrations of the tension between king and prophet – the story of Naboth's vineyard. As with the story of the sacrifice on Mount Carmel (ch. 18) it is very clear that one of the purposes of the story-teller is to establish the distinctiveness of Israel, its God and its traditions, over against the surrounding peoples. How far this really was the case, and how far it was a matter of special pleading, is much debated within contemporary biblical scholarship. Given that attempts are made in some quarters to link the modern-day state of Israel with biblical Israel, it is not difficult to see the relevance of this debate to some of the tensions in the world of today.

Turning to the specific story here told, nothing else is known of Naboth, but he was clearly a figure of at least local importance. Peasants did not own vineyards, and it was accepted quite readily that he might be at the head of the local assembly (v. 9). So this story should not be taken as an example of that frequent prophetic theme, the oppression of the poor by the rich. Rather, it seems that another tension familiar from today's world is here involved: the power of central authority over against local custom. Though the stoning to death of Naboth cannot be excused, much of the rest of the story might be retold in a way that would picture him as an obscurantist standing in the way of progress.

That, of course, is not the viewpoint of our story-teller. In the conflict between royal claims and the prophetic tradition represented by Elijah, Elijah is consistently taken to be the true bearer of God's will, and at the end of our reading and in the following verses a drastic fate is threatened for Ahab. Curiously, however, that is not the whole story, for in vv. 27–29 quite a different tradition is reported – the repentance of Ahab. There is no other tradition relating to this, but it may serve as a warning against the tendency to assume that biblical characters are pictured as wholly good or wholly evil. The biblical world, like the contemporary world, is more complex than that. RC

2 Samuel 11.26—12.10, 13–15

The story of the succession to David for the most part avoids passing judgement on the actions of the characters involved, but here we have a rare exception. We are told that 'the thing that David had done displeased the LORD'. Perhaps the final editor wanted to make certain that readers and hearers got the message right.

However that may be, there follows a parable. Christian readers may associate parables particularly with the teaching of Jesus, but they are found in a variety of religious traditions. Like some of the more extended parables of Jesus this story engages in deliberate exaggeration in order to make the point more vividly. Nathan's story is told in such a way that in effect it demands an immediate response. The king asserts that justice must be done in such a case. Nathan's response is brilliant: 'You are the man!' David is condemned out of his own mouth.

We know little in detail about the status of figures like Nathan who came to be regarded as prophets, but certainly in this story his authority seems to be unquestioned. He is able to spell out all that God had done for David (vv. 7–9), again with a measure of exaggeration (Saul's wives?). This enables him to warn David of the disasters that now lie ahead (vv. 10–12). There is no suggestion that Nathan is under threat when he makes these devastating announcements. Perhaps the intention is to set out with approval the ability of David to recognize when he had done wrong. This provides a contrast with the attempts of later kings such as Ahab who tried to silence the prophet Elijah and others who spoke against them. Certainly our reading ends in the most edifying way, with David acknowledging that he has done wrong. He is assured of God's forgiveness without any requirement that he should offer any form of sacrifice. RC

Galatians 2.15–21

In Gal. 2.15–21, Paul turns to his main argument of the Epistle. Until this point he has been setting out his own credentials as an apostle but here he begins to draw out the theology that underpins the rest of the Epistle. This section functions almost as a table of contents and summary of the rest of Paul's argument. In it he lays out his major points and shows what he thinks about them. The problem is that, because this is a summary of his argument in the rest of the Epistle, the passage only makes sense when read in the light of the whole. Paul unpacks the comments he makes here in the remaining chapters of Galatians. Anyone who wants to get to grips with this passage should read to the end of the Epistle and then return to 2.15–21 afterwards.

Paul's opponents in Galatia were, like Paul himself, Jewish Christians. The point of disagreement between them was whether the Gentiles who converted to Christianity should follow Jewish law or not. In other words Paul questioned whether it was necessary for a Gentile to become a Jew in order to be a Christian. The whole issue was illustrated by circumcision. Circumcision was the first and most demonstrable act of living by Jewish law that a (male) Gentile convert would be expected to undertake. Paul's argument in Galatians began with the practical details of whether a Gentile should be expected to be circumcised after conversion to Christianity but from there moved outwards into a debate about the theology that underpinned this expectation.

In vv. 15–16 Paul makes a statement upon which all Jewish Christians are agreed. They are Jewish by birth and hence differentiated from Gentiles and, more importantly, justification occurs not through works of the law but through faith in Jesus Christ. Upon these two points it seems that Paul and his opponents are in perfect agreement. There is no implication in Galatians that any Jewish Christians thought that they or anyone else would be justified by 'doing works of the law' such as circumcision. The question arises, therefore, about why they were insisting upon circumcision if they did not think it would affect the status of the person concerned. In order to make sense of this we need to ask why Jews in the first century obeyed the law. It seems fairly clear from the literature of first-century Judaism that Jews of the period did not think that doing the works of the law would alter their relationship with God. An interesting quotation from the Jewish historian Josephus illustrates this: 'It is not possible for men to return thanks to God by means of works, for the Deity stands in need of nothing and is above any such recompense' (*Antiquities of the Jews*, 8.111). Instead Jews obeyed the law out of gratitude to a God who loved them and acted on their behalf. Following the law was something that indicated grateful acceptance of what God had done for them. Jewish Christians, according to v. 16, believed that they were justified by Christ and expressed their gratitude at this in the way that they knew, which was by following Jewish tradition.

Verse 17 turns to the points of disagreement between Paul and his opponents. It is here that the condensed nature of Paul's argument leads to confusion about what he really means. Perhaps the simplest way of understanding this very complex passage is to try to hear in our heads the other half of the conversation between Paul and his opponents. Here we have Paul's response but not what the opponents said to him first. The language he uses implies that his opponents are accusing Paul and his followers of sin, presumably because they are not following the law. Paul's response is that the real sin is going back to an old order rather than living fully in the new one. Through Christ's death and resurrection, Christians now live in a new order 'in Christ', no longer in the old order, 'through works of the law'. The sinners therefore are not Paul and his followers but his opponents.

In this passage Paul demonstrates that Christianity is much more far-reaching than the Jewish Christians who oppose him have realized. They recognize that justification comes through Christ but believe that the appropriate response to that was an old response, that of following the law. Paul argues here that this is not possible. The new order established by Christ's death and resurrection is entirely new. Those justified by Christ also live in Christ and Christ in them. The things of the old order cannot feature in this new life in Christ. PG

Luke 7.36—8.3

The version of this beautiful story found in Luke has two foci. On the one hand, two sinners, coming from different circumstances, meet Jesus, and their responses stand in sharp contrast to each other. On the other hand, Jesus is depicted as a unique prophet who is able to see below the surface of things, who teaches, and who forgives sins. No sermon faithful to the text can avoid either focus, and yet particular attention to one or the other may be appropriate.

First, there are the two sinners. One is a nameless woman, who did not accidentally wander in from the streets and happen upon Jesus but who came prepared, with her alabaster jar of ointment. She is identified by the narrator, by Simon, and by Jesus as a sinner, but we are not told what qualified her for such a label. To speak of her as a prostitute is to engage in useless speculation.

The woman says nothing but does plenty – weeping, bathing, kissing and anointing Jesus' feet and wiping them with her hair. Her action fulfils the hospitality neglected by the host, but much more. The parable of Luke 7.41–42 and v. 47 suggest that her lavish display of affection is the result of her having already been forgiven. At some point she has heard a word of divine pardon, and her deep sense of gratitude prompts an extravagant response, in spite of the hostile, critical context. Jesus' statement to her in 7.48 is a necessary (in light of the scepticism of Simon) confirmation of her forgiveness. She has returned like the Samaritan leper to give thanks for her newfound life (see 17.11–19).

The other sinner is Simon the Pharisee. We should anticipate his negative reaction to the woman's extravagance, since the narrator has already made the telling comment that while tax collectors in receiving John's baptism acknowledge the justice of God, the Pharisees by refusing John's baptism reject God's purpose for themselves (7.29–30). The woman has accepted the divine verdict on her life and has received divine pardon. Simon, on the other hand, simply finds such grace offensive and takes the woman's presence at the dinner to be a scandalous intrusion.

Simon's criticism is not spoken aloud, and in fact is aimed more at Jesus' acceptance of the woman's behaviour than at the woman herself (7.39). If Jesus is a prophet, surely he should know about the woman and not let her carry on so shamefully. But then follows Simon's exposure – a simple parable that functions like a trap to snare the unsuspecting predator (7.41–43). Whether Simon failed to get the point of the parable or not, we are not told, but Jesus offers an explanation contrasting the lavish behaviour of the woman with Simon's failure to provide even the basic elements of hospitality (7.44–47).

The two sinners provide a striking contrast. It may be difficult for contemporary audiences to identify fully with either character. The woman is so stigmatized by her sins as to be a public figure, and Simon comes across as a blind, smug religionist, who cannot perceive the genuine gratitude of a forgiven woman. Yet the two figures retain their cutting edge. Like the parable Jesus tells, they serve to expose our modern moralisms and dramatize for us an authentic response to divine grace.

The story of the two sinners makes sense only in light of the words and actions of Jesus, who throughout the whole of Luke 7 functions as a prophet (v. 39). Three features of his prophetic role are highlighted here: his discernment of Simon's unspoken criticism (v. 40), his teaching the truth about the current predicament (vv. 40–47), and his pronouncement of divine forgiveness (vv. 48–49).

Even so, to depict Jesus as a prophet is not somehow to reduce his authority to the level of other prophets and to minimize his uniqueness. Jesus fulfils the promise given to Moses about the raising up of a prophet (Deut. 18.15, 18), and his words become decisive for the destiny of the people of God (see Acts 3.22–23). The rhetorical question of those at table, 'Who is this who even forgives sins?' (Luke 7.49), hangs in the air for the reader to decide.

It is intriguing in the parable Jesus tells to find forgiveness of sins depicted by forgiveness of debts, an experience no doubt well known to Galilean peasants. Their whole lives as well as their futures were bound up with their fiscal obligations. Pardon of debts, then, has nothing to do with guilt but rather with the restoration of life and the renewal of hope.

The suggested reading for this Sunday goes on to include 8.1–3, one of Luke's typical summaries. In many ways it serves to introduce a new section more than it does to conclude ch. 7. It includes among Jesus' followers not only the Twelve, but also three women by name and 'many others' who serve as benefactors to the group. There is no historical or literary reason to connect the nameless woman of 7.36–50 whose sins are forgiven with Mary Magdalene, 'from whom seven demons had gone out' (8.2). CC

Proper 7

(Sunday between 19 and 25 June inclusive, if after Trinity Sunday)

I Kings 19.1–4 (5–7), 8–15a or Isaiah 65.1–9; Galatians 3.23–29; Luke 8.26–39

I Kings 19.1–4 (5–7), 8–15a

Once again we are taken back to an earlier episode in the story of Elijah. The threat to his life posed by Ahab and Jezebel is mentioned at the outset, and there is reference to the persecution of prophets by the Israelites in general (vv. 10, 14), but this really forms the background to our story rather than its main thrust. Those interested in geographical matters will notice that whereas the main tradition about Elijah places him in the northern kingdom of Israel, here he is found at Beersheba, in the far south of Judah (v. 3). More important is the 'theological geography' which brings him to Mount Horeb like a second Moses.

Links with the stories told of Moses are very close. As in Exod. 3, the setting is a solitary tree in the wilderness, where the faithful follower of God is visited by an angel (vv. 4–5). With the angel's support he comes to Horeb, the name for the holy mountain found also at Exod. 3.1. (The relation between Horeb and the more common name, Sinai, remains unknown; it is not even clear whether we should be thinking of different geographical locations or different literary modes of expression.)

If the early part of the story provides links with Exod. 3, its development is closer to Exod. 19—24. The vivid description of the elements (wind, earthquake, fire) is the kind of language regularly used when God is to be shown to worshippers (the technical term is a 'theophany'), but here they are the prelude to an even greater manifestation. The 'still, small voice' of older translations has become a well-known English expression; since the Hebrew phrase is almost a contradiction in terms ('sound of stillness') no translation can be wholly satisfactory.

In the last part of the story there are striking parallels with Exod. 32, where we are told of the apostasy of the people (cf. v. 14 here; it is striking that the story condemns 'the Israelites' rather than the foreign queen). The parallel is taken further in the following verses, with mass slaughter and the survival of a small faithful remnant, but the delicacy of those who compile lectionaries has excluded those verses from public reading. Overall, however, it is clear that the intention of the story is to present the role of Elijah as a second Moses, instrumental in making possible a new beginning for those chosen by God. RC

Isaiah 65.1–9

The reading falls into two parts. In the first (vv. 1–7) the Israelite nation is condemned because of its provocation of God. In the second (vv. 8–9) God promises that he will not reject the people utterly but will preserve some of them partly because of his promises to the ancestors of the people.

The remarkable opening words put the whole matter of election, the choice of Israel as God's special people, in a new light. It was not so much that God chose Israel, as that he constantly made himself available to a people that wilfully did not wish to know him. The mode of speaking implies that the nation was well aware of what God had done and was willing to do for them. In Rom. 10.20–21 the words are understood differently, and taken to refer to the Gentiles who have come to know God through Christ, even though they were not seeking God. Verses 3–5 indicate the ways in which the Israelites have spurned God. They list what the Old Testament regards as pagan practices, although not all can be identified for certain. Sacrificing in gardens probably refers to fertility rites, while offering incense on bricks may be a Babylonian custom. To sit in a tomb was probably to commune with the dead, and this may also be what spending the night in secret places (v. 4) means. Eating pork (v. 4b) offends one of the best-known prohibitions in Judaism. Here, and in connection with the 'broth of abominable things' the reference may be to religious rather than merely dietary practices. Not content with these abuses the people put themselves on a higher religious plane than other nations and say, 'I am too holy for you.' The language is obviously exaggerated. Not *all* Israelites behaved in this way, which is why v. 8 recognizes that something can be rescued from the wayward nation that has been threatened with such dire punishment (vv. 6–7). The reference to 'my chosen' and 'my servants' in v. 9 is ironical in view of the fact that the passage concerns the obtuseness of the chosen nation. But the passage expresses the hope that somehow God will find a way to make his people desire what he promises, and love what he commands. JR

Galatians 3.23–29

Paul the Jew, but now Christ's apostle, must do justice to both God's age-old gifts to his people and his new bestowal of himself in Christ. In particular, Paul, unlike other Christian leaders (chs. 1—2), is wholly convinced that Christ's inclusiveness puts Jews and Gentiles on precisely the same footing. Elsewhere, he expresses this vividly, by seeing him as a new Adam, i.e. going behind Israel's beginnings and special status, grounded in Abraham and Moses. In Christ, God starts the human race off, all over again. In this letter, 6.10 makes the point: there is a new creation.

All the same, the old dispensation cannot be written off as if it had been no more than a divine aberration. In its way, it retains its force and is still a source of pride. For all their newness, the Christian Gentiles are drafted into the 'offspring of Abraham' (3.29) and fulfil the promise to him that in him all nations would find a blessing (Gen. 12.3). It was a promise easily overshadowed in the practicalities of Jewish life – and Jewish survival. More precisely, the law, post-Abraham, created in practice a massive obstacle for both Jews and Gentiles when it came to the blessing's fulfilment. Did it in fact still, in the light of Christ, have any positive role? Yes, says Paul, it had at the least an educative or 'nannying', including a disciplinary, role – to prepare (whom? Israel? the world? all of us?) for Christ who has inaugurated a whole new framework, where 'faith' is the determining factor and freedom the outcome; belief, self-surrender, the new dispensation, takes over the central role for our relating to God. In terms of the image, maturity has arrived.

This new basis sets all on one and the same footing in relation to God, through Christ: regardless of race, class and gender. Verse 28 is Paul's most comprehensive statement of this vision, including, unlike 1 Cor. 12.13, the matter of gender. How it worked out in practice in his communities we cannot tell. 1 Cor. 7.21 advises against Christian slaves stampeding for free status (and we know that the move did not always give the advantages in life that we would associate with it); and 1 Cor. 11.17ff. indicates that the richer Christians were not always to the fore in obliterating social gradations in the Church, and Paul chastises them for it. It may be that there was an eschatological dimension to the new equality. This is indeed how things would be at the end; in the meantime, the Eucharist should be its foretaste, though in everyday life the household must continue, with each doing his or her tasks in the role assigned. A little later, instructions were given under Paul's name to this effect: see Eph. 5.21—6.9; Col. 3.18—4.1. In these passages, we see that convention was to be sweetened by the bond of love. How much satisfaction there was in practice we cannot know. All the same, the true dream, however marred within Christian societies in the centuries ahead in every particular, keeps its freshness and its capacity to amaze and to challenge. In any case, it is easy to forget that Paul's vision is actually less one of social equality than of unity in Christ. Verse 27 may indicate that already baptism involved the outward ceremony of reclothing, to show how radical the move to the new life really is. LH

Luke 8.26–39

This story, not wholly congenial to many modern readers, appears in all three Synoptic Gospels, but the Common Lectionary chooses to expose it to public hearing only once every three years, placing it in the year of Luke. In his version, Matthew (8.28–34), who tended to be fastidious about stories involving gross physical aspects (he dropped Mark 7.31–37, with its use of spittle as a means of healing), reduced it by more than half, giving only the barest outline. But Luke was content to take over Mark's unusually long tale (5.1–20), lock, stock and barrel, making only a few changes of wording, order and detail.

Readers who do not inhabit a first-century mental world, where demons are a regular way of accounting for untoward events and exorcism a recognized way of attempting to deal with them, are liable to be bemused by this episode; and if they have a feel for animal rights, so much the worse. This Sunday is then a challenge, even a nightmare, for the preacher. The only reasonable and virtuous solution is to invite people to face the difference between the present majority culture in the West with that of the near East in the first century – a fact, whether one finds it possible to enter aspects of that ancient thought-world or not. As that issue lurks in many parts of Scripture but can often be sidestepped without too much difficulty (and is in any case full of anomaly), there is no harm in its having to be faced in a case such as this.

The omnipresence of demons, threatening humans and vying with God for control here below, came up in the preceding story of the calming of the storm. Here, it meets us head on, as a shocking scene unfolds. For all his (as it sometimes seems to us) urbanity of outlook, Luke has no trouble with this aspect of the world outlook of his day. He had taken over another Marcan story of exorcism at 4.31–32, and we find the same phenomenon in Acts, in 19.13–20; and in 8.14–21, Simon Magus had seen the apostles as in the same magical trade as himself – and Luke does not quite refute that basic assumption, simply making plain that the apostles are more effective.

Our story, whose precise location is uncertain in the textual tradition, seems to be set in Gentile territory, so giving a foretaste of Acts (cf. Luke 2.32). We see that this region in Jesus' day was part of the wider as well as the narrower world. On the one hand, a severely disturbed man (in our terms) is seen as packed with a whole Roman-style legion of demons – 6,000 at least; and then on the other hand, the demons are banished to a herd of pigs, ritually unclean in Jewish eyes, and so a fit place for their banishment and, as it turns out, destruction in the abyss. But however differently we might describe (mythologize?) an encounter with so sick a man, we are able to join forces with Luke in the final verse, thankful that 'God' can figure as the source of all good, in modern as well as ancient pictures of 'how things are'. LH

Proper 8

(Sunday between 26 June and 2 July inclusive)

2 Kings 2.1–2, 6–14 or 1 Kings 19.15–16, 19–21; Galatians 5.1, 13–25; Luke 9.51–62

2 Kings 2.1–2, 6–14

Most of the stories about Elijah have shown him in conflict with the royal court. Here, however, the concerns are different; indeed, it is not entirely clear whether we are intended to see the primary function of this story as rounding off the story of Elijah with an account of his departure, or as stressing the legitimacy of Elisha as Elijah's successor. (The two names, incidentally, sound confusingly similar in English, but are not so close in Hebrew, either in pronunciation or in structure.)

The double thrust of the story is apparent from the beginning. We are told that it is to be an account of the LORD taking Elijah 'up to heaven by a whirlwind'. (The word translated 'heaven' is the ordinary word for 'sky'; there is no necessary suggestion of a place of bliss, though that meaning came to be applied later.) It is also stressed throughout the story that Elisha accompanies his master and refuses to be parted from him. We may also note that vv. 3–5 speak of companies of prophets at various places, and this seems more characteristic of the stories about Elisha, who is regularly shown as the leader of an (often rather dim-witted) prophetic group, whereas Elijah is characteristically a loner.

Elijah's last miraculous action is to divide the waters of the Jordan just as Moses had divided the waters of the 'Red Sea'. This is surely a development of the parallel between the two figures which we noted last week when looking at 1 Kings 19. The concluding verses take the parallel further. Just as Moses had been buried in an unknown spot, so Elijah is taken from the people without their knowing the place. (Later in this same chapter [vv. 16–18] we are told of a rather crass attempt to find Elijah's burial-place.) In addition to these links, Elisha is the equivalent to Joshua, the successor of Moses; he also divides the Jordan waters just as Joshua had done (Josh. 3).

Overall, then, we may certainly say that an important part of this story is its concern to emphasize that even in unpropitious times a true succession of God's servants continues. In later tradition more attention came to be paid to the manner of the departure of Elijah, and the tradition developed that he had not died but had been taken to be with God. As belief in a future life developed in both Jewish and Christian traditions, the story of Elijah gained an important illustrative function. RC

1 Kings 19.15–16, 19–21

The reading is the conclusion of the story of Elijah on Mount Horeb, whence he has fled from the wrath of Queen Jezebel. The 'still small voice' of God instructs him on what to do when he returns to his country and, interestingly, these instructions touch upon Israel's arch-enemy Aram as well as on the northern kingdom, Israel, itself. Hazael was king of Aram from *c*.842–800 BC and left his mark in Assyrian records as well as the Bible. In 2 Kings 8.7–15 Elisha (not Elijah) is reported to have encouraged Hazael to assassinate Ben-hadad (probably Hadad-'izr). It is also Elisha, not Elijah, who causes Jehu to be anointed king of the northern kingdom, Israel (2 Kings 9.1–13). The fact that Elisha carries out the tasks commanded by God to Elijah indicates that these narratives in 1 and 2 Kings present difficult critical problems to historians. What is relatively secure is that prophetic groups in the ninth century did not shy away from fomenting revolution at home and abroad in the conviction that they were being faithful to God's commands. In the event, Hazael turns out to be more of a curse than a blessing for Israel. For while Jehu's revolution freed the people from the reign of the house of Omri, Jehu himself was humiliated by both Hazael and the Assyrian king, Shalmaneser III.

The incident of Elijah recruiting Elisha has superficial similarities with the Gospel for the day, which is no doubt why this Old Testament passage has been chosen. It is, in fact, more profound than its gospel parallel, for its point is that just as God is active in the political affairs of the nation, so he also takes steps to ensure that the prophetic word is safeguarded, and kept alive from one generation to the next. JR

Galatians 5.1, 13–25

In Galatians 5.1 Paul starts a new section rather abruptly. At the end of 4.31, Paul reminds Christians that they are descendants of Sarah the free woman, not Hagar the slave. Although the word 'free' in 4.31 clearly triggers Paul's reflections on freedom and the nature of Christian freedom, it is hard otherwise to work out what made him change subject so quickly. In one verse he explores the image of Sarah and Hagar as allegories of life in Christianity and life in Judaism; in the next he exhorts all Christians to act as though they are free. A link exists but Paul does not indicate the link in the text itself apart from through word association. Despite this sudden change of tone, 5.1 plays a pivotal role in the Epistle: it summarizes what Paul has been arguing up to this point and looks forward to what will come afterwards. It contains a two-part statement: a declaration and a command. In the declaration Paul gives a pithy summary of the Christian gospel, in the command he states what the effect of this should be on Christians. In other words Christ has set us free, so be free!

The remaining two chapters of the Epistle explore what this freedom is. It is a theme that Paul picks up particularly again in v. 13, where our lectionary passage resumes. It seems that the Galatians in common with many societies teetered between over-legalism on the one hand and libertinism on the other; between too much law and too little law. In this passage Paul reminds the Galatians that although they are not obliged to follow the Mosaic law they are bound firmly to one another in love. Thus he states the paradoxical nature of Christian freedom. True Christian freedom exists not in self-involved individualism but through community. Only in community can the freedom to which we are all called be worked out. Paul himself is fully aware of the irony of what he is saying here and draws this out at the end of v. 13: you are free only when you are 'slaves to one another'. Voluntary slavery to those around us is what grants us true freedom.

Paul backs up this point in a rather surprising way. Having spent most of Galatians arguing that those who are 'in Christ' should not do works of the law, Paul now cites a summary of the law to support his case: 'You shall love your neighbour as you love yourself' (v. 14). This quotation indicates that Paul's attitude to the law is more nuanced than simply being for or against it. Instead what he questions is what should be done in order to fulfil the law. Those who follow the law are required to observe all its commands but those who are 'in Christ' do not need to do so. This single command to love their neighbour as they love themselves is the fulfilment of the law. Another surprising feature of this quotation is that it appears alone. The common summary of the law, which Jesus cited in the Gospels, was love of God and love of neighbour. Here only the second element of this summary is given. Paul concludes this part of his argument with a warning about what will happen if they do not follow this command: those who bite and tear each other are likely to be eaten up.

Having established in brief outline what living a life of Christian freedom is like, Paul begins to explore it in more detail. Here he contrasts living by the Spirit with living by the flesh (v. 16). Paul seems to have in mind here two competing forces: the Spirit and the flesh. It is not possible to live by both at the same time. Although the NRSV translates this verse as two commands, one positive (live by the Spirit) and one negative (do not gratify the desires of the flesh); it is better understood as a command followed by a promise: live by the Spirit and you will not carry out the desires of the flesh. For Paul the contrast was clear: you cannot occupy both spheres, Spirit and flesh, at the same time. In vv. 17–25 Paul unpacks this further. These two forces are implacably opposed to each other and produce different effects. Paul outlines these effects by two catalogues, one of vices and one of virtues. The Galatians will be able to discern easily which one they live by according to the fruits they produce. In sum, however, the catalogue of virtues simply returns us to Paul's initial command to love one another. In the presence of love that binds a community together in Christian freedom, virtues such as peace, joy and patience will abound. PG

Luke 9.51–62

The passage marks a major development in Luke's narrative – in a number of perspectives. Most obviously, with regard to the structure of the Gospel, here Luke stops following Mark consecutively and only begins to do so again at 18.15. Older critics called this section, rather portentously, 'the greater interpolation'. Others call it the Lucan 'travel narrative'. It is true that it seems to cover Jesus' movement in the general direction of Jerusalem, and it begins with an important statement of resolute purpose; but purposive 'travel' is scarcely the main focus of these chapters. Their function in Luke's composition is to enable him to assemble a wide range of Jesus' teaching, some his own, much shared with Matthew (and occasionally Mark). It has been suggested that Luke ordered these items, not haphazardly, but reflecting the sequence in Deuteronomy – also a book about a purposive movement of God's people, to the land of promise. This may be confirmed if the reference in v. 51 to Jesus' being 'taken up' refers, as is likely, to his ascension, the triumphant climax, via the cross and resurrection, of his whole mission as God's Messiah, and our destiny too.

The rest of the passage concerns the call to receive or follow Jesus, which meets various kinds of reluctance (cf. the parable of the sower, 8.4–8). Samaritans refuse Jesus because he is not 'one of them'. In response, Jesus shows restraint (unlike Elijah, earlier man of God, in 2 Kings 1.10). In the rest of Luke-Acts, Samaritans are shown in a positive light: 10.25–37 and 17.11–18, and then in Acts 8, where Samaria is a specific and early stage in the Church's mission, following the programme in Acts 1.8. (Compare John 4: it looks as if Samaritans were a significant component of some parts of the very early Church.) In other words, in Luke's terms, Jesus is here staying his hand in view of positive good in store.

The rest of the passage is made up of three other instances of hesitation to respond to Jesus' call. The first two correspond to Matt. 8.19–22. They testify to a shockingly stringent picture of the urgency of the summons: it even takes precedence over basic pious duties, like seeing to one's father's funeral. So great is the urgency of the mission of the kingdom of God. It is a doctrine worked out, for example, in the restless haste that marks parts of Paul's journeys as he goes from city to city (e.g. Acts 14.19–26).

The final instance (in Luke alone) reproduces Elijah's call of Elisha (1 Kings 19.20, and we note that the latter was ploughing when the call came). Even Elisha's brief respite before obeying the call is now, it seems, not allowable: the day of decision is, emphatically, here. These sayings give the sharpest evidence we have of the urgent character of Jesus' mission. It is a far cry from the steady living of the Christian life, day by day (which Luke also understood, e.g. 9.23). Can we make a unity of both? LH

Proper 9

(Sunday between 3 and 9 July inclusive)

2 Kings 5.1–14 or Isaiah 66.10–14; Galatians 6.(1–6), 7–16; Luke 10.1–11, 16–20

2 Kings 5.1–14

The last in our series of readings from 1 and 2 Kings is the only one where Elisha is the central figure. We saw last week that he is pictured as Elijah's successor, but the traditions relating to him present his role in rather different terms. He is much more closely attached to the royal entourage, as is well illustrated by today's story, where Elisha is well acquainted with affairs at court.

The chapter begins with the remarkable claim, made in almost throwaway fashion, that Aramean military successes were due to Yahweh the God of Israel! We are introduced to Naaman, a chronic sufferer from a condition which most translations call 'leprosy', but was probably some perhaps rather embarrassing form of eczema. True leprosy was not known in this period.

In the rest of the story much is delightfully ironical. The present described in v. 5 is an enormous sum, the kind of amount that defeated nations would have to pay as tribute money; the (unnamed) king of Israel is pictured as a suspicious fool, seeing malice where none was intended. And then Naaman himself is too high and mighty to undergo the simple remedy prescribed by Elisha. (In some respects at least human nature remains remarkably unchanged.) There is probably no point in attempting to explore the rationale of the cure; the story was written in a context in which miraculous developments of this kind were regarded as a real possibility. It is not easy to spell out for a twenty-first-century reader what actually happened.

Though only vv. 1–14 are appointed as the official reading, you will get a fuller picture if you read the whole chapter. It concludes with another superb piece of irony – the fate of the grasping Gehazi (vv. 20–27). Before that, however, in vv. 15–19 a very important issue is raised in a seemingly naive way, as to whether Israel's God might properly be worshipped in a foreign country. ('Rimmon' was the name of an Aramean god.) It would be unwise to construct precise modern analogies, but the issue of inter-religious relations is still a live one. RC

Isaiah 66.10–14

The reading is part of a passage that begins at v. 5 and which explores in various ways the motif of childbearing. In vv. 10–11 the motif is employed initially to stress the certainty of Jerusalem's coming redemption. The present situation (of exiles who have returned to a ruined city) which causes people to mourn is like the preliminaries to childbirth. It will be transformed as surely as joy comes when the child is born (cf.

John 16.20–22). In v. 11 the image changes. Jerusalem becomes a mother who succours her inhabitants, and who will richly supply them when she is transformed. The word 'nurse' in v. 11 is misleading because it gives the impression that the inhabitants will do the nursing, when what is meant is that they will be nursed. The RSV 'that you may suck' better conveys the sense of the Hebrew. The further spelling out in v. 12 of the prosperity to be enjoyed (where 'suck' should again be read for 'nurse') draws upon the images of a river and an overflowing stream. In a land where water was scarce and the rainfall unpredictable, these are images of reliable and abundant fertility. In v. 13 the childbearing motif is altered again so that God becomes the mother who comforts Jerusalem and her inhabitants. The final verse of the reading repeats the promises in a general way. The vindication of Jerusalem, its prosperity and the confusion of its enemies will be signs of the power (hand) of God. Although the passage was directed to people who faced difficult material conditions, its poetic and visionary qualities require an interpretation that transcends the purely material. There is nothing wrong with hoping for a more prosperous world; but to be prosperous in the most profound sense it must include God. It must be the kingdom of God. JR

Galatians 6.(1–6), 7–16

In the final passages of his most outspoken letter, Paul begins to write in the form of semi-random jottings. That does not mean that his words are trivial or uncharacteristic of himself, more that he becomes somewhat aphoristic. He also becomes sharply relevant.

The first six verses express robust pastoral sense. In dealings with individuals, kindly repair is always better than ticking off. And mutual support is essential. As in 1 Corinthians, Paul shows his impatience with those pleased with their religiousness ('the spiritual'). The command to love lies in the background (cf. Rom. 13.9), though it is not actually stated. Verse 5 seems formally to contradict v. 2, but it speaks of modest contentment with one's gifts, whereas the earlier verse is about need.

Verses 7–10 concern the dynamics of personal morality: first the quelling of sin, and then the promoting of goodness. As elsewhere, Paul sees the two competing loyalties: 'flesh', internal to oneself and looking no further, and 'spirit' whose source is God, irrupting into the self and carrying one into new paths and new hopes ('eternal life'). Inevitably, the seeds of one's future are in one's present. But the essence of the moral life is simply – and, to our ears, perhaps narrowly – doing good, especially within the Christian community. Partly, this limitation is explained by the circumstances of the churches of Paul's day – new, small, self-aware – but partly it is a matter of moral realism, for it can be less testing to be good at large than at one's own hearth. All the same, it would be a shame to use this verse as a pretext for shunning Oxfam.

In the final verses, Paul apparently takes the pen from the scribe's hand, and his words tumble forth. They also repeat and summarize what he has said before. No acceptance of those who try to insist on making Gentile converts take on Jewishness. Jesus' cross stands in its own right and is all-sufficient. More than a new law or new basis of identity – it is a whole new start to everything (v. 15; cf. 2 Cor. 5.17). What does 'Israel' refer to here? Does Paul draw back and claim 'God's people status' for the Church in the language most deeply natural to him? Or is it a gesture of peace to those who make his mission so painful with their Judaizing, nearly driving him to despair? LH

Luke 10.1–11, 16–20

Following the call to respond to Jesus at the end of ch. 9, the theme now is mission; but whose and why and to whom? The passage is unique to Luke, but modelled on the instructions for the mission of the Twelve found in Mark 6.7–13 and in Matt. 10 – and reproduced in Luke 9.1–6 (in each case with minor though intriguing variations, especially about footwear).

There is a question why Luke included this passage in addition to that in the previous chapter. It may be that, in his historical way, he felt that the mission of the Twelve belonged to its place, in Jesus' lifetime, as indeed it plainly does in the narrative; and if symbolic of something wider than itself, then it was probably the Church's mission to Jews, whom the Twelve could represent. And for Luke, that certainly required balancing with a foreshadowing of the mission to the Gentiles of which he was the earliest chronicler, both with regard to its progress (Paul lands up in Rome) and its terms (see Acts 15). The hazards endured by the missionaries in Acts reflect the risk of crises referred to in Luke 10.3.

But why 70? Perhaps it was the belief that humanity was made up of 70 nations (see Gen. 10). But perhaps there was an allusion to the 70 elders of Israel in Exod. 24 and Num. 11, in which case the allusion to the Gentile mission is less clear and the duplication of chs. 9 and 10 is harder to understand. However, the point may be more narrowly ecclesiastical and, in the two missions, Luke may be prefiguring the apostles and the elders who are together in Acts as officers of the Church (11.30; 14.23; 15.2, 4). No doubt his first readers knew his code in a way that we do not.

It may seem a pedantic detail, but various good manuscripts give 72 rather than 70 as the number of those sent out. It is a multiple of 12 and indeed it reflects the Septuagint version of Gen. 10 – and it may be original. It would carry the thought of the Gentile mission as aiming at a perfection of a wider 'Israel' – not unlike aspects of Paul's vision at the end of Rom. 11 (as well as various Jewish texts, e.g. Isa. 60).

The final verses affirm, in Johannine language, the identity of Jesus' messengers with himself. So the evident success of their mission is the fulfilment of his own – and occasions the unique visionary experience mentioned in v. 18. We may, however, compare John 12.31 and 16.11; and, as involving sight of the heavenly world, the transfiguration and the angels at Jesus' birth and at his resurrection and ascension. In apocalyptic writings, both Jewish and Christian, the defeat of Satan is variously placed in the envisaged sequence of events; but the vanquishing of evil, however seen, is an essential element in the drama of salvation, assured to Christ's faithful ones (v. 20; cf. Phil. 3.20). LH

Proper 10

(Sunday between 10 and 16 July inclusive)

Amos 7.7–17 or Deuteronomy 30.9–14; Colossians 1.1–14; Luke 10.25–37

Amos 7.7–17

Verses 7–9 are the third of three visions, each of which indicates imminent and devastating judgement upon the northern kingdom, Israel. In the case of the first two visions, Amos intercedes for the people. 'How can Jacob stand? He is so small!' (7.2, 5). God relents and promises that the indicated judgement will not take place. Whether or not the vision of the plumb line indicates a judgement smaller in scope than those of the first two visions is hard to say. At any rate, it is not followed by an intercession from the prophet. The vision means that God is to establish a standard, a means of measuring behaviour. He will no longer be indifferent to how his people lives.

Verse 9, which restricts the coming judgement to the cultic centres and which makes explicit reference to Jeroboam II (782–747 BC) is an editorial transition to the prose account of the attempt to ban Amos from preaching in the northern kingdom. Whether or not Amos publicly predicted Jeroboam's violent death is uncertain. If he did, the prophecy was unfulfilled because, according to 2 Kings 14.29, Jeroboam died a peaceful death after a reign of 41 years, which saw him restore much of Israel's material greatness. The prophecy of Israel going into exile agrees with Amos 3.11–12 and 4.2–3, and would be sufficient to arouse hostility. It was also fulfilled in the events of 734–721, when the northern kingdom was reduced to nothing by the Assyrian Tiglath-Pileser III and his successors.

The attempt of Amaziah to silence Amos leads to a well-known, and much disputed, statement about Amos's relationship to prophets and prophecy. The NRSV margin offers the simple solution, that Amos says in effect, 'I was not a prophet nor a prophet's son; I was a herdsman, and the LORD took me from the flock and said, Go, prophesy.' Although this is attractive, and possibly correct, there is no 'was' in the original Hebrew, and the NRSV text is more faithful to the original. Another solution has presumed that by the word 'prophet' (Hebrew *navi'*), Amos understood someone belonging to a professional guild, and that he wished to dissociate himself from this idea. At the greatest extreme is the suggestion that 'I am no prophet' is a forceful way of saying 'I *am* a prophet'! The view that Amos is dissociating himself from 'professional' prophets can at least be justified by the fact that Amaziah twice used the verb for 'to prophesy' that is directly connected with the word for 'prophet'. Amos is saying, in effect, that he is not doing what Amaziah accused him of, that is, carrying out the normal activity of an institutional prophet.

It is as one called unexpectedly by God out of the tasks of daily living that Amos delivers his message of judgement. JR

Deuteronomy 30.9–14

This passage occurs in the context of God's promise to the people that he will gather them together in one place from all the parts of the earth to which they have been exiled. Although the literary setting of the passage is the threshold of the promised land following the exodus and the wanderings in the wilderness, its actual situation is probably that of the exile to Babylon in the sixth century BC, or that of the returned exiles to a devastated land. The promises of God are conditional upon the obedience of the people (v. 10) because it is the view of the deuteronomic writers that the disaster of the exile was divine punishment for the apostasy of the rulers of the nation and its inhabitants.

Verses 11–14 probably originally existed independently of the rest of the material. They are a noble passage about the availability of the commandment, by which is meant all that God has previously enjoined upon the people. It presumes objections: that the command is too difficult. In reply God (who is the speaker here) insists that the commandment is not remote but accessible and observable. However, the beautiful and poetic language, 'Who will go up to heaven for us...?' led later interpreters to understand the words differently. In Baruch 3.29–30 the verses are quoted in a hymn to Wisdom, which uses them to argue for the inaccessibility of Wisdom. Paul, in Rom. 10.6–7, sees in them a reference to the death and resurrection of Christ. For present purposes they are best taken as a noble statement of the immanence and transcendence of God. The potential remoteness of what comes from God (in heaven and across the sea) indicates his transcendence. His word of commandment being very close to us expresses his immanence. We cannot ascend to heaven or (from an Israelite point of view) cross the sea. Only because God draws near to us, can we draw near to him. JR

Colossians 1.1–14

The passage is far from being alone in the Pauline corpus in conveying a sense of the sheer energy of the early Christian movement, of which he was so significant a leader. Whichever way we look, dynamism is among the first impressions that we receive. As in other letters, in the formal greeting itself, the Christians in Colossae have the high dignity of 'saints'; that is, full members of God's own people. It is a word used for Israel, a 'holy' people, signifying possession by God as a community rather than individual character as in later usage. Then the metaphor moves to that of household, the primary unit of Greco-Roman life: they are brothers and sisters in the Christian clan.

The following formal element, the thanksgiving, soon takes off in anything but formal directions. There is live interaction between the scattered communities that make up the Church – as indeed letters like this one themselves exemplify. It is marked by common *faith* and mutual *love* (v. 4), and by the sharing of *hope* of heavenly fulfilment (v. 5). Note the trio of key qualities, as in 1 Cor. 13.13. The movement is not a one-man show, but a team-enterprise. Epaphras (otherwise unknown) has been apostle to the Colossian church and no doubt to the others in the Lycus valley, at Hierapolis and Laodicea (see Col. 4.13).

In the final part of the passage (vv. 9–14), the writer turns, by way of prayer, to what is in effect a statement of some of his fundamental convictions, his way of seeing what the act of God in Christ has accomplished. It is no less than a transfer or release ('redemption') from 'the power of darkness' to the security and splendour of the rule of 'his beloved Son' (literally, 'the Son of his love'). The destiny, already assured and even given, not merely a promise for the future, is described as 'the inheritance of the saints (= holy ones) in light': perhaps it means that God's people share the status of the angels – all of his own, in heaven and earth, are one community. No wonder that the passage applies to the Church terms that echo the old hopes and assurances of Israel whose heir they are: 'inheritance'; messianic 'kingdom'. The union of heaven and earth, realized inside this Christian enclave within the human race, implicitly excludes the invisible powers hostile to God (whom Christ has defeated, Col. 2.15) and those on earth who refuse the gift in Christ; and this may seem heady stuff. Other Christian writings, including Paul in some passages (e.g. Rom. 11; 1 Cor. 15.22), have a more inclusive vision, or at least have a sense of a difficulty to be dealt with (e.g. Matt. 25.31–46). But wider embrace, though not absent, has not been a common Christian understanding until recent times.

The Christians' position is not one of mindless enthusiasm, but is marked by 'the knowledge of God's will, in all spiritual wisdom and understanding' (v. 9). These terms follow scriptural models and precedents, though there is no sense (as in modern times) that our knowledge of (or about) God can be somehow generated independently by the autonomous human mind. No, it is a divine gift, uniting giver and receiver. We 'know' as 'we are known' (cf. 1 Cor. 13.12); and true wisdom is that which unites us to him. It is about as unmodern an idea as can be imagined; so it is all the more worth troubling to get to the bottom of the sense and feel of it. LH

Luke 10.25–37

The good Samaritan is a preacher's gift. Its thrust is unmistakable. Even so, it repays thought. This first of a number of parables, not found elsewhere, which Luke included in these middle chapters of his Gospel, the good Samaritan started its *literary* life (whatever place it may have had in pre-Lucan tradition) as an illustrative but splendid addendum to Luke's treatment of the question and answer about the two great commandments, found also in Mark and Matthew. And in this Gospel, the lawyer is notably interested in action rather than theory: 'What shall I *do* to inherit eternal life?' (v. 25). And so is Jesus: 'This *do* and you will live' (v. 28) and 'Go and *do* likewise' (v. 37).

The practicality comes out vividly in the parable: loving the neighbour involves risk, trouble and expense. More, it means pushing conviction and prejudice aside. 'Who is my neighbour?' proved a costly question at a number of levels.

The meaning does indeed seem unmistakable. But, to get close, we should say what its meaning is *not*. For example, it is not an anti-clerical story. It is not about a simple layman who is virtuous when the clergy 'pass by' in the staring face of human need. In terms of the Jewish law and culture, priest and levite might plead their case. Their temple duties, for which they were bound, required the preserving of ritual purity, which contact with a (possible) corpse would ruin. But, in any case, 'priests' and 'levites' were not clergymen in any recognizable Christian or modern sense. Their role was hereditary, doing temple duty in their turn, but mostly living as small farmers.

Nor was the Samaritan simply 'doing good' in what we would call a 'neighbourly' sort of way. He was breaking an inherited taboo, and going beyond all recognizable obligation. For Jews and Samaritans, each group with its own tradition of the Law, Lev. 19.18 ('Thou shalt love thy neighbour as thyself') meant by 'neighbour' a fellow-Jew (or Samaritan). So there is a lesson in itself. The achievement of this story was extraordinary: to universalize beyond recall the whole idea of the command. It was Jesus' (and Luke's) greatest and most influential ethical victory. A gauntlet thrown down to us all.

There is a well-known twist in the story as Luke tells it. In v. 29, the neighbour is the one to be helped, the object of care; but in v. 36, he is the one who helps. Is this simply a little Lucan slip of writing (not alone)? And if so, did it perhaps come about when Luke inserted a pre-existing story? Who knows? But it could be that Luke was teaching, cleverly, a major lesson. To love one's neighbour is not a matter of in any way establishing superiority. Carer and cared for live in a mutuality of generosity and love. Doctor needs patient as much as patient needs doctor. Each does good to the other. Both meet in the symbiotic love of God. LH

Proper 11

(Sunday between 17 and 23 July inclusive)

Amos 8.1–12 or Genesis 18.1–10a; Colossians 1.15–28; Luke 10.38–42

Amos 8.1–12

The vision seen by Amos in vv. 1–2 is the fourth of a series of visions, the other three being described in 7.1–9. The incident of Amos's expulsion from Bethel (7.10–17) interrupts the series of visions. The prophet sees a basket full of summer fruits (Hebrew *qayits*) and is informed that the end (Hebrew *qets*) has come upon the people. The point can be made in another way. The summer fruits are the outcomes of a harvest; the nation is about to experience a grim harvest. Precisely what it is, is not stated, but the response to it is that the temple singers wail in mourning (for 'songs' a slight alteration of the Hebrew yields 'singers') as many dead bodies are taken to burial. War or plague may be the cause. The address to the oppressors of the poor (vv. 4–6) can be seen as the reason for the catastrophe. The Old Testament view of creation is that it includes the moral order. If this is abused there are dire consequences. Wrongdoing is not a private matter. It affects the world and human communities. The list of accusations contains a play on the words 'bring to ruin' (Hebrew *lashbît*) and sabbath (*shabbat*). The powerful prey on and profit from the misfortunes of the poor. Three scenes of judgement now follow (vv. 7–8, 9–10, 11–12). The first stresses the link between the moral and the natural order. The land ought to tremble and its inhabitants mourn because of the social injustices. God swearing by the 'pride of Jacob' (v. 7) is an unusual idea. At Ps. 47.5 the 'pride of Jacob' is the land of Israel. Whether 'pride' here means the land or the kind of 'pride' that humans have, it is ironic that God should swear by it, seeing that it merits punishment. The second scene involves the imagery of the 'day of the LORD' as conceived by Amos (cf. 5.18–20). The third scene raises the question why the people should be so concerned to seek for and to find the 'word of the LORD' when their disregard of it has been so blatant. Perhaps the catastrophes that will overwhelm the people will reduce their self-reliance to the point where they turn to God, as a last resort. In these circumstances, not to be able to find him will be the harshest judgement of all. JR

Genesis 18.1–10a

The stories relating to Abraham are essentially a series of separate units, held together by two recurring themes: the land where he was to settle, and the birth of an heir. Earlier, Abraham had been pictured as a wanderer moving from place to place; here he is a settled inhabitant, at the 'oaks of Mamre' near Hebron, the traditional burial-place of Abraham which is still held in reverence by modern Jews and Muslims.

Abraham is said to be visited by 'the LORD' (v. 1). Then quite unexpectedly, verse 2 refers to 'three men'. Christian theology of an earlier period saw in this a prefiguring of the Trinity; more recently and more prosaically scholars have seen the variation as indicative of more than one source. In fact no wholly satisfactory solution to the problem of the variation between one and three, which continues throughout the story, has ever been established.

It will in any case soon become clear that the concern of the visitation is the provision of an heir. Before that topic is raised, however, there are certain proprieties to be observed: proper hospitality is a recurring biblical theme. The preparations described in vv. 6–8 would in fact have taken several hours, but the story is told with such economy that we are tempted to envisage a fast-food setting. The narrator's concern is to stress that due hospitality was observed.

Previous chapters have described the birth of Ishmael to Hagar, taken by Abraham as a sexual partner at his wife's suggestion (ch. 16). But now a different resolution is proposed. Despite her great age Abraham's wife Sarah is to bear a child. This theme – of the birth of a child to a woman whose circumstances should apparently have prevented her from becoming pregnant – is a characteristic biblical one, continued in the New Testament in the story of the birth of John the Baptist. The same motif, differently expressed, underlies the story of the birth of Jesus to a mother who was virgin. The various biblical story-tellers clearly use this as a way of emphasizing God's power in overcoming all human limitations.

In our present episode the announcement of impending birth is almost overshadowed by the wordplay centring on the verb 'to laugh' (vv. 12–15). Such wordplay is characteristic of Hebrew story-telling, but it has an additional function here, in that the verb 'to laugh' is very similar to the name 'Isaac', and so we are prepared for the account of the birth of the son to Sarah, and his naming as 'Isaac' in ch. 21. RC

Colossians 1.15–28

The first six verses of this passage (15–20) are widely recognized as a distinct composition, and are often categorized as 'an early Christian hymn' – which, for want of knowledge and of comparable material, must remain a rather general description. It is often placed in this way alongside Philippians 2.5–11. The two passages are alike in giving, in different ways, a succinct and poetic sweep of Christian faith, in each case largely christological in content. Here, the passage falls into two related halves. The first is about Christ's role in creation and the second about his redemptive work, with the Church as the vehicle and sphere of his continuing life, both parts being cosmic in their visionary scope. The two strophes certainly have a parallelism of idea and structure, and both seem to lean upon the themes and ideas of Jewish 'wisdom' thought. Here, Christ himself (as not infrequently in early Christian reflection) occupies the key place in God's work and self-disclosure that is occupied in parts of Judaism by wisdom, as the reflection of his inner life, rationality and purpose (cf. Prov. 8; Ecclus. 24). He is indeed from 'the beginning' at the heart of God's rational and good purpose: to limit him to lesser roles would seem intolerable to faith and experience. The passage as a whole is remarkable in its universal sweep as it surveys the significance and being of Jesus, seen as superior to all angelic powers (with which in certain ways he might be compared or confused: we are some way from the more 'natural' idiom of the Synoptic Gospels). That the Church shares this exalted role is of a piece with Paul's teaching in Rom. 12 and 1 Cor. 12, but here reaches new heights and sharper definition.

The rest of the passage moves on to consider more fully the nature of Christ's work of salvation. It expresses a width of vision and confidence comparable to the perspective in the earlier 'hymn'. The universality of the Christian message and of its progress already are taken as axiomatic (v. 23). It is a conclusion, no doubt resulting from fervour of heart, but also the reflection of a conviction of Christ's universal sway that results from his exaltation. In that way, it stems from the most basic of early Christian beliefs.

Yet the Christian community also has its vital role. Verse 24 has caused much head-scratching, as it seems to cast doubt on the all-sufficiency of Christ's work, increasingly felt down the centuries to be an axiom of faith. But in truth, from the beginning, in Pauline reflection, the 'oneness' of Christ and his own people had been felt so intensely that a formulation like this, though striking, is not outrageous, except to the literal-minded. The question it seems to us to be answering had simply not arisen, namely how to conceive the bond between Christ and those little communities, scattered ever more widely across the Greco-Roman world, who believe in him and know that bond to mean something more intense and rich than, for example, the relationship between a teacher and his followers; what is here affirmed in the strongest way, is the oneness of Jesus and his people. They live in him and he in them, with heavenly splendour as the sum of their hope. It could only be put in unusual and dramatic terms. LH

Luke 10.38–42

The Gospel readings for the past three Sundays have come from the beginning of Luke's travel narrative (9.51—19.27) and have concerned the theme of discipleship – the sharpness of the call, the vulnerability of those sent, and the practicality of helping and being helped. At a first reading of the story of Martha and Mary (10.38–42), one might reasonably ask what this incident has to do with discipleship. It seems more like a typical family squabble that Jesus settles by giving each participant the right to do her own thing. A careful examination not only of the story but of its location following the parable of the despised Samaritan, however, yields a different conclusion.

Martha comes on the scene first, as a woman who welcomes Jesus into her home. Though the phrase 'her home' can be questioned on textual grounds, Martha's action establishes her as the leader of the household. She is clearly in charge, as women in the first century usually were in the limited world of the home. But the *responsibilities* of the household also fall on Martha. We are not specifically told that a meal is being prepared, but it is not hard to imagine, since the words behind 'many tasks' and 'to do all the work' (*diakonia, diakoneo*) are commonly used for 'waiting at tables'.

Martha very naturally becomes upset that her sister, Mary, spends all her time with Jesus and does not help with the family chores. We miss the point if we caricature Martha as an obsessive type who gets angry because she wants to be sure that everyone works as hard as she does. For the narrator, there clearly are many chores to be done, and Martha seems more distracted by the work that has piled up, with guests in the house, than by some inner need to see to it that if she is working, then, by golly, Mary is going to work too. There are apparently no servants to help, as Martha is working by herself.

Why does Martha go to Jesus with her complaint rather than to Mary? Who knows? Maybe there is a history of Mary's not helping with the housework. Maybe there has been a family rift. Maybe it is simply the narrator's way of having Jesus confirm Mary's choice. In any case, Martha's preoccupations with the household responsibilities are given secondary priority by Jesus' statement that 'Mary has chosen the better part' (v. 42).

What is 'the better part' Mary has chosen? Interestingly, the narrator tells us only two things about Mary. She 'sat at the Lord's feet and listened to what he was saying' (v. 39). Her posture is a way of declaring her a disciple (see Acts 22.3). She has made herself a learner of Jesus. Hearing what he says means that she has received Jesus as a prophet. She is doing what loyal disciples should do – she is listening.

It is hard to overemphasize the importance of 'hearing and doing the word' in the Lucan narrative. It is the decisive activity in building on a solid foundation (Luke 6.46–49), in maturing as in good soil (8.15), in being a member of Jesus' family (8.21), in being truly blessed (11.27–28). Mary, in listening to Jesus' word, has at least begun where faithfulness begins, and this warrants the commendation of Jesus in the face of Martha's complaint.

But what does this suggest? That the life of contemplation is preferred over the life of action? Hardly. The literary context here becomes critical. At 10.25 we encounter the lawyer who ultimately answers his own question to Jesus about eternal life by citing the two commands to love God and to love one's neighbour. Then follows the parable highlighting the action of the Samaritan, who assists the victim left in the ditch by tending to his wounds, carrying him on his donkey to an inn, and paying the costs incurred (10.29–37). He is a model for loving one's neighbour (as well as identifying who the neighbour is).

Then comes Mary, who is distinguished not for her action, but for her attentive listening to the word of Jesus. Her place alongside the Samaritan affirms that discipleship has to do not only with love of neighbour but also with love of God, not only with active service but also with a silent and patient waiting upon God's supreme prophet. The Samaritan and Mary belong together. Doing without listening can easily degenerate into busyness that loses its purpose. Listening without doing soon becomes no more than a mockery of the words.

Consider a footnote that perhaps should be a prelude: the story of Martha and Mary is one in which a stereotypical role of a woman (Martha's concern for the household tasks) is given secondary status. Many women in the congregation can identify with Martha and feel put down by the way she is treated, as if her complaint is only neurotic whining. The critical point is that the text does not so much 'put down' Martha (who certainly is not a neurotic whiner) as it honours Mary's ministry of the word, a ministry Luke consistently elevates to a place of priority and sets alongside ministry, the ministry of the Samaritan. It is proper for a woman to leave the stereotypical role for that of a full and faithful disciple. cc

Proper 12

(Sunday between 24 and 30 July inclusive)

Hosea 1.2–10 or Genesis 18.20–32; Colossians 2.6–15 (16–19); Luke 11.1–13

Hosea 1.2–10

If people know anything at all about Hosea, it is that he is thought to have learned about the love of God for Israel through his own domestic trials; that his wife Gomer became unfaithful and took up the life of a prostitute, but that Hosea bought her back from those whose property she had become. Whether chs. 1 and 3 of the book actually support such a reconstruction is highly questionable. The difficulties presented by the text have led to many, and widely differing, interpretations. For many commentators the chief stumbling block has been the divine command to the prophet to 'take a wife of whoredom and have children of whoredom'. Does this mean that Hosea was commanded to marry a prostitute? Are the 'children of whoredom' Gomer's previous children born out of wedlock, or are they children of Hosea's marriage with her? Would God command a prophet to marry a prostitute? In view of these practical difficulties it is no surprise that alternative views have been put forward, such as that the prophet and his family are engaging in street theatre, and acting the roles of prostitutes. On the other hand, whatever is made of the words 'wife of whoredom' the children born and named seem to reflect real happenings, even though the names given to the children are meant as signs to the people. It is safest not to indulge in speculation about Hosea's relationship with Gomer and better to concentrate on what is certain.

Verses 4–5 are a surprise because they condemn Jehu's *coup d'état*, when he eliminated the house of Omri and Ahab (2 Kings 9). Yet according to 1 Kings 19.16, the anointing of Jehu was commanded by God, and Jehu was not of the royal line. He could only become king by way of revolution. Indeed, his commission is to destroy the existing royal house (2 Kings 9.7–10). The prophetic words in 2 Kings 9 and Hos. 1 are at odds with each other! Yet in another way they are not. They are giving different answers to the same question, which is how the northern kingdom, Israel (the reference to Judah in v. 7 is an addition from a much later period) can be worthy of God. The answer in the books of Kings is that political revolution will effect a change. The response in Hosea is that only a radical act of divine recreation will suffice. This explains the harsh words of rejection of the nation by God symbolized by the children's names 'Lo-ruhamah' and 'Lo-ammi' (meaning 'no mercy' and 'not my people') and the promise in v. 10 (2.1 in the Hebrew) of the people's acceptance by God. Both prophetic words are important. Political revolution may be necessary in some circumstances, but may involve bloodshed and evil. It can never be a final and lasting solution. The other divine word is needed to make that point clear. JR

Genesis 18.20–32

This is a very important passage, for two reasons. First, it is one of a number of passages in the Old Testament where a moral question is resolved not by divine fiat, but by discussion. Second, in this particular case, it is not human moral standards that are under scrutiny, but God's! The extent to which the ten commandments have been central to using the Bible in ethical matters has given the impression that the Bible is a kind of law book, from which absolutes can be derived. There is nothing wrong with this, except that absolutes have to be applied to concrete situations, where they may come into conflict with other absolutes. This is exactly the case in this passage. Two absolutes – that wickedness should be punished, and that the righteous should not be punished because of the wickedness of others – come into conflict. The result is a discussion about how the absolutes can be applied, and in the event, rightly or wrongly, justice for the innocent prevails over punishment of the wicked. Whatever we may think of these absolutes and their resolution in this case, the passage shows that making moral judgements is not a simple matter of applying absolutes.

The second point, that God himself is questioned, albeit by an Abraham who describes himself as dust and ashes in comparison with God, is encouragement for a use of the Bible that is not frightened to question its moral content. It is sometimes supposed that what God commands must be right because it is God who commands it. This is not the view taken in this passage, and the question 'shall not the Judge of all the earth do what is just?' comes from a deep desire that God should be better than us, otherwise we have little to hope for. Provided that we, too, recognize that we cannot be presumptuous when we question the morality of passages of the Bible, we can be encouraged to use it critically. We are engaged in the same quest to know what is right and how to apply it in specific circumstances, as is Abraham in the lectionary reading. JR

Colossians 2.6–15 (16–19)

It is always hard when we are made to hear only one side of an argument, and that is the case here. In fact, it is a number of related arguments, which coalesce in the matter of the uniqueness and all-sufficiency of what God has done in Christ. All-sufficiency both for our understanding of ourselves and the world and for the health of our lives. Both aspects in fact run through this letter as a whole, and in this passage we get echoes of the 'hymn' in 1.15–20, a seminal text for our writer (e.g. 2.9 echoes 1.19; 2.15 echoes 1.16, 20). The forces he sees as threats to the Christian gospel, all operating in the Greek world of the Colossian Christians, are intent on promoting the claims of a number of alternative routes to both the best way to 'see things' with our minds and the best places to look for relief and support in the face of life's ills. In both matters, these people (quite who they are is unclear, but they are certainly articulate and lively of mind, and may include Jews as well as Gentiles) are much beholden to an unseen world of angels, then, for the author as for them, an ever-present reality, governing the affairs of the world for good or ill and heavily influencing humankind and determining its fate. (We must never forget what a relatively small and confined place the universe was for them compared with the apparently infinite space on which we look out; these forces, good and evil, were relatively close at hand.) So of course it was vital to champion Christ, if he were to be seen as effective saviour, as having subjugated these forces and liberated us for direct and free access to God, to serve him in liberty. (We might say, cutting out the middlemen, which is always a desirable objective.) This has, for our writer, been the heart of Christ's work, and it is cosmic in scope – seen with a clarity perhaps greater than anywhere else in early Christian writing (though see Heb. 1, with its emphasis on the relativizing of the angels, and the universal outlook of John's Gospel).

It is not surprising that people subject to the profound fears that came from attributing life's misfortunes to such personalized powers should turn to all kinds of ways out: relief for the mind – 'getting things straight' (cf. the reference to philosophy); relief through rituals (like circumcision in the case of Jews); and through ascetic habits and devout observances (vv. 16, 18). The writer's sole concern is to push this farrago of ideas and practices aside, as he returns time and again to the clear belief in Christ as the plenary expression of the one God to us and to baptism as the way into secure relationship with him, the safe haven given by God. Using metaphors of legal settlement and military triumph (vv. 14, 15), the writer makes plain that the ultimacy and supremacy of God have been established in full. LH

Luke 11.1–13

Luke follows the direction of our attention to the primacy of devotion to Christ over action (Mary over Martha) with formal teaching on prayer. This comes in three parts. First, a normative form for prayer; then (as in the case of the good Samaritan in 10.25–37, following on from the teaching on love of neighbour) a parable to teach us to stick at God in prayer with all tenacity. The message of the parable thus extends the meaning of the prayer itself. The final verses tell us that tenacity is never in vain.

The Lord's Prayer (vv. 2–4) appears in a shorter form than that found in Matt. 6.9–13 (and indeed in the Didache). There is no agreement on which of the two forms is 'original' – whatever that might mean. Conventional source criticism suggests that Luke's briefer version holds that palm, and Matthew filled it out with his own characteristic language. Certainly, as far as church use is concerned, Matthew has won hands down: nobody much prays as Luke says Jesus taught his disciples to pray! But there are signs that the debt may go the other way: Luke chooses (v. 4) 'sins' rather than 'debts' (Matt. 6.12) – but (carelessly?) leaves 'indebted' in the next clause. Luke's simple 'father' (v. 2) – no 'our' – is as typical of him as the pronoun is of Matthew (compare Luke 22.42; 23.34, 46 – three other prayers of Jesus; and Matt. 26.29, 39). And Luke's 'each day' (v. 3) gives a presentness to Christian living also found in the same wording in 9.23. So the question of priority is open. In both evangelists, the petitions add up to a single prayer under successive scriptural images: that the rule of God may come to us, in our inner selves and in our common life. And we are to be glad to address God as Jesus did, 'Father' – that suffices, surely.

The parable in vv. 5–8 teaches a lesson that Luke repeated in the parable of the unjust judge (better, the persistent widow) in 18.1–8. The lesson is strange to modern ears: it seems to be that God, too uncaring to respond to us readily, will only do so under our great pressure. This is the exact contrary of the final verses, 9–13 (cf. Matt. 7.7–11; and in the same vein Luke 12.22–31 = Matt. 6.25–34): no real need to worry, God provides. It may of course be an improper later Christian fad to demand precise consistency in what became Scripture: why should the evangelist be so bound? Contrary images can throw genuine light on different facets of our relationship with God in the light of experience. So, here, we absorb initial bewilderment, and realize that in prayer God is no pushover – but is nevertheless wholly dependable. Our role is to stick with him in persistent love: 'Though he slay me, yet will I trust in him' (Job 13.15, AV). LH

Proper 13

(Sunday between 31 July and 6 August inclusive)

Hosea 11.1–11 or Ecclesiastes 1.2, 12–14; 2.18–23; Colossians 3.1–11; Luke 12.13–21

Hosea 11.1–11

The opening words of the reading: 'Hear the word of the LORD, O people', are not part of the Bible. The passage that follows is one of the most moving in the Bible. Alluding to the tradition of the exodus from Egypt, it grounds the special relationship between God and his people in a response to the needs of a child. The Hebrew word *na'ar* can mean anything up to a lad old enough to be an armour-bearer (1 Sam. 14.1). 'Child' is nonetheless a good rendering. The point is that someone is indicated who is vulnerable without help. This vulnerability calls forth divine love. However, even if this love was initially returned, it was later diverted to other gods who had done nothing for the people.

In v. 4, the Hebrew words translated as 'human' and 'love' may be plays on similar words for 'red leather' and 'leather' (see NEB footnotes). The sense would be that the harness with which God helped the child to learn to walk was made of the very best materials. This would indicate love and kindness, of course. In vv. 5–7 the mood changes. One can almost hear a parent saying, 'If that is what they want, they can have it!' Returning to Egypt means returning to slavery, unless the background is help sought from Egypt when the Assyrians invaded Israel in the reign of Salmaneser V (727–722 BC; cf. 2 Kings 17.3–4).

Another abrupt change comes in v. 8. After all, the bond of love for God's people is so strong that God cannot give them up. Human patience may become exhausted, but not divine patience (v. 9). Admah and Zeboim are mentioned in Gen. 14.8 as cities of the plain, together with Sodom and Gomorrah. In Deut. 29.23 they are said to have suffered the same fate as Sodom and Gomorrah. The closing verses (10–11) are difficult, and may in part derive from the hands of later editors. They presuppose some kind of exile, although there may have already been some deportations by the Assyrians in the ninth and eighth centuries. JR

Ecclesiastes 1.2, 12–14, 2.18–23

It is a pity that this reading is put as an alternative to Hos. 11.1–11, because it is the only appearance of a part of Ecclesiastes in the three-year Principal Service lectionary cycle. It is also a pity that the parts selected omit the great poem of 1.3–11 or do not include 3.1–15. The Teacher (or Preacher or Philosopher – various renderings are possible) quite possibly ran an academy in Jerusalem in the late fourth century BC, when Judaism was having to come to terms with Greek philosophy. He appears to have been a lonely thinker, uncertain about organized religion (5.1–6) and deeply sensitive to the injustice of the world (4.1–3). Adopting the literary fiction of having been a king in Israel (which is why the book was traditionally ascribed to Solomon) he describes the futility of trying to discover the meaning of life by human observation and experimentation. The world of nature with its never-ending annual cycles is inscrutable. Human achievements are temporary, and nothing can be learned from them, except that life is an unhappy business (1.13).

What can be learned from such pessimism? In the first place, Ecclesiastes is a proper antidote to the kind of natural theology that believes that the worlds of nature and human achievement disclose a God of love and power. Ecclesiastes could not have believed in a sacramental universe, i.e. a world pointing to the things of God. Whether we agree with him or not, his voice needs to be heard on this matter. Second, Ecclesiastes is a seeker after truth. It is not doubt but honesty that leads him to question as he does. That the book is in the Bible at all is a testimony to its respect for honest seeking, which is why it is a pity that it figures so little in the lectionary. However, what this honest seeking ultimately achieves is a sense of the awesomeness of God, and the conviction that while the constitution of the world and human dealings can be criticized, God does not have to justify himself. This may not be a complete or a satisfying theology, but that it contains profound elements of truth cannot be doubted. JR

Colossians 3.1–11

We turn, as commonly in the latter part of Paul's letters, to the moral outcome of the new life whose rationale has been expounded in the earlier part. Verse 1 is the hinge between the two: Christian virtue flows straight from the fact of sharing Christ's risen life. This statement recalls Rom. 6.1–11, and makes the point about baptism and resurrection even more firmly. It carries with it the awareness of sharing in the consummation of all things (v. 4). So the scheme put forward is as comprehensive as could possibly be: the 'story' is seamless and, once accepted, wholly satisfying to mind, imagination and heart. There is then the difficulty for later generations, in the long history that in fact ensued, to wonder how to see things quite so starkly and dramatically, for all then was short-term in the mind's eye. Ethics has become more and more a matter of nuance and discussion, and the simplicities that can put human conduct into lists of vices and virtues (the latter follow in vv. 12–14, and it is odd to cut the reading short at v. 11) seem unrealistic. The lists are largely conventional: as far as they go, who could disagree with them? Their conventionality does not mean that they were not taken seriously, rather that they were seen as beyond discussion – and not inviting analysis or entry into the world of case-studies.

But morality here goes beyond the lists: it is seen in terms of the whole 'self', the old, pre-conversion person having been restored to Adamic, paradisal splendour (v. 10), with status and morality fusing in one vision. It is a picture that joins ethics and doctrine together again: that is, in this account, morality is not a separable department, with its own distinguishable agenda, such that it might be seen as independent of one's standing in the universe and before God. In the glorious renewal of humanity pioneered in the Christian community, distinctions of race and culture are naturally transcended, and Christ, the seminal new Adam (cf. 1 Cor. 15.22), presents us with a whole new vision, less of what we might be than of what we are. Who is sufficient for these things? LH

Luke 12.13–21

Once again, we have teaching, followed by a parable that makes the message vividly clear. This is becoming Luke's favourite method of working in this part of his Gospel.

The message is, however, one of his favourite themes. It comes time and again throughout most of his book – though scarcely at all, oddly, in Acts, where the actualities surely come into view: we are to put no trust in wealth and property if we are concerned with the things of God. Are we then simply to surrender our wealth? Perhaps Luke thought so, though the Gospel says nothing about practical policy in this regard. His few references to the subject in Acts do indeed concern church life, and a pooling of Christians' property is enjoined: Acts 4.32—5.11. But was this part of a Lucan ideal world, seen from a distance, a golden age in the Church's youth? We do not know the facts about Luke's church situation, but in Paul's letters, written from inside, contemporaneously with the life they describe, the picture is different. Certainly, he asks for generosity, especially for his collection for the impoverished Jerusalem church (Gal. 2.10; 1 Cor. 16.1–4; 2 Cor. 8—9); but there is no general sense of poverty or common ownership being a Christian duty. In fact, his town churches depended on richer members for biggish houses to meet in and for general sustenance – though he experienced some of the resulting difficulties (1 Cor. 11 makes it plain).

Luke, however, is adamant that money and property are spiritually dangerous, and poverty is a blessing (Luke 4.18; 6.20–24). Our present passage is then typical, putting the matter firmly and at length. It makes as plain to us as anything elsewhere that Luke gives priority to this aspect of morality. Not as a piece of self-sufficient teaching: it is because money is a prime indicator of the heart's loyalty. 'You cannot love God and mammon' (16.13; cf. Matt. 6.24). Luke sees this so clearly, quoting Jesus time and again to make the case, that he does not consider contrary arguments: about the good that money may do, or the ills that poverty often brings, or the inevitable complexity of commerce, even in the first century. But there is enough moral and spiritual sense here for his readers not ever to shrug off his uncomfortable words. In the perspective of the kingdom and of the age to come, which is both Luke's and ours, all else fades from view – and we should be alert. LH

Proper 14

(Sunday between 7 and 13 August inclusive)

Isaiah 1.1, 10–20 or Genesis 15.1–6; Hebrews 11.1–3, 8–16; Luke 12.32–40

Isaiah 1.1, 10–20

Unlike modern books, ancient books do not necessarily begin at the beginning; that is to say, ch.1 of Isaiah is not necessarily the first part to have been written. In fact, the opening verse belongs to the final editing of the book, rather as the title page of a modern book is typed or set up only after the book itself has been written. The verse places the prophecies in a particular period of history, roughly from 740 to 690 BC, a period when Jerusalem was threatened and attacked by successive Assyrian kings. The reading now jumps to one of the famous anti-sacrificial passages of the Old Testament (cf. also Amos 5.21–24; Jer. 7.21–23; Ps. 50.7–15). It begins, however, by offering the greatest insult possible, by calling the rulers of Jerusalem the rulers of Sodom and Gomorrah (v. 10). It is hard to think of a stronger indictment; for the fact that the rulers are named points to human responsibility for the state of affairs. In this situation, it is not surprising that the cultic ceremonies are so repulsive to God, and indeed in modern church life there is nothing more repulsive than the type of hypocrisy that combines pious language with insensitive and cruel treatment of others. The various observances that are listed are best understood as practices that, in normal circumstances, would be acceptable to God. (There is no need to cast doubt on incense as a Canaanite practice!) The 'blood' on the hands of the worshippers can be understood in two ways: as bloodshed, i.e. killing and oppression of innocent people; and as wickedness more generally, which the religious observances are unable to wash away. The command to 'wash yourselves' (v. 16) invites the suspicion of 'justification by works'; but in the context of a city likened to Sodom and Gomorrah a thoroughgoing reformation is necessary if people are realistically to approach God. No doubt the prophetic word of warning and judgement plays its part there. Verse 18 alludes to the idea of a lawsuit, a motif introduced earlier in the chapter (1.2f.). God will not punish the nation without good cause, and he is willing to argue the matter out. Judgement, if and when it comes, will be self-imposed by the nation. JR

Genesis 15.1–6

This passage has presumably been chosen to illustrate the point made in the reading from Heb. 11, that Abraham acted in faith. Of course, the exact passage implied in Heb. 11 is Gen. 12.1–4; but what is interesting is that in the story of Abraham as a whole and in the continuation of Gen. 15, Abraham is presented as finding it hard to trust God's promises! In Gen. 12, having been promised the land of Canaan, Abraham promptly leaves it for Egypt when a famine looms. In spite of the divine promise of becoming a great nation (Gen. 12.2) Abraham feels obliged to place his wife in great danger in order to preserve his own life (Gen. 12.10–20). In the present reading, he appears to have adopted one of his slaves to be his heir, and in the continuation of the narrative (see the Second Sunday of Lent, p. 82 above) he asks the question regarding the promised land, 'How am I to know that I shall possess it?' (15.8).

These falterings on the part of Abraham should give us some encouragement, and help us to see the reading in Heb. 11 in a new light. Having faith is not a simple matter. It includes taking personal initiatives and making practical arrangements. Because we are frail human beings it involves being uncertain about where we are going. Perhaps it is only from the point of view of hindsight that we can say of people that they had faith. There is far more to the statement 'he believed the LORD' (Gen. 15.6) than meets the eye. JR

Hebrews 11.1–3, 8–16

The author returns to the elevated, rhetorical language of the opening of the Epistle for his definition of faith, posing difficult questions of translation and interpretation. Faith is the *hypostasis* of things hoped for: in 1.3 the word means the real being of God, of which Christ is the exact reproduction (a meaning it carries when used in the later definition of trinitarian doctrine). Here, however, it must carry the meaning it had in 3.14, conviction or confidence. Faith does not make real the things hoped for: it is the conviction that they are, or will be, real. The definition raises the issue of the author's cultural and intellectual background: does he think, like a Platonist, of realities that are unseen because they belong to the eternal, immaterial world; or does he think eschatologically of things not now seen because they belong to the future new age? With heaven, it is possible to say both that it is not yet visible as the kingdom of God to be established on earth (12.26–28), and that it already exists as the holy place of the presence of God: and confidence both in its unseen reality and in its future accessibility is founded on Jesus' entry there as the forerunner (9.24; 12.2).

Faith is first demonstrated through an understanding of creation. The world is not to be explained in terms of the material stuff of which it is formed, but in terms of invisible realities. This does not read naturally like a statement of *creatio ex nihilo*, but more like the Platonic dualism of the material world and the world of eternal forms. It is just possible that the author thinks of the words of God, 'Let there be . . .' as the invisible means of creation.

He is on more familiar ground as he begins his roll-call of the heroes of faith. Abraham is the traditional example, used also by Paul and James (Rom. 4.13, 16–22; Jas. 2.21–24). Like Paul, Hebrews sees Abraham's faith in his willingness to believe in God's promise in face of the apparent impossibility of its being fulfilled. (Some versions of the text allow Sarah also to be an example of faith in this respect.) The author, however, adds his own distinctive exposition. Abraham's faith is seen when, in response to God's promise, he commits himself to his journey to an unknown destination. The ambiguity about the author's perspective is seen again. Abraham and the other patriarchs did, in geographical terms, live in the land of promise, but did so only in a temporary way. This could be because the physical land of Israel is only a shadow of the eternal 'promised land' of heaven; or because Israel is only an anticipation of the homeland, or holy city, to come (cf. Heb. 12.22) – or, as above, both. In any event, what the patriarchs looked to in faith is 'better' than what they had: a frequent and characteristic term of contrast in Hebrews (e.g. 1.4; 8.6; 11.40). The passage in general recalls the author's longer exposition of the meaning of 'entry into God's rest' in 3.7—4.11. There he warned of the importance that his readers should persevere and move on from their first acceptance of the gospel, and that warning is implicit here, in v. 15.

The idea of believers as 'strangers and sojourners' in the world draws on the distinction in classical society between the inhabitants of a city who are in legal and political terms full citizens, and those who are 'resident aliens'. It is a theme that appears in other early Christian documents, such as 1 Pet. 1.17 and the Epistle to Diognetus 5—6. SL

Luke 12.32–40

As Luke continues his account of Jesus' journey to Jerusalem, he offers a number of sayings about readiness for God's kingdom. The tension in Luke's narrative is almost palpable. Jesus has already raised the stakes by provoking the ire of the scribes and Pharisees. Now as he teaches his disciples, he is surrounded by crowds in their 'thousands', trampling on one another (12.1). Note the contrast between these vast numbers and his 'little flock' of disciples, who despite their vulnerability have been given the kingdom (v. 32).

The first theme is getting one's priorities right. There are purses that don't wear out, and treasures that can't be harmed by moth or burglar. Luke's 'treasure', like the one in Matthew's field (Matt. 13.44), appears to be the kingdom. But for Luke setting your heart on God's kingdom-treasure has economic implications: it will involve sharing your earthly 'treasures' lest they become a distraction (see Acts 2—5).

Treasures, of course, should be carefully protected (a fact highlighted by the twofold reference to 'thief', bracketing our passage at v. 33 and v. 39). So second there is emphasis upon being alert in the two parables of vv. 35–40. Middle Eastern hospitality is such that wedding-guests could expect to be entertained until the early hours: so slaves must be dressed with lamps burning to open up when their master finally staggers home. Nocturnal burglars are not renowned for announcing their arrival in advance. So the Lord's servants are urged to watch.

But for what precisely? On the narrative level, Jesus' attention is on Jerusalem, and Luke has clearly grappled with the non-acceptance of the messianic king by his own people on his arrival there. The Jerusalemites of Jesus' day are like servants with lamps unlit, or householders who have forgotten to set the burglar alarm.

But Luke's travel narrative also functions as a 'last testament' for the departing Jesus, preparing the disciples for his absence. So, traditionally, these parables have been read as urging the post-Easter Church to watch for the *parousia* of the Son of Man. They echo Luke's awareness that the Lord's final coming has been delayed (though not for so long as to allow his followers to extinguish their lamps). He alerts us to the danger of Christian complacency in such circumstances. Christians cannot afford to rest on their laurels, but must maintain that urgent expectancy as if the master were already at the gates. If they do so, they will be rewarded with seats of honour at the messianic banquet, when in a great reversal the master becomes the servant.

However, Luke's context may also suggest another possibility. Partly in view of the Lord's delay, early Christians came to recognize another, more immediate 'coming' of the Lord in the Eucharist (e.g. Rev. 3.20), anticipating that final banquet. Given Luke's emphasis upon Jesus' scandalous dining habits, which he sees continued in the Church's 'breaking of bread' in Acts (see also Luke 24), perhaps there is a eucharistic echo here too. Already the watchful Christian community can sit at table, where the master dons his apron as one who serves (cf. Luke 22.27). IB

Proper 15

(Sunday between 14 and 20 August inclusive)

Isaiah 5.1–7 or Jeremiah 23.23–29; Hebrews 11.29—12.2; Luke 12.49–56

Isaiah 5.1–7

Because the autumn Feast of Booths was the occasion on which the grape harvest was celebrated, it has been suggested that the prophet sang his song to the people gathered together on this occasion. This may be correct, although there is no direct evidence that this was so. The song acts as a parable; that is, it invites the listeners to make, or agree with, a decision before the implications of that decision are spelled out.

The song begins with the singer acting on behalf of his male friend, describing the infinite care taken with preparing the best possible site for a vineyard, and planting the best possible vines. The hearers will be worried, if not shocked, to learn that the outcome was not choice grapes but wild grapes.

The owner of the vineyard now takes up the song. He asks the listeners, in effect, what they would do in the circumstances (vv. 3–4). He expects them to agree with him when he dismisses the case as hopeless. He will disown the vineyard, remove its protecting wall, no longer prune or hoe it, and will let it become overgrown. He will also tell the clouds that it will be a waste of precious water if they rain upon it.

We must assume that the listeners agree, or that the owner describes what they, also, would do. Verse 7 applies the parable. The vineyard is the house of Judah, and instead of producing justice (Hebrew *mishpat*) it has produced bloodshed (Hebrew *mispach*); instead of righteousness (*tsedaqah*) there has been a cry of the oppressed (*tseaqah*). By agreeing with the song, that the vineyard that produced wild grapes deserves to be left to turn into a wilderness, the listeners have been forced to agree that they deserve an analogous fate.

Within the narrative structure of Isa. 5 the song introduces a set of statements of judgement which spell out in greater detail the accusation that the chosen people have produced the opposite of what could be reasonably expected. Modern readers are entitled to ask, however, whether the action taken in regard to the un-productive vineyard was the only action possible; whether it might not have been worth trying again. Within the context of the original setting of the song, its message is clear: the people deserve and will get judgement because of their wickedness. On a longer term view, the good news is that God did not abandon his vineyard to become a wilderness, but that he gave it, and continues to give it, a further chance. JR

Jeremiah 23.23–29

If readers and hearers find the opening words difficult to understand, they will not be the first to do so! Some of the ancient translations into Greek, Latin and Syriac omitted the initial question marker in the Hebrew, thus producing the rendering, 'I am a God near by . . . and not a God far off.' This is much clearer, although probably not correct, for technical Hebrew reasons that cannot be discussed here. If the question is retained, what does it mean? Suggestions include that God is both near and far off (the same result as if the question marker is omitted), or that God is only far off, and that this is what enables him to see all that happens. Another view is that the false prophets bring God too near (i.e. use God for their own ends), while only the true prophet encounters the sovereign God, the God who is far off. Verse 24, which says that God fills heaven and earth so that no one can be hidden from him, is perhaps the best clue as to how to take the opening words. The remainder of the passage contrasts true and false prophets. Dreams as such are probably not condemned. It is their content that is the problem, if their effect is to lead people away from God. The implication is that these dreams of false prophets lull the people into a false sense of security. In contrast, the message spoken by the true prophet is like fire, and like a hammer that smashes rocks. This is best taken to mean that true prophets feel driven to say things that may threaten the national interest, unmask all hypocrisy and abuse of power, and possibly put the prophets themselves in situations of great danger. This, admittedly, is to look at the prophetic word from a human perspective, and to run the danger of trivializing it. Only from the perspective of hindsight can a true prophetic word be recognized, and even true prophets can be wracked by doubt and uncertainty when compelled to speak. The divine perspective, which is not susceptible to human control or analysis, is preserved by the opening words of the passage – that God is also a God who is far off. JR

Hebrews 11.29—12.2

The catalogue of faith continues from the formative event of the exodus to examples from the more recent past. Among the judges and kings is included the foreign prostitute, Rahab. Her declaration of faith in the God of the Israelites (Josh. 2.8–11) led her to be seen in Jewish tradition as the archetypal proselyte; she appears as an example of faith expressed in works in Jas. 2.25, and in Matt. 1.5 as an ancestor of Christ. The unspecified women and victims of v. 35 must be an allusion to the mother with seven sons martyred in the persecution of Antiochus Epiphanes in 167 BC whose story is told in 2 Macc. 7. It is not necessary to suppose that the author of Hebrews had read that account, written in Greek and so finding its way into the Septuagint but not the Hebrew Old Testament canon; the Maccabees and their contemporaries were popular Jewish folk-heroes whose story was told and retold. In later popular Judaism a tradition also developed that prophets would meet martyrs' deaths, and vv. 36–38 reflect legends, such as the death of Isaiah by being sawn in two. The final note of homeless wandering links these latest examples of faith back to the patriarchs, the 'strangers and sojourners', of vv. 8–16.

All these heroes of faith provide examples for Christians to admire and imitate, as they run their own race (not a native Jewish image, but drawn from the Hellenistic world of the games, as by Paul in 1 Cor. 9.24–26); but the author indicates a closer relationship between them. The saints of the Old Testament are not just figures in a storybook past, but are a present 'cloud of witnesses'. They did not receive the promises in their own time, 'apart from us', but the author implies that they may do so with us. His readers, called to persevere in their own faith, have a responsibility to those who have gone before them. The theme that underlies much of the argument of Hebrews – that the models of the Old Testament, like priesthood and sacrifice, were ineffective and so set aside by Christ's effective action – does not mean that God's chosen people are also set aside. There is a continuity between the old Israel and the new. Paul draws a similar conclusion to his argument in Rom. 9—11. Despite the failures of his kinsmen, and despite his new understanding of the 'children of Abraham', Paul continues to believe that in the end, when the fullness of the Gentiles is gathered in, 'all Israel will be saved' (Rom. 11.25–26).

The prime example of faith to whom Christians look is, of course, Jesus, who 'in the assurance of things hoped for' (Heb. 11.1) was able to endure suffering and death. (This is the only point in the Epistle where the precise form of his death, the cross, is referred to.) He is not, however, the last in a long list of examples, but the 'pioneer', because he is the first to enter into the promised land of heaven itself (11.16, cf. 9.24, the true Holy Place). Furthermore, he did so as the fully human son among many brethren (cf. 2.10–14, where the term 'pioneer' is also used) and as the representative high priest (4.14–15), so that his achievement opens the way for others. He is the pioneer 'and perfecter' of our faith because he has made access to the presence of God not just a hope but a reality. SL

Luke 12.49–56

Certain gospel sayings of Jesus cause embarrassment, and the first part of this passage offers a cluster of such hard sayings. Christ has come to bring not peace but division (v. 51), to set the earth ablaze and sow seeds of dissension within families! Such words seem diametrically opposed to the angelic message to the shepherds, promising peace on earth (2.14).

A good starting-point is to ask what 'fire', 'baptism' and 'peace' mean here, as the prophet Jesus journeys towards his rejection at Jerusalem. Fire in the biblical tradition symbolizes judgement, given its destructive nature, though its capacity to purify offers a more positive image. More positively, Luke also associates fire with the Holy Spirit. The fiery John has already spoken of one who will baptize in 'the Holy Spirit and fire' (3.16), and this promised gift will soon descend as tongues of fire upon the expectant Church (Acts 2.3). The gospel can be encountered as judgement or as salvation.

Baptism too is double-edged. Mark understood Jesus' death as a 'baptism' (Mark

10.38), and Luke develops this theme: Jesus' passion for his mission will lead inevitably to his death in Jerusalem. But for the Christian reader there may also be a reference to Christian baptism (which Paul understands as a sharing in Christ's death, Rom. 6.3–4).

Given other Lucan passages (e.g. 1.79; 7.50; 10.5; 19.42), v. 51 cannot mean that peace on earth is contrary to God's will (though the true 'peace' here probably denotes the Hebrew *shalom*, peace and harmony with God and his people). It is rather a recognition that Christ's life and teaching will inevitably provoke dissension, fulfilling Simeon's prophecy that this child would be a sign of contradiction to divide his people Israel (perhaps better expressed by the alternative translation, 'peace in the land'). Unlike the returning Elijah (Mal. 4.5), whom in other respects the Lucan Jesus resembles, his message will alienate parents from children.

As for Jesus, so for his followers. Luke's form of Jesus' words has been shaped by the bitter experience of (predominantly Jewish) Christians. They reflect the fierce 'family squabbles' of the first generations, in which families were literally torn apart and many Christian Jews found themselves excluded from families and communities. Preachers will want to recognize this historical context, which explains the often-intemperate language. But the divisive nature of the gospel is not restricted to Jewish disciples (cf. 1 Cor. 7.12–16). These harsh words remind all Christians that the urgency of the kingdom takes priority even over family ties.

The final saying (vv. 54–56) concerns humanity's ability to heed the message of the passionate prophet. The ancient world was more adept than our own at weather-forecasting, and Palestinian Jews would have known how to interpret clouds from the Mediterranean or scorching winds from the Negev. All the more damning, then, is the human inability (or unwillingness, given Luke's charge of hypocrisy) to read the signs of God's activity, to recognize that the *kairos*, this time of salvation, has arrived. IB

Proper 16

(Sunday between 21 and 27 August inclusive)

Jeremiah 1.4–10 or Isaiah 58.9–14; Hebrews 12.18–29; Luke 13.10–17

Jeremiah 1.4–10

For the next few weeks the Old Testament reading will be from Jeremiah. It may be helpful at the very outset to refer to some of the debates which have taken place recently with regard to this book. Jeremiah as an individual is mentioned more frequently than any other of the prophets for whom books are named, and we are told many stories about him. Traditionally, therefore, the main interest has been at the personal level – Jeremiah struggling to understand God's purpose and his own role at a time when the nation was being overrun by foreign invaders and the whole religious life of the people was collapsing. In recent years, however, it has been suggested that such a portrait owes more to the literary skill of the author than to real knowledge of an individual. In that case 'Jeremiah' would become a kind of typical figure, embodying the turmoils and anxieties of a time when a whole world order seemed to be under threat. For some, therefore, the book of Jeremiah is better approached as a literary masterpiece rather than as the record of the travails of an individual soul.

These differences of approach already affect the way we approach the account of Jeremiah's call, which is today's reading. We do not know whether there was any formal ceremony of calling, equivalent to an ordination, but the Old Testament certainly contains several strikingly similar accounts of individuals being called to God's service. If you have opportunity you may like to look at Exod. 3 and Isa. 6 alongside today's story. In each case the initiative is taken by God himself. In each case the one called confesses his own inadequacy for the task: Moses was afraid (Exod. 3.6), Isaiah was 'a man of unclean lips' (Isa. 6.5), and Jeremiah here was 'only a boy' (v. 6). To this day in services of ordination those called are first expected to acknowledge their inadequacies.

One feature of Jeremiah's call is unique and continues to puzzle commentators. He is to be a 'prophet to the nations' (v. 5) There are indeed oracles against foreign nations in Jer. 46—51, but they are usually treated as marginal to the book's main concern, and the main thrust of the book as a whole, and of the passages we shall be concentrating on, is Jeremiah's engagement with his own people. Perhaps this unexpected expression is intended to alert us to the fact that many of Jeremiah's own people will be driven into exile among the nations. RC

Isaiah 58.9–14

This reading can only be understood in the context of Isa. 58 as a whole (see Ash Wednesday, p. 73 above). The chapter is a response to a complaint of the people that, in spite of their religious observances, their material situation remains dire. The reference to ancient ruins (v. 12) possibly indicates that the complainants have recently returned from exile, and have begun to restore the outward religious observances of the community. In the verses that precede the reading, a complaint that fast days produce no response from God brings a marvellous definition of the kind of fast that God prefers – one devoted to justice and the support of the hungry and homeless. The reading follows on from, and repeats these sentiments. 'Removing the yoke' (v. 9b) if correct (NEB renders 'if you cease to pervert justice') probably refers to some kind of social injustice, while 'pointing the finger' perhaps means making false accusations. In vv. 10–11 a link is made between assisting the hungry and afflicted and enjoying prosperity and health. The former are to be a priority, not an afterthought. It is implied that the social will needed to tackle poverty and justice will supply the effort needed to rebuild the ruined city. Verses 13–14 may be an addition. Their subject matter is the sabbath and its proper observance. It is to be used as a day for honouring the things of God and not for pursuing human selfish interests. Such space and reflection are needed if the will is to be found to create a community such that God desires. This may seem like 'justification by works' (see also on Isa. 1, Proper 14, p. 213 above), but no spirituality can have any value that is indifferent to injustice and human suffering. JR

Hebrews 12.18–29

The opening verses summarize the description of Sinai in Exod. 20, the place where God was present, but as a frightening, dangerous and inaccessible presence. Even Moses, the only one who could go into the presence of God and bring back his message, was full of fear. By contrast the author of Hebrews invites his readers to Mount Sion, the heavenly Jerusalem. (The contrast between Sinai and Jerusalem is reminiscent of Paul's allegory in Gal. 4, though the purpose of the comparison is very different.) There is now access to God, and to a great community with him. First are the angels, as if at a festival (the word suggests the great public celebrations of the gods in the Hellenistic world). Then there is the assembly (*ekklesia*, the word used for the Church) of the firstborn enrolled in heaven, whose identity is more uncertain. Hitherto Jesus has been called 'the firstborn', but with brothers and sisters (1.6, cf. Rom. 8.29) and in Col. 1.18 and Rev. 1.5 he is the 'firstborn of the dead', so it is possible that the group of firstborn here are the Christian dead who have already followed him to heaven. The 'spirits of the just made perfect' are easier to identify: they are the saints of the Old Testament whose faith was celebrated in ch. 11 but who would not reach the city to which they looked forward 'without us' (11.39–40). The image is like the great west door of a gothic cathedral: the ranks of angels, saints and prophets welcoming into heaven the Church on earth.

In the midst of them is God: he is still judge, but with Jesus not Moses as the mediator between him and his people. Moses in Exod. 24 sprinkled the blood of sacrificed oxen on the altar and the people, and the author has already alluded to this in Heb. 9 in the course of his explanation of the sacrifice of Jesus; the blood of sacrifice that Jesus presents in the true Holy of Holies that is heaven, is his own. Here, in another link in a chain of allusions, the sprinkled blood of the covenant at Sinai suggests to him the shed blood of Abel (Gen. 4). That blood called on God the judge to avenge it in punishment of the brother-slayer; Jesus is the brother whose blood gives forgiveness of sins (a comparison drawn in Edward Caswall's passiontide hymn, 'Glory be to Jesus'). Finally, this access to God through Jesus is not a vision of the future but an experience of the present: the author twice uses the perfect tense, we 'have come' there, so there we are.

All this gives assurance and confidence, but is not a ground for carelessness or complacency.

The argument of Hebrews has been punctuated by warnings of the dangers of failure and the impossibility of a second chance (e.g. Heb. 6.4–6). These warnings are now given added urgency in terms of time, and of the prophecy of Hag. 2.6. The language sounds apocalyptic: the shaking of earth and heaven like the removal of heaven and earth in Rev. 21.1; but it seems to be translated into platonic terms, for it is the created, material order that will suffer change while the eternal and permanent endures. As in other parts of the New Testament, Christians are seen to stand between the times: already receiving the kingdom, but in expectation of its future revelation. In this situation God must be worshipped appropriately: the imagery of fire is still relevant, and so is the fear of God: not the terror of Moses at what he could not approach, but an awe inspired by that very access to the presence of God which Jesus has given. SL

Luke 13.10–17

Stories of Jesus' healing carry differing meanings depending on how an incident is related and in what context it appears. Some highlight Jesus' capacity to accomplish remarkable deeds; others precipitate controversies with the religious authorities; still others take on a didactic function as Jesus instructs about the way of discipleship.

Luke 13.10–17 is one of those accounts which reflect at least two 'interests'. On the one hand, since the healing occurs on the sabbath it becomes the occasion for a sharp exchange between Jesus and the leader of the synagogue, which puts the latter to shame. It becomes a controversy story and ultimately a judgement on the Jewish authorities. On the other hand, it is the story of Jesus' authority over the forces of Satan that have left this woman badly crippled for 18 years. It demonstrates the inbreaking of God's rule in human life. The two 'interests' of the story, of course, belong together and mesh with the thematic thrust of the context.

First, we look at the conflict between Jesus and the leader of the synagogue. The account begins with the observation that Jesus 'was teaching in one of the synagogues on the sabbath' (13.10). He was doing what a prophet should be doing on the sabbath. While we are not told from what text Jesus was teaching, his healing of the crippled woman may have been no more than a carrying out of the implications of the text.

The indignant and persistent protest of the leader of the synagogue ('kept saying to the crowd') was based on a reading of Exod. 20.9 and Deut. 5.13 that categorized Jesus' actions as work that should have been done on a weekday. Challenged, Jesus responds with a sharp criticism of the synagogue leader's reading of the fourth commandment. He uses a clear and homely example to expose the fallacy of ignoring the woman's infirmity on the sabbath. The crowds immediately get the point, and the leader of the synagogue and his cohorts are 'put to shame'.

But Jesus' retort indicates that the issue is more than an academic difference of opinion about the interpretation of texts. 'You hypocrites!' raises the moral issue of interpretation. The charge is levelled in Luke at those who are blind to the real meaning of things, those who cannot perceive their own weakness (6.42) and cannot discern the present evidence of God's rule (12.56).

One of the things to which the leader of the synagogue is blind is the remarkable restoration of a 'daughter of Abraham' (13.16). The illness this woman had had meant the disruption and loss of social relationships, exclusion and therefore loneliness. What Jesus' action did was not only to bring physical wholeness to the crippled woman, but also to reinstate her to legitimate membership in the community of Israel, a fitting behaviour for the sabbath.

A second aspect of the account leads to the other major 'interest' of the story. A teaching of Jesus in ch. 12 chided the people for their failure to discern the significance of the present. They knew that a cloud in the west meant rain and a strong wind from the south suggested a heat spell, but they could not perceive the clear signs of God's rule, nor did they realize that the present was a time of crisis, a time for repentance and changed lives (12.54—13.9).

The leader of the synagogue and his colleagues fail to see that Jesus has taken the initiative in releasing the woman from the bondage of Satan. By forbidding such conduct on the sabbath, they put themselves on Satan's side in the struggle for human lives, and they become enemies of Jesus. They badly misjudge the conflict taking place between the rule of God and the rule of Satan (see 11.20). Not surprisingly, ch. 13 concludes with Jesus' anguish over Jerusalem, 'the city that kills the prophets and stones those who are sent to it!' (13.34). The authorities' blindness leads to their final rejection of the prophet who could save them.

It is important that the story leave us with a vivid picture of a divided Israel. The religious leaders are shamed. Their failure to detect the signs of God's presence condemns them. Homiletically, it is easy to let the leader of the synagogue symbolize Israel and stoke the fires of anti-Judaism. At the same time, the text says that the woman ('a daughter of Abraham') praises God for her healing (v. 13) and the crowds rejoice at the wonderful things Jesus is doing (v. 17). Rather than a judgement on Israel, the story becomes a fulfilment of the prediction that Jesus brings division (12.49–53), a phenomenon all too modern, when the present is discerned as a time for repentance. CC

Proper 17

(Sunday between 28 August and 3 September inclusive)

Jeremiah 2.4–13 or Ecclesiasticus 10.12–18 or Proverbs 25.6–7; Hebrews 13.1–8; 15–16; Luke 14.1, 7–14

Jeremiah 2.4–13

This piece of poetry is typical of much in the early chapters of Jeremiah. The community is being condemned for its failure in matters relating to its practice of worship. The Lord's saving power was characteristically seen in the Old Testament in the way in which he had delivered his people from Egypt, led them through the desert and so brought them into the promised land. Those saving acts are rehearsed in vv. 4–7. Such generosity should have led to an appropriate religious response, but the leaders of the people had totally failed in that respect: priests, those responsible for the Torah (law), rulers and prophets are all condemned in v. 8. We cannot be certain whether Torah here refers to law in general, or more formally to a collection which we might describe as 'Scripture'.

The accusation that follows is directed against the whole community, with the clear implication that it has been involved in this wrongdoing. But such an accusation owes much to the desire for dramatic effect: not only are the ancestors condemned (v. 5), but also 'your children's children' (v. 9) will be no better. So we should perhaps not worry too much about the illogicality of the fact that the house of Jacob and families of Israel addressed at the beginning (v. 4) are now invited to reflect on the evils done by 'my people', who are surely identical with those being addressed. But poetry of this kind has its own logic; the appropriate mode of reading is to see this as part of the search for an explanation of the miseries that had befallen the community. Elsewhere in the book of Jeremiah there is no hesitation in holding God himself responsible; here the stress is on the religious failures of the worshippers. Either way the impression comes over very powerfully of a community utterly bewildered by the troubles that have come upon it. Unhappily such situations are not confined to the ancient world. RC

Ecclesiasticus 10.12–18

This is part of a longer passage (10.1–18), which states that all sovereignty comes from God and that failure to recognize this leads to disaster. The opening phrase (v. 12a) differs in the Hebrew remains from the Greek (which is what is translated here) and is to be preferred. For 'to forsake the Lord' read 'stubbornness'. The Hebrew is also more illuminating in v. 13a where it has 'sin is the reservoir of pride', a thought which connects well with 'pours out abominations'. It has been suggested that vv. 14–17, which speak of the overthrow of thrones and nations, reflect recent events in the writer's experience. Around 200 BC, two decades before Ecclesiasticus was written, the Greek rulers of Egypt had been defeated by the Greek rulers of Syria, and Palestine had passed from the one jurisdiction to the other. This may be correct. But v. 14 is to be noted, which speaks of God replacing the (arrogant) rulers with humble people, and the same thought appears in v. 15. A more likely source for this is the Song of Hannah in 1 Sam. 2.7–8. The Hebrew of v. 18, 'pride is not fitting' makes better sense than 'pride was not created', and the entire verse looks as though it should follow v. 6. If the reading is meant to complement the Gospel for the day, it is not an entirely happy choice. JR

Proverbs 25.6–7

This short passage, with its obvious parallels with the Gospel for the day, indicates the link between some of the material in Proverbs, and royal circles and protocol (cf. Prov. 25.1). The art of being a courtier involves knowing how to behave according to one's station. In the presence of the king one waits to be called, and does not put oneself forward. Similarly, where a procession or similar gathering is assembled strictly according to rank, knowledge of who is present will prevent the embarrassing situation of occupying a place higher than one's rank deserves. The religious value of this advice needs to be questioned. Does it sanction the kind of hierarchical society that fits ill with New Testament teaching about true greatness? Does it stifle a person's creativity and result in a subservient and self-interested attitude? After all, does it point to a God who, we are assured, is no respecter of persons (Rom. 2.11)? JR

Hebrews 13.1–8, 15–16

The final chapter of Hebrews contains the same kind of direct instructions and warnings with which Paul concludes his letters, but there were of course no comparable opening greetings. It is possible to argue that it was added to the original document in an attempt to 'Paulinize' it and so append it to a growing Pauline collection. Hebrews is not, however, merely an exercise in abstract theological argument, but assumes a situation to which the theology is addressed, and there are some similarities between that situation and the admonitions in the present passage. The instructions on marriage and money have no obvious connection, but the encouragement to mutual love and hospitality is relevant to a community that has been criticized for neglecting to meet together (10.24–25); and the reminder to remember fellow-believers in prison and suffering torture may be necessary for those who are not themselves at present called to face such an ordeal (12.4) or who may see it as something in their past (10.32–34). Verse 7 looks back to former leaders, and suggests that the readers are second-generation Christians or, at any rate, not recent converts, and this also would fit with the caustic observation that they ought by now to be teachers themselves, and that there is no time to go over the basics again (5.12—6.2).

Echoes of the author's characteristic thought may also be found: v. 2 alludes to Abraham's hospitality to the three strangers, traditionally understood as angels, at the oaks of Mamre (Gen. 18.1–8), and so chimes with his interest in angels in Heb. 1.4–14, and in the earlier parts of the story of Abraham, like his encounter with Melchizedek (7.1–10; Gen. 14.18–20). The ringing statement of v. 8 can be seen to summarize and reaffirm the argument that because Jesus as the perfect high priest has offered the one effective sacrifice in the true Holy of Holies, he remains there for ever (7.24–25). His priestly sacrifice, because it was effective, is unrepeatable, but there is still room for Christian offerings to God, which may be called 'sacrifice': praise and sharing with each other; effectively obedience to the great commandment to love God and one's neighbour. SL

Luke 14.1, 7–14

The gospel readings from Luke for today and next Sunday come from the critical ch. 14, where much of the action and teaching is set on the sabbath in the house of a leader of the Pharisees. As if that setting were not enough to make readers anticipate conflict, the narrator adds that the Pharisees were watching Jesus closely (v. 1). As the various incidents unfold, it turns out, however, that Jesus is really the aggressor – the one who challenges the lawyers and Pharisees (v. 3), who repudiates the guests who jockey for the 'first couches' at the meal (v. 7), who instructs the host whom to invite to his next meals (vv. 12–14). By both ancient and modern standards, Jesus might be called a rude guest. The wary Pharisees are reduced to silence.

One can hardly overstate the importance of the meal as the setting for this section. Eating is essential for life; no one can manage for very long without it. But a dinner with guests is an occasion of social importance, to which people of one's class are invited and where there is an implied sharing of values and ideas. The status and rank of individuals are legitimated by their inclusion in the guest list and their location on the seating chart. For readers of Luke's narrative, meals are also symbols for the inbreaking and anticipated rule of God. In 13.29 we hear of people coming from east and west, north and south, to 'eat in the kingdom of God'. The Lord's table becomes a foretaste of the eschatological banquet (22.14–20).

There are four incidents that occur at this particular meal in the house of the leader of the Pharisees: Jesus' healing of the man with dropsy (14.2–6), his counsel about finding a place at the table (vv. 7–11), his instructions about what guests to invite (vv. 12–14), and the parable of the great dinner (vv. 15–24). The assigned lection focuses only on the two middle sections.

Jesus' warning about striving for a prominent seat and risking humiliation by being sent to a lower seat seems at first blush like no more than a piece of common-sense, home-grown wisdom. In fact, it can be paralleled by a variety of texts in both Jewish and Greco-Roman literature. There is nothing particularly distinctive about Jesus' counsel – until one reaches 14.11: 'For all who exalt themselves will be humbled, and those who humble themselves will be exalted.'

The saying is what the literary critics call a polar reversal. It is not just that the exalted will be humbled; we know about that from the story of Job. Nor is it simply that the humble will be exalted; we know about that from the story of Joseph. This is a complete reversal in which those who exalt themselves will be humbled and those who humble themselves will be exalted. When the north pole becomes the south pole and the south pole becomes the north pole, a world is overturned.

What starts out in the narrative as a breach of etiquette for a number of guests ends up with a prediction about a radical change. The passive voice of the two main verbs in v. 11 suggests that God is the real actor, the one who humbles the pretentious and exalts the humble. God is at the root of this polar reversal, a theme Luke will not let the readers forget (e.g. 1.51–53; 6.20–26; 13.30).

The second section (14.12–14) spells out one of the revolutionary features of God's polar reversal. A guest list is usually composed of those closest to the host or hostess – relatives, friends, and rich neighbours – and it tends to foster a cycle of reciprocity. Hospitality takes on a self-serving purpose. Jesus abruptly proposes inviting a different group to the next 'power lunch' – the poor, the crippled, the lame and the blind. These are not only beyond the usual categories of family, friends and rich neighbours; they are by Jewish law unclean.

The host is being urged to cross a big boundary and offer hospitality that cannot be repaid, at least in this life. As one writer puts it, 'Jesus urges a social system without reciprocity' (Halvor Moxnes, *The Economy of the Kingdom: Social Conflict and Economic Relations in Luke's Gospel*; Philadelphia: Fortress Press, 1988, p. 132). Through such activity these marginalized people become members of the group. Symbolically they are no longer outside the circle of power.

But why the poor, the crippled, the lame and the blind? In the upcoming parable, they are the outsiders who end up being the insiders at the great dinner (14.21). They seem to be Jesus' favourites, his kind of people. They are those for whom he came (4.18–19). Because he likes them, his disciples cannot ignore them.

There is no doubt that Jesus is a disturbing, even rude, guest at this dinner party, upsetting standard protocol, but his presence and his words open the way for the transformed structures of the kingdom of God. CC

Proper 18

(Sunday between 4 and 10 September inclusive)

Jeremiah 18.1–11 or Deuteronomy 30.15–20; Philemon 1–21; Luke 14.25–33

Jeremiah 18.1–11

Within the poetry that constitutes the greater part of Jer. 1—25 there are a few narratives such as today's reading. The making of pottery was an important part of everyday life in the ancient world, and provided the biblical writers with an obvious source of illustration for stories of creation (the second creation story in Gen. 2 is reminiscent of a potter shaping a series of products) and of destruction (pottery was very liable to be broken, and such broken pottery provides archaeologists with valuable evidence relating to the ancient world). In addition the potter could reshape anything that, as we might say, failed to pass quality control.

So it is here: the potter was dissatisfied with the appearance of his first product and decided to rework it. The figurative language seems to run out of control in the latter part of the story, for Israel is presented as a vessel that has already been fully created and yet can be re-created – not easy for even the most skilful potter! By v. 11, too, the metaphor has changed. Though God is still described as a potter the main concern is with the divine plan, in deciding the fate of nations and kingdoms. But we are probably not intended to pay too much attention to detail. The point is that the writer wants to stress the community's complete dependence on its God.

The reading ends with a call to repentance: 'amend your ways and your doings'. The Old Testament prophets are sometimes described as preachers and it is assumed that preachers will regularly summon their hearers to repentance. In fact the call to repentance is much less frequently found in the prophets than we might expect; only as here in Jeremiah and in Ezekiel is it a major motif. It is also important to recognize that the call to repentance is addressed to the whole community; it is not primarily an appeal to individuals. Some may feel that preachers in our own day spend too much time in exhorting individual repentance when what is far more basic is that society as a whole should be shown the need to reshape its ways. RC

Deuteronomy 30.15–20

Deuteronomy 28 to 30 form a conclusion to the legal section of the book (chs.12—26) and are concerned to set before hearers/readers the logical conclusion that follows from the laws: that they can be obeyed or ignored. The set passage presents at least three difficulties. The first is that it seems to be pure 'justification by works'. Obedience to God will bring prosperity. The second difficulty is the opposite of the first. Not only will disobedience entail divine disfavour; it will bring down curses upon the disobedient. Is the wish to avoid curses an adequate reason for serving God? Will it not lead to a grudging and half-hearted religion? The third difficulty is that life in general and many passages of the Old Testament disprove any simplistic correlation between doing good and enjoying prosperity. The psalms are full of complaints about the prosperity of the wicked!

These problems can be partly, but not wholly, explained in terms of the kind of material that Deuteronomy and our passage are. They are based upon vassal treaties which defined the relationship between powerful kings and their subject nations in the ancient Near East of the seventh century BC. The treaties set out the obligations (laws) of the subjects to the king, demanded absolute loyalty, and threatened severe reprisals if this loyalty was broken. Gods were invoked as witnesses to the agreement between the parties (cf. v. 19, where heaven and earth are called on as witnesses). The deuteronomic legislators utilized the vassal treaty form to articulate a covenant between God and the people of Judah, using the literary device of an address of Moses to the people as they were about to enter the promised land.

In defence of the passage it can be said that the fact that there is no automatic, or necessarily demonstrable, link between goodness and a material prosperity does not mean that no attempt should be made to obey God and seek his way. If we hope for a better world it will be one in which evil will be corrected and punished in the way it deserves. Further, if we seek God's way in a world in which goodness is not automatically rewarded, we do so not for the reward but because of the intrinsic value of God's laws. In Deuteronomy, there are laws designed to promote compassion towards the needy and to articulate what I call 'structures of grace'. Obedience to God's ways is then no grudging service designed to avoid punishment. It is a creative and loving service which can justifiably be called 'life'. JR

Philemon 1–21

This lection offers the rare opportunity to deal with virtually an entire Pauline letter. Since the letters are occasional writings, written as part of the ongoing conversation between Paul and other early Christians, reading them 'whole' brings us at least a step closer to the experience of Paul's correspondents. It also decreases the danger that we will read a passage out of context or overemphasize a particular theme.

Even if we read the entire letter, however, we still have only half of the conversation. Whether or not Paul accurately portrays the situation, what Philemon's attitude was toward Onesimus prior to the letter, what Onesimus's own attitude and actions were, and what response Philemon made to the letter – all these factors remain securely hidden away. Indeed, even what Paul says remains somewhat hidden, since he writes with such diplomacy that he does not plainly state his own hopes for Philemon's action.

These are not observations born of scholarly timidity and concerning small details in the letter. Essential dimensions of Onesimus's story are unknown. Traditionally, we refer to Onesimus as a slave who has run away from Philemon's household in search of his freedom. Somehow he has encountered Paul, who is coincidentally the 'father' of Philemon's own faith, and has become a Christian. The letter does not identify Onesimus as a fugitive, however, and contemporary investigations of ancient slavery suggest that Onesimus may have fled because he had a significant problem in Philemon's household. In that circumstance, a slave would normally go to a trusted third party to appeal for intervention. Such a slave was not legally regarded as a runaway.

The more difficult question regarding the letter has to do with the nature of Paul's request. Does he anticipate that Philemon will free Onesimus? Does he want Onesimus assigned to himself as a helper? Or is Onesimus simply to be restored to his position without punishment? Given that slaves in the Roman Empire were very often set free by the time they were thirty, some suggest that Paul has in mind early manumission.

Despite these serious unclarities in the letter, several features of it are both clear and significant. First, only here among the letters generally regarded as authentically Pauline does Paul write a personal letter. Even if Apphia, Archippus and the church are addressed, the letter is nevertheless personal. It concerns the affairs of a single individual, Philemon, with regard to his slave, Onesimus, which explains why Paul moves so delicately through his appeal.

In this sense, the letter contrasts sharply with 1 Cor. 5.1–8, where Paul addresses the sin of an individual but does so in the context of addressing the larger congregation. Paul castigates what he takes to be the gross immorality of a man who is living with his father's wife, but he employs equally harsh language for the congregation and its failure to discipline this individual. In Philemon, perhaps because of local circumstances or perhaps because Paul does not see the same risk of 'infecting' the larger congregation, he addresses an individual.

At the very same time that Philemon is a personal letter, it is also profoundly ecclesiastical. The slender references to the church in v. 2 and to other Christian workers in vs. 23–24 open this possibility, but the ecclesiastical dimension of Philemon enters primarily through Paul's own mission. Philemon's previous faithfulness has given refreshment to 'the hearts of the saints' (v. 7). Onesimus has now become an embodiment of his own name, useful to Paul in the service of the gospel (vv. 11, 13). Because he is a new brother in Christ to Philemon, Onesimus should be received and treated as such. The church forms the horizon within which this personal matter must be addressed and settled.

Philemon also provides us with a glimpse of the way in which Paul's pastoral sensitivity intertwines with his theological convictions. Even if theological argumentation is largely absent from the letter, what permeates the letter is the knowledge that the Christian lives in profound connection to Jesus Christ and that Christian behaviour must reflect that connection. Paul's imprisonment belongs to Jesus Christ (v. 1). Philemon's faith will be effective as he 'perceive[s] all the good' he may do for Christ. By virtue of his conversion, Onesimus has become a brother in Christ, which necessitates that he be treated as brother. Paul concludes his request: 'Yes, brother, let me have this benefit from you in the Lord! Refresh my heart in Christ' (v. 20).

Contemporary Christians can scarcely read this letter without longing for Paul to take the argument yet another step. Why not assert the profound immorality – the impossibility – of one human being owning another? Why not demand the release of Onesimus, the release of all slaves everywhere? With Paul's own convictions that the eschaton was imminent, such demands may have seemed unnecessary. In light of the pervasiveness of slavery in the Roman Empire, such demands may have been unthinkable for a single, obscure individual. The implications of vv. 15–16, however, should not be overlooked. One who is a brother in the Lord can scarcely be a slave in the flesh. BG

Luke 14.25–33

The assigned lection for this Sunday from the travel section of Luke's Gospel specifically reminds us of the theme of discipleship that pervades the section. It is not an easy passage, because of the rash and exclusive way statements are made, but just for this reason it is important for contemporary audiences. It confronts us with hard choices and jars any notion that being a Christian leads to social enhancement or personal betterment. While there are texts that comfort the disturbed, this one disturbs the comfortable.

The location of the passage in the narrative is critical. The preceding parable of the great banquet (Luke 14.15–24) depicts previously invited guests who offer excuses for their refusal to attend the party and then relates the host's persistence in seeing that his dining hall is filled and his meal eaten. Two groups are recruited: first, the poor, the crippled, the blind, and the lame and second, those in the countryside. It is a remarkable story of the divine grace, which reaches beyond traditional bounds to include those otherwise excluded.

But it is easy to be presumptuous about grace. The three who send excuses for their absence illustrate just how easy it can be to take lightly God's gracious invitations, and there is no reason to think that the outsiders brought in at the last minute are going to be any less vulnerable to such presumptuousness. Therefore, to the 'large crowds' who 'were travelling with him', Jesus delivers these sharp words about the demands and priorities of discipleship. If they are contemplating being more than hangers-on and intend to be regular diners at Jesus' table, they need to know what they are getting into and to decide whether they can sign on for the long haul.

The passage is cleanly structured. The introductory verse (14.25) is followed by three parallel statements about the nature of discipleship (vv. 26, 27 and 33). The middle one provides the clue for understanding the first and last. In between the second and third statements are two analogies (building a tower, waging a war) that raise the question whether would-be disciples can follow through on their initial commitments (vv. 28–32). The final words about salt and the potential loss of its usefulness, while outside the lection, provide a fitting conclusion to the chapter (vv. 34–35).

How are we to understand 14.26? It includes a piece of Semitic hyperbole that Matthew has softened a bit ('Whoever loves father or mother more than me . . . and whoever loves son or daughter more than me is not worthy of me', Matt. 10.37). Jesus is clearly not telling the crowds to hate their parents and abandon their children. He is sharply confronting them with the priority of their commitments and implicitly pointing them to the new surrogate family they join as they become disciples. It is a note repeatedly sounded in Luke's narrative (Luke 8.19–21; 12.52–53; 21.16) and needing to be heard in a society that talks much about family values.

The second statement about discipleship is the familiar word about cross-bearing (14.27). By putting the verb 'carry' in the present tense, Luke tends to stress the everydayness of this identification with Jesus (cf. 9.23). By including *'one's own cross'* (not clearly rendered in the NRSV), Luke underscores the need for a personal acknowledgment of such an identification.

The third statement about discipleship, with its inclusive 'all', reiterates another Luke theme (14.33). Material possessions have a seductive appeal that can turn them quickly from being servants to being masters (12.13–34; 18.18–25; 19.8). They become excess baggage that makes the journey with Jesus difficult to negotiate. Thus, at the outset, choices have to be made. 'You cannot serve God and wealth' (16.13).

The intervening analogies of assessing resources before building a tower and doing feasibility studies before going to war vividly argue the case for a commitment that is made with eyes wide open to the cost (14.28–32). A hasty or casual decision leaves one vulnerable to ridicule and defeat. The warning is not meant to encourage a calculating wariness about discipleship (which would certainly seem incongruous with the daring, risk-laden calls to follow Jesus), but a sober realism about what it entails.

In light of the hardness of the text and the overwhelming demands made, one is tempted to give the two analogies a further twist. In answer to the questions, 'Which of you would fail to make an assessment before building a tower? Which of you would bypass reconnaissance before starting a war?' the responder of course says, 'None of us.' But then neither would God! God has counted the cost. God knows what it takes to build a tower. God knows how strong the enemy's forces are. The rule God has inaugurated will not be left unfinished. It may have a rather unpromising beginning, but do not be deceived: God means to win. It is just this certain and conclusive cause we are called to join. CC

Proper 19

(Sunday between 11 and 17 September inclusive)

Jeremiah 4.11–12, 22–28 or Exodus 32.7–14; 1 Timothy 1.12–17; Luke 15.1–10

Jeremiah 4.11–12, 22–28

One of the great changes that has taken place in study of the Bible in recent years is a new interest in what it has to say about the created world. Sometimes, as in the creation story of Gen. 1, creation is pictured as very good, but in the main part of today's reading a very different understanding is found. We might almost regard vv. 23–26 as a kind of 'un-creation'; there are enough verbal links with Gen. 1 to make it possible that this is a terrifying vision of the possibility of the complete breakdown of the whole created order.

In its present setting it seems as if this vision is to be read in the context of the collapse of Judah under the onslaught of the Babylonian invaders, which culminated in the destruction of Jerusalem and the deportation of many of its leading citizens. That impression is heightened by the reference to the people and Jerusalem at the beginning of the reading, and the reference to 'desolation' at the end. In particular the note there that this is not to be 'a full end' suggests a later addition when hope for a renewal of life in Jerusalem was emerging.

It would probably be wrong, however, to suppose that this is the main or only point of the middle verses. The book of Jeremiah is best conceived of as an anthology, originating from a variety of sources, and brought together under the name 'Jeremiah' when he came to be understood as the typical representative of the suffering community at a time of great crisis. We do not know what brought about such a bitter view of the created world. We may find it a positive benefit that the poem is not to be tied too precisely to one historical situation. We live in a time when the different Christian churches are just beginning to take seriously the need for a responsible attitude to the created world, and a reminder such as this, of the possibility of drastic dis-order bringing a good creation to ruin, may be very appropriate as a contemporary reading. RC

Exodus 32.7–14

A comparison of this passage with 1 Kings 12.25–33 makes it likely that, at one stage in the development of Israel's faith, Israelite sanctuaries contained bull images that served as the throne of the invisible YHWH. When Jeroboam I said of the golden calves in Bethel and Dan 'Here are your gods' (or, 'Here is your God') 'who brought you up out of the land of Egypt' (1 Kings 12.28) he was arguably appealing to Israel's traditional faith as opposed to Solomon's new-fangled temple designed and built by a foreign architect.

If this is correct, a long period has elapsed between the time when a golden calf was legitimately to be found in an Israelite sanctuary, and the story of the golden calf in Exod. 32. That period will have seen the bitter war waged by the prophets against the bull as a fertility symbol, as well as Josiah's attempt in 622 BC to reform the cult (2 Kings 23). What was once commonplace will have become a symbol for the worst kind of idolatry.

In the narrative structure of Exodus, this chapter is a turning point. Hitherto, the people have complained against God and Moses and demanded signs and wonders, including water made sweet (Exod. 15.22–25), the manna and quails (Exod. 16) and water from the rock (Exod. 17.1–7). In ch. 32, however, the ultimate apostasy occurs when the Israelites make a golden calf and worship it. This later leads to civil war (vv. 25–29) and to the destruction of the tablets of stone (vv. 19–20).

A notable feature of the narrative is the role of Moses in averting God's wrath, and of his refusal to let God destroy the people so that God can make a great nation out of Moses (v. 10). Moses reminds God of his promises to Abraham, Isaac and Israel (Jacob). While there are no doubt deep currents running here, which reflect disputes within the Jerusalem community in the post-exilic period, Moses' action can be taken at its face value at the surface of the narrative – as refusal to profit personally at the expense of others to whom promises had been made.

In the history of interpretation this incident has been used by the churches to justify the belief that not all of the Old Testament law is binding upon Christians. It has been argued that all the sacrificial laws follow Exod. 32 and were directed to faithless Israel and designed to prevent any further apostasy.

Thus they are of no concern to Christians, who need only to heed the Old Testament laws that precede Exod. 32. At a deeper level, the story is a contrast between two types of religion – that which demands that the divine be made immediate, visible and accessible, and that which waits upon a God who seems to tarry when human impatience demands action (v. 1). JR

1 Timothy 1.12–17

If one tends to believe, on good grounds, that the Pastoral Epistles were the work of a follower of Paul rather than Paul himself and probably come from the later years of the first century, this passage seems at first sight to be among those that tell against such a view. It is personal, heartfelt and, it seems, autobiographical. In its main lines it is paralleled in Paul's undoubted letters: his revolutionary change from persecutor to apostle in 1 Cor. 15.8–10 and his utter dependence on unmerited grace in Phil. 3.4–10 (cf. also Gal. 1.11–17). Here as elsewhere, Paul's theology was no abstract construct; it was compelled by his experience, his story.

There are, however, reasons for seeing in our passage not just simple fidelity to Paul's own testimony but subtle (and probably unconscious) shifts in the way of expressing it that are even destructive of Paul's clear vision. They are, moreover, symptomatic of this writer's own church 'world' and its perspectives.

So: could Paul have said that Christ had chosen him because he 'judged' him 'faithful', i.e. saw him as fit for the job? No, it was in and despite his wretchedness that he was 'called'. Could Paul have said that Christ, like an indulgent magistrate, excused his persecuting activity and his (in Christian terms) blasphemy on the grounds of his ignorance and unbelief? Luke, it is true, was inclined to mitigate Jewish guilt for Jesus' death on this basis (e.g. Acts 3.17). So the writer here sees Christ as exercising headmasterly 'patience' towards Paul, as an 'example' to others. It is all very different from Paul's sense of dependence on sheer unmerited grace acting in the face of inexcusable sin. The profundity and drama of Paul's awareness of God's dealings with us are sacrificed for the sober considerations of a human appointing board. The picture is in line with the admirable but unexciting qualities required of church officers in ch. 3. But we cannot crow; for the instincts and interests that begin to creep in here, in the Church's second generation, are both understandable and persistent. Would it be faithless to say they are inevitable? But the question is: at which level ought Christian life before God to be pitched? And is the preacher always a lone voice, preaching of course always to himself or herself as well as to the others? LH

Luke 15.1–10

These two parables of the lost sheep and lost coin (together with the following parable of the 'prodigal' son, called by Germans the 'lost son') highlight the Lucan emphasis upon joy, forgiveness and repentance (cf. 24.47). Luke's immediate context is the grumbling of the Pharisees and scribes over Jesus' eating with tax-collectors and sinners.

Historically, Jesus seems to have scandalized his contemporaries by eating with sinners before they had shown evidence of 'repentance' or 'changing their lives', and without demanding the prescribed means of atonement. 'Sinners' here are those who deliberately placed themselves outside God's law by their manner of life, rather than being pushed to the margins by others. They are linked with the tax-collectors (toll-collectors), who probably caused offence not for their collaboration with the Romans – Jesus' Galilee was governed directly by the Jewish tetrarch Herod Antipas – but for their dishonesty.

Luke partly tones down this scandalous aspect by adding qualifying words about repentance to Jesus' teaching. Nevertheless, he more than the other evangelists describes Jesus' *actions* of sharing table-fellowship with tax-collectors and sinners. In doing so, he reveals something of the compassionate heart of the Father, which is picked up in these two memorable parables.

The first, that of the lost sheep, Luke shares with Matthew. However, whereas Matthew applies it to waverers within the Christian community (in the context of his so-called 'Discourse on the Church' in Matt. 18), for Luke it describes God's concern for the morally dubious considered outsiders by religious people. These 'lost' are objects of special concern to the shepherd, and the joyful celebration of the 'finding' with friends and neighbours evokes the joyful, even riotous atmosphere of Jesus' dinner parties.

A similar sense is found in the uniquely Lucan parable of the lost coin, which closely parallels the first in structure and vocabulary. Here God's extravagant behaviour towards the 'lost' is emphasized by the woman's desperation in locating the silver coin. Whether the lost drachma is part of her wedding headdress, or rather a substantial part of the family's hard-earned savings, she is one of God's poor (one drachma represented a day's wage for agricultural workers). Her relative poverty is also suggested by her lighting a lamp: her dark, windowless house is a far cry from the light, airy villas of the wealthy. No wonder she cannot rest until she finds her drachma! In her persistent determination, we see in her (no less than in the Christ-like shepherd) something of what God is like.

Finally, in their context, these parables turn the spotlight on Jesus' accusers. Sometimes the Church's message of repentance can appear rather like the words of the grumbling Pharisees and scribes. In these striking parables, Jesus challenges the narrow, even idolatrous view of God held by his critics within the religious community. God is far more generous than we would often allow him to be. In contrast, it is often those 'beyond the pale' who are best able to see the depths of God's generosity, and to respond joyfully to it themselves. IB

Proper 20

(Sunday between 18 and 24 September inclusive)

Jeremiah 8.18—9.1 or Amos 8.4–7; 1 Timothy 2.1–7; Luke 16.1–13

Jeremiah 8.18—9.1

This is a poem of a kind very typical of the book of Jeremiah: a lament, bewailing the unhappy state of the community, apparently deprived of any awareness of God's presence with them. The poem gives no indication of its author. Some readers will find it helpful to take this as one of the 'words of Jeremiah' mentioned at 1.1 and see here the outpourings of a deeply troubled soul. Others may prefer not to be concerned about authorship, and to reflect on this as the kind of poem that is applicable to a great variety of circumstances.

The basic anxiety expressed here seems to be the complete break-up of the established order of society. The poet empathizes with the desperate concerns of the community, and three quite different metaphors are employed to bring out those concerns. First, there is no awareness of God's presence in Zion. This might be because of the destruction of the temple by the Babylonian invaders, but we need to remember that this sense of absence is found in a number of psalms, not all of which seem to relate to the Babylonian period. Second, the completion of harvest was normally a time for communal rejoicing; here, by contrast, summer and harvest-time have gone by without any sense of rescue from their plight. (The word 'saved' should not be given the strong theological sense that it often has in Christian contexts.) Third, there is no sign of restored health. Physicians did not always have a good reputation in the ancient world, but their different balms might soothe pain. Of that there is no sign. (Some readers may have come across older translations of the Bible, which at 8.22 had 'treacle in Gilead', a charming picture, but not the required sense.) The poem ends, as it had begun, with the wistful acknowledgement that the poet can see no grounds for hope of improvement in the people's sad state.

The last part of v. 19 is put in brackets by NRSV and other translations. It looks as if this brief note was added by an early editor who felt that he knew the reason for the people's distress and must put that over to those who read or heard the poem. On this reading, images and foreign idols were the problem. This is the same viewpoint as that expressed in the books of Kings, and many will feel that it is much too neat and tidy a solution; religious folk in the ancient as in the modern world have often been ready to demonize what clashes with their particular world view and blame all society's troubles on that cause. RC

Amos 8.4–7

See Proper 11, p. 201.

I Timothy 2.1–7

This passage marks an early stage in Christian accommodation (if that is the right word for it) to the institutions of the surrounding society. It is one of the evidences for what is often seen as the bourgeois character of the Pastoral Epistles, their tendency to sober respectability (cf. the qualities urged for Christian ministers in 1 Tim. 3), and their lack of a sense of the deeper and more dangerous aspects of Christian allegiance. At the same time, political loyalty of what we (in a very different world) are likely to see as a rather naive and uncritical kind is commanded by Paul (Rom. 13.1–7) and indeed (with whatever sense) in the tradition of Jesus' teaching (Mark 12.13–17). Here, a Pauline inheritor states the attitude more unequivocally than ever, and the general disposition is plain. Here is the charter for all civic services and prayers for royal families and rulers that have ever been – the kind of open Christian ministry often disliked by Catholic and principled Protestant alike. Yet its justification here lies in something deeper than the tendency to live at ease in one's social niche; and it goes beyond even the great and gracious good of social stability that only those who enjoy it can take easily for granted and which later Christian thinkers were to make much of. The doctrine is that God desires the salvation of all and Jesus gave himself for all. The only question then is how best to further the divine purpose in the societies of which we are part. LH

Luke 16.1–13

Having challenged his opponents with his three 'lost and found' parables, Jesus turns again to his disciples. He recounts an obscure parable, followed by a number of sayings. But where does the parable end and this group of sayings begin? It is unclear whether *ho kurios* of v. 8a is the steward's 'master' or 'the Lord' Jesus. If the former, then we are still in the parable; if the latter, then v. 8a begins Jesus' (or Luke's) application of it. Given the 'I' of v. 9, vv. 1–8a most likely form the parable proper, vv. 8b–9 the application, and vv. 10–13 are related sayings.

The parable describes a rich man, perhaps an absentee landlord, who employs a manager to oversee his affairs (including the right to rent out land to tenant-farmers and make loans). Faced with being sacked from his post, the manager strikes a deal with his master's debtors to ensure a friendly welcome on his dismissal.

His initial action is certainly dishonest or 'wicked': he squanders not his own property but his master's. It is less clear whether his subsequent action of rewriting the debtors' bills is equally dishonest. He is probably cooking the books in order to win influence, though he may simply be removing his own commission from the final figure.

Either way, it is not his dishonesty that receives praise, either from his master or from Jesus. Rather, he is praised for acting 'shrewdly' or 'prudently'. Faced with a life-changing crisis, he musters all his managerial acumen to meet that crisis. He may not have much potential either as gardener or professional beggar ('I cannot dig; I am ashamed to beg'); but he is a shrewd manager!

This theme of crisis may provide the key to the application. The 'children of light' ought to learn from the 'children of this age' in their ability to respond shrewdly and effectively to coming crises; in the same way, God's people ought to respond to the crisis of the coming kingdom.

Second, there are Christians who, like this manager, have 'mammon' entrusted to them in this world. They too are to use it wisely, to make friends for themselves. In their case, however, it is to be used in the service of the poor and needy, who will welcome them into 'the eternal tents': almsgiving was an accepted Jewish way of storing up capital for the world to come (see 12.33).

The remaining verses pick up themes from the parable. 'Mammon', a Hebrew word denoting 'money' or 'wealth', has an essentially neutral meaning. But Luke, recognizing its corrupting potential, calls it 'dishonest' or 'unjust'. It can be used prudently, to assist others (as in the case of the shrewd manager). And those who are 'reliable' with such things may be entrusted with greater, the true riches of the kingdom. But slippery is the slope from possession of wealth to idolatry. Thus Luke concludes with Jesus' provocative saying about the impossibility of serving two masters. IB

Proper 21

(Sunday between 25 September and 1 October inclusive)

Jeremiah 32.1–3a, 6–15 or Amos 6.1a, 4–7; 1 Timothy 6.6–19; Luke 16.19–31

Jeremiah 32.1–3a, 6–15

The greater part of Jeremiah 1—25 is in poetry; chs 26—45, by contrast, contain many prose narratives set at around the time of the Babylonian invasion and the fall of Jerusalem. The opening verses of this reading make it clear that that is the setting of this story; the dates given in v. 1 suggest a setting around 588 BC. When the Babylonians first conquered the country in 597, Zedekiah had been set on the throne, with the requirement and expectation that he should be a faithful vassal, but he had rebelled. By this time Jerusalem was again under siege, and Jeremiah had been put under house arrest – not surprisingly, since it appears from vv. 3b–5 that he was announcing that Jerusalem would be destroyed and the king sent into exile.

For our reading, however, this is no more than the setting. Verses 6–15 give quite an unexpected twist to the tale. A piece of family land becomes available in Anathoth, Jeremiah's home village (1.1), and he is urged by his cousin to exercise his right and buy the land. We might have supposed that Jeremiah's gloomy prognosis of events would lead him to regard this as a useless exercise. Instead we are told that Jeremiah knew that he was to buy the field (how he knew it we are not told), and the story spells out in solemn detail all the appropriate legal procedures, which were duly carried out despite the continuing Babylonian threat. The deeds were sealed in an earthenware jar, to ensure that they would be preserved despite the inevitable ravages that Jerusalem would undergo. And the story ends by laying down the basic point that this was to be seen as a sign of a future restoration.

We need not argue here about how much of this story actually goes back to the life of Jeremiah, or indeed reflects the details of the condition of a city under siege. Those who told the story and handed it down were convinced that the destruction of Jerusalem had not been simply a random act, for which no explanation was possible. As we saw in last week's reading (8.19) the editors of the book of Jeremiah took the view that false religious practice had been the basic cause for the disasters that had taken place. But they were equally convinced, as today's reading shows, that that was not end of story. After a period of punishment there would be restoration. It is an interesting subject for reflection, and one on which agreement can hardly be expected, to ask whether events in the present-day world can be explained in the same kind of way. RC

Amos 6.1a, 4–7

Although v. 1 is addressed to Jerusalem (Zion) and Samaria, all that follows is pertinent to Samaria only, and it is likely that the reference to Zion is the work of a later editor who wanted to extend the scope of Amos's words to the southern capital. Samaria became the capital of the northern kingdom, Israel, early in the ninth century BC when Omri built the city on an imposing hill (1 Kings 16.24). Excavations there have revealed artistically engraved and shaped ivories that decorated the royal palace ('beds of ivory' means that they were decorated with ivory), as well as ostraca (administrative accounts written on broken pottery) that show how neighbouring villages supplied the capital with foods and wine. 'Eating lambs from the flock' was an extravagant misuse of resources, granted that Palestinian sheep usually produced only one offspring per year in Old Testament times. The reference to David (v. 5) is probably a later addition. It overloads the metre and was not, apparently, in the Hebrew used by the translators who produced the ancient Greek version. Verses 5 and 6a describe a wealthy, privileged group whose life is one long round of parties, unconcerned with the people for whose welfare they are supposed to be responsible ('the ruin of Joseph'). The harshness of Amos's judgement is proportionate to the arrogance of the people condemned. There is a pun in the Hebrew on 1b (not included in the reading) 'the notables of the *first* of the nations' and 7a, 'they shall now be the *first* to go into exile'. When disaster strikes (as it did in 722/1 when Samaria fell to the Assyrians) they can retain their status of being first, by going first into exile. Power involves responsibility. To use it for personal enjoyment is not part of God's design, and will lead to judgement. JR

I Timothy 6.6–19

As so often in the Pastoral Epistles, we have in this passage what feels like abrupt movement from rather commonplace ethical instruction to inspiring exhortation and then to the example of Jesus himself. The moral teaching concentrates on the subject of the snare of wealth. Rather oddly, the writer reverts to the topic in the latter part of the passage. (The Letter of James has the same feature in relation to the same subject; it comes in ch. 5 as well as ch. 1.) In itself, it is an ethical commonplace, with parallels in Stoicism and the Jewish 'wisdom' tradition. Religious teachers and sages of all kinds favour the simple life and attack dependence on money and other property. The New Testament abounds with it, most strikingly in the lifestyle of Jesus himself, and it comes with special force in the Gospel of Luke. In the case of Jesus it surely has eschatological motivation: in the light of the kingdom, now being brought into being among us, of course worldly concerns fall away and can on longer claim our attention. Here, that dimension and that motivation no longer fill the picture.

The attack on wealth is, of course, and always has been, a lost cause – for the most part; Christian heroes take it truly on board, the rest of us in hope and by fits and starts. Even the Letter of James, attacking the rich and welcoming a poor visitor to the community, thus reveals that the Christians themselves were mostly of the 'middling sort'. So, surely, it has chiefly been throughout history with Christian groups of all kinds. The fact is that the Church has from early times lived with an uneasy conscience on the subject of wealth, depending on at least a measure of property for its very survival (certainly for its flourishing) and then tending to accumulate wealth on the grand scale, with poverty as a fitful ideal and relief of the poor as one policy among many. So the passage we read is inescapably offensive to our way of life – yet makes us feel helpless. Economics (including church economics) defeats us. At least we can thereby know that, sinners, we depend wholly on grace. Virtue, here as in other areas, is generally beyond us, and the charge of hypocrisy is our just penalty. But there is no area where virtue is more commonly ignored than this, self-interest coinciding with despair.

The heroic qualities listed are less problematic, in theory. Again, nobody would disagree with them. But the appeal here is to the decision of baptism (mostly adult at the time of writing) – 'the good confession'. It is baptism that carries the obligation to the life of goodness. That act is compared not with Jesus' baptism but with his stand at his trial, which was his occasion for making the good confession. Perhaps the Johannine account, which majors on the trial before Pilate rather than that before Jewish authorities, was chiefly in mind; and the creeds were to make the same choice. The outcome of Christian commitment in solid, conventional moral be-haviour is characteristic of the Pastorals and of most of the later New Testament writings, but with an eye always on the distinctive Christian hope: Christ's return. Christian survival was to depend on solid and decent goodness in the life of the Christian communities and on the assurance of heavenly acceptance. So these Letters go a long way towards setting the agenda for Christian life in the years that lay ahead. LH

Luke 16.19–31

The issue of material possessions appears and reappears in the section of Luke's Gospel called the travel narrative (12.13–34; 14.12–24; ch. 16). Four of the lections in recent Sundays have focused on the deceptiveness of wealth (enticing the rich to presume they can ensure a secure future), the potential idolatry of possessions, the importance of attending to the poor, and the critical importance of the manner in which one gives alms (Propers 13, 14, 17, 20). The climax of this Lucan interest comes in the lesson for this Sunday, the dramatic story of the rich man and Lazarus.

Why is so much attention given to material possessions? Some commentators would argue that the narrative is directly aimed at Luke's community, which either is composed of predominantly rich people needing to be reminded of their obliga-tions to the poor or is a community in tension between rich and poor. This may or may not be true. More evident than the sociological contours of Luke's community, however, are the sociological implications of the Christian message. At the heart of the gospel is the great reversal in which the rich and powerful, who in this life perceive no need for divine grace, are cut off from the people of God, while the poor, the lowly and the outcasts are given a proper place in the community of faith. In any and all communities, the promise is that God reverses the social and economic scale in surprising ways. (This, of course, is a Lucan theme not limited to the travel narrative. See, for example, Mary's Magnificat, 1.46–55.)

Nowhere is this reversal more vividly put than in the story of the rich man and Lazarus. While there are at least two themes developed in the plot, the changed circumstances of the primary characters dominate the story. Right at the beginning we are faced with a sharp contrast – rich man, poor man. What is mentioned about the rich man are the signs of his lavish wealth, his well-stocked wardrobe and his sumptuous diet ('every day'). Lazarus is depicted in gross terms that we would rather not hear. The mention of dogs licking his sores identifies him as not only poor but also unclean, and thus an outcast.

It is only after the death of both characters and their reversed positions in the afterlife that we begin to discover the real problem with the rich man. He is not harshly condemned. He is not indicted because he is rich, as if there were something inherently evil about money. We are not told that he persecuted Lazarus or deliberately refused him food or sponsored legislation to rid his gates of beggars.

Perhaps the clue, as John R. Donahue notes, is the fact that now he *sees* Lazarus for the first time (16.23). The difficulty with their relationship all those years on earth is that the rich man never sees Lazarus. 'One of the prime dangers of wealth is that it causes "blindness"' (John R. Donahue, *The Gospel in Parable: Metaphor, Narrative, and Theology in the Synoptic Gospels*; Philadelphia: Fortress Press, 1988, p. 171). The rich man's wealth has so distorted his vision that he is unable to perceive the plight of the beggar at his gate, to identify with his predicament and to ease his suffering. Unfortunately, prosperity has a way of limiting our perspective, of closing down the shades on the distasteful so as not to disturb our enjoyment. It is an age-old story.

And so the reversal occurs. The rich man's plea from Hades to 'Father Abraham' recalls John the Baptist's warning to the crowds that they not glibly claim Abraham as their father. They are, rather, to bear fruits worthy of repentance (3.8). But all the entreaties of the rich man now are resisted. He can think of Lazarus only as an errand boy to assuage his thirst or to warn his brothers. Tragically, he seems beyond the time for repentance. In sharp contrast, Lazarus is sitting by Abraham's side.

The other theme of this parable, often overshadowed, comes at the conclusion. The rich man's request to send Lazarus, a person from the dead, to alert his brothers is denied on the ground that they already have Moses and the prophets. The Scriptures are important to Luke (see e.g. 24.25–27, 32, 44–49). What is happening in the advent of Jesus is the fulfilment of prophecies contained in the holy writings. There are a host of texts in those writings that remind Israel of its covenant responsibility to the poor in the land. If the brothers pay no heed to them, then they will pay no heed to one from the dead. The continuity is affirmed between the Scriptures and the witness of the community of the resurrection.

One of the dilemmas in preaching this passage is that it is hard to identify with either the rich man or Lazarus. It is difficult to picture oneself as affluent as the rich man in all his opulence or to imagine oneself as catastrophically devastated as Lazarus. They both represent people other than us. It may be, then, that contemporary audiences can most easily associate with the five brothers, those of us who still have an opportunity to be instructed by the Scriptures and to see the beggar at our gates. If so, then the parable itself becomes a word to the rich man's siblings to 'warn them, so that they will not also come into this place of torment' (16.28). CC

Proper 22

(Sunday between 2 and 8 October inclusive)

Lamentations 1.1–6 or Habakkuk 1.1–4; 2.1–4; 2 Timothy 1.1–14; Luke 17.5–10

Lamentations 1.1–6

How do communities react to great disasters? The answer is that it depends on the traditions and culture of a given community. In countries of the Middle East today, grief can be expressed communally through crying accompanied by violent physical gestures, and by angry outbursts among great crowds. Western secular societies, especially those traditionally encouraged to have a stiff upper lip, find it more difficult to cope with disaster or grief, except that British society has increasingly resorted to leaving bunches of flowers or even toys at the sites of tragedies. In ancient Israel, mourning was much better organized (if it is appropriate to use that verb), and 2 Chron. 35.25 provides a glimpse of what could happen. Singing men and women are mentioned, who spoke and recorded their laments on the tragic death in battle of King Josiah. The destruction of Jerusalem by the Babylonians in 587 BC was undoubtedly a national disaster of the first order. That it should have resulted in gatherings of people to lament communally, and probably annually, is to be expected.

The book of Lamentations may well have been used at, or have been produced because of, such gatherings. In its present form the book is a sophisticated literary composition, including four acrostic poems; that is, poems in which each verse (in ch. 3 every three verses) begins with a successive letter of the Hebrew alphabet. Today's reading opens by portraying Jerusalem as a widow mourning for her husband (cities and countries are grammatically feminine in Hebrew); yet in one respect the simile is inappropriate. A newly bereaved widow would be surrounded by friends and neighbours. Jerusalem is alone, deserted by those who would have comforted her had she been a woman. The plight of the city is thus strikingly emphasized. In v. 3 the attention switches to the country, to Judah. If Jerusalem is alone and deserted, Judah's inhabitants are scattered and unable to hide or get respite from their pursuers. The scene shifts back to Jerusalem (v. 4). No one comes to the city to celebrate. The roads are deserted, the gates (i.e. public spaces) empty. Priests cannot minister, girls of marriageable age have no prospects. Verse 5 attributes the city's situation to divine punishment. The word translated 'transgressions' has the sense of 'rebellions'. The city's wrongdoings stemmed from a fundamental desire to go its own way and do its own thing apart from God. In effect, God has let the city have its own way. It has become a victim of the human pride that expresses itself in warfare and conquest. JR

Habakkuk 1.1–4, 2.1–4

Nothing is known about the prophet Habakkuk. The editorial introduction gives his name, but no setting in time; not even his father's name. Within the book, the statement that God is stirring up the Chaldeans (1.6) has led many commentators to date Habakkuk to the period 626–605 BC, when the Babylonians (Chaldeans) began the expansion that would ultimately entail the destruction of Jerusalem. Even if this is correct, it does not contribute much to understanding the lectionary reading. The opening verses are similar to the numerous psalms that cry out to God in despair. Why is God apparently indifferent to, or powerless to prevent, wrongdoing? Such is the situation that the law becomes slack (v. 4). The Hebrew verb translated 'becomes slack' can mean to 'be or become numb' and the NEB 'grows effete' (i.e. worn out, feeble) gets the sense well. As in the psalms of lament, the complaints are not sufficiently specific for the wrongdoings or their perpetrators to be identified. Does v. 4b ('The wicked . . .') refer to wicked Israelites or to foreign nations?

Habakkuk 2.1–4 is about faithfulness – the kind of fortitude born of the conviction that God's justice will ultimately prevail. The prophet sees himself as a watchman who looks for the arrival of good tidings. He is commanded to write down something that will encourage faithfulness in others. This vision for the future will provide hope and action for the present. Faithfulness to God and hope in his future will become a way of living. JR

2 Timothy 1.1–14

In this passage we are apparently in touch, for the first and only time in the New Testament, with what has ever since been the basis of the stability of the Church's life: Christian families, one generation after another, handing down their 'sincere faith' (v. 5) from mother to child. New converts are of course always to be sought, always welcome, but it is in solid Christian families, both guarding and passing on the art and the skill of Christian observance, that we meet bedrock. This tends naturally to be a conservative force – and our writer commends it as such. That is both its strength and its limitation.

At the same time, by this very emphasis the writer gives away the pseudonymous character of these letters. In Paul's day, such inheriting of faith had not had time to take place. His Christians were converts from Judaism or paganism, and stability was still precarious, still awaited formation, as is evident from the genuine letters.

Yet it is in 2 Timothy (especially here and in ch. 4) that the writer adopts Paul's mantle most convincingly and most personally, with many small details of life and story. (So it is here that he offers those who still maintain Pauline authorship, in whole or in part, what is perhaps their strongest argument.) The writer is certainly a devotee of Paul and Paul is his hero and model – and his authority for his message. This is Paul the prisoner for the Christian cause and for his apostolic charge, and this status as a sufferer for Christ gives him his standing. Naturally, as often in these letters, Paul urges Timothy to hold fast to what he has inherited and to pass it on intact. On the ground that one only fights when there is a real enemy, we read the sign to indicate that one motive for these letters lay in the rise, by the later first century, of dissident styles of faith or Christian life, which the writer feels to be inimical to what Paul could have countenanced. The passage then raises the highly relevant question: is fidelity the same as conservatism? Or how much (and what sort of) development and adaptation can the gospel bear without ruin, or, alternatively, can it really survive by seeking to stand still? LH

Luke 17.5–10

As Luke's lengthy travel narrative draws towards its close, this final section focuses once again upon the disciples. After teaching about 'occasions for stumbling' and forgiveness (vv. 1–4, oddly omitted from the lectionary), we are presented here with a saying about faith and another parable of the master/slave relationship. On the surface, it is hard to see any obvious link connecting these various sayings.

However, the context may help us. The request that provokes the saying of v. 6 comes from 'the apostles' (for Luke synonymous with 'the Twelve') rather than the wider group of disciples. So Jesus' reply, and possibly also the parable, may be particularly directed towards those exercising leadership within the Church. Those with a certain status in the community may fall prey to the temptation of superiority, or even presumption of God's favour, and what follows challenges both.

The request concerning faith (literally 'Add to us faith') is ambiguous. The apostles could mean 'increase our faith!' (as in our NRSV translation). In this case they are challenged for their fixation on quantity rather than quality: even as much as a tiny mustard seed would be sufficient to do incredible things (and Jesus gives a sufficiently ludicrous example). However, another possible translation is 'Give us faith!', suggesting that the apostles currently have none at all, and this alternative is strengthened by the 'unreal' condition of Jesus' reply ('you could say . . .').

Luke continues with the short parable of the 'unprofitable servant' (which may embarrass modern Christians for its disinterest in the morality of slavery). It is unlikely that Jesus originally addressed such a parable – which assumes that its hearers would have a farm, a flock or slaves – to his disciples or especially to the Twelve, given his prior demands upon them. But these are the audience in its present context. They are reminded that they are 'unworthy' slaves, whose pleasure is to do the master's bidding, and who should not expect thanks or favours at the dining table.

Yet there remains a puzzle. For Luke has already told a very different parable, in which watchful servants were assured that their master would sit them down for dinner and wait on them himself (12.35–38). Has the Lord now gone back on his promise? This is not necessarily so, if today's parable is seen as challenging presumption of favourable treatment, a sense that God owes us something. Yes, God is indeed a gracious God, who liberally feeds his people in the messianic banquet of the kingdom. But this divine generosity should not be presumed upon as a reward for good behaviour. Again, Luke may be thinking especially of Christian ministers. Like the servant of the parable, they can be spoken of as shepherds (1 Cor. 9.7; John 21), or as those ploughing a field (1 Cor. 9.10). But ultimately they must remember that they are slaves, like the one who himself took the form of a slave, *doulos* (Phil. 2.7), Christ the Lord. IB

Proper 23

(Sunday between 9 and 15 October inclusive)

Jeremiah 29.1, 4–7 or 2 Kings 5.1–3, 7–15b; 2 Timothy 2.8–15; Luke 17.11–19

Jeremiah 29.1, 4–7

In these verses we are presented with the first, and most agreeable, part of a letter said to have been sent by Jeremiah to those who had been deported to Babylon. The latter part of the chapter reveals deep divisions within that exiled group, but for better or worse the prescribed lectionary readings limit themselves to the safer and more acceptable elements. The letter is written in prose, and its style is very different from the poetic fragments in the early part of the book, some of which we have looked at in the last few weeks. The letter in the form in which we have it has been shaped by the editors of the book, often spoken of as Deuteronomists because the style and theological standpoint is very close to that of the book of Deuteronomy.

Verse 1 provides the context. The situation is that many of the leaders of the community had been deported following Nebuchadnezzar's capture of Jerusalem in 597 BC. 'All the people' may give a misleading impression; certainly not all had been taken away. We saw from last week's reading that a sizeable community remained in Jerusalem, including of course Jeremiah himself, but an influential group was now in Babylon.

In the ancient world gods were often very closely linked with the place in which they were worshipped. Yahweh the God of Israel might be supposed to be quite irrelevant to those taken away to another land; surely they should now worship the Babylonian gods? The message of the letter is very different. First of all, vv. 5–6 stress that the community are to take every opportunity to build up as normal a life as possible. But it is clear that this is intended as more than a message to get on with life. The underlying message is theological. They are to understand their exile as brought about by Yahweh ('whom I have sent into exile', v. 4, repeated in v. 7), not by the superior military power of Babylon. And a very strong claim is implied at the end of the reading: that the welfare of Babylon is dependent not upon its own gods but upon the favour of Yahweh. We know little in detail of the nature of Israel's religion and belief from an earlier period, but the signs are that they did not differ in any very fundamental way from the practices of other surrounding peoples. Here we can trace the beginnings of the astonishing claim made within the Jewish and later the Christian tradition, for the universal power of the God whom they worshipped. RC

2 Kings 5.1–3, 7–15b

See Proper 9, p. 193.

2 Timothy 2.8–15

This passage is almost a model of exhortation for martyrs. It is full of brief, sharp statements that few, still, can find unmoving (vv. 11–13). For Paul (in whose persona, if not by the real self, the letter is written), it was a question of imprisonment whose outcome, it is true, could not be foreseen; so that facing it as the ultimate crisis makes perfect sense.

Christian spirituality has, wisely if dramatically, seen the ethos of martyrdom as less a remote possibility than, in its essence, an everyday challenge (cf. 1 Cor. 15.31, 'I die daily'; and Luke 9.23, on the daily taking up of the cross); so that the attitudes here enjoined are to be part of the Christian's internal system, day by day, formed by disciplined prayer. Our passage is preceded by verses that see Christian disciple-ship in military terms, which catches perfectly the spirit that is involved. The point is so strongly made that we may suppose that the readers could not be assumed to see things this way without encouragement.

The actual statement of the beliefs (v. 8) at stake is, as everywhere in these letters, terse in the extreme. By comparison with Paul's undoubted writings, it gives us only the barest idea of what doctrine is actually to be maintained. It is almost as if the writer is keener to slap down dissidence for its own sake than to say precisely what beliefs are involved and how a Christian really ought to think and believe. Our writer was not one for seminars, tossing ideas about for the fun of it (v. 14). A modern parish course on the faith, surely involving discussion and finding one another's views 'interesting', would have tested his patience to the limit. To be faithful (to whatever is held to be 'basic') is the greatest and perhaps even the only virtue that is really required of the church-member. We are to live as stripped for action of the most stringent kind. And the basic relationship with Christ is utterly sure, wholly dependable. Though there are some signs in these letters of the Church begin-ning to 'settle into society' (cf. 2.2), this tendency in no way detracts from the perceived need to resist any such temptation – the writer recognized it all too well and saw it as a threat to the purity of Christian corporate life. How far are we to live still in the first century? LH

Luke 17.11–19

The message is the duty, both morally and theologically rooted, of gratitude to God. In context, the story exemplifies once more Jesus' positive discrimination in favour of outcasts of society: for 'leprosy' (whatever precisely was meant in the way of skin diseases) was accounted ritually unclean (Lev. 13) and a ground for exclusion from ordinary social intercourse – probably more for its abnormality than for medical reasons.

The gratitude of the single Samaritan further accentuates the theme of Jesus' indiscriminate welcome, and highlights the location of the positive response to him, anywhere but in mainstream Israel. The story has its eye on the future situation of the Christian mission, of which Luke was the narrator; and this concern leads Luke to a failure in realism, for no Samaritan could surely report to the Jerusalem priesthood to certify recovery (v. 14; cf. Mark 1.40–45, perhaps a prototype for this story).

As often, Luke's Gospel shadows what is to come in his second volume. In Acts 1.8, we read that Samaria, as schismatically Jewish, is an early stage in the foreseen spread of the Christian mission, out from Jerusalem to 'the ends of the earth'; and Acts 8 describes this development in some detail. It is presented as a major move, marked by an apostolic visit from Jerusalem (so that it has the aspect of a centuries-long breach now, in the Christian movement, repaired: Jesus' healing work goes on); marked too by the Spirit's ratifying and empowering gift. From the Gospel of John (ch. 4) too we have evidence of early Christian interest in and accommodation of Samaritans. This is the practical face of early Christian universalism.

But gratitude to God is the theme: he is the giver of all good, including reconciliation of the estranged back to the human race as a whole – a gift which merits its appropriate and necessary response. LH

Proper 24

(Sunday between 16 and 22 October inclusive)

Jeremiah 31.27–34 or Genesis 32.22–31; 2 Timothy 3.14—4.5; Luke 18.1–8

Jeremiah 31.27–34

Whether or not these words derive from Jeremiah (scholarly opinion inclines to the view that they are not his work) they wrestle with a profound problem: how can God relate to us in such a way that he does not compel us to serve him on the one hand, but prevents us from spurning him on the other hand? The answer is that such an arrangement is virtually impossible. The problem with the covenant with the Israelites was that the latter were human beings, and it belongs to human nature to wish to be self-sufficient of any outside power, for all that humans constantly create outside powers in their own image. In the ancient world these were stars and planets, and magical forces. The modern world continues with astrology, to which it adds extra-terrestrial aliens and concepts such as Gaia.

It would be easy to suppose that the new covenant has been fulfilled in the New Testament and the Church, but this would be premature. Can the Church be said to have been more faithful to God in its history than the people of Israel? In what sense is God's law written on the hearts of Christians? And if everybody knew God, from the least to the greatest, would there be any need for missions?

From a Christian perspective it can be said that Jesus fulfils the new covenant in his own person and his obedience to God. His followers, alas, fall far short of this.

The Jeremiah passage must therefore be seen as a precious hope for a future kind of existence in which all mankind will love what God commands and desire what he promises. One of the forces most likely to bring about such a state of affairs is the self-giving love exhibited in the passion of Jesus. JR

Genesis 32.22–31

Jacob's marital adventures in the East are over; he is returning to his homeland. Just as there had been a divine encounter on the outward journey (ch. 28), so on his return he is confronted with 'a man', who is quickly shown in the story to be no ordinary human being. We were told in Gen. 1 that human beings were made in the image of God, so it is not surprising that on more than one occasion in Genesis divine appearances take human form (cf. Abraham's visitor(s) in ch. 18).

The powerful description of the present encounter can be read at many different levels. There are what are known as 'aetiological' elements, that is to say, explanations of such matters as unusual place names ('Peniel' = 'face of God') or eating habits (the verse following our reading, 32, refers to this). More important, the story functions in several different ways as a 'rite of passage'. It begins with Jacob 'left', bereft of 'everything that he had' – wives, children and possessions. Jacob is then pictured as being required to make the crossing which was the only means of access to the holy land. That land was occupied by his brother Esau, whom he fears will be hostile; can it be that the blessing was after all intended for him? Jacob receives a new name, 'Israel'; both in the Bible and in many human situations the giving of a new name is an important symbol of a changed status. (In a Christian context the giving of a name in baptism is the most obvious example.) The name given here is a clear pointer to the identity of the community of Israel which will be the main concern of the Old Testament and, in another sense, of the New. Another 'passage' underlying the story is that it all takes place as night becomes day; God's help is regularly pictured as coming 'in the morning' (e.g. Ps. 30.5).

Basic also to the story is the presentation of fundamental human experiences in terms of a struggle with the divine. This is an element played down in some Christian traditions, which emphasize submission to God's will, but the portrayal of Jesus in the New Testament several times pictures his relation with God in terms of struggle (e.g. in the passion narratives). Jacob's persistence is finally rewarded, 'I have seen God face to face and yet my life is preserved'. We have moved a long way from the cunning and treacherous Jacob of the earlier part of his story. RC

2 Timothy 3.14—4.5

We focus on the commendation of 'Scripture' in 3.15–17. But it is as well to be clear what is referred to: the expression 'sacred writings' (v. 15) is a standard Hellenistic Jewish way of referring to Scripture. In context, that means the Septuagint; that is, (in Protestant Christian terms) the Old Testament (= Hebrew Bible) plus, more or less, the Apocrypha. We are still some decades away from collections of Christian writings and a sense of such collections as 'Scripture', that is, authoritative writings, to be used in liturgy and decision-making. (Nevertheless, one might say that the use of Mark as a source by Matthew and Luke, combining acceptance with additions and alterations, was not unlike the way Jewish writers had, in the past, developed existing authoritative works in the furtherance of quasi-canonical use; cf. the dependence of Ephesians on Paul's undoubted writings and our present writer's appeal to the authority and example of Paul, whose mantle he wears.) This text, if viewed in context, is then of only modified usefulness to an unsubtle modern propagandist for the authority of Scripture.

Moreover, there is irony in the fact that this writer is notable in the New Testament for his scant use of what Christians came to call the Old Testament whose merits he advocates: 2.19 stands alone in this book. In that way, his appeal to Scripture is on all fours with his campaign for true doctrine – whose content he states only in brief formulas and does little to expound. 'All scripture', v. 16, conceals a multitude of problems that are never touched here, and 'inspired by God' is in practice too general to solve them, and has often served more as a weapon than a serviceable tool.

No, our writer's overwhelming concern is for unity and for the elimination of dissent. It is evident that at this time, probably around the end of the first century (note the hint in v. 15), the Christian movement was at a dangerous stage in its development (4.3–4), looking for criteria of true faith and authorities to define and legitimate it, whether in terms of documents or dependable human leaders (cf. 1 Tim. 3). Gone is the time when a chief task was how to define oneself over against Judaism; here, the problems are internal to the Church and the old Scriptures are part of the Christian equipment. Wearing his Pauline hat, the writer, having leaders especially in view, urges sober fidelity in the task of holding the line, before the Lord returns. His is the predicament, endlessly replicated, of the person of goodness and sound sense trying to grapple with the strident and the eccentric. Or at least, we can be sure that that is how he viewed the situation – and it does beg the question. Even the neutral commentator risks showing his colours. LH

Luke 18.1–8

This Sunday's parable, and next's, address Luke's favourite theme of prayer. But here is no general exhortation to 'pray constantly'. The parable is closely linked with the preceding chapter, which focuses on the delay of the Son of Man's coming. So we should expect teaching about prayer in this urgent 'in-between time'.

We are probably meant to appreciate the comedy of the parable with its colourful characters: an arrogant judge, and an annoyingly persistent widow who drives him to distraction. Moreover, there is surely humour in the ambiguous Greek of v. 5 (obscured by NRSV's 'wear me out'). Does the judge relent lest the widow accost him in the street and literally punch him in the face ('give me a black eye')? Or is he concerned, metaphorically, with potential damage to his reputation?

Nevertheless, there is a more serious side. The two characters are poles apart in their society's power structures. The judge, perhaps a local magistrate, wields considerable authority. Yet given the Law's requirement that judges have a particular concern for the weak, he is letting the side down. Widows were one of the most vulnerable groups in Jewish society, often mentioned alongside orphans for their precarious economic position. This makes this widow's dogged persistence all the more understandable. Yet as so often in Jesus' parables, we find a shocking reversal of roles, as the apparently weak and defenceless woman is shown to wield real power.

Verses 6–8 provide the interpretation for Luke's readers. It has an allegorical aspect: the widow is like God's elect who pray for vindication (perhaps in the face of the expected hostility and persecution of the 'last days'). Yet it is not straightforwardly allegorical: God is not like an unjust judge!

Two difficulties are raised by these verses, one linguistic, the other theological. First, the translation of v. 7b is disputed. The verb could refer either to God's current slowness to act (see NJB), or to his patience towards his chosen (AV). Moreover, the sentence could be a question expecting a negative answer (as NRSV), or a concessive clause to v. 7a (*kai* meaning 'though'). Given v. 8, NRSV may have it about right here: the judge's slowness to act is contrasted with God's willingness to vindicate his people 'speedily'.

More theologically, some may read the parable's language as encouraging a desire for vengeance. But the emphasis is rather on the present injustice, which in God's world cannot be allowed to continue indefinitely. The NRSV perhaps helps with its translation ('And will God not grant justice...?'). Luke knows that Israel's God sides with the victims of injustice and ultimately acts on their behalf.

Finally, v. 8b has an expected twist. The eschatological prayer of God's elect has been at issue here. But Luke's Jesus concludes with a provocative question, which challenges the presumption of those who consider themselves faithful. When God sends his agent the Son of Man in answer to their persistent prayers, will they ultimately be found wanting? IB

Proper 25

(Sunday between 23 and 30 October inclusive)

Joel 2.23–32 or Ecclesiasticus 35.12–17 or Jeremiah 14.7–10, 19–22; 2 Timothy 4.6–8, 16–18; Luke 18.9–14

Joel 2.23–32

This passage is part of the divine response to the people's prayer and fasting (2.15–17) in the face of disaster (1.2—2.11). The exact nature of the disaster is disputed. It is possible to see it wholly in terms of a devastating plague of locusts (cf. 1.4; 2.25) or to see a series of disasters, including drought, locusts, fire and invasion by an army. The reading begins with reassurance to the people of Jerusalem in material terms. Whatever may have caused the lean years, they will now be replaced with years of plenty. An intriguing question of translation and interpretation is raised by the Hebrew of v. 23a ('early rain'), which mentions the Instructor, or Teacher in, or for, Righteousness. Jewish and some older Christian interpreters saw a reference to the Messiah; and because a 'Teacher of Righteousness' is known from the Dead Sea Scrolls, it has been asked whether Joel 2.23a is the origin for this title. Most modern versions take the Hebrew *moreh*, which can mean 'teacher', to be the 'former rain', the rain that falls ideally in October. However, the NIV margin has 'the teacher for righteousness' here. Verse 28 (3.1 in the Hebrew) introduces words familiar from the speech of Peter on the day of Pentecost (Acts 2.17–21). God will pour out his spirit on all flesh, which presumably means upon the descendants of the people addressed, rather than all humanity everywhere. There is a similar thought at Ezek. 36.25–27. If there is a link between human wickedness and the failure of the natural world to produce food (cf. Gen. 4.11–12) it follows that, ideally, a renewal of the fertility of the world of nature demands a new type of humanity. This will be done by the pouring out of God's spirit, and by the dreams and visions that will disclose the things of God to those who experience them.

However, this raises the question whether such action on God's part destroys human choice. Will people be forced to become faithful to God? Whether or not the final verses (Joel 2.30–32) are intended to answer this question, they introduce a new dimension. They stand in the tradition that the day of the LORD is a day of darkness rather than light (Amos 5.18), a day on which the divine appearing will bring fear to the world of nature as well as to human inhabitants. If v. 28 gives the impression that the spirit of God will come upon all (Israelites), v. 32 implies that only those will survive on the great and terrible day who call upon God's name. It is further implied that this calling cannot be a self-interested plea to God when all else has failed. It must be a genuine desire for God. The survivors will be those whom God calls (v. 32d). There can be no satisfactory human answer to the question of how God brings people to faith without violating their integrity and freedom to choose. JR

Ecclesiasticus 35.12–17

This passage is part of a larger section (34.21—35.26) dealing with sacrifices brought to the Jerusalem temple during the author's time (early second century BC). At 34.21f. it is stated as strongly as possible that God will not accept sacrifices if they have been come by illegally. An example would be the offering of an animal that had been unlawfully taken from a poor man (34.24). The opening verse of the reading indicates that a sacrifice is only a giving back to God of what God has given in the first place, and the profligacy of a person's giving (literally, 'giving with a cheerful eye') will indicate how much God's giving has been recognized and appreciated. For this reason, any thought of sacrifice as a bribe to God is profoundly misconceived (v. 14) while v. 15 repeats the point that the sacrifice of something obtained dishonestly is not acceptable. The thought now shifts naturally to justice, because the God who will not accept a sacrifice obtained dishonestly is the God who expects justice to be impartial. To say that he does not show partiality to the poor does not mean that he disregards the poor. Indeed, v. 17 indicates solidarity with the orphan and widow. The point is that justice should be even-handed and should not, in this regard, exhibit a 'bias to the poor', even if such a bias is appropriate and justified in other spheres. JR

Jeremiah 14.7–10, 19–22

The two poems that comprise this reading are very similar to one another, though they are separated by a section in prose. The poems are of a type found in a number of psalms, and are often described as 'communal laments'. In them the community is pictured as bewailing the troubles that have come upon it. On the one hand it is ready to acknowledge the wrongs that it has committed (vv. 7, 20), but it also feels that God has let his people down (vv. 8–9a, 21). In the psalms of lament God is some-times thought to have gone to sleep and is needing to be roused (e.g. Ps. 44.23); here the picture is that he may have lost his way, like a traveller in a foreign land. Jewish tradition down the ages has been much more ready than most Christians to blame God for the way in which things have gone wrong. It would be an interesting subject for reflection whether it might be helpful, at either the psychological or the spiritual level, for Christians sometimes to follow Jewish practice here.

The sense of frustration and rejection is not the whole of these laments. Each of our poems ends with the confidence that God can and will act to put right the miseries of his worshippers. The two passages differ, however, in their emphases. The first recognizes the continuing wrongdoing of the people, and that there can be no real change as long as that continues (v. 10); punishment is inevitable. The second also acknowledges the sin (v. 20), but sets out a hope for the future beyond present misery: God remains in control. It is interesting, and somewhat unusual, that the evidence of that control is seen in the provision of rain and showers (v. 22). This is one of the passages in the Hebrew Bible that invites us to think not just of our fellow human beings but also of the natural world in which we all live. Recently, and many will think somewhat belatedly, the Christian Church has begun to pay more attention to environmental issues. If climate change takes the form of which we are warned by some experts, human behaviour, right or wrong, will be seen in a very different way, for the world as we know it will have been fundamentally changed. RC

2 Timothy 4.6–8, 16–18

The dramatic force of Paul as example and inspiration, which is so prominent in this letter, reaches its climax in this final chapter – as indeed does the poignancy of his ordeal. In all of it, however, he remains steadfast and valiant, in the sure hope of Christ's victory and his own vindication. The imagery of struggle comes from the games that were so prominent a feature of the city life of the ancient world (vv. 7–8): Paul will win and the Lord, his 'emperor', will award him the victor's garland-crown. It is an image that has remained attractive, chiefly perhaps in hymns. His endurance has indeed been exceptional. At his 'first defence' (v. 16: we cannot be sure which trial it refers to), he was left alone (like Jesus at his trial, as the Gospels emphasize). Whether 'the lion' is meant figuratively (cf. Ps. 22.21) or not, we cannot tell: if literally, then his survival was indeed remarkable, though now seen to be only temporary.

Inspiring as all this is, the basic understanding by 'Paul' of his relationship with Christ is very different from that in Paul's genuine letters and similar to the picture of the ascended Christ and his followers on earth that we find in Acts. It is, in a word, more detached or external (Christ is in heaven, they below), less intimate or 'mystical'. There is none of the sense of 'Christ in you, the hope of glory' (Col. 1.27) or of the Christian as living 'in Christ' that is so pervasive in Paul. We are in an era, however dramatic its possible risks might be, of a more 'plain' theology (deckered universe and all), where the drama of Christ, past, present and future, is well, even neatly, laid out in the mind. It is no surprise that in these writings the term 'the faith' (v. 7) comes to mean (as only very rarely, if ever, in Paul) the body of Christian beliefs, a sense it has carried prominently ever since. 'Christianity', 'the Christian faith', as an identifiable entity, is born; and we are in at the birth. LH

Luke 18.9–14

Luke continues his teaching about prayer with a second parable, addressed now not to the disciples, but to 'those who trusted in themselves that they were righteous and regarded others with contempt'. While on the narrative level 'the Pharisees' are probably Jesus' particular target, this less specific designation already suggests a broader application of the parable. The setting is the Jerusalem temple, central to Jewish piety during Jesus' ministry, and important for the early Jerusalem church, but probably in ruins by Luke's time. The two characters go up for personal devotion, probably at one of the set times for prayer.

This parable deals in stereotypes, and though this gives the story its punch, it has its dangers. It is important to remember that its present form has been shaped by ongoing Jewish–Christian debate, as well as the hostility experienced by Jesus himself. Attention to first-century historical sources suggests that this particular Pharisee was not typical of the Pharisaic party, which according to Josephus was highly regarded by the people. Preachers should beware of perpetuating the portrait of the Pharisees as hypocritical legalists.

Moreover, there is no suggestion that this particular Pharisee is being criticized for hypocrisy. Indeed, on one level, his claim not to be like other people seems justified (though cf. 11.39). He goes beyond the strict requirements of Torah in tithing 'all' his income (cf. Deut. 14.22f.), and in his twice-weekly fasting. Nor is there any indication that the tax-collector is not what he claims to be, a sinner whose sins need dealing with (the Greek verb translated 'be merciful' is the verb used for expiating sin).

Perhaps this is less a parable about two kinds of people than about two kinds of prayer. The Pharisee's prayer reveals how piety can so easily lapse into self-satisfaction. Though he begins by thanking God, he does so first for what he is not ('like other people'), and second for what he has done for God rather than what God has done for him. An alternative translation of v. 11 heightens the sense that God is peripheral to his prayer: 'The Pharisee, standing, was praying these things *to himself.*'

The tax-collector's prayer is revealed as more authentic, leaving him, rather than his Pharisaic accuser, justified before God. He does not speak of himself by reference to others. He does not even raise his eyes to heaven, let alone raising his hands in the traditional posture of prayer. Like the repentant crowds at the cross of Jesus, he beats his breast in sorrow. But this should not be understood as motivated by a sense of his own worthlessness, but rather by an overwhelming sense of God's mercy. His prayer is honest, and it is God-centred, rather than self-centred.

The parable concludes with a saying of gospel reversal (shared, though in a different context, by Matthew). It echoes Luke's Magnificat theology, into which tax-collectors seem to have particular insight: the proud will be scattered, and the lowly exalted. IB

Bible Sunday

Isaiah 45.22–25; Romans 15.1–6; Luke 4.16–24

Isaiah 45.22–25

This passage has provoked much discussion about whether it envisages universal salvation. Because texts have latent meaning – meaning in excess of what their authors might have intended – it may be legitimate to interpret the reading universalistically, as offering salvation to all mankind. Within its context, however, it is addressed to Jews in exile in Babylon, and being 'saved' means inviting the 'ends of the earth' to witness God's vindication of Israel. This may lead, of course, to their 'salvation' in the sense that they come to acknowledge that the God of Israel is God alone and that 'there is no other'. In vv. 23–24a God issues a promise in the form of an oath sworn by himself, since there is no greater one by whom he can swear. The Hebrew in v. 24a is awkward, and the two words rendered 'it shall be said of me' are best altered to 'saying' and transposed to follow 'swear' in v. 23. Verse 24a 'Only in the Lord are righteousness and strength' then becomes the content of the oath that is sworn by 'every tongue'. Again, the words 'every knee' and 'every tongue' raise the question of universality. The safest answer is to say that it is every knee of the Jewish exiles that is envisaged, but that this can have a wider application: first to foreign nations that see the vindication of the exiles, second to those who read the Scriptures that exist because of the exiles' vindication, including today's readers. The final verses (24–25) are a prophetic comment that sum up what has been said. It is not clear whether 'all who were incensed' is restricted to Jewish exiles or can include nations that despised Israel's God because his people went into exile. Whoever is meant will acknowledge that they were mistaken. The triumph will not be a nationalistic orgy of feeling superior to other nations, but an expression of joy that justice has been demonstrated by a God whose justice is longed for by all right-minded people. JR

Romans 15.1–6

This passage concludes a long section of exhortation that has run from 14.1 to this point. In it Paul has been encouraging the different sections of the Roman church to live with each other in tolerance and respect. One section of the community Paul calls 'the weak' and in this passage for the first time he names the other section, 'the strong'. Although it is possible to work out a general profile of these two opposing groups that is not Paul's purpose here. Throughout this section Paul addresses the strong and counsels them on their attitude to the weak. What becomes clear therefore is that this group is not a defined group within the community who call themselves 'the strong', instead this is a general term designed to include all those who for some reason or another consider others to be weaker than themselves. In vv. 1–6 Paul summarizes the case he has made throughout the previous chapter.

Verse 1 gives us a fascinating insight into what Paul is saying here. The NRSV gives a rather grudging translation of what Paul says, 'the strong should put up with failings of the weak'. A better reading of the verse is 'the strong must support the weaknesses of the weak (literally the un-strong)'. Weakness here is not something to be tolerated with barely concealed irritation but supported and celebrated. It is not even the weak that the strong are to support but their weaknesses. The very things that make 'the strong' despise them are what they are to support. Here we encounter the radical nature of Paul's message. The language he uses implies that he himself is one of the strong in their patronizing of the weak. Then, with a rather clever rhetorical flourish we discover that Paul never was on the side of the strong; what he considers to be important is the support of weakness.

The reasons for this are given in vv. 2–3. The first reason Paul gives is the building up of the community. The weaknesses of the weak are to be supported so that the weak might be built up. Paul's concern, as ever, is the welfare of the Christian community, the building up of a neighbour is a good purpose and reason itself for supporting the weaknesses of the weak. He follows this first reason rapidly with a second one, which is even more important: it is that Christ did the same. Here we encounter the heart of Paul's message. The real reason for supporting the weaknesses of the weak is because the whole Christian gospel, as borne out in the person of Christ, is one of weakness. The strong may pride themselves on their own superiority but the essence of the gospel lies not in strength but in weakness. The real reason for supporting the weak is because in gospel terms they are, in fact, the strong.

This message is proclaimed not only in the person of Christ (v. 3) but also in the Scriptures (vv. 4–5). Reading and learning from the Scriptures will, Paul says, give all Christians hope. This hope he defines in v. 5 as the encouragement of God to live in harmony with one another. The vision Paul has of a mutually supportive and harmonious community is one that he believes can be seen in the pages of the Scriptures. This is unusual. The Scriptures are regarded as important for many things but rarely are they seen as a manual for building up community life. Paul, however, sees the Scriptures as the blueprint for the behaviour that he is exhorting his readers to pursue. On Bible Sunday this is a powerful message. One of the reasons why the Bible is so important is because within its pages we can catch a glimpse of what a community, living as God intended, would look like. Paul ends this passage with a vision of what a harmonious Christian community might be able to do. The language he uses here is reminiscent of the body of Christ language that we encounter in Rom. 12. Paul states in v. 6 that when the Romans are living in harmony with each other they will glorify God 'with one voice'. It is only when Christians are living and working together in harmony that they will be able to achieve a single voice of praise to God. At the end of this passage therefore we encounter a third reason why the strong should support the weaknesses of the weak: then the Body of Christ on earth will be able to praise God as God deserves. PG

Luke 4.16–24

Luke's expanded account of Jesus' rejection at Nazareth dominates the beginning of the public ministry in his Gospel. He regards this episode as so important that he has rearranged the order of Mark, so that it precedes the call of the first disciples and accounts of Jesus' first healings. The resulting editing is not seamless: v. 23 now seems out of place, for Jesus has not as yet visited Capernaum.

Clearly Luke wants this episode to be understood as the key to Jesus' ministry. First, it sets Jesus firmly within the tradition of Israel as an observant Jew. He frequents the synagogue on the sabbath (Luke's narrative suggests a developed synagogue liturgy, though it is unclear how far the evangelist has read his own knowledge of diaspora synagogues back into the earlier period in Palestine). The Isaiah passage he reads aloud is probably not selected by Jesus himself, but the lectionary portion from the prophets set for that sabbath.

Second, the Isaiah reading reveals the focus of his ministry, and the kind of Messiah ('anointed', v. 18) Luke's Jesus is. The text largely follows the Septuagint version of Isa. 61 (with some omissions, including the negative 'day of vengeance', and an addition from Isa. 58.6 about the oppressed being set free). Some have interpreted this passage as announcing the year of Jubilee ('the acceptable year of the LORD'), promising liberty to all the inhabitants of the land. Thus Jesus' teaching is given a political edge. Others have understood it as a more spiritual 'release' from the oppression of sin. While forgiveness of sin is certainly important for Luke, more is surely meant here, given Jesus' subsequent ministry. From the start, Luke highlights a concern for the poor, disadvantaged and oppressed that will be a recurring theme of his Gospel.

More significantly, he presents Jesus as the *prophet* Messiah. Not only does Jesus cite the saying about a prophet not being accepted in his own town. He is also portrayed as the fulfilment of Isaiah's shadowy prophecy about the Spirit-filled figure. As a prophet as well as a king, Christ will challenge his people with the word of God.

Yet there is a twist in the tail. In Luke (unlike Matthew and Mark), Jesus' fellow townspeople do not immediately take offence at him. Rather, they speak well of him, recognizing the 'words of grace' he has been given. He is the local boy made good, 'Joseph's son', 'our prophet'. It is only when he goes on to remind them of the prophetic activity of Elijah and Elisha among the Gentiles that they take offence, for they realize that God's prophet Messiah cannot be confined or controlled.

This passage highlights several themes appropriate to Bible Sunday. It provides an opportunity to reflect upon the relationship between Old and New Testaments, and how Christ might be said to be the 'fulfilment' of the former. Or it presents a challenging view of God's prophetic word, which despite our best efforts can never be tamed or domesticated. IB

Dedication Festival

(The First Sunday in October or Last Sunday after Trinity)

I Chronicles 29.6–19; Ephesians 2.19–22; John 2.13–22

I Chronicles 29.6–19

The account in the books of Chronicles of the last days of David, of the transfer of power from David to Solomon, and of the building of the temple, differs considerably from the account in the books of Kings. There, Solomon's accession comes from a power struggle between him and an elder son of David, Adonijah, each of whom is supported by a different royal and priestly faction. There is no mention of preparations by David to build the temple. In Chronicles, David knows well in advance that Solomon will succeed him (1 Chron. 22.9) and, because Solomon will be young and inexperienced (22.5), David makes all the preparations for building the temple, including organizing its personnel (1 Chron. 23—26). The reading describes the culmination of David's efforts. In a way probably deliberately reminiscent of Moses gathering materials for the building of the tabernacle in the wilderness (Exod. 35.20–29), David gathers offerings from the people via their ancestral leaders. The sums of money involved are astronomical, and while they are a product of the writer's imagination, their purpose is to indicate how generous the response was and how magnificent the temple must have been. The mention of the daric (v. 7), a Persian coin probably named after Darius I, places the composition of the narrative in the Persian period (539–333 BC), probably towards the end of that period. Whatever the temple looked like then, it is unlikely to have matched up to the wealth implied in the reading. The passage therefore looks back to a kind of golden age. The prayer put into the mouth of David is a noble composition, and indicative of the piety of the late Persian period. It contrasts the eternity and majesty of God with the smallness and transitory nature of humankind. Yet the temple – and this is the point of describing its original building in such superlative terms – is a visible symbol of God's enduring nature, and of the surety of the promises made to the people. The prayer asks not that the people should be concerned with the building, but that their hearts should be directed towards God (v. 14). It is difficult to think of a better theme for the dedication festival of a church building. JR

Ephesians 2.19–22

It is not in the least surprising that the early generations of Christians, reflecting on their faith, turned to the image of the temple. Most of them were Jewish in upbringing and formation, and what was usually in mind was the Jerusalem temple. From a 'comparative religions' angle, it was not greatly different in design and, partly, in function from the temples of paganism, common in all the cities of the Greco-Roman world and, in real life, more familiar to the readers of the New Testament writings than that of Jerusalem. This was not only because, at least if they were Gentiles, they had neither cause nor much opportunity to visit the latter but, once we move (as perhaps in the case of Ephesians) into the period after AD 70, it was no longer there to be visited. It was a ruin, desolated by the Romans as the rebellion that began four years before was coming to its later stages. So for both Jews and Christians, the temple was becoming a memory, known less by the testimony of the eyes than from scriptural and other descriptions of its structure and its solemn role, and also from a quasi-poetic or symbolic sense of its importance as a place where, in prayer and ceremony, God's people assembled to meet him, ritually (above all in sacrifice) expressing their oneness and their relationship with him.

The use of the image among Christians took many forms. In today's Gospel, for example, Jesus is shown defining his risen body as, like the temple, the true place of meeting for God and his human creatures who believe. Elsewhere, in Paul, both the Christian individual (1 Cor. 6.19) and the community (3.16) are spoken of as 'temples' where the Holy Spirit dwells, and various lessons are inferred as a result.

Here, however, in Eph. 2, the writer applies the image differently. In line with one of his leading concerns, it refers to the Church, indwelt by God, as the union of both Jews and, now, Gentiles. In this way, the passage is not unlike the sense of Christ's quoting of Isa. 56.7 at the 'cleansing of the temple' in Mark's version (11.17): 'My house shall be called a house of prayer for all nations.' The theme of Eph. 2 is indeed not without Jewish antecedents, notably in those last ten chapters of Isaiah. Here, however, the image sits, appropriately, alongside those of citizenship and household; the Jewish precedents make the flow of ideas wholly understandable. In what ways does the Church now fulfil such a comprehensive role for its members' sense of themselves? Would it really be desirable? Perhaps it was scarcely quite like that for Christians in a city like Ephesus in the first century, especially where some aspects of citizenship were concerned.

We note that apostles and prophets stand together as fundamental. If the latter refers to the old prophets rather than Christian preachers, it speaks, in giving such venerability to the apostles as already figures in Christian memory, for a post-Pauline origin for this writing. It speaks with his voice but in tones that are partly new and thoroughly eirenic. And it is more institutionally minded than 1 Cor. 3.11, where it is Christ who is the Church's one foundation. Here, he is the corner-stone holding all together. LH

John 2.13–22

At this point John's Gospel presents us with a choice. The episode of 'the cleansing of the temple' in the Synoptic Gospels (and so in most people's minds) stands at the beginning of Holy Week, straight after Jesus' entry into Jerusalem. Here it is at the other end of Jesus' ministry, his very first moment of public confrontation with the religious authorities. From the point of view of chronology there is no way of reconciling the two accounts. We just have to choose.

But is chronology the most important thing? By the time the Gospels were written the exact sequence of events may have been forgotten (it is usually the first thing to get muddled in people's memories). The two traditions may represent two decisions on how best to tell the story. The Synoptics chose to separate Jesus' confrontations in Jerusalem from his preaching and healing ministry in Galilee by grouping them all together at the end, whereas John wove these two aspects of Jesus' activity together through relatively frequent visits to Jerusalem (which is in fact the more plausible pattern historically). The point, at any rate, is not so much to determine exactly when these events took place, but what they *meant*.

And John packs a great deal of meaning into his account. Jesus' action against the traders was in the tradition of the Old Testament prophets, a physical demonstration (of a distinctly aggressive kind in this Gospel) followed by a verbal explanation. He was explicitly fulfilling a prophetic protest made by Zechariah (14.21): 'There shall no longer be traders in the house of the LORD' – there is some evidence that trading had begun to exceed proper limits in the precincts, even if certain commercial activities (such as changing money into the special coins required for temple dues) were necessary and perhaps officially sanctioned.

But the Gospel goes on to offer more meanings than this. 'Zeal for your house will consume me' is an allusion to Ps. 69.9, the song of a nameless righteous sufferer who had had even his devotion to the temple turned against him. The disciples are said to have begun to see a similar destiny for Jesus. But there is a further meaning introduced in a way typical of this Gospel. On several occasions something Jesus says is taken in a literal and superficial sense by his hearers, only for Jesus to confound them by showing that it has a deeper meaning. Jesus certainly made some prophecy about the temple's destruction: there is a number of reports of it scattered through the New Testament. Here his opponents are the ones who take it literally. Jesus does not immediately correct them; it was his disciples who gradually came to see what he may have meant when, after the resurrection, they experienced that, through their life in the Church, they belonged to the 'body of Christ', a 'temple not made with hands'. AEH

All Saints' Day

(1 November)

Isaiah 56.3–8 or 2 Esdras 2.42–48; Hebrews 12.18–24; Matthew 5.1–12

Isaiah 56.3–8

The community centred upon Jerusalem that rebuilt the temple around 515 BC and restored the religious life of the people, was one split by deep divisions, if Isa. 56—66 is anything to go by. There were those who seem to have questioned whether there was any need for the temple to be rebuilt at all (Isa. 66.1–4) while others were sharply critical of some of the religious observances (Isa. 58.1–9).

The present passage, with its inexplicable omission of vv. 2–5, is evidently concerned with the problem of non-Jews belonging to the chosen people and participating fully in its temple worship. Its sentiments are only understandable if there were people in the Jerusalem community at the end of the sixth century BC who maintained that non-Jews could not belong to the Jewish community.

We can only speculate about who these non-Jews were who had joined or who wanted to 'join themselves to the Lord' (v. 6). They may have been non-Jews who had moved into Palestine during the exile, from southern Trans-Jordan, or they may have been Babylonians who had been involved in the administration of Judah during the period 597 to 548. It is less likely that they were Babylonians who deliberately journeyed back to Jerusalem because they wanted to embrace faith in the God of Israel.

On the face of it, that there were such people should have been a cause for satisfaction if not joy. After all, Isa. 45.2 contains a call to 'all the ends of the earth' to turn to God and to be saved. Foreigners, however, cause problems in all societies in all ages. If they are too successful they arouse resentment; if they perform below the average they are blamed for a society's troubles. We may also detect in the passage disputes about the layout and accessibility of the rebuilt temple. Unfortunately, we know nothing about its layout; but the temple that Herod the Great enlarged and rebuilt at the close of the first century BC certainly allowed access to certain parts only to Israelite males. The passage certainly promises to non-Jews who observe the sabbaths and hold fast to the covenant that they will be able to join fully in the worship of the temple, and that their sacrifices will be acceptable. We do not know how the dispute over non-Jews was resolved at the end of the sixth century. Sixty years later, Ezra and Nehemiah made a determined, and apparently successful, attempt to exclude the non-Jewish wives of Israelites from the community (Ezra 9.1–4; 10.1–15; Neh. 13.1–3, 23–29). The implications of the passage for today's churches with regard to their attitude to all 'outsiders', especially those of African and Asian ethnic origins, should not be difficult to discern. JR

2 Esdras 2.42–48

2 Esdras (also known as 4 Ezra) is a composite work. Chs. 3—14 were written in Hebrew or Aramaic around 100 AD as a response to the destruction of the second Jerusalem temple by the Romans 30 years earlier. The Semitic original is lost and the chapters are known only in translation, in Latin, Syriac and Ethiopic to name only three languages. The Latin version contains additional material in the form of chs. 1—2 and 15—16 which are often referred to as 5 Ezra and 6 Ezra respectively.

Chapter 2, from which today's reading is taken, is a Christian addition, probably dating from the second century AD. We therefore have the phenomenon of the Old Testament (Apocrypha) reading being later than the New Testament readings!

A comparison of the reading with parts of the book of Revelation (cf. Rev. 7.9–14) indicates that Revelation is the probable source for the material in 2 Esd. 2. However, 2 Esd. 2 is more explicitly Christian than Revelation in the sense that it features a young man of taller stature than any other, who places crowns on the heads of the martyrs (v. 45). He is later identified (v. 47) as the Son of God. In this reading the focus is arguably mostly upon the tall young man. In Rev. 7.9–14 the focus is more upon the martyrs. JR

Hebrews 12.18–24

See Proper 16, pp. 222–223.

Matthew 5.1–12

Matthew has arranged his Gospel in alternating sections of narrative and teaching. There are five sections of teaching, each ending with virtually the same formula that marks the transition from direct speech to narrative (see e.g. 7.28–29). The first of these speeches is the Sermon on the Mount (5.3—7.27), and today's gospel is the beginning of it.

In the previous narrative (chs. 1—4), Matthew has prepared his readers for this section of his book by comparing Jesus to Moses: both were threatened by wicked kings; both escaped, one out of Egypt and the other into Egypt; Moses received, and now Jesus commends and revises, the Law of God, on a mountain.

John the Baptist and Jesus have proclaimed the coming of the time when God will rule and the need for repentance (3.2; 4.17); so the first speech addresses the question that this raises: who is it that will enter this new age?

There are eight Beatitudes, marked out by an *inclusio* – the repetition of the promise: 'The kingdom of heaven is theirs' (5.3, 10). Each beatitude consists of two parts: the statement that certain people are blessed, and the promise of their reward. After the eighth beatitude, the form of the language changes, from third person plural ('Blessed are the . . .') to the second person ('Blessed are you . . .'); these eight sayings can be read as the 'text', or as a kind of prologue, for the rest of the Sermon, which then begins at 5.11.

The order of the eight sayings is different in some of the manuscripts and ancient versions from that which is found in most printed editions of the New Testament, and it is not certain which arrangement is original; there is much to be said for following the witnesses that place v. 5 before v. 4. If this is done, then the Beatitudes form four pairs: the poor and the meek; those who mourn and those who fast; the generous and the single-minded; the peace-makers and those who are persecuted.

The seven different promises in the second halves are in effect all one promise (just as the petitions in the Lord's Prayer are in effect one and the same), because each of them refers to entry into the kingdom of heaven, the time when God will rule on the earth (see 6.10). They are not alternative options, so that one cannot choose some and reject others, for example preferring comfort and mercy to seeing God. The future passive verbs (shall be comforted, filled, receive mercy, be called God's children) are all ways of describing God's actions in the coming end-time of fulfilment; he will comfort, fill, be merciful, and he will declare who are his children.

Similarly, the eight statements in the first halves of the Beatitudes refer to everyone who is to enter the coming age: all of them are poor, meek, mourning for the way things are in the world, longing for God to rule, abandoning status and privilege, peace-makers, and (inevitably) persecuted by those who do not want God to rule. Again, these are not alternatives.

A major theme that runs through the Beatitudes and the Sermon on the Mount, and indeed this Gospel as a whole, is: many who are first will be last, and the last first (19.30; 20.16). Discipleship means the acceptance of a life that is not what the majority choose. What is required of those whom God will bless is poverty and the giving up of any compensating 'religious' rewards in the present (see. 6.1–21; 23.1–33). The character of the follower is, of course, the same as that of the one whom we follow. JF

All Saints' Sunday

Daniel 7.1–3, 15–18; Ephesians 1.11–23; Luke 6.20–31

Daniel 7.1–3, 15–18

The prescribed passage is the climax of the vision, written in Aramaic, in which the seer sees four beasts emerging from the sea (a symbol of chaos). Each beast, representing an empire, is more terrible than the one that precedes it, and on the head of the fourth beast there appears a little horn that displaces three horns, and which has eyes and a mouth.

The scene switches from the source of the chaos and the destruction wrought by the beasts that emerge from it to a judgement scene on earth. The plural 'thrones' implies that there will be a panel of judges; but the dominating feature is the Ancient One (Aramaic, 'One ancient of days' i.e. years). The figure of white clothing and pure wool hair is meant to denote eternity and wisdom, and certainly not senility. The wheels of the throne are reminiscent of those of Ezek. 1, and the fire symbolizes purity and holiness. The fact that the beasts are only partially destroyed, even if their dominion is taken away, is an attempt to account for the persistence of evil in the world even after the judgement.

The climax is reached in v. 13 with the coming on the clouds of heaven of the 'one like a human being' (Aramaic, 'like a son of a human'). That this figure is in some sense 'heavenly' is indicated by his coming on the clouds of heaven, and by the qualifier 'like'. He is thus best thought of as an angelic figure. However, in the explanation of the vision in vv. 19–27, the dominion is given to 'the people of the holy ones of the Most High' (v. 27) in language almost identical with that of v. 14. These 'holy ones' are evidently those Israelites who have been persecuted and martyred by the little horn, usually taken to be Antiochus IV (175–164 BC) who banned Judaism from 168/7 to 164.

How can the persecuted ones be the same as the 'one like a human being'? This is the language of vision and symbols in which precision may not always be possible. The angelic figure may be a personification or may be a kind of heavenly guardian of the persecuted ones.

The fundamental message of the vision, however, is that the evil personified by the beasts, and embodied partly in the actions of desperate rulers, is ultimately subject to divine judgement. It is overcome not by greater, similar force, but by faithfulness to goodness and truth, which may lead to persecution and death. The dominion that is therefore given to the 'one like a human being' or the holy ones, is not based upon human ideas of power, but the experience of those who have drunk deeply from the well of suffering. JR

Ephesians 1.11–23

See Ascension Day, pp. 147–148.

Luke 6.20–31

Luke's Beatitudes, which form the opening of his 'Sermon on the Plain', present a challenging portrait of what the community of believers is called to be. Luke has four 'blessings', which only partially overlap with the nine of Matthew's better-known version. Each of his four has a corresponding 'woe', underlining the prophetic aspect of Jesus' preaching.

The immediate context is significant: having selected the Twelve from among his disciples after a night of prayer, Jesus now descends from the mountain to 'a level place'. Here he addresses the wider band of disciples, with a much larger group of people listening in. Given the parallels with Moses (e.g. Exod. 24), the reader may expect to find here the foundation of a new or renewed people of God.

Luke's Beatitudes then describe the ones who have particular priority in this renewed people, with his characteristic emphasis on the lowly and disadvantaged. Though 'poor' could refer to the pious, those who recognize their need for God (hence the self-designation of the Qumran community as 'the poor ones'), this does not seem to be Luke's primary usage here. Whereas Matthew's Beatitudes address those who cultivate particular dispositions ('poor in spirit', 'hunger and thirst after righteousness'), Luke's speak of God's saving action for those who find themselves in desperate circumstances through no fault of their own: the poor, the hungry, those who weep. His beatitudes do not glorify poverty, but proclaim the gospel reversal when the compassionate God acts on behalf of the disadvantaged to bring in his kingdom.

Luke's fourth 'blessing' (and its parallel 'woe') recognizes that popularity is not the ultimate yardstick. Jesus' followers, like the one they follow, are called to exercise a prophetic ministry. Therefore, they can expect to be excluded and despised even by their co-religionists, as were the prophets of old. What is more surprising is that the woes are apparently addressed to the disciples: the rich, well-fed, laughing, and those spoken well of may also be found within the community of faith. Luke's harsh prophetic critique suggests that some of Christ's followers may manifest a closer family resemblance to him than others.

The remaining verses of our reading (vv. 27–31) offer concrete teaching for those who would be blessed, culminating in the so-called Golden Rule (also found, in its negative form, at Tobit 4.15 and in traditions about the Pharisee leader Hillel). But in fact, Jesus urges his disciples to go beyond this Rule's straightforward reciprocity. When struck on the cheek (regarded as an insult), they are to turn the other as well. When a robber tries to steal their cloak, they are to give up their inner tunic as well (Matthew's reverse order of tunic and cloak suggests the rather different situation of legal proceedings). But such 'going beyond' could be regarded as a provocative challenge by one's opponent; hence it calls for a particular kind of heroism, which is celebrated on a day such as All Saints. IB

The Fourth Sunday Before Advent

Isaiah 1.10–18; 2 Thessalonians 1.1–4 (5–10), 11–12; Luke 19.1–10

Isaiah 1.10–18

See Proper 14, p. 213.

2 Thessalonians 1.1–4 (5–10), 11–12

Although the pulpit is no place for a lecture on any given authorship or the historical circumstances that produced any given letter, the preacher must have some understanding of each lest the text appear to have floated down from the heavenly places. Arriving at some sense of the authorship and circumstances behind 2 Thessalonians is particularly difficult, as a survey of commentaries will readily indicate. This letter has many formal elements in common with the other Pauline letters, especially with 1 Thessalonians, which suggests to some scholars that Paul also wrote 2 Thessalonians. Others call attention to the substantial conflicts between the two letters, particularly regarding the time of the *parousia* (compare 1 Thess. 4.13—5.11 with 2 Thess. 1.5–12), and conclude that 2 Thessalonians was written in order to counter a kind of misguided eschatological fervour. The latter argument accounts better for the differences between the two letters, but scholarly opinion remains deeply divided on this matter.

In addition to this set of historical problems that plague any reading of 2 Thessalonians, the editors of the lectionary have created another problem by their decision to confine the reading to 1.1–4, 11–12, excising vv. 5–10. Even a quick glance at these verses reveals the probable reasoning of the editors, for they make claims about retribution and eternal punishment that can be misleading and difficult. Eliminating them, however, results in serious distortion of the text.

In the first place, in Greek all of vv. 3–12 constitute a single complex sentence. English translations cannot reflect that structure without producing something virtually unreadable, but the section represents a single unit of thought, so that excluding this central section is difficult to support. In the second place, and more important, vv. 5–10 introduce what is certainly the central topic of the letter, the *parousia* of Jesus Christ. However uncomfortable we may find vv. 5–10, then, we probably should include them in considering this lection.

Following the customary salutation, identifying the church with God and with Jesus Christ, the thanksgiving (vv. 3–12) first lifts up the growing faith and love of the Thessalonians. This recalls the passionate thanksgiving of 1 Thessalonians, with its celebration of their 'work of faith and labour of love and steadfastness of hope' (1.3); it also recalls 1 Thess. 3.12, Paul's prayer that the Thessalonians would continue to 'increase and abound in love for one another'.

Because of this growth, Paul and his colleagues are able to 'boast' about the Thessalonians. Despite Paul's strong cautions about boasting on the basis of one's own accomplishments (see e.g. Rom. 3.27 and 1 Cor. 1.29, 31), he regards boasting about the churches as right and proper, indeed, as a means of proclaiming the work of the gospel (2 Cor. 8.24) and as a basis for eschatological hope (1 Thess. 2.19).

The particular basis for boasting here moves us toward the central concern of 2 Thessalonians. Paul boasts of them because of their 'steadfastness and faith' in the face of their 'persecutions' and 'afflictions' (v. 4). Both the context and the use of this language elsewhere in the New Testament strongly suggest that these 'persecutions' and 'afflictions' are to be understood eschatologically. Mark 13.3–37 and its parallels express this connection narratively, but it appears also in Paul (e.g. Rom. 8.18–25). While no timetable may be deduced from such sufferings, early Christians do identify them as signs of the eschaton.

The grammatical connection between 2 Thess. 1.5 and what precedes is ambiguous, for it is unclear whether 'this' refers to the church's faithfulness, to the persecutions themselves or perhaps to both. Whichever alternative is in view, the writer quickly moves to the expectation of the glorious return of Jesus. Both the detailed depiction here ('when the Lord Jesus is revealed from heaven with his mighty angels in flaming fire') and the anticipation of retribution toward unbelievers require careful handling. Because contemporary preachers know the damage inflicted when such passages are read literally and judgementally, we often wish to ignore them altogether. Their insistence on the faithfulness of God to God's own people, the final protection afforded humankind by God and the ultimate triumph of God belong among the fundamental elements of Christian proclamation.

The topic of the *parousia* and the appropriate attitude toward it will dominate the second chapter of this letter. For the time being, the thanksgiving concludes with the prayer that God will make the Thessalonians worthy of their calling. The focus here is not on the attitude Christians are to have toward outsiders, but on their own worthiness, itself a gift of God. The final aim, of course, is the glory of Jesus (v. 12). BG

Luke 19.1–10

The story of Zacchaeus is found only in Luke's Gospel, and for good reasons commentators are inclined to label it a masterpiece. The way the details subtly hint at Lucan themes and invite comparison with other characters, the colourful connections drawn within the story itself make for an interesting text. Even the gaps in the story tantalize the reader. (Why is Zacchaeus so interested in Jesus? How does Jesus know Zacchaeus's name? What transpired to prompt Zacchaeus to make such excessive restitution to the poor and to victims he may have defrauded? When is Zacchaeus's speech in Luke 19.8 made – on the way to his house or after Jesus' visit?) The homiletical richness of the passage is hard to overestimate.

We shall indicate three possible approaches to the story, none of which excludes the others. First, Zacchaeus seems a perfect antitype to the rich ruler of 18.18–23. The one is genuinely respectable and religious, honoured in the community. His question about inheriting eternal life no doubt reflects a sincere restlessness, a desire for something more in life than his present situation offers. His problem lies in his attachment to his riches and, when instructed by Jesus to contribute his money to the poor, he becomes 'sad'. Jesus' response is that nothing short of a divine miracle will enable rich people to enter the kingdom of God.

Zacchaeus, then, represents the miracle. Like the ruler, he too is rich and yet clearly unhappy with his lot in life. Dishonoured in the community, he takes the initiative in seeking out Jesus, despite the obstacles of a large crowd and his short stature. He is only too happy to welcome Jesus into his house. (The Greek says, 'He welcomed him, rejoicing.') Unlike the ruler, Zacchaeus's encounter with Jesus enables a distancing of himself from his riches. He gives to the poor and promises restitution to any he may have cheated.

The similarities, but mainly the contrasts between the two characters, are remarkable, particularly regarding the matter of wealth – the idolatry of the one versus the freedom of the other, the sadness of the one versus the joy of the other. According to 18.24–27, what explains the difference is the powerful action of God, Luke's only reason for extraordinary occurrences (cf. 1.37). Zacchaeus's response to Jesus illustrates that the miracle *can* occur, that the wealthy *can* gain freedom from possessions that possess them, just as the blind come to see, the lame to walk, the demon-possessed to be restored, and the dead to be made alive.

A second approach to this story pays attention to the gift of salvation pronounced by Jesus. The repeated use of 'today' (19.5, 9) indicates that this is not an eschatological hope Zacchaeus is being given, but a change in his immediate life, an experience of salvation now.

What does this salvation entail? Four dimensions of the experience stand out. First, Zacchaeus welcomes Jesus, implying hospitality and friendship. In a sense, by doing so Zacchaeus cooperates with the divine will, since the urgency of Jesus' intent to come to his house includes a 'must'. (The impersonal Greek verb *dei* ['it is necessary'] 19.5 is an example of Luke's characteristic expression for God's will.) Second, the mood of the experience is joy. Third, Zacchaeus is restored. The crowd has unanimously labelled him 'a sinner' (v. 7), a common and understandable designation for a chief tax-collector who profits from the tolls he (over)charges. He is excluded from the community and is to be avoided at all costs. In a curious aside to the crowd (since the third person is used), however, Jesus declares Zacchaeus 'a son of Abraham' (v. 9b; cf. 13.16), making him part of the community and an heir of all the promises given to Israel. Fourth, Zacchaeus makes more than adequate restitution, symbolizing his independence from his money.

A third approach to the story highlights the strange paradox of salvation. At the beginning, Zacchaeus is depicted as a seeker. 'He was trying' (also translated 'seeking') 'to see who Jesus was' (v. 3). He is not deterred by his inability to peer over the heads of the throngs who line the road, but finds a way to catch a glimpse of Jesus. As an adult, especially one the object of disdain, Zacchaeus no doubt presents a comic figure sitting in the branches of a sycamore tree. But he persists.

At the end of the story, however, we learn that it is the Son of Man who seeks and saves the lost (v. 10). The divine 'must' that sent Jesus to Zacchaeus's house (v. 5) coheres with this declaration of Jesus' purpose and mission. Reading the story in this light, one is reminded of the anonymous old hymn.

> I sought the Lord, and afterward I knew
> > He moved my soul to seek him, seeking me;
> It was not I that found, O Saviour true;
> > No, I was found of thee.

CC

The Third Sunday Before Advent

Job 19.23–27a; 2 Thessalonians 2.1–5, 13–17; Luke 20.27–38

Job 19.23–27a

The words added to the Bible at the beginning, 'Job said to his companions', are unfortunate if they give the impression of solidarity between Job and the others. The whole book has shown them to be at loggerheads with Job about the reason for his extreme misfortune, which is why Job explains that he wishes that his words were written down in such a way that they would never be lost. He believes in his integrity, and that his defence of himself, if read by posterity, will be seen to be compelling. However, in v. 25 his certainty of vindication rises higher, as he explains that he knows that there exists one who will vindicate him. The word rendered 'Redeemer' (Hebrew *go'el*) usually means a kinsman whose duty it is to avenge the death of a member of a family who is murdered, and who has other tasks of support and solidarity. In his own case, Job believes that God himself will take on this role. There will be double vindication: in the permanent record left behind, and in action taken by God as Job's vindicator. Verse 26 raises the question whether Job is expressing a hope for the future, whether he expects to see God's vindication in his lifetime, or whether he will see vindication after death. The Hebrew is notoriously corrupt and difficult, and the NRSV translation (in the lectionary) though traditional, makes no sense. If Job's skin has been 'thus' (how?) destroyed, how will Job be able, 'in his flesh', to see God? Not surprisingly, many subtle alterations to the Hebrew text have been proposed. One possibility (NRSV margin) is to understand 'in my flesh' as 'without my flesh' (i.e. without my body); but it is doubtful whether the writer had in mind a post-mortem, bodiless, existence. A good case can be made for slightly altering the Hebrew word for 'my skin' to a word meaning 'my witness', and for taking the line in accordance with the remainder of the passage as in the REB 'I shall discern my witness standing at my side.' This shifts the passage towards Job seeing God as his vindicator in this life; but this does not matter. The important point about the passage is not that it might prove the existence of life after death, but that it affirms God as the vindicator of a man who has a just cause. This truth is a much surer basis for hope beyond our earthly life. JR

2 Thessalonians 2.1–5, 13–17

This lection stands at the heart of 2 Thessalonians. Because it also contains apocalyptic imagery and expectations that may be elusive and complex, contemporary readers may miss the urgent pastoral worries that drive the passage. When the author, whether Paul or a later writer, refers to the possibility that the Thessalonians have been 'shaken in mind or alarmed', he refers to a situation of considerable anxiety. 'Shaken in mind' may be translated a bit more literally as 'shaken out of mind', as if they were quite distraught. It is not surprising, then, to find strong language being used in the pastoral response (e.g.'we beg you', in v. 1; 'Let no one deceive you', in v. 3; 'Do you not remember . . . ?' in v. 5). Whatever the cause or the exact fears, the author believes that the Thessalonians are beside themselves.

The precise contours of the problem are hidden from our view, although it clearly concerns not only the *parousia* of Jesus but the disposition of believers as well ('our being gathered together to him', v. 1). Somehow the Thessalonians have been instructed that this 'day of the Lord' is already at hand. They may have been informed by some supposed prophetic utterance ('by spirit'), by some argument in the community ('by word'), or by a letter, whether 1 Thessalonians misinterpreted or a forged letter from Paul ('by letter').

Verse 3 begins to counter these fears with a reminder about previous teaching. First, the Day of the Lord is to be preceded by 'the rebellion' and the appearance of 'the lawless one'. Several strands within the New Testament anticipate a rebellion (literally, 'apostasy') prior to the *parousia* of Jesus. Matt. 24.11–14 refers to the false prophets who will mislead the faithful and the time when 'the love of many will grow cold'. The pastorals likewise connect deceptive teachings with the last times (1 Tim. 4.1; 2 Tim. 3.1–5). Jude 17 recalls that the apostles themselves predicted that 'scoffers' would appear in the last days.

The expectation that a period of increased lawlessness and opposition to Christ will precede the *parousia* likewise occurs elsewhere in the New Testament (see e.g. Matt. 24.23–24; 1 John 2.18; Rev. 13). The identification of this lawlessness with a particular figure ('the lawless one') is almost certainly influenced by Old Testament passages such as Isa. 14.12–15, with its celebration of the fall of the king of Babylon, or Ezek. 28.1–10, with its indictment of the king of Tyre. That the lawless one exalts himself but acts in accord with a divine timetable recalls Dan. 11.36 and its polemic against Antiochus IV.

The details of 2 Thess. 2.6–12 (which, of course, stands outside the limits of the lection) serve as further verification that the *parousia* has not yet occurred. What precisely the author means about the restraint on the lawless one or by the 'mystery of lawlessness' being 'already at work' remains completely unclear. Does he refer to some figure or event commonly known to the community? Or is this a general reference to evil in the environment, evil that impinges on the life of the church? Whatever the precise nature of the situation, the author understands it to be a means of testing the community, 'so that all who have not believed the truth but took pleasure in unrighteousness will be condemned' (v. 12). This period of trial serves to divide true believers from false.

Verse 13 abruptly returns to the language of thanksgiving. The sudden transition heightens the contrast between the faithful and the unfaithful. What awaits those who are led astray by lawlessness need not be frightening to those who remain faithful. They give thanks to God, confident in God's love, in God's choice of them 'for salvation through sanctification by the Spirit and through belief in the truth' (v. 13). Unlike the Pauline letters, where we would expect to see salvation through belief or faith in Jesus Christ, here it is important to identify the faith with truth, as distinct from untruth.

The thanksgiving yields, in v. 15, into an exhortation to steadfastness to what has previously been taught 'by us, either by word of mouth or by our letter'. As with the earlier designation of faith as 'belief in the truth', here also the particular kind of teaching becomes important. Not all teachers who purport to be Christian may be trusted. This central section of the letter concludes with a prayer-wish that focuses on the comfort of believers and their strength in 'every good work and word' (v. 17).

Few contemporary pastors will have encountered an anxiety quite like that addressed in 2 Thessalonians. Even the eschatological fervour that occasionally manifests itself in the assigning of a particular date and place for the *parousia* does not claim that 'the day of the Lord is already here'. This lection may nevertheless be helpful to pastors and teachers who encounter the various forms of anxiety that are born of misunderstanding – whether concerning eschatology or some other aspect of Christian faith. Here the teacher (Paul or someone else) moves straightforwardly, first naming the anxiety for what it is, then recalling the teaching previously offered on this topic, reminding of God's fundamental love and salvation, exhorting to confidence, and praying for growth. Taken together, these steps make for a powerful response to fear and alarm. BG

Luke 20.27–38

Luke 20 contains the remarkable stories of controversy between Jesus and the religious authorities, stories found also in Mark and Matthew but here adapted to Luke's purposes. Jesus' triumphal entry into Jerusalem (Luke 19.28–40), his tears shed over the blindness of the city (vv. 41–44), and the expulsion of the money changers from the temple (vv. 45–48) set the stage for the dramatic encounters – three questions put to Jesus with hostile intent (20.1–2, 20–22, 27–33), and one question of Jesus put to the religious authorities (20.41). The chapter concludes with a denunciation of the scribes for their pretentiousness (vv. 45–46) and a vivid contrast between their foreclosing on the houses of defenceless widows and one widow who elicits extravagant praise from Jesus for her gift at the temple (20.47—21.4).

There are at least two tacks the preacher could take in preaching this assigned lesson. First, the context invites careful attention to the conflict between Jesus and the religious power structure. This is the third time in the temple that a trick question has been put to Jesus in hopes of shaming him before the people. The questioners this time are Sadducees, described as 'those who say there is no resurrection'. Josephus tells us they were the urban aristocrats, conservative in their beliefs and claiming a connection with Zadok, a priest during the time of David (2 Sam. 8.17). Their query is no genuine seeking of knowledge, since it assumes what in fact the Sadducees explicitly deny. Furthermore, the question turns out to be a rather complex riddle that contains an absurd scenario (the deaths of seven brothers), a sure-fire strategy to embarrass Jesus.

As with the chief priests and scribes who challenge Jesus' authority (Luke 20.1–2) and with the spies sent by the chief priests and scribes to trap him with the tax issue (20.20–22), Jesus uncovers the insincerity of the Sadducees. The riddle is easily solved. The narrator concludes the vignette by noting that the religious authorities 'no longer dared to ask him another question' (20.40). Their strategy of posing trick questions had not only failed, it had backfired, leaving Jesus as the lone authoritative figure.

In a culture where the honour of an individual is attacked by challenges like these, the importance of a retaliatory retort is critical. The narrator presents Jesus as a master of riposte, cleverly throwing the question back to the questioners (20.3–4) or offering answers that expose the perverted intent of the question (20.34–36). Here in Jerusalem in the court of the temple, on the home turf of the chief priests, scribes and Sadducees, the questioners turn out to be no match for Jesus.

But Jesus' answer is more than merely clever. It shows the Sadducees as belonging to 'this age', so preoccupied with the details of the levirate marriage system that they are unable to contemplate something radically new, the miracle of the resurrection. Their question ties them to a period that ultimately must give way to 'that age', where there is no death and where the children of the resurrection are children of God.

A second tack that might be taken with this passage is to focus on Jesus' teaching about the resurrection. In moving in this direction, of course, one must recognize that we simply do not have the language or concepts to depict what life 'in the resurrection from the dead' will be like. Literalism with the text will not work. Nevertheless, it is instructive to follow the line Jesus takes in answering the question of the Sadducees. It encompasses the themes of both discontinuity and continuity.

Initially, Jesus calls attention to the difference between life in the here and now and life after the resurrection (20.34–36). In this world people regularly die, and the future of the human race is sustained by sexuality. Beyond the resurrection, however, there is no more dying and thus no more need for the same type of sexual relationships that now pertain. (Describing the children of the resurrection as being 'like angels' and as 'children of God' merely depicts them as immortal.) Jesus' point is simply that God's future cannot be understood as an extension of our present existence. It is not the case that we can take what we like out of our current life, raise it to the nth power, and call it heaven. Resurrection entails transformation.

Then, using a rabbinic form of interpretation, Jesus makes a case for the resurrection based on the account of Moses' experience at the burning bush. The declaration that 'I *am* the God' of patriarchs who have died (Exod. 3.6, emphasis added) means that in some sense they still live; 'for to him all of them are alive' (Luke 20.8). The proof of resurrection, then, is the living God. While there is a radical discontinuity between the present and the resurrection, the continuity is to be found in God, the One who transcends death.

To be sure, the themes of discontinuity and continuity will not satisfy the curiosity of those who wonder about the particulars of life in the resurrection and who long to see parents and loved ones who have died before them. But such speculation is exactly what the Sadducees would like to have heard from Jesus. He would have been an easier target to combat. CC

The Second Sunday Before Advent

Malachi 4.1–2a; 2 Thessalonians 3.6–13; Luke 21.5–19

Malachi 4.1–2a

The passage is part of a larger section (3.16—4.3), which describes the coming day of the LORD. A shift away from prophecy and towards apocalyptic can be detected in the fact that in earlier prophecy (e.g. Amos 5.18–20; Isa. 2.13–22) little or no hope is offered to the chosen people that they will escape when the terrible day comes. In Malachi the terror is not mitigated (v. 1) but there is definite hope for God's people. This is associated with the 'sun of righteousness' – a dense phrase which needs to be unpacked. While the sun may not be as welcome in a hot country as it is in a country such as Britain, it dispels all shadows and exposes everything to the light. In this sense it can be linked to justice, which is what 'righteousness' means here. The sun was widely regarded as a symbol of justice in the ancient world, and its wings (v. 2) may refer to the way in which the sun or the sun god were represented in the art of the time. In this context, healing is to be understood as the healing of social divisions and the removal of wickedness rather than the healing of illnesses. It is not impossible that 'sun of righteousness' is meant to imply a personification, a looking forward to the coming of a heavenly figure who will restore what is good when the day of wrath has destroyed what is evil. Within the passage is an interesting contrast: between heat and burning that consume the refuse of human activities, and the sun that restores human harmony. It is a fitting end to what for Jews is the conclusion of the law and the prophets, and for Christians is the last book of the Old Testament. JR

2 Thessalonians 3.6–13

'Anyone unwilling to work should not eat.' Preachers may cringe when they read this lection, knowing that they are entering a minefield. The moralism that constantly threatens to turn the Christian faith into a rulebook waits anxiously to take over a sermon on this particular text. Congregations eager for some answer to massive homelessness and hunger may see this passage as a step toward addressing those social issues.

Before we flee to some safer territory, several aspects of the text need to be noticed. First, and perhaps most important, 2 Thess. 3.6–13 concerns matters *within* the Christian community. On this point, there is no ambiguity. Verse 6 introduces the problem with a command to ('keep away from *believers* who are living in idleness' (emphasis added). The use of the example of Paul's own behaviour reinforces this conclusion, for it is precisely Christians – and only Christians – to whom Paul serves as an example. Although vv. 14–15 fall outside the lection proper, they also pertain to the same problem, and there again it is clear that this is an issue within the Christian community ('Do not regard them as enemies, but warn them as believers', v. 15). The problem here is how Christians treat one another, not how hungry people in the world are to be fed. (That is not to say that the Bible is indifferent to hunger, but that we need to turn elsewhere for those discussions.)

Second, the words 'idle' and 'idleness', which certainly reinforce our tendency to moralize on this passage, may not be the best translations of the Greek. The word *ataktos* primarily describes behaviour that is insubordinate or irresponsible; perhaps these are individuals who rebel against the community itself, chafing at the constraints imposed by the needs and wishes of others. Apparently, one form that irresponsibility takes is that they eat the food of others 'without paying for it' (v. 8) and are unwilling to work. We would rightly refer to this as idleness or laziness, but the underlying problem may be their rebellion against the church itself.

The passage does not hint at the reasons for such behaviour. Some have speculated that fervent eschatological expectations, such as the author feels obliged to correct in 2.1–12, have fuelled a kind of retreat from engagement with the world. If Jesus is coming back at any moment, the logic might run, then why would Christians continue to labour for food, when they know that their needs will be met?

Whatever the cause of this behaviour, the response is sharp and unequivocal. If the author is Paul, then Paul calls on earlier tradition (perhaps similar to 1 Thess. 5.14); if we assume the author is a later follower of Paul, this follower employs Paul's example forcefully. The response opens with the language of command, and this 'in the name of our Lord Jesus Christ' (v. 6). Those who engage in such behaviour have violated 'the tradition that they received from us'.

The appeal quickly turns to the need to imitate Paul. Interestingly, Paul does often urge believers to imitate him (as in 1 Cor. 4.16; 11.1; Phil. 3.17; 4.9; 1 Thess. 1.6), but that imitation generally is an imitation of attitude and disposition rather than of specific behaviours. And in 1 Cor. 9, where Paul speaks about his own pattern of self-support (v. 15), he insists that he has the right to be supported by the congregations but refuses to take advantage of that right. Here, Paul's tradition of self-support and his admonition to imitation come together in a new way in order to address a new situation.

The reasons for such a sharp response become clear in 2 Thess. 3.8 and especially in v. 12. Those who eat the bread of others, as v. 8 suggests is occurring, place an unnecessary burden on the community. Other Christians are being harmed by this undisciplined behaviour. Verse 12 concludes that all must 'do their work quietly' and 'earn their own living'. The little adverb 'quietly' speaks loudly here. Christians who do not live 'quietly' may attract the sort of attention that compromises the community as a whole.

Initially, this passage seems remote from the nature and experience of contemporary Christian churches, for our massive individualism would not permit a situation in which Christians could choose not to work and count on other believers to feed them. Examined more closely, however, the perspective of these Thessalonians looks more familiar. Faith has become, for them, an excuse for irresponsible behaviour. This particular form of irresponsible behaviour is idleness of body, but we know also idleness of mind and spirit, that attitude that manipulates faith, expecting it to supply the missing pieces of life.

The stern response of this early Christian writer, whether Paul or another, insists that faith may not become an excuse for our own idleness. Faith does not wait for another to labour, for another to think, for another to pray. Faith plunges us into the reality of everyday life, even as it also insists that this life is not the whole story. BG

Luke 21.5–19

The New Testament is ambiguous about Jesus' relationship with the Jerusalem temple. Luke shows him, both as a child and as an adult, on pilgrimage to 'his Father's house', and records that his disciples continued to worship there after his ascension. On the other hand, ominous words speak, as here, of the sanctuary's impending destruction. In his version of Jesus' eschatological discourse, Luke uses Mark 13 (the so-called 'Little Apocalypse') as his main source, though his alterations and additions place his own distinctive slant on the passage.

What remains of the platform of Herod's temple in Jerusalem today gives some indication of how magnificent the complete structure must have appeared, with its white marble gleaming in the sun. It is not surprising that Jesus' companions comment on its beauty. But Luke knows from Mark of Jesus' enigmatic saying about stones not being left one upon another, and interprets this as a reference to the (now past) destruction of this temple by the Romans (this will become explicit in vv. 20–24). The 'terrors and great signs from heaven' (v. 11) may refer to the extraordinary occurrences that Josephus claims accompanied the destruction of the city in AD 70. Given that many Christians plunder passages such as Luke 21 to construct their scenarios of what is to happen in the future, it is salutary to recall that Luke looks not forwards but back.

As if to make this clear, he omits the phrase 'this is but the beginning of the birthpangs' (Mark 13.8), clearly separating these historical events from the truly eschatological events heralding the Son of Man's return (vv. 25–28). Moreover, his Jesus warns the disciples of the folly of following would-be messiahs who announce that the time is near. Using the full panoply of apocalyptic imagery (wars and revolutions, earthquakes, plagues and famines), Luke paints a portrait that many who lived through the turbulent years following Nero's death would recognize. Still, even such cosmic upheaval is to be firmly distinguished from the future events that will mark the End.

Another key Lucan addition is 'Before all this' of v. 12. Even prior to the traumatic events of AD 70, Christians have faced persecution, appearance before synagogues and imprisonment (Acts will work this out in detail through the figure of Paul). Luke's ability to show the historical fulfilment of Jesus' words is significant. It gives the reader confidence that his other words will also be fulfilled, particularly those concerning the coming of the Son of Man, whose apparent delay may have caused some to question their trustworthiness. More importantly, these words reassure believers facing hostility and persecution of Christ's presence and inspiration (giving them 'words and a wisdom'). Those who endure, even if this means rejection and even death at the hands of family and friends for belonging to Christ's 'alternative family', will paradoxically win their lives. IB

Christt the King

Jeremiah 23.1–6; Colossians 1.11–20; Luke 23.33–43

Jeremiah 23.1–6

The use of the figure of the shepherd to indicate a king is well established in the ancient Near East. Some Egyptian pharaohs included the shepherd's crook among the symbols that denoted their royal status. Jeremiah has already criticized shepherds; that is, rulers, in poetic oracles at 10.21 and 22.22, and the present passage in prose may be a reworking of these ideas. At any rate, only vv. 1–2 of ch. 23 probably derive from Jeremiah, with vv. 3–4 and 5–6 constituting two enlargements from later times. There are two ways of understanding vv. 1–2, depending on whether the translation 'concerning' is retained, or whether 'to' is preferred. In the second case there is a direct address to the condemned rulers. Another matter of translation that affects the interpretation is whether to follow the NRSV in v. 1 or to prefer the REB 'who let the sheep of my flock scatter and be lost'. The REB implies negligence, whereas the NRSV conveys the sense of deliberate oppression on the part of the rulers. Again the NRSV 'driven them away' suggests a different image from the REB's 'dispersed'. The NRSV also raises more acutely than REB whether the verbs used are to be confined to the shepherd imagery or whether they have wider reference. Are vv. 1–2 saying that the (or an) exile has already occurred? If they are, then the whole passage will be post-exilic.

Verses 3–4 certainly envisage the exilic or post-exilic situation, with their promise to gather the remnant of the flock 'out of all the lands' where they have been driven. It is noteworthy that this disaster is attributed to the rulers of Judah and Israel, and not to foreign powers.

The opening words of v. 5 'the days are coming' look to the longer-term future. The tree imagery (cf. Isa. 11.1) suggests that the defunct Davidic line will sprout once again. The king provided by God will do all that the condemned shepherds failed to do, and his name will sum up the longed-for situation. The word 'righteousness', which probably looks back to the phrase 'righteous branch', has the active sense of vindication in Hebrew. God's righteousness is what he does to vindicate and uphold what is right. The GNB's 'the LORD is our salvation' gets the flavour of this. JR

Colossians 1.11–20

Although it has already appeared earlier in Year C, this passage has particular relevance for Christ the King Sunday (see the discussions of Col. 1.1–14 under Proper 10 and Col. 1.15–28 under Proper 11). As the church celebrates the reign of

Christ over all creation, the early Christian hymn found in the second section of this lection (Col. 1.15–20) asserts Christ's priority through a variety of images. First, along with other passages in the New Testament, the hymn asserts that Christ bears the very image of God (see also 2 Cor. 3.18; 4.4; Phil. 2.6; Heb. 1.3). Second, and more elaborately, the hymn proclaims Christ's connection with creation itself: he is firstborn (Col. 1.15b,), he is an agent of creation (v. 16a), he is the origin and goal of creation (vv. 16b–17). Third, Christ is the head (or origin) of the Church and the firstborn from the dead (v. 18).

Verses 19–20 move from these assertions about the priority of Christ to take up more directly his salvific role. It is through Christ that God reconciles 'to himself all things, whether on earth or in heaven, by making peace through the blood of his cross'. The theme of reconciliation returns to the reason for introducing the hymn in the first place, namely, the reference in the thanksgiving to God's rescue of human beings through God's Son (v. 13).

Taken together, the two parts of this lection draw attention to both the reign of Christ in all creation and the implications of that reign for humanity. Through Christ, God transfers humankind from 'the power of darkness' and into 'the inheritance of the saints in the light' (v. 12). The commemoration and celebration of that transfer carries with it, of course, the obligation to gratitude and endurance (see vv. 11–12). LH

Luke 23.33–43

The account of the crucifixion of Jesus in Luke abounds with themes characteristic of the whole Gospel, so much so, in fact, that commentators wonder whether Luke has reworked a Marcan source or has used an entirely different source. Since the twists and turns of the narrative seem strategic and rich in meaning, they provide a plentiful lode to be mined by the preacher who is interested in more than relating bare facts.

For example, on this Sunday labelled 'Christ the King' it is instructive to trace through the narrative the royal motif. Already the narrator has related the political charges brought against Jesus – that he perverts the Jewish nation, advocates a tax revolt against Rome, and calls himself 'the Messiah, a king' (Luke 23.2). The hearings before Pilate and Herod exonerate him of the accusations, but nevertheless lead him closer and closer to crucifixion (vv. 1–16). A murderous political insurrectionist is released instead of Jesus (vv. 18–25).

It is in the mocking words of the scoffers – the leaders (v. 35), the soldiers (vv. 36–37), and an unrepentant criminal (v. 39) – and in the inscription put over the cross (v. 38) that readers are faced with the true nature of Jesus' Kingship. On the one hand, the repeated demand, 'Are you not the Messiah? Save yourself and us!' functions as yet another temptation for Jesus. Just as the devil had earlier challenged his vocational identity three times and offered him a different, less painful option (4.1–11), so now Jesus is being invited to save himself, to avoid the cross and in the process to save the criminals as well. He is being tempted to choose another vocation, to be a different sort of king from his distinctive calling, perhaps a political figure not unlike the one depicted in the false charges brought against him. By his lack of response to the scoffers, however, Jesus clearly remains steadfast in fulfilling the divine will.

On the other hand, the words of the scoffers ironically pose the paradox of his kingly mission. He is a Messiah who saves others only by not saving himself (v. 35). He is resolutely committed to God's plan, which includes betrayal and death (22.22, 37). Only in the powerlessness of the cross can he demonstrate the authority that ultimately rescues criminals, scoffers and religious leaders. Refusing the voices of temptation, Jesus then defines for us what sort of king he really is.

This means that the constituting event of the Christian faith is not a power play that follows the rules and logic of most of the power plays we know – retaliation, competition, self-protectiveness, and the like. Instead, Jesus dares to trust and obey the divine will that takes him to the cross – and beyond.

There is, perhaps, irony here in that the religious authorities lead the cries for Jesus' death, whereas the one person in the text who perceives the truth and dares to speak it is the second criminal being crucified alongside Jesus (23.40–43). He acknowledges that he justly deserves his punishment, in contrast to Jesus, who is innocent. Furthermore, he sees that Jesus will enter his kingly realm not by coming down from the cross, but by dying. His request, 'Jesus, remember me when you come into your kingdom' (v. 42), is a plea not to be forgotten. Yet it is also a confession of faith and an indication that he has understood the mystery of the gospel – that mockings, insults, floggings and crucifixion are necessary to the prophetic plan that leads to resurrection (18.31–34). While other actors in the drama suppose that Jesus' fortunes are coming to an end (albeit for some a tragic end), the second criminal perceives that God will vindicate the King and will bring him into his proper rule.

A critical verse underlying the interchange with the criminals unfortunately remains, textually speaking, an uncertain one (23.34a). It is omitted in some ancient and trustworthy manuscripts and included in others. The notion that Jesus forgives his murderers because they are ignorant of what they are doing is certainly appropriate to the Lucan story. A case can be made for the theory that it is more likely that a scribe (who would tend to be anti-Jewish?) in copying would have omitted the verse than that he would have made it up. (See the critical commentaries for a fuller discussion.)

If the verse belongs in the text, then it becomes a watershed for the two criminals. They are specifically introduced in vv. 32–33; then Jesus speaks these words of pardon on his crucifiers. One criminal 'kept deriding him' and joined the group of scoffers. But the other criminal hears in the words something more and different – the words of a King, whose authority is like no other, who prays for those who spitefully abuse and persecute him. He seeks a place for himself in a realm where the keynote is pardon and not recompense, where condemned criminals can be fully restored. CC

Harvest Festival

Deuteronomy 26.1–11; Revelation 14.14–18 or Philippians 4.4–9; John 6.24–35

Deuteronomy 26.1–11

See the First Sunday of Lent, p. 78.

Revelation 14.14–18

The dominant tone of a harvest festival is one of thanksgiving and rejoicing at the 'harvest home', yet this passage shows that the imagery of harvest and vintage can be violent and threatening: the sharp sickle, the fire and the crushing of grapes. (The effect would be even more horrific were the reading to include the next two verses, which properly belong to the passage.) Both aspects of harvest are drawn on in the Old Testament: harvest as the joy of the new kingdom in Isa. 9.3 and harvest as judgement on the nations (Jer. 51.33; Joel 3.9–14, which is echoed here; and Isa. 63.1–6, to be drawn on in Rev. 19.13–15). The same is true of the Gospels, where Jesus uses the image of harvest for the kingdom of God in Mark 4.26–29 (cf. John 4.35–36), but also for judgement in Matt. 13.24–30. It is not immediately obvious which idea is uppermost here. The preceding verses of Rev. 14 have announced, in anticipation, the fall of 'Babylon', the great and persecuting city (v. 8, cf. 17.5–6); but have also shown the Lamb with his army of those redeemed as 'first fruits' (vv. 1–4); and have given reassurance to those called to endure and face death (vv. 12–13).

In fact, however, the two ideas of harvest cannot be separated: the act of reaping is a means to the collection of grain and production of the staple, bread; and the crushing of grapes provides that other staple, wine. So even if one idea is uppermost in an image, the other will not be forgotten – especially by those whose lives were still closely linked to the rhythm of agriculture.

The Apocalypse is an uncomfortable book. It looks forward to God's vengeance on his enemies and his people's oppressors. They will suffer for their wickedness. But the harvest imagery shows that God's judgement is not just retribution. In the judgement there is hope, because it is 'the harvest of the earth', and from it will come the ingathering of God's people. Even suffering and death contain hope, for the ingathering has already begun with the martyrs who are the 'first fruits' that guarantee the rest, and who have already been presented in the temple of heaven from which the angels come, and wait beneath its altar (6.9).

Even before the deaths of the martyrs, though, was the slaughter of the Lamb, the basis for the hope of redemption for the people of God to be gathered from throughout the earth (5.6, 9). 'The Lamb' is the most characteristic term for Christ in

Revelation, but here he reappears as 'one like the Son of Man' as in the opening of John's vision (1.13), coming on a cloud like the figure of Dan. 7.13. The judgement theme has presumably reawakened this image, and Christ the Son of Man comes with his angels as he does in Matt. 25.31. SL

Philippians 4.4–9

See the Third Sunday of Advent, pp. 10–11.

John 6.24–35

Somewhat mystified by Jesus' apparent disappearance from the site of the miraculous feeding, the crowd followed him as soon as they could to the other side of the lake. Whatever their motives may have been – the hope of more such miraculous provision, a chance to see another sensational 'sign', or just sheer curiosity – Jesus sees the need to lead them towards a deeper understanding.

He begins at a level they do not find difficult. The contrast between 'food that perishes' and 'food that endures' sounded like conventional religious teaching – short-term materialism over against lasting spiritual benefits. And if they were familiar with the Son of Man of Daniel 7, they would have known that he might well be instrumental in securing long-term rewards for the faithful. So they responded by asking what kind of conduct would assure them of these rewards. The same question is asked of Jesus in the Synoptic Gospels, and the answer is to 'follow' Jesus. Here (in typical Johannine fashion) it is to 'believe in' him.

But how were they to know that they *should* believe in him? They needed some 'sign' that would decisively identify Jesus as the person he claimed to be. Moses, after all, had secured many days' provision of manna in the wilderness. Could Jesus claim similar credentials, such that a sentence from Scripture would fit him as well as it fitted Moses, 'He gave them bread from heaven to eat'?

Oddly enough, this sentence does not exactly occur in the Old Testament, though it was close to a more or less standard formula for summarizing the manna episode (Neh. 9.15; Ps. 78.24). But it becomes, in effect, the text of Jesus' sermon and is treated as preachers have always tended to do, a word or two at a time. First, Jesus comments on 'He'. *He* does not mean Moses. It was God who provided the manna; and possibly there is some resonance here with the Lord's Prayer (not given in John's Gospel), where the Father is prayed to 'give us this day our daily (or perhaps it meant "our special") bread'. Second, Jesus interprets the word 'bread'. The manna may have been supernatural, but it was merely to satisfy physical hunger. The *bread* of the scriptural text meant more than this, just as what Jesus had just provided was more than an emergency supply of bread. But the crowd still does not get the point. They ask to be given this bread 'always', just as the woman at the well had asked Jesus to give her a supply of water that would prevent her having to come for it each time herself (John 4.15).

Instead Jesus offers true bread, indeed he is himself (as he will go on to show) 'the bread of life'. And this is for any- and everyone who will genuinely ask for it – the invitation deliberately evokes the figure of Wisdom crying out, 'Come, eat of my bread and drink of the wine I have mixed' (Prov. 9.5). AEH

Biblical Index